'Preparing for Power'

'Preparing for Power'

The Revolutionary Communist Party and its Curious Afterlives, 1976–2020

Jack Hepworth

BLOOMSBURY ACADEMIC
LONDON • NEW YORK • OXFORD • NEW DELHI • SYDNEY

BLOOMSBURY ACADEMIC
Bloomsbury Publishing Plc
50 Bedford Square, London, WC1B 3DP, UK
1385 Broadway, New York, NY 10018, USA
29 Earlsfort Terrace, Dublin 2, Ireland

BLOOMSBURY, BLOOMSBURY ACADEMIC and the Diana logo are trademarks of
Bloomsbury Publishing Plc

First published in Great Britain 2023
This paperback edition published in 2025

Copyright © Jack Hepworth, 2023

Jack Hepworth has asserted his right under the Copyright, Designs and Patents Act, 1988,
to be identified as Author of this work.

For legal purposes the Acknowledgements on p. viii constitute an extension of this
copyright page.

Cover image © Irish Freedom Movement Demonstration, London, c. 1984,
Joan Hoey, Private Collection.

All rights reserved. No part of this publication may be reproduced or transmitted in any
form or by any means, electronic or mechanical, including photocopying, recording,
or any information storage or retrieval system, without prior permission in writing
from the publishers.

Bloomsbury Publishing Plc does not have any control over, or responsibility for, any third-party websites referred to or in this book. All internet addresses given in this book were correct at the time of going to press. The author and publisher regret any inconvenience caused if addresses have changed or sites have ceased to exist, but can accept no responsibility for any such changes.

A catalogue record for this book is available from the British Library.

A catalog record for this book is available from the Library of Congress.

ISBN: HB: 978-1-3502-4237-1
PB: 978-1-3502-4240-1
ePDF: 978-1-3502-4238-8
eBook: 978-1-3502-4239-5

Typeset by Deanta Global Publishing Services, Chennai, India

To find out more about our authors and books visit www.bloomsbury.com and
sign up for our newsletters.

Contents

List of figures   vii
Acknowledgements   viii
Acronyms and initialisms   xi

'Who are these people?' The Revolutionary Communist Party and its curious afterlives   1
   'There's an RCPer everywhere you look. What the hell's going on?'   1
   'I can't keep up with whether I'm supposed to be a hard-left fanatic or an alt-right apologist'   4

1   'We take the very unpopular position of giving unconditional support to the republican movement'   13
   Questioning everything: The origins of the Revolutionary Communist Party   13
   'Unconditional support' for 'Irish freedom'   27

2   'Fight back with the party of the future': Militant anti-racism, c.1981–6   43
   Building the Revolutionary Communist Party   43
   'We must be prepared to put our lives on the line'   55

3   From the miners' strike to 'moral panics', c.1984–9   71
   'Universally condemned by the British left'   74
   'Moral authoritarianism' and the AIDS crisis   88
   'Young, angry, thinking people'   95

4   'The empire strikes back': Anti-imperialism and the Gulf, the Balkans and Ireland, c. 1989–95   101
   'The left . . . no longer exists'   102
   'The moral rearmament of imperialism'   109
   'A historic defeat for the liberation movement'   119

5   'Class politics cannot be rebuilt, regenerated or rescued': Reorientation and renewal, c. 1993–2000   129
   'Rescuing the subject'   131

	'No easy solutions'	146
	'Ban nothing, question everything'	154
6	'Encouraging the unsayable to be said': *spiked* and the Institute of Ideas, c. 2000–2010	163
	'A prevailing climate of misanthropy'	164
	'Let's replace capitalism with something even more dazzlingly cocky and human-centric'	173
	A 'pre-political' epoch	182
7	From the 'demise of ideologies' to a 'people's decade', c. 2010–20	185
	'Democracy: The unfinished revolution'	186
	'The dangers of the new anti-racism'	198
	'The lockdown has done untold damage'	202
	'A better world is possible'	210

'Pessimism of the intellect, optimism of the will': The Revolutionary Communist Party and its curious afterlives — 215

Continuity and change — 221

An experience of defeat? — 229

Bibliography — 237

Index — 264

Figures

1	'Ireland Must Win!', 1981	29
2	RCP and IFM activists at County Hall, London, during an IFM demonstration, *c.*1985	38
3	Party for Joan Phillips. Members of *the next step* editorial board at a party in London given for Joan Phillips on her appointment as the RCP's Yorkshire organizer, 1986	86
4	Anti-Section 28 demo, 1988	92
5	Irish Freedom Movement, 1992	133
6	Claire Fox and Helene Guldberg, 2000	158
7	Claire Fox, 2019	191

Acknowledgements

The idea for *Preparing for Power* emerged during a lectureship at Newcastle University, when I was researching the British left and the Northern Ireland conflict, and has concluded during a Junior Research Fellowship at St Catherine's College, Oxford. It is a pleasure and a privilege to thank the many colleagues and friends, in Newcastle, Oxford and beyond, whose support and wisdom made this book possible.

My first thanks are to all of the interviewees. Invited to review their complex political careers, several were circumspect. Yet many went above and beyond to participate, and all were generous with their time and their candour. I thank them all: Jon Bryan, Dolan Cummings, Mike Fitzpatrick, Paul Flewers, Claire Fox, Ann Furedi, Frank Furedi, John Gillott, Joan Hoey, Alan Hudson, Rob Killick, Kirk Leech, Norman Lewis, Tim Martin, Para Mullan, Phil Mullan, Linda Murdoch, James Woudhuysen and all of those who chose to remain anonymous.

Like all research projects of its scale, *Preparing for Power* draws upon the valuable resources of multiple archival collections. I thank the librarians and archivists of the Bodleian Libraries in Oxford – especially at the Old Library, the History Faculty Library, the Weston Library and the Social Science Library – and of the Ahmed Iqbal Ullah Race Relations Resource Centre in Manchester; the Mining Institute in Newcastle; Lancashire Records Office in Preston; the Linen Hall Library in Belfast; West Yorkshire Archives Service in Bradford; and all of the volunteers at the Working Class Movement Library in Salford. Additional thanks are due to the Special Collections teams at Leeds University, Manchester University, the University of Edinburgh and the University of Glasgow. At London Metropolitan University, Special Collections manager Peter Fisher was especially obliging, facilitating my work both with the institutional collections and the vast Archive of the Irish in Britain.

It has been a great privilege to complete this study while pursuing new projects at St Catherine's College, Oxford, where Fellows, students and staff sustain a tremendous collegial atmosphere. Special thanks to the Master, Professor Kersti Börjars; to the president of the Senior Common Room, Professor Sam Wolfe; and to my fellow historians, Professor Marc Mulholland, Dr Amanda Power and Dr Helen Sunderland, who challenge and encourage me in the best possible spirit. For their inspiration and humour, thanks also to my Catz colleagues Dr Tom Adams, Dr Mark Coen, Professor Andrew Dickinson, Dr Jeremy Dimmick, Andy Elliott, Naomi Freud, Leo Geyer, Dr Jess Goodman, Professor Ashok Handa, Dr Emma James, Professor Marc Lackenby, Dr John Lynch, Waqas Mirza, Dr Cayenna Ponchione-Bailey, J. C. Smith, Professor Goran Stanivukovic, Dr Alex Teytelboym, Dr Colin Thompson, Professor Richard Todd and Professor Laura Tunbridge. I am extremely grateful to the custodians of the Murray Fund, which supports the Canon Murray Fellowship in Irish History. For generous research grants, I am also delighted to thank the Research Fund Committee in the School of History, Classics and Archaeology at Newcastle University, and, in Oxford, the History Faculty Research Committee.

While any errors and shortcomings are, of course, my own, the book bears the imprint of many inspiring scholars from whom I have had the pleasure of learning, especially Dr Alex Barber, Dr Sarah Campbell, Professor Ludmilla Jordanova, Dr Alexandros Koutsoukis, Dr Stephen Meredith, Dr Eve Morrison, Dr Connal Parr and Dr Matt Perry. For illuminating conversations and correspondence throughout the research and writing process, I am grateful to Dr James Heartfield, Dr David Renton, Kevin Rooney, Michael Savage and Dr Evan Smith, and thanks also to Joan Hoey and Pandora Kay-Kreizman for granting permission to feature their photographs. At Bloomsbury, it has been a pleasure to work with Emily Drewe, Abigail Lane and Meg Harris. Thanks are also due to Bloomsbury's anonymous readers for their thorough and entirely constructive feedback on an earlier manuscript.

Members of the Newcastle University History Research Seminar and the Oxford Modern British History Seminar alike asked perspicacious questions about preparatory papers – special thanks to Dr Shane McCorristine in Newcastle and Dr Aled Davies, Professor Ben Jackson and Alfie Steer in Oxford for convening these thought-provoking forums. An earlier article in *Contemporary British History* informed this book's opening chapters: I thank Professor Tony Shaw of the University of Hertfordshire and the journal's editorial board and reviewers for their erudite advice.

I owe much to the expertise of members of the Newcastle University Oral History Unit and Collective, especially Dr Alison Atkinson-Phillips, Sue Bradley, Rosie Bush, Dr Andy Clark, Dr Niamh Dillon, Silvie Fisch and Professor Graham Smith. In Oxford, the Irish History Seminar continually represents a dynamic and exciting forum for discussions spanning modern Ireland and Britain – thanks to Dr Lia Brazil, Dr Deirdre Foley, Dr Rachel Kowalski, Dr Anna Lively, Professor Ian McBride, Seamus Nevin, Josie Richardson and Maura Valenti.

Throughout the research and writing process, I have had the pleasure of teaching many undergraduates and postgraduates in Newcastle and Oxford. Teaching across modern Irish and British history and on thematic papers interrogating historiographical theory and practice, I have been fortunate to find multiple synergies between research and teaching. Throughout these years, students' energy, acuity and inquiry have produced some of the most intellectually exciting moments.

My parents have been a source of steadfast support throughout the preparation of this book: it is a delight to record my love and gratitude. Friends across these islands continually offer inspiration and joy: thanks in particular to Aldo, Alex and Becci, Andrew, Annie, Ben, Chris, Dan, John, Josh, Manon, Mark and Amanda, Sam, Steven and Chris, and Tanya. Heartfelt thanks to Joan for sage counsel and crucial encouragement, and to Bob for always inspiring me to take ideas and inquiry seriously.

While this book was under preparation, I lost my dear friend Andy Corkhill and my wonderful Auntie Gerry Murphy. Both Andy and my Auntie Gerry were heroes of mine; both taught me more than they could have realised. I know that these two very special people, with their brilliant wit, warmth, and wisdom, would have delighted in debating the ideas discussed here. I dedicate this book in loving memory of Andy and Auntie Gerry.

Acronyms and initialisms

AAM	Anti-Apartheid Movement
ANC	African National Congress
ANL	Anti-Nazi League
BLM	Black Lives Matter
BNP	British National Party
CAM	Campaign Against Militarism
CND	Campaign for Nuclear Disarmament
COVWAR	Coventry Workers Against Racism
CPGB	Communist Party of Great Britain
CSWG	Committee to Stop War in the Gulf
DUP	Democratic Unionist Party
EEC	European Economic Community
ELWAR	East London Workers Against Racism
EU	European Union
GLC	Greater London Council
HOME	Hands Off the Middle East Committee
IFM	Irish Freedom Movement
IMG	International Marxist Group
IRA	Irish Republican Army
IRSP	Irish Republican Socialist Party
IS	International Socialists
ITN	Independent Television News
LCI	Labour Committee on Ireland

MEP	Member of the European Parliament
NALGO	National and Local Government Officers' Association
NCB	National Coal Board
NUM	National Union of Mineworkers
NUPE	National Union of Public Employees
NUS	National Union of Students
NUT	National Union of Teachers
PLO	Palestine Liberation Organisation
PNL	Polytechnic of North London
PTA	Prevention of Terrorism Act
RCG	Revolutionary Communist Group
RCP	Revolutionary Communist Party
RCS	Revolutionary Communist Students
RCT	Revolutionary Communist Tendency
SOLWAR	South London Workers Against Racism
SPTAC	Smash the Prevention of Terrorism Act Campaign
StWC	Stop the War Coalition
SWP	Socialist Workers Party
TGWU	Transport and General Workers' Union
TOM	Troops Out Movement
TUC	Trades Union Congress
UCATT	Union of Construction, Allied Trades and Technicians
UDM	Union of Democratic Mineworkers
UN	United Nations
WAR	Workers Against Racism
WRP	Workers Revolutionary Party

'Who are these people?'
The Revolutionary Communist Party and its curious afterlives

'There's an RCPer everywhere you look.
What the hell's going on?'

One Saturday morning in the late 1980s, the Irish Society at London's South Bank Polytechnic hosted a conference on the Northern Ireland conflict. After twenty years of 'the troubles', such events were regular features of student activist calendars in Britain: there seemed little to distinguish the sparsely attended South Bank seminar. An eyewitness takes up the story:

> Not many people turned up – about 20 people during the morning. Then, all at once, about six or seven more turned up [. . .] They proclaimed themselves as RCP, and proceeded to take over the meeting. They were very heavy, physically and intellectually. We went to the pub at lunchtime and said to each other, 'Who are these fucking people?'[1]

In the same city some twenty years later, the author Jenny Turner paid £80 to attend a weekend of public debates at the Royal College of Art. Hundreds of visitors heard discussions on topics ranging from euthanasia to the global recession, from abortion rights to freedom of speech. For Turner, however, the organizers represented the main subject of interest:

> I've been watching these people off and on for years now, since I was a student in the 1980s and they called themselves the Revolutionary Communist Party. I find them fascinating, peculiar, entertaining. . . . Who are these people, what on earth do they think they're up to?[2]

This book seeks answers to these questions which, for several decades, have generated considerably more heat than light.

1   Andy Beckett, 'Licence to rile', *Guardian*, 15 May 1999.
2   Jenny Turner, 'Who are they?', *London Review of Books*, 8 July 2010.

Although it officially existed for barely two decades and its core cadre membership did not surpass 300 at any given time, the Revolutionary Communist Party (RCP) left a curiously lasting imprint on British politics. The RCP disbanded in 1996, and its former house magazine *Living Marxism* (latterly rebranded as *LM*) closed in 2000 after a well-documented libel case brought by Independent Television News (ITN).[3] But the end of the party and its publication did not precipitate obscurity. Former cadres resolved to keep in touch as they pursued their own initiatives. In 2000, Mick Hume and Claire Fox, respectively, founded *spiked*, an internet magazine, and the Institute (later the Academy) of Ideas, a debating forum. After the millennium, many former members proceeded to public prominence in the media, technology and innovation, policymaking and academia. By 2020, Oliver Kamm of the *Times* could remark that the former party network had 'completed an extraordinary infiltration' of 'British public life'.[4] Although Kamm was exaggerating, his comments indicated how the party and its organizational afterlives have simultaneously bemused, nettled and fascinated observers.

Formed as the Revolutionary Communist Tendency in 1978 ('Party' replaced 'Tendency' in 1981), the RCP emerged from the Trotskyist left of the 1970s. Formulating a distinct and often controversial critique, the new organization deliberately distinguished itself from the twenty-one Trotskyist organizations active in Britain at the turn of the 1980s.[5] Espousing an independent revolutionary politics, party cadres charged the Labour Party, the trade union leadership and the radical left with perpetuating reformist illusions. Only independent revolutionary politics, the RCP asserted, could supersede capitalism with a superior alternative.

From the late 1990s, the ITN libel case prompted several media commentators to excavate the RCP's curious history. Tracing *LM*'s origins to its foundation in 1988 as the party's monthly review, Julia Hartley-Brewer noted that the magazine's critics considered its positions 'wilfully perverse'.[6] For others, former

---

3   The libel case against *LM* magazine is discussed in Chapter 5. For a detailed account of the trial, see David Campbell, 'Atrocity, memory, photography: Imaging the concentration camps of Bosnia – the case of ITN versus *Living Marxism*, part 1', *Journal of Human Rights*, 1 (2002): 1–33 and David Campbell, 'Atrocity, memory, photography: Imaging the concentration camps of Bosnia – the case of ITN versus *Living Marxism*, part 2', *Journal of Human Rights*, 1 (2002): 143–72.
4   Oliver Kamm, 'The extraordinary journey of the Revolutionary Communist Party is a lesson in politics', *CapX*, 14 August 2020. Available at capx.co/the-extraordinary-journey-of-the-revolutionary-communist-party-is-a-lesson-in-politics (accessed 12 January 2021).
5   John Kelly, *Contemporary Trotskyism: Parties, Sects and Social Movements in Britain* (Abingdon: Routledge, 2018), 40, 53.
6   Julia Hartley-Brewer, 'One man band with "big mouth and broad mind"', *Guardian*, 15 March 2000.

RCPers espoused a libertarian anti-statism which signalled a damascene shift from the radical left to the new right. The US literary magazine *Lingua Franca*, for example, suggested that *LM* had 'adopted some of the language of right-wing cultural critique'.[7] Narrating the party's journey through the interpretive prism of left and right, commentators perceived profound contrasts between the RCP's Trotskyist origins and its supposedly reactionary offshoots. For environmental activist George Monbiot, the RCP-*Living Marxism* network propagated 'perversities and cheap controversialism', with 'less in common with the left than with the fanatical right'.[8] Scorning *Living Marxism*'s 'very right-wing bedfellows' in 1998, Monbiot likened the party network to 'far-right' libertarians.[9] Writing in 2002, Nick Cohen asserted that the RCP had moved 'ever rightward' to become 'media-friendly Tory extremists'.[10] Ranking Claire Fox among the 100 'top left wingers' in UK politics in 2007, the *Daily Telegraph*'s selectors admitted their puzzlement:

> Is she left wing or right wing? Having spent twenty years in the Revolutionary Communist Party you'd think the former, but she's a stout defender of freedom of speech and small government.[11]

When the RCP had dissolved in the 1990s, observers scarcely anticipated its political and intellectual traditions enduring into the twenty-first century. Writing during the *LM* libel trial, radical commentator Dave Walker suggested that individuals among the former party network might harbour hopes of 'carving out a career in the academic or media world, having a book published, or getting a website put on-line'. But Walker ultimately anticipated the magazine and its exponents fading into obscurity:

> So where can the former members and supporters of the now-defunct RCP go now? [. . .] Whilst cultural issues are obviously an important area for study, you can't maintain for long anything resembling a political organisation solely on these grounds. . . . I can't see *LM* attracting any wealthy sponsors who will help keep it going. . . . Even if the ITN court case doesn't finish *LM* off, lack of direction and a declining audience could well do so.[12]

---

7 Matthew Price, 'Raving Marxism', *Lingua Franca*, March 1999.
8 George Monbiot, 'Marxists found alive in C4', *Guardian*, 18 December 1997; George Monbiot, 'Far left or far right?', *Prospect*, November 1998.
9 George Monbiot, 'Free speech? Excuse me', *Guardian*, 27 October 1998.
10 Nick Cohen, 'The rebels who changed their tune to be pundits', *New Statesman*, 12 August 2002.
11 'The left list', *Daily Telegraph*, 23 September 2007.
12 Dave Walker, 'Libertarian humanism or critical utopianism? The demise of the Revolutionary Communist Party', *New Interventions*, 8, Issue 3 (1998).

'I can't keep up with whether I'm supposed to be a hard-left fanatic or an alt-right apologist'[13]

Especially among the party's former foes on the left, the RCP's afterlives have been a subject of bewilderment, suspicion and considerable animosity. Adam LeBor's recent analysis highlighted how the party's offshoots, especially *spiked*, had provoked hostility among 'the *Guardian* and its bien-pensant allies'.[14] Noting several former cadres' rising media profiles, David Aaronovitch claimed in 2004 that 'the contrarian Institute of Ideas has become the first number called by lazy radio producers wanting a five-minute argument'.[15] For one left-wing critic, the 'ex-RCP group', having dispensed with class struggle, had undergone 'a wrenching shift in political orientation' towards 'thoroughgoing bourgeois libertarianism'.[16] In 2015, *Guardian* columnist and self-declared 'leftie', Tim Lott, suggested that enjoying *spiked* seemed 'like a dirty little secret'.[17]

The former RCP network especially piqued popular curiosity in 2019, when several candidates associated with its milieu stood as Brexit Party candidates in elections to the European and UK parliaments.[18] In the national press, commentators juxtaposed 'former communists' standing alongside Nigel Farage.[19] Claire Fox was subject to particular criticism concerning the party's 'unconditional support' for Irish republicanism in the 1980s and 1990s. When Fox stood in the European elections in 2019, Colin Parry – whose son, Tim, was killed in the Irish Republican Army's (IRA) Warrington bombing in March 1993 – condemned Fox as an 'apologist for the IRA'.[20] When Fox was granted a

---

13   Julia Llewellyn Smith, 'The Brexit Party's Claire Fox on why she's fighting for Farage', *Sunday Times*, 28 April 2019.
14   Adam LeBor, 'The Marxist cell in Number 10', *Critic*, December 2020.
15   David Aaronovitch, 'The thinking classes: Too clever by half', *Observer*, 12 September 2004.
16   James Turley, 'Boris gets spiked', *weekly worker*, 21 May 2008.
17   Tim Lott, 'If leftwingers like me are condemned as rightwing, then what's left?', *Guardian*, 11 March 2015.
18   Otto English, 'My trip down the Brexit Party rabbit hole', *Politico*, 2 September 2019. Available at politico.eu/article/my-trip-down-the-brexit-party-rabbit-hole-nigel-farage/ (accessed 2 July 2020). In the European elections of 23 May 2019, Claire Fox, James Heartfield, Alka Sehgal Cuthbert and Stuart Waiton stood as Brexit Party candidates. Until party leader Nigel Farage announced that the Brexit Party would not stand against Conservative incumbents in the general election of 12 December 2019, John Fitzpatrick and Yasmin Fitzpatrick were the prospective candidates for North Thanet and East Surrey, respectively. James Woudhuysen stood for the Brexit Party in Carshalton and Wallington.
19   Peter Walker, 'Former communist standing as MEP for Farage's Brexit party', *Guardian*, 23 April 2019; David Aaronovitch, 'The shadowy past of Farage's motley crew', *Times*, 24 April 2019; Nick Cohen, 'The twisted truth behind Nigel Farage's Brexit Party', *Spectator*, 16 May 2019.
20   'Brexit party candidate responds to IRA bomb comments "disgrace"', *Western Mail*, 2 May 2019.

peerage in August 2020, the *Sunday Times* asked why a 'champion of terror' was being elevated to the Lords.[21]

Much of the journalistic commentary implies that the former RCP network has undergone a dramatic conversion from radicalism to reactionary politics. Former RCP activists' positions in the public sphere today have kindled widespread media intrigue. Coining an 'RCP-*Living Marxism-spiked* network', commentators have contrasted the party's Trotskyist roots and heterogeneous afterlives. In 2020, the *New Statesman* ranked Munira Mirza, head of the Number 10 Policy Unit and a former *spiked* contributor, as 'the third-most influential adviser in Downing Street'.[22] In the *Guardian*, Evan Smith noted Mirza and the *spiked* network becoming 'increasingly known' for 'contrarian takes on current events'. *spiked* writers with RCP backgrounds, Smith argued, were

> popping up in various places across the media landscape with rightwing views. Famed for its right-libertarian and iconoclastic style, Spiked has gained notoriety for arguing against numerous progressive positions.[23]

Renewed interest in the RCP and its former exponents has not been confined to Britain. In 2019, the Australian political commentator Guy Rundle highlighted the 'amazing story of how the Revolutionary Communist Party got into No. 10 Downing Street, Brexit and News Corp':

> As the UK slides towards a genuine institutional crisis, there's an RCPer everywhere you look. What the hell's going on?[24]

With only two notable exceptions, the RCP features only peripherally in contemporary historiography. Even in major studies of the British radical left, the organization receives only a cursory mention: Keith Laybourn's extensive *Marxism in Britain* (2006), for example, contains a singular passing allusion.[25] In a section of his book *No Platform* (2020), Evan Smith, the only historian to assess the RCP in any depth, details the party's commitment to free speech. Like Monbiot and Cohen, Smith plots a trajectory between distinct poles, from

---

21 Rosie Kinchen and Hannah Al-Othman, 'From champion of terror to peer of the realm: Who put Claire Fox in the House of Lords?', *Sunday Times*, 16 August 2020.
22 Harry Lambert, 'Who's in charge inside No 10: The maverick advisers running Britain', *New Statesman*, 4 March 2020.
23 Evan Smith, 'How a fringe sect from the 1980s influenced No 10's attitude to racism', *Guardian*, 23 June 2020.
24 Guy Rundle, 'The little party that could', *Crikey*, 16 August 2019. Available at crikey.com.au/2019/08/16/revolutionary-communist-party-boris-johnson/ (accessed 8 July 2020).
25 Keith Laybourn, *Marxism in Britain: Dissent, Decline and Re-emergence, 1945–c.2000* (London: Routledge, 2006), 9.

'ultra-left Trotskyist group to libertarian contrarianism'.[26] Although essentially sympathetic to the RCP's ideological positions and modus operandi, former RCP cadre Michael Fitzpatrick's essay helpfully periodizes the party's evolution. Fitzpatrick schematizes its origins as a dissenting tendency which 'emerged out of the left' but 'in many ways . . . was not of the left' and 'developed in a struggle against it'; its subsequent attempts to build a vanguard; and its reassessments and dissolution in the 1990s.[27]

Much of the historiography of the British radical left since the 1970s has comprised organizational studies[28] – especially of the Communist Party of Great Britain (CPGB)[29] – and activist memoirs.[30] Occasionally these genres have overtly overlapped. Institutional histories and autobiographical works alike have helpfully illuminated organizational cultures and the dynamics of intra-movement debate. Furthermore, in the past decade, Evan Smith and Matthew Worley have jointly edited two valuable collections of essays combining activist accounts and thematic studies of left ideas and strategies.[31] Thanks to their sensitivity to intra-left ideological controversies, these compelling volumes raised important questions about the political ecology of the British left between the radical furores of the 1970s, Thatcherism and its discontents in the 1980s and the post–Cold War order of the 1990s. Nevertheless, compared to the wealth of scholarship examining, for example, the intellectual legacies of the 1960s New Left, the post-1970s British radical left has not yet received the same degree of synoptic scrutiny.[32]

---

26 Evan Smith, *No Platform: A History of Anti-fascism, Universities and the Limits of Free Speech* (Abingdon: Routledge, 2020), 179. See also 174–83, 196–200.
27 Michael Fitzpatrick, 'The point is to change it: A short account of the Revolutionary Communist Party', in Evan Smith and Matthew Worley (eds), *Waiting for the Revolution: The British Far Left from 1956* (Manchester: Manchester University Press, 2017), 218–37.
28 See, for example, Ian H. Birchall, *'The Smallest Mass Party in the World': Building the Socialist Workers Party, 1951-1979* (London: Socialists Unlimited, 1981); Michael Crick, *Militant* (London: Faber & Faber, 1984); Michael Crick, *The March of Militant* (London: Faber & Faber, 1986).
29 Geoff Andrews, Nina Fishman and Kevin Morgan (eds), *Opening the Books: Essays on the Social and Cultural History of the British Communist Party* (London: Pluto Press, 1995); Geoff Andrews, *Endgames and New Times: The Final Years of British Communism* (London: Lawrence & Wishart, 2004).
30 Tony Cliff, *A World to Win: Life of a Revolutionary* (London: Bookmarks, 2000).
31 Evan Smith and Matthew Worley (eds), *Against the Grain: The British Far Left from 1956* (Manchester: Manchester University Press, 2014); Evan Smith and Matthew Worley (eds), *Waiting for the Revolution: The British Far Left from 1956* (Manchester: Manchester University Press, 2017).
32 See, for example, Lin Chun, *The British New Left* (Edinburgh: Edinburgh University Press, 1993); Michael Kenny, *The First New Left: British Intellectuals after Stalin* (London: Lawrence & Wishart, 1995); Madeleine Davis, 'The Marxism of the British new left', *Journal of Political Ideologies* 11 (2006): 335–58; Madeleine Davis, 'The origins of the British new left', in Martin Klimke and Joachim Scharloth (eds), *1968 in Europe: A History of Protest and Activism, 1956-1977* (Basingstoke: Palgrave Macmillan, 2008), 45–56; Wade Matthews, *The New Left, National Identity, and the Break-Up of Britain* (Leiden: Brill, 2013).

By focusing upon an organization which emerged from the left yet self-consciously positioned itself as a distinct critique of that tradition, *Preparing for Power* seeks to elucidate not only the history of a peculiar group but more broadly the left's contested terrain since the 1970s, most notably in relation to the Northern Ireland conflict, anti-racism, industrial militancy and the end of the Cold War. Moreover, extending the chronological focus beyond the dissolution of the vanguardist organization, the book unpacks critical left perspectives since the turn of the 1990s, probing radical humanist critiques of technocracy, environmentalism, critical race theory and the contemporary political conjuncture in toto.

In sum, *Preparing for Power* examines how, over almost five decades, a network of revolutionaries who convened in the late 1970s navigated changing political conjunctures and adapted their strategies. These wide chronological and thematic parameters unpack critical debates which remain sharply contested. More broadly, the book examines both ideological continuity and change among a network of radicals who espoused a distinct constellation of ideas and critiques. It elucidates how, amid transformed circumstances, radicals maintained their central political ideas and philosophical precepts through modified tasks and methods.

Probing the evolving components of political ideologies, this book's methodological and analytical framework fuses Quentin Skinner's influential critique of the history of ideas and Michael Freeden's morphological approach. Both taxonomies provide a felicitous optic for assessing a network whose core concepts – to borrow Freeden's term – have largely endured while their assessments of external conjuncture, and therefore of political possibilities, have modulated significantly. Dismantling a 'mythology of doctrines', Skinner's clarion critique warned scholars against exaggerating historical thinkers' clarity, continuity or prescience. Moreover, upbraiding intellectual historians for attempting to 'resolve' seeming contradictions in historical thinkers, Skinner positioned these antinomies not as obstacles to be circumvented but as compelling themes meriting scrutiny.[33] Freeden's morphological method, meanwhile, posited that political ideologies must be understood as hybrid forms, comprising conceptual components which fluctuate, mutate and interact differently according to unfolding circumstances. Adapting Skinner's emphasis upon excavating authorial *intent*, Freeden further signalled attention to the

---

33 Quentin Skinner, *Visions of Politics, Volume I: Regarding Method* (Cambridge: Cambridge University Press, 2002), 59–65, 71–2, 77, 176–9.

social context, reception and political contestation of historical ideas.[34] In this spirit, *Preparing for Power* examines diachronically both the internal dynamics of a distinct political tradition and the broader external conjuncture.

Scrutinizing the legion writings and words of ex-RCP members and supporters since the late 1970s, this analysis spans party propaganda as well as former activists' political engagements in the twenty-five years since the party dissolved. Tracing veterans' political trajectories, the book elucidates how the milieu has delineated an increasingly adverse conjuncture while sustaining a decidedly distinct critique. Drawing upon a comprehensive analysis of the RCP's propaganda and theoretical literature, *Preparing for Power* also examines a small collection of internal documents from private collections. Together, these sources offer valuable insights into the political and formal foundations of the party and its project. Locating this network's interventions in their thematic and temporal complexity, the analysis is grounded in a thorough archival study of the left and student press, political periodicals and radical agitprop. The book further examines the post-party writings and activities of more than 250 former members or supporters of the RCP. Especially in relation to the most prominent post-party forms – chiefly the web magazine *spiked* and the Battle of Ideas – *Preparing for Power* examines activists' publications, speeches and online media. Assessing how veterans have formulated their radical critiques, the book considers how, over the past five decades, former RCPers have differentially envisioned political alternatives.

To unpack further how veterans retrospectively evaluate their trajectories, *Preparing for Power* also analyses twenty-four original life-history interviews with former activists. The sample of seventeen men and seven women spans a range of generational cohorts and levels of organizational seniority, including founder members alongside younger activists who joined in the 1980s and 1990s and ranking from leading Political Committee cadres to supporters who refrained from becoming full members of the party.[35] Although the former RCP milieu has largely avoided major intra-group divisions, the interviewees nevertheless differ to a degree in how they narrate their network's legacies and contemporary evolution. Throughout the book, these oral testimonies reconstruct qualitative aspects of activist experience not usually elucidated

---

34 Michael Freeden, *Ideologies and Political Theory: A Conceptual Approach* (Oxford: Clarendon Press, 1996), *passim*, especially 100–8, 131–6.
35 In its gender profile, the interview sample probably slightly over-represents male activists (29 per cent): for a point of reference, women constituted some 109 of the 297 activists (37 per cent) whose words and writings feature, directly or indirectly, throughout the book.

in documentary sources. More resonantly, however, the oral histories elicit veterans' critical reflections upon how and why their network forged a distinct ideological praxis but failed to realize its revolutionary objectives. Following the pioneering oral history work of Graham Dawson and Penny Summerfield, testimonies are refracted here through the valuable lenses of subjective (dis)composure. Developing Dawson's concept of composure – which mapped how subjects drew upon 'public discourses' and strove for 'personal equanimity' in their narratives[36] – Summerfield accentuated how interviewees also negotiated *dis*composure. When narrators could not attain what Dawson called 'psychic comfort', Summerfield argued, they confronted dissonances in their stories, often manifested in anger, discomfort or self-contradiction.[37] As such, the interviews yield valuable insights not only into activist trajectories through mobilization and politicization but into how veterans appraise their historical ideas and activism in relation to their contemporary self and networks.

As an exploratory history of ideas, *Preparing for Power* argues that routine portrayals of former RCP activists moving from the revolutionary left to the reactionary right obscure salient features of the network's complex evolution. Situating important ideological themes in their specific historical context, this analysis explains how the radical humanist core of the RCP network survived its strategic and formal modification. In line with Freeden's multifaceted method of ideological analysis, understanding the milieu's complicated career requires close attention to the precepts which defined and distinguished the RCP from its origins. The organization's curious afterlives, this book contends, are indivisible from its founders' independent political philosophy.

Situating activists' critiques historically in their contested contexts, the following chapters are organized to assess the RCP's lifespan and legacies both chronologically and thematically. This introduction and Chapters 1–5 inclusive broadly chart the origins and development of the RCP, while Chapters 6 and 7 trace post-party forms since the turn of the millennium. Connecting these sections, the concluding chapter evaluates both continuity and change in the network's political prognoses and assessments of external conjuncture. Whereas the analytical threads through Chapters 1–5 are fastened more firmly to specific issues with which the party engaged, Chapters 6 and 7 probe more general

36 Graham Dawson, *Soldier Heroes: British Adventure, Empire and the Imagining of Masculinities* (Abingdon: Routledge, 1994), 11–26, 34–43.
37 Penny Summerfield, *Reconstructing Women's Wartime Lives: Discourse and Subjectivity in Oral Histories of the Second World War* (Manchester: Manchester University Press, 1998), 16–23; Penny Summerfield, 'Culture and composure: Creating narratives of the gendered self in oral history interviews', *Cultural and Social History* 1 (2004): 65–93.

themes among the post-party milieux – most notably the enduring critique of diminished subjectivity. Nevertheless, to cohere the discussion, these closing chapters retain episodic focal points, such as the referendum on the UK's membership of the European Union in 2016.

Introducing the RCP's origins as a self-consciously upstart critique of the radical left of the 1970s, Chapter 1 proceeds to dissect the organization's strategic emphasis upon expounding 'unconditional support' for the Irish republican movement during the Northern Ireland conflict. Assessing the party's militant anti-racism, Chapter 2 similarly explicates how the nascent organization simultaneously prioritized its work on Ireland and racism to expose and challenge reformism in the labour movement and the working class. Examining the party's controversial interventions with the miners' strike and the AIDS epidemic, Chapter 3 unpacks further the organization's critique both of 'collaborationist' trade unionism and of what theoreticians considered radical illusions in the state. Throughout, these chapters trace how RCP cadres envisioned a Leninist revolutionary vanguard developing political independence in the working class. Inspecting the RCP's assessment of the 'new world order' of the early 1990s, Chapter 4 explains why party strategists postulated that class vanguardism was no longer viable.

Bridging the RCP's dissolution and the emerging post-party forms through the mid-1990s, Chapter 5 analyses how revolutionaries who considered class politics in abeyance retreated to a more foundational struggle defending radical humanist precepts. Concluding with an analysis of the libel trial which precipitated the closure of erstwhile party magazine *LM*, the chapter connects the party's demise and the wider network's initiatives in the twenty-first century, chiefly the online magazine *spiked* and the Institute (later the Academy) of Ideas. Tracing former activists' critiques during their political wilderness years in the 2000s, Chapter 6 explores how ex-RCPers fulminated against a 'pre-political' epoch and upheld the history-making potential of the human subject.

Finally, Chapter 7 traces former RCP activists' energetic engagements with the referendum on the UK's membership of the European Union in 2016. For the many ex-cadres who advocated a Leave vote, the referendum result represented the first political advance in a generation. The chapter explains why veterans celebrated Brexit as an epochal advance for national sovereignty and, crucially, as a prerequisite for a challenge to globalist technocracy. Chapter 7 concludes with veterans' more dismayed assessments of the 'new anti-racism' of Black Lives Matter and of the British government's lockdowns during the Covid-19 pandemic. Echoing Gramsci's 'pessimism of the intellect' and 'optimism of the will', the conclusion reviews veterans' conflicting assessments of the contemporary moment: a robust and enduring emphasis upon the human potential to remake the world, mitigated by an unflinching analysis of the political obstacles to formulating a cohesive or compelling alternative.

Engaging critically with polemics both of the RCP's staunchest defenders and its fiercest critics, *Preparing for Power* illuminates the ideas which propelled the party, how they evolved and how they have been remembered. Striving for historical empathy – seeking at least to understand why historical actors thought and acted as they did – *Preparing for Power* will doubtless dissatisfy partisan readers of varying stripes seeking either vindication or castigation. The book's thematic and chronological breadth necessarily runs the risk of frustrating specialists on particular aspects of the contemporary history discussed here: it is no more a comprehensive history of the British left than it is a dedicated analysis of, for example, anti-racism, libertarianism or radical humanism. Rather, as a dispassionate analysis, the book seeks principally to understand dynamically the ideas which defined the network. It does not presume to be the final word on the topic. But in training a critical, analytical eye towards the RCP and its afterlives, it is hoped that the present book will stimulate further interest and discussion surrounding this peculiar political tradition and its complex historical contexts.

1

'We take the very unpopular position of giving unconditional support to the republican movement'[1]

Questioning everything: The origins of the Revolutionary Communist Party

The Revolutionary Communist Tendency (RCT) originated among a small group of radicals expelled from the Revolutionary Communist Group (RCG) in 1976. A product of a split from the International Socialists (IS) in 1974, the RCG charged the radical left with perpetuating 'nationalism' and 'reformism' in the labour movement. According to the group's foundational text, *Our Tasks and Methods* (1975), the prevailing trends on the left – subordinating workers' interests to those of the state or asserting that state-led reforms could ameliorate capitalism – occluded independent revolutionary politics.[2] Among the RCG's few dozen cadres, prominent theoretician Frank Richards expressed the critique especially starkly: 'The greatest threat facing the labour movement is its own reformist consciousness.'[3]

Charging the British left with hubris, the RCG – and, subsequently, the RCT – emerged dissenting against radicals who were nostalgic for the militant

---

1 'The Irish War: Which side are you on?', *the next step: review of the Revolutionary Communist Tendency* (hereafter *tns*), February 1981.
2 'Our tasks and methods – the founding document of the RCG', *Revolutionary Communist: Theoretical Journal of the Revolutionary Communist Group*, 1 (January 1975).
3 Frank Richards, 'The question of fascism and racism in Britain', in *Revolutionary Communist Group Discussion Bulletin*, 3 (April 1975): 48–60. For security reasons, members of the RCG, RCT and RCP generally used 'cadre names', which often took the form of a false surname. For example, the RCP's central founding figure, Frank Furedi, employed the cadre name Frank Richards. Sometimes, activists assumed entirely new monikers: serving on the Political Committee at the turn of the 1990s, avid Newcastle United supporter Kirk Leech became 'Mick Quinn', in homage to the team's burly goalscorer. Following standard practice, in each instance, this book simply refers to individuals by the names they publicly used in the given context. Kirk Leech to the author, 13 April 2022.

peaks of the early 1970s. After the ferment of the global 1968 – when student protesters, anti-war activists and industrial militants especially swelled the ranks of Trotskyist groups – fringe organizations to the left of Harold Wilson's Labour Party rose in confidence. At the zenith of industrial unrest in 1971, the leaders of the official labour movement – in the Trades Union Congress (TUC) and the Labour Party alike – joined forces to oppose the Heath government's Industrial Relations Act, designed to restrict workers' ability to strike. Although the act became law in August 1971, the labour movement remained galvanized: after unsuccessfully imploring the electorate to renounce industrial militants as a menace to democracy – 'who governs Britain?' – Heath was expelled from Downing Street in the election of February 1974. At the forefront of the emboldened radical left, Tony Cliff – whose International Socialists grew after 1968, before becoming the Socialist Workers Party in 1977 – later remembered the early 1970s as 'the best years of my life'.[4]

From the vantage point of the late 1970s, however, the founders of the RCT arraigned British revolutionaries for overestimating their strength and coherence. In 1974, with Labour returned to power, the TUC leadership had settled a 'social contract' with Wilson's government, agreeing to limit inflation and industrial unrest. Whereas trade union bureaucrats largely endorsed the concordat with Labour, the more radical left – especially around the International Socialists – were left dismayed by the collaboration.[5] In this context, the RCT's founders postulated that the radical left had been hoist by its own reformist petard. Expounding their 'tasks and methods', the RCT's founding cadres denounced reformism and envisioned instead a Leninist vanguard, organized around the principles of democratic centralism, to establish an independent revolutionary movement in the working class.

To challenge reformism and invigorate independent class politics, the RCG aspired to forge a revolutionary vanguard in the working class. Its foundational priority was to develop ideological independence: 'our aim', leading cadre Judy Harrison wrote in 1974, 'is to widen the political consciousness of the working class as a whole'.[6] Expelled from the Brighton branch of the International Socialists in 1973, Sussex University physics undergraduate James Woudhuysen aligned with a dissenting milieu around David Yaffe in Brighton and Frank

---

4   Cliff, *A World to Win*, 124.
5   Stephen Meredith, 'A "brooding oppressive shadow"? The Labour Alliance, the "trade union question", and the trajectory of revisionist social democracy, c. 1969-1975', *Labour History Review*, 82 (2017): 251–76.
6   Judith Harrison, 'Political work amongst women – perspectives', July 1974. *Revolutionary Communist Group Discussion Bulletin*, 2 (December 1974).

Furedi in London. In 1974, he became a founder member of the RCG, attacking 'economism, chauvinism and left-reformism' in the labour movement.[7] Some five decades on, Woudhuysen recalls a moment when an alternative to left-wing sloganizing seemed possible:

> In those days, at Sussex in particular, the left was quite intellectual.... There were some heavy, quite good scholarly Marxists.... I liked all that. The atmosphere was right for it. The curiosity was part of the sixties. And I rapidly ran into this sort of faction, the [David] Yaffe/Frank [Richards/Furedi] faction.... that wasn't satisfied with the left's failure to respond to the charge that wage rises caused inflation [. . .] It was also clear to me and to us that more militancy and 'Heath out' just wasn't a solution, just like the left's political economy on wages and inflation.[8]

By 1978, Harrison, Richards/Furedi and Woudhuysen, veterans of the RCG, would be among the founders of the RCT.

The new organization emerged from an RCG schism rooted in abstruse theoretical and programmatic differences. Dissenters within the RCG had criticized their leading figure, David Yaffe, especially in relation to his position on the South African anti-apartheid movement. In November 1976, tensions within the RCG peaked at a conference discussing the liberation struggle. Several cadres accused Yaffe of drawing the RCG towards the Communist Party of Great Britain (CPGB) and its affinity with the Stalinist tendency in the South African liberation movement. Charging Yaffe with abandoning an 'independent working-class standpoint', three cadres – Chris Davies, Judy Harrison and Frank Richards – left the group acrimoniously.[9] Barred from an RCG meeting in Manchester in December 1976, the trio began organizing an independent propaganda group with a small coterie of comrades.

Styling themselves the Steering Committee of the RCT, a cell of approximately twelve comrades spent the opening months of 1977 producing the first edition of their theoretical journal. Published in March 1977, this formative text ('Revolutionary Communist Papers No. 1') presented the dissenters' version of the RCG's fracture. For the RCT's founders, most notably Mike Freeman and Frank Richards, the RCG had latterly failed to challenge chauvinism in the

---

7   James Wood, 'The crisis of the bourgeoisie: The European Economic Community', in *Revolutionary Communist Group Special Discussion Bulletin, July 1975* (London: RCG Publications, 1975), 43.
8   James Woudhuysen interview with the author, 7 December 2022 (hereafter, James Woudhuysen, 7 December 2022).
9   Revolutionary Communist Group Executive Committee, *Statement on the Expulsion of a Chauvinist Grouping in the RCG*, 17 November 1976. Copy in author's possession.

labour movement. Committing, by contrast, to 'the struggle for proletarian internationalism', the RCT's founders began developing and documenting their revolutionary critique.¹⁰

The intensiveness of the RCT's early theoretical work reflected the perceived scale of its world-historical objectives. In July 1979, reissuing the RCG's *Our Tasks and Methods*, the RCT's founding Political Committee echoed its ambitious imperative: 'to **transform** the present consciousness . . . [and] win and train a vanguard in the working class movement'. The fledgling organization vowed to act on the most adverse political terrain. Noting the 'absence of a Marxist tradition' in the working class, the RCT's founders anticipated that their politics would 'often be met with indifference'.¹¹ Deliberately challenging orthodoxies in the working class, the RCT would prioritize campaigning on issues 'which most clearly reveal the necessity for a break with reformism'.¹²

Like the RCG before it, the RCT was founded upon a critical analysis of the radical left. For revolutionary cadres eschewing reformism and statism, it was crucial to develop ideological independence among activists and, in time, among the working class. Identifying reformism not as a diluted version of their own revolutionary objectives but as an entirely different political project, cadres echoed Rosa Luxemberg's resonant contempt for reformism's essential conservatism.¹³ Writing as a member of the RCG Political Committee in 1975, Richards had asserted that a revolutionary alternative must supplant left-wing tendencies which bore the imprint of successive working-class defeats.¹⁴ Similarly, repudiating the Moscow-aligned CPGB, the founders of the RCT

---

10 Pat Morris, *Open Letter to All Members of the Revolutionary Communist Group*, 1 February 1977. Copy in author's possession.
11 Chris Davies and Judith Harrison, 'A retrograde step for the Marxist movement – a reply to Cde Yaffe', in Revolutionary Communist Tendency, *Documents on the Split within the Revolutionary Communist Group* (Revolutionary Communist Papers, No. 1, March 1977), 5, 7, 20. Emphases in original.
12 Revolutionary Communist Tendency, *Our Tasks and Methods* (Revolutionary Communist Reprints, No. 1, August 1979), 2.
13 In the 1890s, the German radical Eduard Bernstein had intimated socialism could be achieved constitutionally by democratic methods. Lambasting Bernstein's reformism, Luxemberg's pamphlet *Social Reform or Revolution?* (1899) underscored the imperative of the revolutionary overthrow of capitalism: 'People who pronounce themselves in favour of the method of legislative reform in place and in contradistinction to the conquest of political power and social revolution, do not really choose a more tranquil, calmer and slower road to the same goal, but a different goal. Instead of taking a stand for the establishment of a new society they take a stand for surface modifications of the old society.' Marc Mulholland, *Bourgeois Liberty and The Politics of Fear: From Absolutism to Neo-Conservatism* (Oxford: Oxford University Press, 2013), 142; Rosa Luxemburg, *Reform or Revolution*, reprinted in Helen Scott (ed.), *The Essential Rosa Luxemburg* (Chicago: Haymarket, 2008), 90.
14 Frank Richards, 'The Question of the International', *Revolutionary Communist: Theoretical Journal of the Revolutionary Communist Group*, 2 (May 1975): 40.

scorned the 'reactionary consequences' of 'official communism'.[15] Diagnosing the 'ideological weakness' of the radical left, they positioned themselves rebuilding from scratch 'independent' revolutionary politics.[16] As Evan Smith has noted, from its foundations, the RCT disavowed the 'no platform' tactics of the left and the student movement and opposed all forms of censorship.[17] For revolutionaries envisioning a herculean struggle for revolutionary ideas, inviting authorities to police expression was anathema.[18]

The RCT's vanguardist methods tasked cadres with winning class-conscious workers to a revolutionary standpoint. In microcosm, vanguardism epitomized the momentous modus operandi: galvanizing a dynamic subjective force to defy adverse objective circumstances and change the world. Founding activists held that revolutionary independence would not emerge spontaneously from working-class institutions but rather required the compelling leadership of a vanguard organization. Echoing Lenin's critique of economism in *What Is to Be Done?*, RCT theoreticians asserted that without the vanguard's inspired leadership, workers could attain only limited trade union consciousness, fighting sporadically against the bosses but not holistically establishing their class interests. Addressing the RCP conference of October 1982, for example, Frank Richards again invoked Lenin's pamphlet: only a class vanguard, Richards told cadres, could transform trade unionism's defensive 'subservience to spontaneity'.[19] Underlining the connection between formal discipline, strategic independence and theoretical clarification, James Woudhuysen reasserts the importance for the RCT's founders of *What Is to Be Done?*

> I really loved it. Some people find it very hard to understand, and the bourgeoisie particularly: they think it's a blueprint for secret organisation. It isn't. It's all about ideology: shades, nuances, not falling into 'the marsh', and the defects of the economists – a word that had a special meaning in Russia in 1905. . . . So the willingness to polemicise against our opponents, the willingness to talk tough

---

15 Frank Richards and Phil Turner, 'Stalinism, the Communist Party and the RCG's New Turn', in Revolutionary Communist Tendency, *Documents on the Split within the Revolutionary Communist Group*, 28, 42.
16 Revolutionary Communist Tendency, *Isolation and the Radical Left – Statement on the Split within the RCT* (May 1977). Copy in author's possession.
17 The National Union of Students (NUS) conference of April 1974, for example, codified the no-platform tactics which were already widely employed on the left. Labour leftists and members of the CPGB, IS and International Marxist Group (IMG) supported the successful motion stipulating that students' unions should deny platforms 'by whatever means necessary' to 'openly racist or fascist organisations or societies'. Smith, *No Platform*, 4–5.
18 Revolutionary Communist Tendency, *The Recession, Capitalist Offensive and the Working Class* (20 July 1978).
19 *Building the New Leadership*. RCP conference bulletin (1982); V. I. Lenin, 'What is to be done?', in V. I. Lenin, *Collected Works, Volume 5* (Moscow: Progress Publishers, 1977), 417–18.

with each other about what we really understood and believed and identified with – that was also a very refreshing part of it all. It kept you on your toes.[20]

In that spirit, the RCT committed to train a vanguard in the working class to transform 'anti-capitalist potential' into 'independent class politics'.[21]

Members of the new organization developed their theory and propaganda in a period of feverish activity through 1977 and 1978. The febrile and hectic atmosphere triggered a brief schism. On 7 May 1977, after disagreements relating to the pace of organizational development, a minority of the RCT's founders left the group. Those who remained insisted that the defectors underestimated the requirements of political elaboration and cadre-training.[22] Styling themselves as the 'Committee for a Communist Programme', the departed activists vowed to maintain 'fraternal relations' with the Tendency.[23] Within months, several had rejoined.

Cohering approximately twenty cadres, the new organization mostly comprised dedicated full-time revolutionaries.[24] According to a founding member, most of the RCT's early recruits were students or graduates, and all were under the age of thirty.[25] Training a vanguard, they asserted, required a rigorous education programme. From the outset, cadres regarded their challenging educationals as a mark of organizational distinction. Sabina Norton and Keith Tompson, for example, contrasted their organization's intellectual demands with those of rival leftists:

> The S[ocialist] W[orkers] P[arty] doesn't even want to see its members regularly. . . . [It] can play no role in the development of an independent working class vanguard.[26]

Founders also distinguished their theoretical literature from what they considered the perfunctory sloganizing of the radical left. In 1978, previewing proposals to

---

20 James Woudhuysen, 7 December 2022.
21 Revolutionary Communist Tendency, *Our Tasks and Methods*, 1.
22 Revolutionary Communist Tendency, *Isolation and the Radical Left*.
23 Committee for a Communist Programme, *On the Split in the Revolutionary Communist Tendency and the formation of the Committee for a Communist Programme*, May 1977. Copy in author's possession.
24 Codifying their party constitution in the 1980s, RCP activists agreed that full members were entitled to twenty-eight days per calendar year off party activism. Members booking leave were required to give at least fourteen days' notice to the Political Committee. *Notes for a constitution* (internal RCP document, 1985). Copy in author's possession.
25 Mike Fitzpatrick interview with the author, 15 August 2020.
26 Sabina Norton and Keith Tompson, *The Struggle for a Revolutionary Propaganda Group* (London: Revolutionary Communist Tendency, October 1977), 10. Emphases in original.

publish a regular review, the RCT insisted that 'unlike the newspapers of the radical left it will not simply describe strikes or issue lists of abstract demands'.[27]

As a programmatic corollary of their vanguardist strategy, cadres aspired to maximal ideological independence, by which workers would clearly and consistently identify their class interests. Distinguishing their politics from the nationalist, reformist and statist tendencies that they abhorred, cadres trumpeted 'independent' working-class politics. Recalling Trotsky's rejoinder to 'ultra-leftists' on revolutionary tactics, 'independence' became a mainstay of the RCP lexicon.[28] Challenging workers to identify and act upon their class interests, the few dozen cadres who formed the RCT elevated a struggle for revolutionary subjectivity. Correspondingly, they accused radical left organizations, most significantly the Socialist Workers Party (SWP), of abdicating responsibility for developing ideological independence in the working class.[29] Tony Allen denounced the SWP's 'narrow trade unionist focus',[30] while Frank Richards opined that Tony Cliff's party tailed the 'reformist leadership of the working class' and failed to recognize that 'the shop stewards are far from revolutionary'.[31]

Vowing to transform working-class consciousness,[32] the RCT attacked 'opportunist' leftists who merely tailed present forms of trade union militancy.[33] Borrowing from Lenin's wartime critique of the labour movement, cadres adopted an avowedly confrontational approach towards the institutions of the working class.[34] Mike Fitzpatrick's account of a Labour Co-ordinating Committee conference in March 1980 encapsulated how the RCT's determination to

27 Tony Allen, Gareth Evans, Mike Freeman and Kate Marshall, *The Recession: Capitalist Offensive and the Working Class* (Revolutionary Communist Papers, No. 3, July 1978), 2.
28 Writing in 1938 during the escalating international crisis, Trotsky defended the nascent Secretariat of the Fourth International. Trotsky's famous dictum lambasted contrarian radicals who mechanically determined their position by inverting the contingent position of the bourgeoisie. Revolutionary tactics, Trotsky insisted, must flow from class independence: 'In ninety cases out of a hundred the workers actually place a minus sign where the bourgeoisie places a plus sign. In ten cases however they are forced to fix the same sign as the bourgeoisie but with their own seal, in which is expressed their mistrust of the bourgeoisie. The policy of the proletariat is not at all automatically derived from the policy of the bourgeoisie, bearing only the opposite sign – this would make every sectarian a master strategist; no, the revolutionary party must each time orient itself *independently* in the internal as well as the external situation, arriving at those decisions which correspond best to the interests of the proletariat'. Leon Trotsky, 'Learn to think: A friendly suggestion to certain ultra-leftists', *The New International* 4, no. 7 (July 1938): 206–7.
29 According to former activist Jim Higgins, by March 1974, after a period of growth, the International Socialists (IS) had 3,310 members. The IS became the SWP in January 1977. Jim Higgins, *More Years for the Locust: The Origins of the SWP* (London: IS Group, 1997), Chapter 11.
30 Tony Allen, 'World in recession', in Revolutionary Communist Party, *World in Recession* (Revolutionary Communist Papers, No. 7, July 1981), 21.
31 Frank Richards, 'One or two things Tony Cliff forgot', *tns*, December 1979.
32 Richards and Turner, 'Stalinism', 41.
33 Davies and Harrison, 'A retrograde step', 2.
34 V. I. Lenin, 'British pacificism and the British dislike of theory', V. I. Lenin, *Collected Works, Volume 21* (Moscow: Progress Publishers, 1974), 260–5; Frank Richards, *Under a National Flag: Fascism,*

transform working-class consciousness underpinned cadres' sense of formal and strategic uniqueness. Billed as a 'debate of the decade' identifying socialists' priorities for the 1980s, the event included among its platform speakers representatives of the Labour Party, SWP and International Marxist Group (IMG). Reviewing the discussion, Fitzpatrick charged the gathered leftists with sharing illusions in the labour movement, where 'the grip of reformism' was 'tightest':

> The radical left may worship the shop floor . . . [but] it is not *where* you operate that makes revolutionary politics distinct, but the final objective and the political strategy.[35]

Above all, the critique of the left arraigned its orientation towards the state. Amid a deepening recession, the RCT's founders charged radicals with prioritizing the national economy over working-class interests. RCT theoreticians railed especially against the Labour left's Alternative Economic Strategy, by which Tony Benn and his parliamentary colleagues expounded a programme for industrial democracy, founded upon major nationalization, increased public spending and controls on prices and imports.[36] Emerging from the theoretical work of the academic and party adviser Stuart Holland, most notably *The Socialist Challenge* (1975), the Alternative Economic Strategy continued to percolate Labour's programme until the party's cataclysmic defeat in the general election of 1983.[37]

For Frank Richards, trade unionists calling for the state to restrict the movement of goods and capital demonstrated the deplorable 'strength of British nationalism' in the labour movement.[38] As James Callaghan's ailing Labour government toiled in economic crisis, the RCT's first public meetings and day schools exhorted workers to identify with their class rather than with their nation. Addressing a meeting in 1978, Richards attacked Labour grandees and Trades Union Congress (TUC) officials who posited that workers shared with their bosses an interest in repairing British capitalism.[39] Cadres found their theoretical analyses substantiated in contemporary labour disputes. In the spring of 1980, when the right-wing leadership of the steelworkers' union struck

---

Racism and the Labour Movement (Revolutionary Communist Pamphlets, No. 2, second edition August 1978 [first edition January 1978]), 3.
35 'A night out for the left', *tns*, April–May 1980. Emphases in original.
36 Andrew Friend and Andy Metcalf, *Slump City: The Politics of Mass Unemployment* (London: Pluto Press, 1981), 178–80.
37 Paul Auerbach, *The Left Intellectual Opposition in Britain, 1945-2000: The Case of the Alternative Economic Strategy* (London: Kingston University, 2003), 5–10.
38 Richards, *Under a National Flag*, 24.
39 Revolutionary Communist Tendency, *The Trade Unions and the Struggle Against Racism* (1978). Copy in author's possession.

a deal with British Steel, ending a fourteen-week strike, the RCT condemned the TUC for the 'sell-out . . . [a] setback to the entire labour movement'.[40]

The RCT's hostility towards left-wing statism dovetailed with its antipathy to reformism. Cadres who vowed to dismantle workers' illusions in the state were especially hostile to trade union hierarchies vying to collaborate with the government. In January 1981, for example, the leaders of the steelworkers', miners' and railway workers' unions commended to the government a 'strategy for economic recovery'. Imploring the Conservatives to subsidize and protect nationalized industries against foreign competition, the union organizers positioned their respective sectors 'at the heart of the nation's struggle for economic survival'.[41]

RCT cadres inveighed against trade union hierarchies, which equated workers' interests with those of 'the nation'. Richards, for instance, scorned the reformist assessment of the state as an 'essentially neutral agency', which radicals and trade unionists could positively transform.[42] At a public meeting at London's Conway Hall in July 1978, Mike Freeman and Kate Marshall castigated 'state socialists' who implied that capitalism could be made 'humane and efficient' and therefore obstructed revolutionary politics.[43] RCT cadres instead expounded the necessity of a vanguard committed to smashing the state and establishing a dictatorship of the proletariat. Following Lenin's critique of 'social-chauvinism', theoreticians fulminated against the 'national-reformist' tradition, by which British leftists endorsed the state apparatus of immigration controls, trade quotas and bans on capital export.[44]

Early theoretical work juxtaposed the revolutionary potential of the working class and the perceived reformism of its institutions. The organization emerged in an epoch of substantial labour militancy: in the year 1972 alone, some

---

40 Members of the Iron and Steel Trades Confederation (ISTC) had initially demanded a 20 per cent pay rise. Resolving the strike, the ISTC leadership negotiated a more modest pay rise – tied to local productivity deals – below the rate of inflation, and accepted redundancies. 'The price of TUC leadership', *tns*, April–May 1980.
41 Iron and Steel Trades Confederation, *What Is the Future? Steel – Rail – Coal* (London: Iron and Steel Trades Confederation, 1981), 10–12. The leaders of the Iron and Steel Trades Confederation, the National Union of Mineworkers and the National Union of Railwaymen authored the document.
42 Richards, *Under a National Flag*, 9.
43 Revolutionary Communist Tendency, *The Recession*.
44 *Racial Oppression: How to Fight It* (Revolutionary Communist Pamphlets, No. 4, April 1979), 21. Lenin coined 'social-chauvinism' in 1915, repudiating socialists in the Second International who espoused 'national defence' at the outbreak of the First World War. For Lenin – who called for the defeat of the imperial powers – social-chauvinism signified 'the justification of an alliance between the Socialists and the bourgeoisie and governments of "their own" countries in this war, the refusal to preach and support proletarian-revolutionary action against "one's own" bourgeoisie'. V. I. Lenin, 'The collapse of the Second International', Lenin, *Collected Works, Volume 21*, 241.

twenty-four million working days were lost to strike action.[45] In a resonant assessment, four founding activists counterposed the 'organisational strength' and the 'political weakness' of the British working class.[46] Norton and Tompson contrasted the labour movement's 'courage and militancy' and its failure to 'advance an independent political response to the capitalist assault . . . the workers' movement is in ideological disarray'.[47] Such a dialectical relationship between subjective possibility and objective reality defined the vanguardist project, which configured a leading role for the revolutionary party.

Promising an antidote to the baleful influence of reformism, cadres condemned leftists' habitual electoral support for Labour. Anticipating the general election of 1979, for example, the SWP's magazine editorial attacked the Callaghan government's record but concluded that in the absence of a credible radical alternative, socialists were 'forced, reluctantly and against their wishes, to call for the return of a Labour government'. Although the SWP proposed rank-and-file organizing, independent of Labour, to build a socialist movement, its leadership maintained that 'to abstain in a situation where the mass of workers continue, despite everything which has happened, to support Labour would be the worst sort of irresponsibility'.[48] By contrast, espousing revolutionary abstentionism, Mike Freeman and Kate Marshall fulminated against Labour's 'classless strategy', which had ensnared the working class in 'the service of the nation', 'suppressed class contradictions' and buttressed capitalism. Rather than voting Labour faute de mieux, Freeman and Marshall asserted, an 'uncompromising struggle' against its reformism was vital.[49] Reflecting four decades later, one of the authors of *Who Needs the Labour Party?* (1978) positioned the pamphlet as an 'important marker' of cadres' distinct critique and tasks, 'defining our relationship with the left. [. . .] We came out of the old left but we were no longer part of it'.[50]

For its rivals on the radical left, the RCT was a utopian sect in thrall to idealistic abstraction. More established left-wing groups regarded the new organization's cadres as dogmatic ideologues, whose theoretical absolutism would repel workers. Distributing propaganda at an RCT day school in August 1978, the Spartacist League portrayed the Tendency as a doctrinaire faction 'not

---

45 Satnam Virdee, 'Racism and resistance in British trade unions, 1948–1979', in Peter Alexander and Rick Halpern (eds), *Racializing Class, Classifying Race: Labour and Difference in Britain, the USA and Africa* (Basingstoke: Macmillan, 2000), 138.
46 Allen et al., *The Recession*, 42.
47 Norton and Tompson, *The Struggle for a Revolutionary Propaganda Group*, 2–3.
48 'The left's choice', *Socialist Review*, April 1979.
49 Mike Freeman and Kate Marshall, *Who Needs the Labour Party?* (Revolutionary Communist Pamphlets, No. 3, September 1978), 9, 26, 30.
50 Mike Fitzpatrick, 15 August 2020.

seriously interested . . . in building a party to struggle for state power'.[51] For Alex Callinicos of the SWP, training cadres in the primacy of ideas and theory represented a 'fallacy', indicating the RCT's aloofness from the vital class struggle. Animosity towards the labour movement leadership, Callinicos contended, rendered the RCT irrelevant: 'revolutionaries should look for every opportunity to involve themselves in whatever struggles are taking place'.[52] Reflecting today, Mike Fitzpatrick avers that the emphasis upon ideological independence underpinned a fundamental strategic difference between the RCT and its left-wing counterparts:

> Whereas the left adapted to the prevailing outlook of the labour movement, we always tried to promote an independent line. . . . The left mistook our commitment to polemic as sectarian and divisive, when it was all about ideological clarification.[53]

The RCT commenced an intensive period of internal education and theoretical clarification during the late 1970s. Cadres joined rigorous educationals and convened events to attract class-conscious thinkers. In February 1979, for example, during the 'winter of discontent', Kate Marshall, Mary Masters, Frank Richards and Keith Tompson coordinated a series of public forums in north London, elaborating a distinct definition of revolutionary independence.[54] Although at this juncture the core membership remained confined to a network of between twenty and thirty activists, the RCT's organizational flair engendered contact with wider metropolitan left milieux. In September 1980, for instance, more than 200 activists attended the RCT's first major conference, which addressed imperialism and the global economic crisis.[55]

Meanwhile, cadres forensically researched detailed pamphlets elucidating their polemical critiques of the left, the state and imperialism. In 1979, the RCT launched *the next step* as its monthly review. The newspaper represented a vital propaganda output and a focal point for organizational activity. Renouncing the 'pompous calls to action', which they considered typical of the left-wing press, members of the editorial board published polemical analyses of contemporary politics and essays adumbrating the inadequacies of reform and the historical

---

51 'RCT: Wrong tasks, wrong methods' (1978) quoted in 'Born-again Cliffites on the move', *Spartacist Britain*, July–August 1983.
52 Alex Callinicos, 'Politics or abstract propagandism?', *International Socialism*, Winter 1981, 111–28.
53 Mike Fitzpatrick, 15 August 2020.
54 Revolutionary Communist Tendency, *Public Forums* (n.d. [1979]). Copy in author's possession.
55 Revolutionary Communist Party, *Malvinas Are Argentina's* (Revolutionary Communist Pamphlets, No. 13, June 1982), 33.

imperative of revolution.⁵⁶ Stylistically, the newspaper adopted what its founding editor remembers as an 'austere look': close-typed Times Roman, unbroken by images.⁵⁷

The establishment of the RCP in May 1981 signalled a new phase in the organization's development. Approximately eight-five activists gathered in London, elected a Political Committee and vowed to take their propaganda into the working class with renewed vigour. According to an undercover police officer infiltrating the organization in its foundational stages, the conference, which launched the RCP in May 1981, hosted twenty-nine 'cell members' – core cadres comprising the leadership and its inner circle – as well as approximately forty 'ordinary' members and a further fifteen 'contacts'. The most recent recruits, 'contacts' were typically individuals who had demonstrated particular interest in the organization's politics at a public meeting or attended a follow-up meeting after buying literature at a street sale.⁵⁸ Recruitment typically arose from personal contacts between activists and interested individuals who bought the organization's literature or attended demonstrations and meetings.⁵⁹ By September 1981, when the RCP convened its first national conference – ambitiously titled 'Preparing for Power' – the party's founding cadres had spent several years developing their ideas and strategy.⁶⁰ The following chapters trace the RCP's efforts to supersede the past defeats of the international working class through a revolutionary movement 'to establish the dictatorship of the proletariat in Britain' and realize 'communism throughout the world'.⁶¹

Forming the RCP in May 1981, cadres embarked upon their vanguardist project in a spirit of profound seriousness combined with realistic self-assessment. Activists perceived themselves attempting to rescue revolutionary politics six decades since the defeat of the Bolshevik revolution: their foundational critique held that the struggle would be arduous and against the odds. A leading cadre recorded that the party was 'small and marginal' and 'did not reflect any

---

56 'Breaking new ground', *tns*, December 1979.
57 Mike Fitzpatrick interview with the author, 22 August 2020.
58 Undercover Policing Inquiry (hereafter, UPI) I0000015575: 'Special Branch report on an internal conference of the Revolutionary Communist Tendency to discuss forthcoming policies and actions', 1 September 1981. Available at ucpi.org.uk/publications/special-branch-report-on-an-in ternal-conference-of-the-revolutionary-communist-tendency-to-discuss-forthcoming-policies-and-actions/ (accessed 12 July 2021).
59 Mike Freeman, 'The road to power', *Confrontation*, 1 (Summer 1986): 83.
60 Frank Richards, 'Editorial: Their alternative and ours', in Revolutionary Communist Party, *World in Recession*, 2.
61 RCP founding statement (May 1981), quoted in Mike Fitzpatrick, 'Waking from the nightmare' (unpublished manuscript). Copy in author's possession. I am grateful to Mike Fitzpatrick for sharing this unpublished manuscript.

significant trend in the working class'.⁶² Similarly, founding members noted with dismay that nationalism, reformism and social-chauvinism pervaded the labour movement. As secretary of Tameside Trades Council, RCT activist Dave Hallsworth delineated the importance of challenging the CPGB's influence in the working class and supplanting its reformist strategies 'in the factories where . . . they dampen down struggles'.⁶³ Sabena Norton admitted that the party's leftist rivals, most notably the CPGB, remained the most 'organised left-wing force in the trade unions'.⁶⁴ With three million British workers unemployed and real wages falling in 1981, *the next step*'s editorial board lamented that 'the hold of the labour bureaucracy over the working class remains intact'.⁶⁵

Some four decades on, cadres remember the early RCP as an attractive milieu defined and distinguished by the clarity and freshness of its analysis. Kirk Leech, who joined the party in 1982, evokes the impression of formal and ideological independence:

> We never saw ourselves as being part of the left. We were organisationally in it, but probably politically and even emotionally outside of it.⁶⁶

Positioning themselves as a revolutionary alternative, activists drew inspiration from their critique of the left:

> We spent a lot of our time arguing against the rest of the left. . . . We really weren't part of that world. *On the left but not of it*, I think Frank once said. . . . That was part of the appeal of it for me, was being separate from that kind of morass and having, I thought, the arguments to take them apart.⁶⁷

The historical momentousness of their project energized cadres who believed that their organization was capable of advancing revolutionary politics despite adverse circumstances. Rob Killick, who met the RCT in Canterbury in the late 1970s, depicted the frisson of excitement during these foundational stages:

> It was exciting intellectually, and it was exciting to feel committed to something, and to feel that you were building something important.⁶⁸

---

62 Freeman, 'The road to power', 53.
63 Dave Hallsworth quoted in 'Fight TUC line on Ireland', *Socialist Press: Weekly Paper of the Workers Socialist League*, 9 July 1980.
64 Sabena Norton, 'Communist Party conference: A knife in the back of us all', *tns*, December 1979.
65 'No turning back!', *tns*, December 1981.
66 Kirk Leech interview with the author, 7 September 2020.
67 Former RCP member interview with the author, February 2021.
68 Rob Killick interview with the author, 20 August 2020.

Early recruits revelled in their commitment to a cadre organization, which aspired ambitiously to overcome the left's past defeats:

> What attracted me was just the rigour of their analysis, the fact that it wasn't like the rest of the left. It was very serious and had theoretical depth, but not in an academic sense: they were doing things, and they were out on the street arguing, selling, organising. But what impressed me was their intellectual seriousness, depth, and rigour.[69]

Adopting the Leninist organizational principles of democratic centralism, RCP organizers instilled a culture of internal debate and discipline.[70] At national conferences, cadres would discuss and determine the party programme. Once strategic priorities and campaigning tactics were agreed, activists worked locally and 'collectively under the discipline of a Branch organiser' – who, in turn, was directly accountable to the elected Political Committee. Cadres committed to 'understand, accept and fight for the RCP programme'.[71]

Some of the earliest recruits first encountered the party through its organizers on university campuses in Canterbury, Coventry and Manchester. Throughout the organization's lifespan, students would remain an important constituency. Affiliating to their local party branches, the RCP's student societies connected issues on campus to broader political controversies: at Newcastle University in 1986, for example, rallying around two Libyan students who had been detained and threatened with deportation, the Revolutionary Communist Students (RCS) amplified their anti-imperialist opposition to the US air strikes on Tripoli.[72] For an activist who met the RCP as a student in Manchester in the early 1980s, the nascent party's self-conscious brio and waspish intellectual culture promised to supplant weary left-wing orthodoxies:

> It was pretty much love at first sight. The RCP were everything I was looking for in terms of political engagement. They were young, they were sexy, they were intelligent, they were active, they put pressure on you. What I particularly liked was the provocativeness. Whatever I thought, they would sort of challenge. They weren't interested in platitudes or being nice for the sake of it. . . . I liked that sort

---

69 Norman Lewis interview with the author, 16 February 2021.
70 Delineating 'party unity' in March 1921, Lenin asserted that democratic centralism married rigorous theoretical discussion *within* the party, with organizational cohesion and 'strict discipline . . . to secure the maximum unanimity in eliminating all factionalism'. Lenin adumbrated these principles in his resolution to the Tenth Congress of the Bolshevik Party. V. I. Lenin, *Collected Works, Volume 32* (Moscow: Progress Publishers, 1973), 241–4.
71 *Notes for a Constitution* (internal RCP document, 1985). Copy in author's possession.
72 George Napier, 'In defence of Libyan students', *Courier: Newcastle University Students' Newspaper*, 15 May 1986.

of provocation, and for many, many years afterwards I tried to employ the same approach myself.[73]

The revolutionary ideals which inspired RCP activists represented, above all, a profoundly humanist radical politics. Aspiring to a communist society, cadres pursued what Hartley Dean and Sabeen Ahmed, conceptualizing Marx's vision of human emancipation, have termed 'eudaimonia' – translated variously to signify happiness, fulfilment or flourishing.[74] As the following chapters will demonstrate, eudaimonic humanism formed the bedrock of the party's project. Marx posited that under capitalism's strictures, the 'alienated' worker was forced to subjugate their affective subjectivity – spanning their talents, desires and emotions – to the dictates of the social system.[75] Impelled by this central critique, RCP cadres pursued a movement capable of realizing an emancipatory society in which human activity would no longer be alienated: in Freedenian terms, these aspirations represented the core concepts, interwoven at the outset with a vanguardist form and strategy. Freed from want and capitalism's inhibitions, the liberated subject would be able to maximize all facets of their true potential.

'Unconditional support' for 'Irish freedom'

Pursuing the project adumbrated in *Our Tasks and Methods*, the RCP committed to campaign on the issues which most sharply arraigned the perceived nationalism and social-chauvinism of British working-class institutions. In 1980, a national conference agreed unanimously to prioritize strengthening working-class anti-imperialism. Accordingly, the party pinpointed militant anti-racism and 'unconditional support' for 'Irish freedom' as campaigning focal points.[76] They would remain the party's foremost campaigns for over a decade.

---

73 Former RCP member interview with the author, November 2021.
74 Hartley Dean, 'Eudaimonia and "species being": A Marxist perspective', in Joar Vittersø (ed.), *Handbook of Eudaimonic Well-Being* (Cham: Springer, 2016), 507–20; Sabeen Ahmed, 'Communism as *eudaimonia*: An Aristotelian reading of human emancipation', *International Journal of Philosophy & Social Values*, 1 (2018): 31–48.
75 Since labour under capitalism was '*external* to the worker, i.e. does not belong to his essential being', the worker 'does not confirm himself in his work, but denies himself, feels miserable and not happy, does not develop free mental and physical energy, but mortifies his flesh and ruins his mind. Hence the worker feels himself only when he is not working; when he is working he does not feel himself. . . . His labour is therefore not voluntary but forced, it is *forced labour*'. Karl Marx, 'Economic and philosophical manuscripts', 1844. Karl Marx, *Early Writings* (Harmondsworth: Penguin, 1976), 326.
76 *tns*, June–July 1980. The RCP's anti-racist campaigns are the subject of Chapter 2.

Since the turn of the 1970s, republican guerrillas, constituted primarily in the Provisional IRA, had waged what they considered a 'war of National Liberation' against British rule in Northern Ireland.[77] For revolutionaries combating social-chauvinism in the British working class, 'the Irish war' was supremely, if instrumentally, significant. Cadres acknowledged that their emphasis upon Ireland reflected their 'programmatic heritage' in the RCG,[78] which similarly challenged the 'pro-imperialist . . . stranglehold' in the labour movement.[79] Writing in 1976, a senior member of the RCG had underlined the imperative of campaigns for 'Irish freedom' to challenge the 'chauvinism' of the British working class.[80] 'Unconditional support' for 'Irish freedom' originated in a theoretical conviction, following Lenin's dictum:

> The English working class will never be free until Ireland is freed from the English yoke. Reaction in England is strengthened and fostered by the enslavement of Ireland.[81]

As far as RCP theoreticians were concerned, British workers who failed to call for the defeat of 'imperialism' could not identify their class interests.[82] Vowing to confront workers' illusions in the state, cadres anticipated a monumental struggle: at a demonstration in Hyde Park in July 1978, RCT speakers declared that 'the absence of opposition to the oppressive role of the British state in Ireland consolidates the political weakness of the British working class'.[83] Founding RCT activist Pat Roberts similarly acknowledged the onerousness of challenging 'anti-Irish prejudices fostered by the labour bureaucracy'.[84]

---

77 *Republican News*, 13 October 1972.
78 Revolutionary Communist Tendency, *Special Issue on Ireland* (Revolutionary Communist Papers, No. 2, May 1978), 2 n. 3.
79 *Fight Racism! Fight Imperialism!* January–February 1981.
80 Chris Davies quoted in 'August 22nd 1976 demonstration', *Hands Off Ireland!*, 1 (December 1976).
81 V. I. Lenin, 'The right of nations to self-determination', V. I. Lenin, *Collected Works, Volume 20* (Moscow: Progress Publishers, 1977), 440.
82 From the mid-1970s, a substantial proportion of the British electorate favoured withdrawal from Northern Ireland: a series of Gallup polls and British Social Attitudes surveys suggested between 50 and 65 per cent support. Pro-withdrawal opinion, however, reflected British self-interest more than anti-imperialist conviction. In 1974, for example, the Bring the Boys Back from Ulster campaign received 120,000 petition signatures from soldiers' concerned relatives. Paul Dixon, '"A real stirring in the nation": Military families, British public opinion and withdrawal from Northern Ireland', in Graham Dawson, Jo Dover and Stephen Hopkins (eds), *The Northern Ireland Troubles in Britain: Impacts, Engagements, Legacies and Memories* (Manchester: Manchester University Press, 2017), 41–56.
83 Revolutionary Communist Tendency, *Ireland: It's a War, Not a Question of Human Rights*, 9 July 1978. Copy in author's possession.
84 Pat Roberts, 'The Revolutionary Communist Group: On the backs of the oppressed', *tns*, June–July 1980.

Figure 1 Organized by the Smash the Prevention of Terrorism Act Campaign on 31 October 1981, this day school formed part of a series of early RCP events on the Northern Ireland conflict. Credit: Author's possession.

The RCP's assessment of Northern Ireland echoed the orthodox anti-imperialist strand of Irish Marxism epitomized by Michael Farrell's book *Northern Ireland: The Orange State* (1976).[85] British imperialism, cadres averred, dominated Ireland north and south, denying the island's populace self-determination. In this analysis, Northern Ireland's Protestant workers allied with the British crown and unionist bourgeoisie to enjoy 'limited but definite advantages' over their Catholic counterparts. Since their sectional privileges derived from maintaining the union, the argument ran, Protestant workers could not act independently as a class until British imperialism was defeated.[86] Assimilating Lenin's taxonomy of imperialism as the 'highest stage' of capitalist development,[87] the RCP's founders asserted that during a recession, imperialist

---

85 Michael Farrell, *Northern Ireland: The Orange State* (London: Pluto Press, 1976).
86 Andrew Clarkson and Phil Murphy, 'The loyalist working class', in Revolutionary Communist Party, *World in Recession*, 31.
87 V. I. Lenin, *Imperialism: The Highest Stage of Capitalism* (London: Junius/Living Marxism, 1996). During the imperialist epoch, Lenin argued, monopoly and state intervention replaced free competition, while economic growth became increasingly uneven and volatile. Frank Richards, 'Revisionism, imperialism and the state: The method of *Capital* and the dogma of State Monopoly Capitalism', in *Revisionism, Imperialism and the State* (Revolutionary Communist Papers, No. 4, February 1979), 17.

powers would intensify their colonial exploitation but could only mitigate and delay the crisis.[88]

Cadres interpreted the Northern Ireland conflict straightforwardly as a war between Irish republicans and British imperialism.[89] Positioning working-class unionism as precariously dependent upon British jurisdiction in Northern Ireland, party theoreticians cleaved to the republican orthodoxy that loyalism would wither when Britain withdrew. The RCP diverged entirely from those leftists, such as the members of the Militant tendency, who considered the republican insurgency a major barrier to class unity between Northern Ireland's Catholic and Protestant workers.[90] Insisting that the British state could play no progressive role in Ireland, the IFM also contradicted the strategic emphasis of the CPGB, which envisaged British trade unionists pressurizing Westminster to implement reforms felicitous to developing class unity in Northern Ireland.[91]

Writing in the late 1980s, the historian John Callaghan asserted that the RCP invoked its stance on Ireland to distinguish itself from leftist rivals.[92] 'Unconditional support' functioned as a polemical challenge to British leftists who qualified their support for republican objectives or criticized guerrillas' methods. As Marc Mulholland has demonstrated, most British radicals endorsed republicanism's militant content but were reluctant to endorse explicitly the IRA, lest they alienate working-class patriots.[93] Socialists who idealized Irish unification were wont to criticize republican tactics. The International Socialists, for example, had supported the Provisionals to the extent that they defended the Catholic community against British troops and sectarian attacks but argued that the lack of a social programme prevented republicans from winning a critical

---

88 *Workers against Imperialism: The British Labour Movement and Ireland* (Revolutionary Communist Pamphlets, No. 5, May 1979), 34.
89 Revolutionary Communist Tendency, *Special Issue on Ireland*, 1.
90 Founded by the Trotskyist Peter Hadden and his comrades in the Militant tendency in the late 1970s, the Northern Ireland Labour and Trade Union Group charged republicans and loyalists alike with exacerbating sectarian divisions. Militant espoused instead 'neither nationalism nor unionism – but workers' unity'. Moreover, Hadden and his comrades arraigned the Provisionals with prosecuting 'individual terrorism' and enabling the state to sharpen repression. Labour and Trade Union Group, *Northern Ireland Labour and Trade Union Group* (Belfast: Labour and Trade Union Group, 1985); Peter Hadden, 'Workers Unity against THE REAL ENEMY', *Militant: Marxist Paper for Labour & Youth*, 552 (15 May 1981).
91 In 1983, for example, the CPGB conference envisioned the labour movement compelling the British government to rescind repressive legislation, underwrite a Bill of Rights unifying Protestant and Catholic workers and 'create in the speediest time possible the political, social and economic conditions for the reunification of Ireland'. Chris Myant, *Common Cause: Trade Unionists and Ireland* (London: Communist Party of Great Britain, 1984), 6–8.
92 John Callaghan, *The Far Left in British Politics* (Oxford: Basil Blackwell, 1987), 145.
93 Marc Mulholland, 'Northern Ireland and the far left, c. 1965-1975', *Contemporary British History*, 32 (2018): 549–50.

mass among Protestant workers or the southern proletariat.⁹⁴ The SWP backed the republican 'right of self-determination' but stipulated

> this does not mean that we necessarily support the politics of the Provisionals, nor that we consider them socialists, nor that we support all the tactics they use.⁹⁵

With bases in Liverpool and London, the revolutionary group Big Flame upheld Irish republicanism's challenge to the British state but explicitly criticized republican politics: the Provisionals' 'petit-bourgeois' leadership and military 'elitism', the argument ran, lacked a social programme capable of sufficiently mobilizing the Catholic working class.⁹⁶ Lambasting the Provisional campaign more sharply still, the Workers Revolutionary Party (WRP) denounced IRA bombings in Britain – 'a political gift to Thatcher' – for enabling the government to justify repression.⁹⁷ For the CPGB, meanwhile, the IRA campaign could only alienate the Protestant working class and prevent class unity in Northern Ireland.⁹⁸

In a Leninist tradition, RCP cadres insisted that revolutionaries must support unconditionally the oppressed nation against the imperial oppressor, irrespective of the methods and programme of the liberation movement. Delineating the right of nations to self-determination, Lenin distinguished between 'oppressed' and 'oppressor' nations under imperialism. Writing during the First World War, the Bolshevik leader urged revolutionaries in oppressor nations to expedite the defeat of their imperialist rulers and to unite with the workers of the world's oppressed nations.⁹⁹ As such, the RCP espoused 'unconditional support' not to align specifically with the Provisional IRA per se but to endorse without reservation the republican threat to the British state. The RCT's foundational position on 'the Irish war' elaborated the principle:

> The RCT gives unconditional support to national liberation movements and we particularly give such support to the movement for Ireland's liberation. We have our criticisms of the programmes of the organisations leading the movements....

---

94 'Northern Ireland: Background to the crisis', *International Socialism*, 70 (June 1974).
95 Socialist Workers Party, *Why We Say Troops Out of Ireland!* (London: Socialists Unlimited, 1980), 7, 9.
96 Big Flame, *Ireland: Rising in the North* (Birmingham: Big Flame Publications, no date [1975]), 16, 26–7.
97 *News Line*, 27 July 1982.
98 *Ireland: A Question for Us All: Report of a London District Communist Party Delegation to Belfast* (London: Communist Party of Great Britain, 1983), 10.
99 V. I. Lenin, 'The revolutionary proletariat and the right of nations to self-determination', Lenin, *Collected Works, Volume 21*, 407–14.

But we have never used our review to criticise the IRA. . . . Today any criticism of the IRA only gives succour to the forces of British chauvinism.[100]

The party's anti-imperialism inflamed controversy on the British left. Radicals who envisaged influencing republican politics accused the RCP of misguidedly tailing the Provisionals. For the *Leninist* faction of the CPGB, the RCP's 'unconditional support' meant 'automatically' acclaiming the British state's heterogeneous adversaries, from the 'Argentinian fascist junta that butchered thousands of progressives' to the 'petty bourgeois' Irish republican movement.[101] *Leninist* cadre Alan Merrik stipulated that British radicals should 'confront' the republican leadership's classless nationalism, rather than simply upholding their right to resist British rule.[102]

For leftists who advocated more interventionist engagement with the 'petit-bourgeois' republican movement, the RCP's position represented a dereliction of duty.[103] The Trotskyist organization Workers Power, for example, scorned the RCP's 'unconditional support' and argued that it behoved British revolutionaries to cultivate a revolutionary vanguard in the republican movement.[104] The Spartacists, meanwhile, accused the RCP of 'tailing . . . petit-bourgeois Green nationalism':[105] according to the Spartacist organizers, British imperialism would only be defeated when a 'revolutionary vanguard' in Ireland supplanted the 'national sectoralism [*sic*]' of Sinn Féin.[106] Criticizing the Provisionals' socialism as a deviation from the 'Marxist theory of Permanent Revolution', Simon Pirani of the WRP implored leftists to 'fight out battles with all political tendencies', including the 'nationalist, Republican movement'.[107]

From the vanguardist perspective, opposition to British rule in Ireland contained a revolutionary dynamic only insofar as it fundamentally challenged the state. Eschewing liberal reforms, revolutionaries called explicitly for

---

100 Mike Freeman, 'The Irish Republican Movement: Why we give unconditional support', *tns*, February 1981.
101 James Marshall, 'The Revolutionary Communist Party: Prepared to defend workers' power?', *Leninist*, July 1984.
102 Alan Merrik, 'Class questions', *Leninist*, 27 December 1987.
103 Across the British left, the pejorative 'petit-bourgeois nationalism' invoked Marx's formulation of the 'petty bourgeoisie' as a 'transitional class' between the bourgeoisie and proletariat, 'in which the interests of two classes are neutralised'. RCP cadres and rival leftists alike employed 'petit-bourgeois nationalism' as an epithet for nationalists who submerged class differences to rally the masses to a national liberation struggle. Karl Marx, 'The Eighteenth Brumaire of Louis Bonaparte', in Terrell Carver (ed.), *Marx: Later Political Writings* (Cambridge: Cambridge University Press, 1996), 62.
104 Workers Power, *The British Left and the Irish War* (London: no date [1983]), 41–2.
105 'Born-again Cliffites on the move'.
106 'We remember Bloody Sunday!', *Spartacist Britain*, 54 (February 1984).
107 Simon Pirani, 'On Sinn Fein', *Workers Press: Weekly Paper of the Workers Revolutionary Party*, 3 October 1987.

imperialism's defeat.[108] Protesting against the Prevention of Terrorism Act (PTA), activists picketed courts and police stations not to 'quibble about civil rights' but to animate class opposition to British rule in Ireland.[109] Developing a position formulated by their former comrades in the RCG, cadres charged the Troops Out Movement (TOM) with failing to confront imperialism.[110] Solely calling for British troop withdrawals, the RCG Political Committee had postulated in 1976, did not challenge 'the dominant chauvinist position' in the working class.[111] Any individual or organization calling for troop withdrawals and all-Ireland self-determination could affiliate to the TOM. As Manchester TOM activist Geoffrey Whittle acknowledged in 1983, his organization was open to 'right-wing' elements who jingoistically implored the government to 'bring the boys home' from a supposedly tribal conflict.[112]

The RCP's vanguardist emphasis upon class-conscious anti-imperialism codified 'solidarity' more discerningly than did the republican movement itself. Straightforwardly envisaging in Britain the largest, most influential pro-withdrawal constituency, Provisional strategists candidly admitted that they welcomed all forms of 'troops out' sentiment. Interviewed by British radicals in October 1978, leading Belfast Provisional Gerry Adams epitomized the movement's pragmatic support for all British strands of pro-withdrawal politics:

> We're very satisfied . . . to receive whatever support we can get for the short-term Republican objectives from the British left and the British working class, regardless of the motives. From a purist point of view, we would prefer that it be a conscious solidarity action; from an expediency point of view we are only

---

108 *Ireland's Victory Means Britain's Defeat* (Revolutionary Communist Pamphlets, No. 7, June 1980), 14.
109 Revolutionary Communist Tendency, *Smash the Prevention of Terrorism Act!* (June 1979). Labour Home Secretary Roy Jenkins introduced the PTA in 1974, after Provisional IRA bombers killed twenty-one civilians in Birmingham in 1974. Illegalizing support for proscribed organizations, the PTA allowed for suspects to be arrested without a warrant and detained for up to forty-eight hours – and, with the Home Secretary's permission, for a further five days. By December 1992, 7,192 persons had been detained under the PTA in relation to the Northern Ireland conflict. Some 6,200 of those arrested were released without charge. Paddy Hillyard, 'Irish people and the British criminal justice system', *Journal of Law and Society*, 21 (1994): 48.
110 Until an internal schism in 1977, the Troops Out Movement had over 1,200 active members across Britain, and a wider affiliate membership numbering more than 10,000. The TOM's demands for British withdrawal and Irish 'self-determination' gained traction among British leftists in the International Socialists, IMG and CPGB and enjoyed substantial support in the trade union movement: 326 union branches attended TOM's conference in 1974. Aly Renwick, '"Something in the air": The rise of the Troops Out Movement', in Dawson, Dover and Hopkins (eds), *The Northern Ireland Troubles in Britain*; Jeremy Tranmer, 'A force to be reckoned with? The radical left in the 1970s', *Revue Française de Civilisation Britannique*, 22 (2017): 7.
111 Jim Johnson, 'Lessons of TOM', *Hands Off Ireland!*, 1 (December 1976).
112 'Call to unite', *An Phoblacht/Republican News*, 24 March 1983.

interested in the dismantling of the British imperialist structures and whatever volume of support for that dismantling, we would welcome it.[113]

Determined to expose the social-chauvinism of the trade union bureaucracy, the RCT inaugurated its Smash the Prevention of Terrorism Act Campaign (SPTAC) in 1979. Highlighting the authorities' powers of summary arrest and detention, the SPTAC challenged trade union branches and area committees to declare outright opposition to British rule in Ireland. At this juncture, the TUC endorsed the Better Life For All Campaign, which denounced violence in Northern Ireland and shunned the national question. Launched in Belfast in January 1976 by the Northern Ireland Committee of the Irish Congress of Trade Unions, the Better Life For All Campaign condemned paramilitarism and advocated reforms in employment, housing, education and social services.[114] Initially, SPTAC activists lobbied trades councils only in areas where the RCT had a presence, such as Tameside in Greater Manchester, and Battersea, Lambeth and Wandsworth in London. In 1980, to enhance the campaign's public profile, the National Organisation of Revolutionary Communist Students moved the National Union of Students (NUS) to condemn the PTA.[115] Picketing courts and detention centres, SPTAC pickets garnered publicity and a degree of organizational growth: in 1981, for example, the Nottingham TOM branch defected to the SPTAC.[116]

Taking its anti-imperialism into the trade union movement represented a dominant theme of early RCP activity. A founding member of the RCT, Dave Hallsworth was also an elected executive official on his local trades council in Tameside, Greater Manchester. In 1980, when Tameside provocatively endorsed the RCT slogan – 'Bring the war to Britain' – the TUC ordered a recantation. When Tameside refused, the TUC leadership disaffiliated the council. Imploring trade unionists nationwide to raise motions supporting Tameside, Hallsworth and his comrades publicized the controversy to expose and challenge what they considered a reactionary union bureaucracy:

113 'interview with Gerry Adams: Vice-President Provisional Sinn Fein', *Hands Off Ireland!*, 6 (January 1979). For a detailed analysis of republicans' and British leftists' divergent ideals of 'solidarity', see Jack Hepworth, '"The moral rearmament of imperialism": The Revolutionary Communist Party, the Northern Ireland conflict, and the new world order, 1981-1994', *Contemporary British History*, 36 (2022): 591–621.
114 A Better Life For All Campaign, *The People's Declaration: 'A better life for all'* (Belfast: A Better Life For All Campaign, 1976).
115 Kate Marshall, 'The Smash the PTA campaign', *tns*, January 1980.
116 UPI0000015575: 'Special Branch report on an internal conference of the Revolutionary Communist Tendency to discuss forthcoming policies and actions', 1 September 1981.

Whenever workers organise independently, union bureaucrats reply with bans and proscriptions. . . . The reaction of the labour bureaucracy to the Tameside conference shows the importance of Ireland for British workers.[117]

Similarly, in March 1981, as the SPTAC, cadres coordinated a national conference at Coventry's Lanchester Polytechnic, imploring union branches to lobby the TUC to express 'support' for the 'national liberation struggle against British rule'.[118] The TUC's draconian response – threatening all 440 British trades councils with disaffiliation if they attended the Coventry event – provoked a furore in the labour movement.[119] Only six trades councils officially defied the TUC diktat, but the conference nevertheless assembled 260 workers who passed resolutions condemning the TUC's nonpartisan position on Northern Ireland.[120]

In September 1981, the RCP's Workers March for Irish Freedom provoked a similarly hostile response from the leadership of the labour movement. Proceeding from Manchester to Blackpool, marchers arrived in the Lancashire seaside town to picket the TUC's annual conference and highlight its failure to support the Irish republican hunger strikers in Long Kesh.[121] Pledging to 'bring the war to England', leading cadres Fran Eden and Carol Taggart told local reporters that marchers were 'fighting the establishment' as republicans fought the British state.[122] Gaining limited traction in the labour movement, the march won formal endorsement from only two trades councils nationwide. Nevertheless, twenty-six organizers from union branches and area offices across the country joined in a personal capacity, and the regional media afforded the Workers March for Irish Freedom considerable coverage.[123]

Throughout the 1980s, cadres who were active in the labour movement endeavoured to win their colleagues to support the 'liberation struggle'. Picketing the Labour Party conference in 1986, IFM activists collected the

---

117 Archive of the Irish in Britain, London Metropolitan University: *Ireland and the British Labour Movement* (London: Smash the Prevention of Terrorism Act Campaign, n.d. [1980]).
118 'TUC hands off Ireland!', *tns*, February 1981.
119 Michael Bromley, 'TUC alert over H-block meeting', *Belfast Telegraph*, 23 February 1981.
120 '"TUC hands off Ireland" Coventry conference', *The Irish Prisoner*, March–April 1981.
121 In March 1981, five years after the Labour government withdrew politically motivated prisoners' special-category status, republican prisoners in Long Kesh/HMP Maze commenced a hunger strike for five demands: the right not to undertake prison work or wear a prison uniform; the right to free association; the right to one visit, one letter, and one parcel per week; and the right to full remission. The strike continued until October 1981, by which point ten prisoners had died, comprising seven Provisional IRA volunteers and three members of the Irish National Liberation Army.
122 Kevin Keenan, 'Strong arm squad on march: Karate experts to guard H-block demo', *Lancashire Evening Post*, 4 September 1981; 'March backs death fasts', *Lancashire Evening Post*, 5 September 1981.
123 'Workers march for Irish freedom', *tns*, July–August 1981.

names of more than 200 Labour activists who were willing to raise IFM motions in party and trade union branches.[124] Occasionally, leading RCP activists with substantial union cachet won support in their branches for party positions on Ireland, piquing the TUC hierarchy. As secretary of Tameside Trades Council, for example, Dave Hallsworth convinced his union comrades to host an RCP film screening in 1983. Banning the event, senior TUC official John Monks threatened to expel Tameside for 'irresponsible' behaviour 'not worthy of genuine trade unionists'.[125] Similarly, as president of Hammersmith National and Local Government Officers' Association (NALGO), RCP veteran John Fitzpatrick persistently campaigned for his union branch to oppose British rule in Ireland.[126] In 1988, when Fitzpatrick's branch finally endorsed Irish self-determination, he revelled in the opportunity to convene a contentious debate including republican speakers: 'for the first time in years we have drawn hundreds of members into a full discussion on Ireland'.[127]

From 1982, the RCP generally pitched its campaigns on Ireland under the banner of its front organization, the Irish Freedom Movement (IFM). Regularly coordinating demonstrations, marches and conferences, the IFM brought the party into contact with class-conscious workers in the trade union movement and the Irish diaspora. Urging workers and their institutions to take sides against Britain in 'the Irish war', participation in the IFM's activities went beyond the core cadre membership of the RCP. The 450 activists at the London conference, which launched the IFM in February 1982, explicitly distinguished this 'anti-imperialist movement' from 'liberal pressure groups' which lobbied parliamentarians for a British withdrawal.[128]

Exhorting British workers to take sides against the state formed an important component of the IFM's challenge to labourism.[129] Distributed in the labour movement and among higher education student societies in the 1980s, IFM agitprop films were designed to win British militants to the RCP's position on Ireland. Combining documentary footage in Belfast and Derry and interviews with republican activists, *No British solution* (*c.* 1984) purported to disabuse

124 'In the unions', *IFM News: Bi-Monthly Bulletin of the Irish Freedom Movement*, 1 (November–December 1986).
125 'TUC wall of silence', *tns*, April 1983.
126 Fitzpatrick was embroiled in controversy in March 1988, when he reportedly used union notepaper for a letter of sympathy to the families of three IRA volunteers killed in Gibraltar. 'Full house for IRA', *Fulham Chronicle*, 21 April 1988.
127 'Debating Ireland in the unions', *tns*, 29 April 1988.
128 Mike Wall, 'A tale of two conferences', *tns*, March 1982.
129 Following the usage of RCT and RCP theoreticians throughout the late 1970s and 1980s, the uncapitalized 'labourism' is employed here to connote the strategies of the Labour Party and the wider trade union movement.

British workers of 'imperialist' illusions.[130] Similarly, featuring extended testimony from IFM activist Dave Hallsworth, *The longest war* (*c.* 1985) documented how Tameside Trades Council's 'unconditional support' for the republican campaign had piqued the hostility of the union bureaucracy. Offering the video for hire to youth groups, college and university student societies, and trade union branches, the IFM also sent speakers to accompany screenings.[131]

Cadres sought to highlight the Labour Party's record on Ireland as a marker of its essential reformism. For example, when Sheffield City Council refused to allow the IFM to use the City Hall for a rally in 1984, IFM organizer Keith Tompson unsuccessfully challenged Labour council leader David Blunkett to a debate on Northern Ireland.[132] The RCP's polemical purposes for championing 'Irish freedom' were not lost on Blunkett. Responding to a letter from a Spartacist League activist in 1983, the future Home Secretary noted that the RCP had 'declared their main enemy to be the Labour Party and Labour Movement'.[133] Blunkett recognized the IFM's modus operandi: 'I think they use the issue of Ireland to pursue their avowed aim of smashing the Labour Party'.[134] The strategic determination to explode Westminster's bipartisan consensus on Northern Ireland underpinned the IFM's notoriety on the reformist left. In 1985, for example, when the Cambridge University Fabian Society invited the Labour Committee on Ireland (LCI) to join a debate on Ireland, LCI secretary Niall Power stipulated that he would send a speaker on condition that they did not share a platform with the IFM:

> such groups as the IFM and the RCP cause such harm to the question of Ireland and indeed British socialism we would decline to give them any credibility.[135]

At the turn of the century, reviewing a century of uneasy interactions between British leftists and Irish republicans, a former RCP activist commented acidly upon how the Labour Party

---

130 Linen Hall Library, Belfast: Northern Ireland Political Collection: Irish in Britain Box 1. Irish Freedom Movement, *No British solution* (n.d. [*c.* 1984]).
131 Linen Hall Library, Belfast: Northern Ireland Political Collection: Irish in Britain Box 1. Irish Freedom Movement flyer (n.d. [*c.* 1985]).
132 *Star*, 13 January 1984.
133 North of England Institute of Mining and Mechanical Engineers: Dave Douglass Archive: Miners' Strike Box 1: David Blunkett to David Douglass, 8 June 1983.
134 Sheena Clarke, 'An interview with Sheffield council leader David Blunkett', *Labour & Ireland*, 2, no. 3 (n.d. [1984]).
135 Archive of the Irish in Britain, London Metropolitan University: Anne Waring to Labour Committee on Ireland, 5 April 1985; Niall Power to Anne Waring, undated [1985].

Figure 2 RCP and IFM activists at County Hall, London, during an IFM demonstration, c. 1985. Credit: Joan Hoey/Revolutionary Communist Party.

in orientating itself towards the institutions of State, has consistently subordinated the aspirations of Irish Nationalists to the interests of either strategic advantage, the co-operation of the Ulster Unionists or the continuance of bipartisanship.[136]

The IFM positioned the republican campaign as an inspiration for working-class independence against the state and the ruling class in Britain. During the miners' strike, leading RCP cadre Mick Hume asserted that republicans' militant anti-statism bore 'important lessons for the labour movement'.[137] Vanguardists implored British workers to emulate the ideological independence which characterized republican resistance. Writing in 1986, an RCP organizer in Stockport hailed the republican campaign as a salutary example of a

> fight-back against the British state. . . . British workers have nothing to gain by supporting the British state . . . but everything to gain by supporting the fight for Irish freedom.[138]

By the end of the 1980s, the IFM's twenty branches comprised the largest radical solidarity movement in Britain.[139] Each August, its annual march in London typically attracted an estimated 3,000 demonstrators, including activists beyond

---

136 Cronain O'Kelly, 'British socialists and Irish republicans', *Studies in Ethnicity and Nationalism*, 1 (2001): 18.
137 Mick Hume, *After the Brighton Bomb* (London: Junius, 1984), 15.
138 C. Moore, Revolutionary Communist Party, Reddish, 'Workers and the Irish agreement', *Stockport Express Advertiser*, 1 May 1986.
139 *Irish Freedom: Bulletin of the Irish Freedom Movement*, May–June 1990.

the RCP's inner circle.[140] For Rob Killick, the August march represented an organizational highlight. As a leading cadre, Killick organized the stewards for marchers running the gauntlet of fascist counter-protesters:[141]

> We'd have a core of about twenty blokes who were all ready and willing to get stuck in. So there was a physical-force element to it, which was also very good. I loved all that stuff. And I loved organising the demonstrations.[142]

As fixtures in the radical calendar, IFM demonstrations galvanized diverse militants against British rule in Ireland. In 1986, alongside nine MPs and two Members of the European Parliament (MEPs), some 115 Labour Party councillors joined the march. Trade union branches in Durham, London and Nottingham were among the affiliated sponsors, while the CPGB's *Leninist* faction and the WRP also endorsed the rally.[143] The *Leninist*'s correspondent at the IFM march in August 1991 noted 'many contingents . . . freely handing out different literature'.[144]

Refusing to criticize publicly republican politics or tactics reflected the RCP's conviction that social-chauvinism pervaded the British working class. In a climate of anti-Irish hostility, cadres argued, rebuking republicans could only galvanize nationalist prejudices and reformist politics.[145] Contrary to superficial appearance, however, 'unconditional support' did not imply specific approval for particular republican policies or actions. For RCP activists, 'Irish freedom' was not, in itself, a strategic terminus but rather a campaigning point to polarize debates in the British working class. The party's rationale anticipated conditions in which revolutionaries would censure republicans' political limitations: when 'large numbers' of British workers celebrated the IRA offensive, Mike Freeman wrote, '*then* there will be a time to criticise the programme of Provisional Sinn Fein'.[146] As a senior cadre told an internal party debate in 1981, the ultimate objective was to establish an independent Marxist alternative to the republican movement: once British workers en masse demanded Irish freedom,

---

140 'Anti-internment rally, Whittington Park', tns, 19 August 1988; *Green Left Weekly*, 4 September 1991; Stuart Sharpe, '3000 support anti-war march', *Irish Freedom: Bulletin of the Irish Freedom Movement*, Winter 1993.
141 In 1988 and 1989, for example, British National Party and National Front contingents attacked the IFM marches and fighting broke out. More than eighty people were arrested in total. *Illustrated London News*, 1 September 1988; 'Arrests as rivals clash', *Sunday Life*, 6 August 1989.
142 Rob Killick, 20 August 2020.
143 *Workers Press*, 26 July 1986.
144 'Irish Freedom Movement demonstration', *Leninist*, 13 July 1992.
145 Revolutionary Communist Tendency, *Smash the Prevention of Terrorism Act!*
146 Freeman, 'The Irish Republican Movement: Why we give unconditional support'.

revolutionaries would move to supplant Sinn Féin.[147] Reviewing the memoir of former IRA Chief of Staff Seán Mac Stíofáin, Andrew Clarkson stipulated that in an independent Ireland, a revolutionary party must develop the class politics which Sinn Féin could not.[148] If republicans forced a British withdrawal, Frank Richards opined, a 'consistent anti-imperialist' vanguard would have to organize.[149]

The Leninist distinction between a struggle's *form* and *content* underpinned cadres' 'unconditional support'. Members of the RCP endorsed Irish republicanism's anti-imperialist content rather than its particular tactical or political forms. Concomitantly, rhetorical 'unconditional support' coexisted with criticisms of the movement's programme. Mary Masters and Phil Murphy lauded the republican challenge to the British state while positioning republicanism in a tradition of 'petit-bourgeois nationalism'.[150] RCP vanguardists regarded the republican movement as a nationalist alliance which would settle for a domestic transfer of power without transforming class relations. Éire Nua ('New Ireland'), Sinn Féin's programme between 1971 and 1982 – when it was unceremoniously dropped after a leadership faction fight – proposed a federalized Ireland built upon redistributive economic nationalism. Private property rights would remain, albeit subordinated to local industrial and agrarian co-operatives.[151] Invoking a fabled *Comhar na gComharsan* philosophy of neighbourhood co-operation and mutual aid, Éire Nua's architects aspired to transcend both the individualism of Western capitalism, 'with its poor and hungry amid plenty', and the dictatorial repression of 'Eastern Soviet' Stalinism, 'with its denial of freedom and human rights'.[152] Sinn Féin's *ard fheiseanna* (annual conferences) of 1979 and 1980 further underlined the programme's 'democratic socialist' credentials, championing co-operatives above 'capitalist plundering' and 'private enterprise', which would have 'no place in industries' in the new Ireland.[153] Reviewing Sinn Féin's erstwhile social and economic programme, Mike Freeman noted republicanism's 'middle

---

147 UPI0000015575: 'Special Branch report on an internal conference of the Revolutionary Communist Tendency to discuss forthcoming policies and actions', 1 September 1981.
148 *Revisionism, Imperialism and the State* (Revolutionary Communist Papers, No. 4, February 1979): Andrew Clarkson, 'Review: Seán MacStiofáin: Memoirs of a revolution', 35.
149 Frank Richards, 'No equivocation!', in Revolutionary Communist Tendency, *Special Issue on Ireland*, 25.
150 Mary Masters and Phil Murphy, 'British imperialism and the Irish crisis', 5, 16.
151 *Éire Nua: The Social and Economic Programme of Sinn Féin* (Dublin: Sinn Féin, 1971).
152 The Secretary, Belfast Executive Sinn Fein, 'What Sinn Fein means by a socialist federal Ireland', *Irish News*, 25 October 1973.
153 Sinn Féin, *Éire Nua: Updated text* (n.d. [c. 1980]); Sue O'Halloran, PRO Sinn Féin (Britain), 'Provisional Sinn Fein Ard Fheis 1980', *Ireland Socialist Review*, 7 (Spring 1980).

class traditions'. Through the mid-1980s, as Sinn Féin extended its experimental electoralism, Freeman criticized the movement's 'opportunist' tendencies.[154]

While cadres seldom publicly criticized republicans in the 1980s, the RCP leadership openly declared that it had no illusions in the Provisionals' ambiguous political ecology. Endorsed at the party's annual Preparing for Power conference in 1985, the Political Committee's position bears quoting at length:

> As the IRA has pointed out, it is not a Marxist organisation.... The Revolutionary Communist Party's support for the republican movement has nothing to do with its politics. We support the republican movement because it is leading the fight against British rule in Ireland.... We would support the republican movement if it was led by a collection of Catholic priests and nuns, so long as it was leading resistance against British domination.... The RCP will continue to give unconditional support to the republican movement irrespective of its programme, its strategy, or its tactics. As long as it remains the leading force in the struggle against British imperialism and the biggest threat to the stability of the United Kingdom, that's good enough for us.[155]

An internal document circulated to party members and supporters the following year similarly separated the struggle's 'inner essence' and 'the movement leading it'. Activists were reminded that the RCP did not sloganize specifically for the IRA, and the party 'reserved the right' to criticize the republican movement if they deemed that it ceased to threaten Western imperialism. Endorsing republicanism's content rather than its forms, cadres did not pronounce upon particular tactics. Theoreticians differentiated specific guerrilla actions – such as 'planting a bomb in a Birmingham pub ... a stupid thing to do' – and the broader revolutionary dynamic of an anti-imperialist campaign.[156]

In recent media coverage of the RCP, the party's historical position on Ireland has featured among its most controversial facets. In 2020, when the Conservative government nominated Claire Fox for a peerage, journalists in Britain and Ireland alike underscored Fox's past association with the RCP and its 'unconditional support' for Irish republicanism.[157] The *Sunday Times*, for example, vilified Fox's journey 'from champion of terror to peer of the realm'.[158] Describing Fox as an 'IRA apologist', the *New European* noted that when an

---

154 *tns*, February 1985.
155 Frank Richards, 'Comrades of the IRA', *Times*, 14 August 1985.
156 'The RCP and the Irish struggle (1986)', reprinted in *tns*, 20 November 1992.
157 See, for example, Lauren Harte, 'Bomb victim's father slams peerage for MP whose former party "defended" the IRA', *Belfast Telegraph*, 3 August 2020; 'IRA sympathiser's Lords peerage is "insult" to town', *Liverpool Echo*, 9 October 2020.
158 Kinchen and Al-Othman, 'From champion of terror to peer of the realm'.

IRA bomb killed schoolboys Johnathan Ball and Tim Parry in Warrington in 1993, the RCP upheld the 'right of the Irish people to take whatever measures necessary in their struggle for freedom'.[159]

In subsequent years, cadres sombrely declared the demise of class politics and the defeat of the republican struggle.[160] Yet for most former RCP activists, the rationale for espousing 'Irish freedom' remains clear. Underlining the historical specificity of 'unconditional support' – in an era preceding the Provisionals' strategic reorientation in the 1990s – one veteran reasserts the vanguardist imperative of campaigning on 'the Irish war':

> The reason why the issues of Ireland and racism were so important is, again, they were issues where the establishment could get people to rally round the flag by being British. If you supported the actions of the British state in Ireland, how are you ever going to be capable of fighting for your independent interests within Britain? If you support the suppression of democratic rights, think the British state has the right to do that, withhold the rights of the Irish people and suppress them, use violence to do that – if you accept that, then how do you stand up for your rights in Britain?[161]

Claire Fox evokes more starkly still how the RCP instrumentalized the conflict in Ireland to implore British workers to clarify their class interests:

> The RCP's Irish politics actually didn't have very much to do with the Irish. . . . It really had to do with encouraging people to not side with the British state against the Irish . . . even where you thought that particular tactics were ridiculous, barbaric, stupid, vile, abhorrent.[162]

Rather than expounding a sentimental or thoroughgoing affinity with the Irish republican movement per se, the IFM's affinity rested upon republicanism's fundamental antagonism towards the British state.

In addition to imploring workers to take sides against Britain in 'the Irish war', the RCP's militant anti-racism was similarly intended to expose and counter left-wing nationalism, reformism and illusions in the state. From the formation of the RCT in 1978, cadres espoused and enacted anti-capitalist, anti-racist politics. The organization's anti-racist activism forms the basis of the following chapter.

---

159 Jonathon Read, 'Brexiteer and IRA apologist Claire Fox joins House of Lords', *New European*, 8 October 2020; 'The response to Warrington', *tns*, 2 April 1993.
160 See Chapter 4.
161 Former RCP member interview with the author, August 2021.
162 Claire Fox interview with the author, 1 September 2020.

2

'Fight back with the party of the future'[1]
Militant anti-racism, c.1981–6

Building the Revolutionary Communist Party

The conference which launched the RCP in May 1981 affirmed two enduringly salient features of the new party. First, it confirmed that in its struggle to supersede left-wing reformism and social-chauvinism, 'unconditional support' for 'Irish freedom' and militant anti-racism would remain the campaigning priorities.[2] Second, it reinforced cadres' sense of ideological and formal distinction from the radical left. Activists agreed that their front groups – the SPTAC and East London Workers Against Racism (ELWAR) – clearly articulated their organizational independence and political alterity.[3]

By the end of 1981, the RCP had instituted new branches in Coventry, Leeds and Manchester, where activists were detailed to focus upon campaigning against racism and the PTA.[4] Cadres aspired to break the influence of social democracy in the working class. Echoing the Hungarian Marxist Georg Lukács's critique of the state, Frank Richards implored the party's founders to confront workers' illusions in reformism and nationalism.[5] In retrospect, Frank Furedi evokes the sense of strategic distinction, which defined the RCP's project from the outset:

---

1   'Hitting back with the RCP', *tns*, July 1983.
2   Enduring throughout the 1980s, the dual campaigning focus upon racism and Ireland reflected Frank Richards's dictum that the revolutionary party's activities must mirror its theoretical emphases. FR, *Introduction to Preparing for Power to be discussed in branch educationals: Marxism in our time* (1983). Copy in author's possession.
3   UCI0000015575: 'Special Branch report on an internal conference of the Revolutionary Communist Tendency to discuss forthcoming policies and actions', 1 September 1981.
4   'RCP action: Around the branches', *tns*, January 1982.
5   Frank Richards, 'The united front', *tns*, May 1981. Lukács posited that the state represented not a mere 'mediation' of capitalist social relations but constituted 'that *unmediated dominance* itself'. Georg Lukács, *History and Class Consciousness: Studies in Marxist Dialectics*, trans. Rodney Livingstone (London: Merlin, 1971), 56.

We called *them* the radical left. We didn't call *ourselves* the radical left – and that wasn't done entirely, you know, in a hostile kind of way. We just felt that people who were kind of moving to the left were trapped in this outlook that had been around for generations and generations and was based upon an ideal of Marx and that kind of Bolshevik tradition that they didn't understand was fundamentally flawed. And so we felt that . . . our job was in the first instance to set up an alternative left-wing kind of approach.[6]

Cadres embarking on their party-building project through the early 1980s evinced considerable confidence in their programme. Activists contrasted their own sense of purpose against the perceived bankruptcy of jaded left-wing institutions. For *the next step*'s editorial board, the clarity of its principles distinguished the RCP from the 'weak and isolated' British left. Asserting the primacy of their ideas, cadres eschewed a short-term, opportunistic 'quest for popularity'.[7] In retrospect, Mike Fitzpatrick traces the theme of 'intellectual and ideological independence' throughout the party's lifespan:

That was crucial to our sense of building a sense of independence and agency, to forge a party which can express the independent interests of the working class on all these different issues. . . . You'd always find that the traditional left thing was to adapt whatever line was more or less what people thought already. . . . Whereas we would say, *it doesn't matter if it moves, the question is what is this political direction, what's the trajectory, how does it relate to the wider picture? What kind of position expresses an independent position?*[8]

As far as RCP vanguardists were concerned, the only popularity worth having would be based upon a clear-sighted critique of reformism and statism. Training a vanguard, cadres asserted, meant challenging workers to clarify and act upon their independent class interests. Seeking to attract an imagined 'average worker', Frank Richards warned, would inevitably result in opportunism. Instead, revolutionaries must aspire to train workers at 'the highest level of class consciousness. . . . The vanguard party is not elitist but *selective*'.[9] After an unacquainted reader complained about *the next step*'s specialist terminology, James Wood conveyed the vanguard's intellectual premises and aspiration: 'We

---

6 Frank Furedi interview with the author, 18 August 2020.
7 'Why we are not "popular"', *tns*, February 1983.
8 Mike Fitzpatrick, 22 August 2020.
9 Frank Richards, 'Our instrument for change: The revolutionary party', *tns*, November 1982. Emphases in original.

refuse to talk down to workers. The working class must master all aspects of bourgeois culture'.[10]

The titanic scale of the vanguardist task energized cadres, who were determined to transform working-class consciousness. Activists who considered themselves developing a vital revolutionary alternative relished their campaign for radical subjectivity. A senior cadre involved in recruiting and training new members in the 1980s, Phil Mullan evokes how activists sensed their capacity to effect change through the upstart organization:

> We could see that we were making gains in terms of building up a national organisation . . . and we could see we were slowly making progress. And sometimes, you know, rapidly making progress. But we could see that there was movement. . . . That gave people reassurance that this was the right thing, the right way to spend our lives.[11]

The perception of organizational progress and cohesion, Mullan suggests retrospectively, helped a relatively small group of cadres to persevere in adverse objective conditions:

> We had a coherence and we had a collective strength . . . which was much more than the numbers that we had. We had that sense that while few in number, we were making a disproportionate impact.[12]

Ann Furedi similarly contends that the frenetic quality of party activity motivated members with supreme self-belief. Despite the knowledge of subsequent events, Furedi candidly maintains that when she joined the party in 1981, she firmly believed that the organization was capable of growing and spearheading a revolution:

> Absolutely, at the time. Absolutely. The conference where the Revolutionary Communist Tendency changed to become the Revolutionary Communist Party – it was at that conference that I joined. I think there were thirty-six people in the room. When I look back you almost ask yourself the question, *did you never think that this was possibly quite a small starting point? [. . .] Wasn't it odd that there was only that number of people there?* I have to say, at the time it did not strike me as being the slightest bit absurd. I think that was partly because every great movement has to have a small beginning to it. I think that one of the things that you kind of felt was that, because we were so focused on the idea of

---

10 'What's in a word?', *tns*, January 1982.
11 Phil Mullan interview with the author, 11 March 2021.
12 Ibid.

developing ourselves and developing the party, possibly that other big part of the objective circumstances outside, and what was going on outside of what you could do through the sheer force of your own will, wasn't really something that I was thinking about.[13]

The boldness of the RCP's clarion critique provoked the suspicion and wrath of a host of British radicals. Rival leftists interpreted the party's declarations of independence variously as petty sectarianism or dogmatic idealism. For Luton SWP activist Keith Copley, for example, the RCT's hostility to the left represented 'political purism' precluding 'united activity' against, for example, public sector cuts or repressive laws.[14] Similarly, charging the RCP with abstract utopianism, Workers Power argued that the party's criticism of prevailing left trends could only precipitate isolation and 'separation from the [working] class'.[15] Throughout the decade, on occasions, disagreements escalated to violent rancour. In Newcastle in 1986, for instance, fighting broke out between RCP and SWP activists selling papers in the city centre. RCP national organizer Ann Burton alleged that members of the SWP on Tyneside were 'conducting a personal vendetta' against the RCP's branch organizer, spreading malicious rumours that she 'only sold so many copies of *t[he] n[ext] s[tep]* because she "touched men up" on sales'.[16]

As the party steadily attracted new recruits in the early 1980s, cadres enjoyed a growing audience for their politics. By the end of 1982, the RCP had inaugurated new branches in Liverpool and Sheffield, while *the next step*'s circulation had risen to 12,000 – equivalent to *Tribune* and the CPGB's *Marxism Today*, and close to the SWP's *Socialist Worker* (16,000).[17] At the centre of the organization, the RCP's ascendancy appeared unabating. Addressing the party's national congress in October 1982, leading cadres declared themselves 'convinced that for the first time in over 60 years we can confidently say that the future is ours'.[18] In this heady atmosphere, party chair Frank Richards warned against self-

---

13 Ann Furedi interview with the author, 7 October 2021.
14 'yes to Wright? Not us!', *tns*, October 1980.
15 'Who needs the RCP?', *workers power: monthly newspaper of the Workers Power Group*, July–August 1981.
16 Ann Burton, 'Trouble on the left', *tns*, 26 September 1986.
17 'Subscribe now!', *tns*, November 1982. The British left's most popular newspaper, however, remained *Militant*, with a regular circulation of 25,000. At this juncture, Militant maintained an uneasy but substantial presence in the Labour Party. Addressing the Labour Party conference in October 1982, party leader Michael Foot condemned Militant as a 'pestilential nuisance'. Labour's National Executive Committee, meanwhile, ruled that as a 'party within the party', Militant contravened the Labour constitution. Henry Pelling, *A Short History of the Labour Party* (Basingstoke: Macmillan, 1985), 183.
18 'Building the Revolutionary Communist Party', *tns*, November 1982.

congratulation – 'too many RCP supporters are complacent . . . satisfied with our theoretical achievements' – and urged activists to extend their influence in the working class.[19]

Activists' experiences of taking uncompromising positions into the working class viscerally reinforced a sense of organizational and ideological distinction. A long-serving veteran of the party recalled, for example, the barbs of the far right and radical left during the Falklands War, when the RCP called unequivocally for the defeat of 'British imperialism':[20]

> Fascists would turn up and attack marches. But the left were extremely hostile to what the RCP was saying. . . . They even called the police on us to try to get the police to kick us off the march. In Manchester that's what they did. It was quite funny, because on the one hand you've got the fascists turning up to attack you, on the other hand the Labour Party and all the left are also attacking you and trying to shout you down, telling you to fuck off, and trying to get police to throw you off the march. Obviously experiences like that told you very quickly that the RCP's got a particular point of view which is very different to everybody else, and there's an extreme hostility to that. Obviously what that meant was you had to be very clear about what you were saying, and very sure it was the right thing. In the face of that hostility, you're not going to stand up to that unless you're sure of yourself and your position and what your ideas are. Because you're under a lot of pressure straight away to stand up for them.[21]

During this phase of party-building, the Bermondsey by-election of February 1983 constituted one of the first major tests. Employing tactical electoralism, activists welcomed the by-election as an opportunity to publicize their positions. Cadres were especially eager to challenge working-class reformism in Bermondsey, where Bob Mellish – the former Labour Chief Whip whose resignation as Member of Parliament triggered the poll – had typified the labourist nationalism which the RCP abhorred. In 1976, for example, during parliamentary debates about Asian refugees arriving from Malawi, Mellish had infamously declared 'enough is enough'.[22] Until Mellish finally resigned in protest against Michael Foot's left-wing Labour leadership, the block votes of the trades unions – in particular, the Transport and General Workers' Union (TGWU) – had secured his position in the London Labour hierarchy.[23] The by-election of

---

19 Richards, 'Our instrument for change: The revolutionary party'.
20 Revolutionary Communist Party, *Malvinas Are Argentina's*.
21 Former RCP member interview with the author, August 2021.
22 Chanie Rosenberg, 'The Labour Party and the fight against fascism', *International Socialism*, Summer 1988, 55–93.
23 Duncan Campbell, 'The real mafia man', *New Statesman*, 6 August 1982.

1983 was notorious for Labour's infighting – Mellish's ally John O'Grady stood as a 'Real Bermondsey Labour' candidate – and for the virulent homophobia directed against official Labour candidate Peter Tatchell.[24]

Fran Eden, the RCP's candidate in Bermondsey, had been a committed ELWAR organizer for two years, patrolling the streets of Hackney and Tower Hamlets and organizing physical defence.[25] Eden had also campaigned on behalf of immigrants threatened with deportation and coordinated opposition to police repression in Brixton.[26] While Eden and her comrades asserted that they harboured no illusions in 'bourgeois democracy', they nevertheless hailed an opportunity to amplify the party's critique of labourism. A week before polling day, the RCP organized a public meeting in Rotherhithe, where Mike Freeman reinforced the party's hopes of corroding significantly the Labour vote. Campaign coordinator Judy Harrison told the eighty attendees to expect substantial support for Eden.[27]

When Eden received only thirty-eight votes – sixty-nine fewer even than 'Screaming Lord Sutch' of the Monster Raving Loony Party[28] – cadres were left to reflect on a recurring problem of the party's first decade: the stubborn persistence of labourism. Eden lauded the spike of party activity in Bermondsey, where the RCP recruited twenty new supporters and sold more than 2,000 copies of *the next step*. But the wider lesson of the by-election, Eden maintained, was that cadres needed to intensify their efforts to break workers' traditional allegiance to Labour:

> Our low poll showed that the Labour Party still retains an effective grip over active sections of the working class . . . even when the [Labour P]arty is disintegrating, workers' gut loyalty to Labour remains immensely powerful. . . . Next time the RCP must do better. To loosen the grip of Labourism over active workers we need a much sharper critique of reformism. . . . We have begun to challenge Labourism. What we have to do now is to drive a wedge between Labour and its disenchanted but loyal left-wing supporters.[29]

---

24   For a detailed analysis of the Bermondsey by-election, see Lucy Robinson, *Gay Men and the Left in Post-war Britain: How the Personal Got Political* (Manchester: Manchester University Press, 2007), 154–64.
25   'Fran Eden to contest byelection', *Guardian*, 11 November 1982.
26   Nicholas Timmins, 'Brixton blacks question police demolition role', *Times*, 3 November 1982.
27   UPI MPS-0731471: 'Special Branch report on an RCP public meeting as part of their campaign in the Bermondsey by-election', 18 February 1983. Available at ucpi.org.uk/publications/special-branch-report-on-an-rcp-public-meeting-as-part-of-their-campaign-in-the-bermondsey-by-election/ (accessed 12 July 2021).
28   Receiving 17,017 votes (57.7 per cent), Liberal candidate Simon Hughes won the seat, while Tatchell received 7,698 votes (26.1 per cent).
29   Pat Roberts, 'Reflecting on Bermondsey', *tns*, April 1983.

Viewed retrospectively, Bermondsey captured in microcosm some of the most salient features of the RCP's career: on the one hand, cadres' strategic single-mindedness and self-confidence; on the other, the magnitude and difficulty of their tasks. 'The experience of the campaign', says Mike Fitzpatrick, 'was a positive one for a growing number of supporters who engaged in lively public meetings and doorstep debates'. But workers' 'residual loyalty to Labour', Fitzpatrick reflects, proved to be a 'familiar feature of the labour movement' throughout the 1980s.[30]

Disappointment in Bermondsey confirmed to cadres the acuity of their critique of labourism, enunciated some five years earlier in *Who Needs the Labour Party?* Vowing to sharpen their own offensive, the RCP stood four candidates in the general election of June 1983, winning 988 votes in total.[31] If the results reaffirmed the difficulties of winning workers to independent revolutionary politics, the election also reinforced revolutionaries' assessment of labourism facing terminal decline:[32] losing sixty seats, Labour recorded its worst electoral performance since 1918. RCP strategists maintained that a vanguard had a pivotal role to play in supplanting left-wing reformism and transforming British politics.[33]

Forming a major part of life in the party, educationals and debates were the internal corollary of the RCP's external challenge to the British working class. To equip cadres to advance their arguments for a revolutionary alternative, branch organizers designed rumbustious discussions of Marxist theory. Members read widely on twentieth-century politics and history, especially on the Bolshevik Revolution and the Left Opposition. Foremost, however, was a thorough analytical grounding in the Marxist canon. As for other radical organizations, *Capital* reading groups were an integral feature of internal party education. Weekly sessions were treated with great seriousness: any individual who missed any of the first four sessions, or two consecutive sessions, was liable to expulsion.[34] Veterans regularly remember educationals as an expression of the party's emphasis upon ideological clarity. 'You'd sometimes spend an hour

---

30 Mike Fitzpatrick, 15 August 2020.
31 The RCP candidates in the general election of 1983 were Farehk Afzal (who received fifty-four votes in Southwark and Bermondsey), Cathy Barrett (222, Sheffield Central), Fran Eden (305, Birmingham Sparkbrook) and Dave Hallsworth (407, Ashton-under-Lyne). Afzal, Barrett, Eden and Hallsworth all accentuated the party's demands for an immediate end to immigration controls and to British rule in Ireland and also called for a universal minimum wage and access to safe abortion on demand.
32 *Preparing for Power: The Programme of the Revolutionary Communist Party* (third edition, London: Junius, 1984 [first edition, London: Junius, 1983]), 5, 12, 16–17.
33 'Out of the ashes', *tns*, July 1983.
34 RCP Yorkshire *Capital* Reading Group schedule (n.d. [c.1986]). Copy in author's possession.

discussing those footnotes and arguing', John Gillott recalled.[35] 'The most important thing that I ever got from all this', Norman Lewis reflects,

> was a very serious reading of *Capital*. . . . That was phenomenal. . . . Mainly because of the way that we read it. We had these very stringent educationals where we had to read it together and we discussed it once a week almost paragraph by paragraph over a period of about six months.[36]

The tradition of rigorous reading remains emblazoned in the memories of former activists, who locate the intensity of discussion in the world-historical role which the party envisioned. The writings of Lenin, Trotsky and Lukács, for example, were debated not in academic abstraction but to hone strategy and method. Cadres read Left Oppositionists such as Christian Rakovsky to excavate the Bolshevik tradition and to understand its perceived defeat in the Stalinist counter-revolution.[37] Reading Henryk Grossman and Paul Mattick, activists seeking to reverse the 'liquidation' of Marxism pursued a dialectical understanding of the Marxist theory of crisis.[38] For one former member of the Political Committee, the 'emphasis on education' distinguished the party's determination to overcome the counter-revolutionary regression of previous decades. Cadre-training was based upon

> reading history, reading Lenin and Marx and Trotsky and Rosa Luxemburg and many more besides – knowing the history, understanding the history of the revolutionary movement but also the radical left, the British tradition, and the European tradition. . . . To really understand the evolution of radical and revolutionary political thought and organisation, and to understand the contemporary moment and where we were and how to situate our own movement and that of others as well – that was a huge endeavour.[39]

---

35 John Gillott interview with the author, 6 October 2020.
36 Norman Lewis, 16 February 2021.
37 From the late 1920s, the Bulgarian Left Oppositionist Christian Rakovsky argued that isolated functionaries had supplanted the working class in the Soviet Union and accused the Stalinist elite of propelling the revolution's 'bureaucratic degenerations'. For Rakovsky, the rise of the bureaucracy stemmed not only from external capitalist encirclement but from a counter-revolutionary social stratum within the party: 'We had the hope that the party leadership would have created a new, truly worker and peasant apparatus; new, truly proletarian trade unions; a new morality of daily life. We have to recognise it frankly, clearly and in a loud and intelligible voice: the apparatus of the party has not accomplished this task . . . it has become bankrupt: it is insolvent. . . . And it continues to follow this road'. In April 1930, with his fellow exiles Kasparova, Kossior and Muralov, Rakovsky demanded that Stalin's position of general secretary be abolished, Trotsky and his imprisoned comrades be released and 'free discussion' initiated to rebuild the Communist Party of the Soviet Union. Christian Rakovsky, *Selected Writings on Opposition in the USSR, 1923–1930* (London: Allison & Busby, 1980), 124–36, 166–79.
38 Revolutionary Communist Party, *Prolonging the Death Agony: The Rise, Fall and Reconstitution of Social Democracy* (Revolutionary Communist Papers, No. 8, September 1981), 17.
39 Joan Hoey interview with the author, 6 August 2022.

New recruits were persistently challenged to justify their ideas. Oral testimonies testify the intellectual formation, which many veterans attribute to meeting the party in early adulthood. Claire Fox, for example, contrasts the directness of party culture from the more polite superficiality of her seminars at Warwick University:

> I'd spent a lot of time at university bullshitting. . . . I was able to get away with a lot. I was never able to get away with anything in the RCP. I'd go to an educational and I'd be waxing lyrical, and I was constantly challenged: *what are you talking about?* [. . .] I was held to account. I couldn't just ramble on. . . . So this was fantastically important to me. I really loved the fact that I met a group of people that didn't condescend to me, didn't patronise me: took me seriously, in other words. Took me seriously intellectually and politically.[40]

For revolutionaries seeking not only to understand the world but to revivify revolutionary Marxism and transform it, educationals were vital to personal and political development. Purposive engagement with an eclectic range of texts endured throughout the party's lifespan, as an activist who joined in the early 1990s attests of 'absolutely brilliant' education in the RCP:

> We would read and discuss, and read and discuss. . . . The RCP really took the world seriously. They actually want to understand the world. They don't just want to go shout empty slogans. If you want to change the world, you have got to be able to understand it in all its ugliness and all its contradictions and all its complexity. We read a range of different books and genres, historical and contemporary – books that reflected current sensibilities as well as those that challenged them. . . . We read a range of books that we disagreed with. It was not a bubble of the like-minded; internal discussions were really engaged and critical.[41]

Former cadres asserting the party's emphasis upon the primacy of ideas frequently attest a combative yet collegial culture:

> Educational meetings were a total eye-opener. I enjoyed it. I was never particularly theoretically brilliant but I loved the idea that I was learning stuff and I loved the idea that I somehow had found a bunch of people who wanted to make a difference to society.[42]

Challenging debates were designed to enable cadres to train a vanguard. For Linda Murdoch, who joined the party in Glasgow in the mid-1980s, tempestuous

---

40   Claire Fox, 1 September 2020.
41   Former RCP member, interview with the author, October 2021.
42   Ann Furedi, 7 October 2021.

discussions were vital for equipping activists with the conviction to challenge prevailing tendencies in the working class:

> They really encouraged you to speak your mind and not hold back, and tell you that your opinion mattered.... You got to the stage where if you didn't say something, you felt bad, because you knew your opinion mattered, and you felt it was your responsibility to clear things, or ask the questions that helped clear things up for other people, or answer questions to clear things up for other people. We were always working hard to try and explain things... We equipped each other with the ideas and the ways to challenge other people.[43]

Underpinning the organization's stress upon ideological independence, the RCP's educational programmes were a defining feature of its party tradition. Implicitly recalling Georg Lukács's dictum that Marxist orthodoxy resides exclusively in method,[44] Frank Furedi argues that questioning orthodoxies, especially on the radical left, fuelled cadres' intellectual and political development:

> We didn't have a party line. We had positions. But the idea was that you are responsible for developing that position, rather than to repeat what you heard somebody else had said. That was something that I was very proud of.... Because it's very tempting to fall back upon a line. And to repeat what you heard somebody else had said, you know. We all do it sometimes.... But we really pushed people not to say, *we've got a line*.... I kind of felt that that was one of our biggest strengths, because it meant that we were able to have a group of individuals around who could think on their feet, who had the flexibility and the capacity to seize the moment and do, you know, incredibly interesting things.[45]

Reflecting in 2005, a former RCP supporter who had become disenchanted with the network's post-party trajectory evoked the ideological certainties which had underpinned activists' zeal:

> Outsiders often talk about it being cultish, but it wasn't cultish at all. You were allowed to disagree with what the line was. They were just so confident in their theoretical knowledge that they were confident that they could convince you.[46]

---

43 Linda Murdoch interview with the author, 21 December 2021.
44 'It is not the "belief" in this or that thesis, nor the exegesis of a "sacred" book. On the contrary, orthodoxy refers exclusively to *method*. It is the scientific conviction that dialectical materialism is the road to truth and that its methods can be developed, expanded and deepened only along the lines laid down by its founders'. Lukács, *History and Class Consciousness*.
45 Frank Furedi, 18 August 2020.
46 David Webb quoted in Chris Bunting, 'What's a nice Trot doing in a place like this?', *Times Higher Education Supplement*, 28 January 2005.

The vanguardist project demanded extraordinary commitment from RCP members, who numbered between 80 and 120 by the mid-1980s. In 1983, branches were formed in Brighton, Bristol, Glasgow and Portsmouth. Typically, directed to establish a cell in a new city, two or three trusted cadres were detailed to establish a political profile around local estates, workplaces, trade unions and left-wing milieux in the hope of attracting 'contacts'. Frequently deployed to initiate new branches – 'during a period of about fifteen years, my mother had twenty-three addresses for me' – Kirk Leech recalls being sent to Nottingham and briefed: 'it'll just be you, and there are a couple of contacts'.[47]

Attaining and sustaining full party membership was a consuming commitment. According to a police informer within the organization, to be considered for membership, 'candidate' members typically required between six and nine months of party activity. Full-time cadres could expect to devote between twelve and sixteen hours per day to party work.[48] Branch organizers populated cadres' diaries with demanding schedules spanning paper sales, engaging with 'contacts' and convening demonstrations and events. In this small organization's Stakhanovite atmosphere, the party centre urged activists to develop their connections in the working class.[49] The 'average RCP member', Frank Furedi remembers,

> would be doing far more political work than other organisations. That was seen as being the norm. And I'm sure it put a lot of people off because obviously not everybody wants to make that kind of commitment.[50]

To support party activity, members also paid dues proportionate to their income: cadres who undertook waged work alongside their activism paid more than social security claimants, who would donate nominal sums.

Warning against the dangers of lapsing into perfunctory routinism, party leaders asserted that raising the party's profile was paramount. In a communique circulated to branches in 1983, the Political Committee complained of 'an underlying work-to-rule mentality [which] prevails at all levels of the party'.[51]

---

47 Kirk Leech, 7 September 2020.
48 UPI0000034280: 'Debriefing of a Revolutionary Communist Party (RCP) Source', 17 October 1983. Available at ucpi.org.uk/wp-content/uploads/2021/04/UCPI0000034280.pdf (accessed 22 April 2021).
49 According to John Kelly's authoritative account, by the mid-1980s, there were more than 20,000 Trotskyist activists in Britain. The RCP had considerably fewer full members than the leading radical organizations, such as the Workers Revolutionary Party (WRP) (9,000), Militant (7,000) and SWP (4,000). Kelly, *Contemporary Trotskyism*, 40, 46, 53.
50 Frank Furedi, 18 August 2020.
51 *The RCP and the Problem of Democratic Centralism*. RCP conference bulletin (1983). Copy in author's possession.

Elected as the RCP's first general secretary in December 1983, Kate Marshall vowed to 'turn the party outwards' to augment its influence.[52] By the mid-1980s, the RCP's networks had grown steadily. Although membership never exceeded 300, during the miners' strike *the next step* became a weekly newspaper, with circulation rising to between 14,000 and 15,000.[53] The party also significantly expanded its ranks of 'supporters', with 238 joining in the first two months of 1986 alone.[54]

The party's bifocal outlook held that while capitalism continued to buckle under its own contradictions, only the conscious revolutionary agency of the working class could effect social transformation. Elevating the radical potential of the subject enabled the RCP to project itself boldly – annual conferences were 'preparing for power' with the 'party of the future' – while acknowledging the enormity of its tasks. At the party's national summer school in 1986, Frank Richards's keynote address underlined the historical role of the revolutionary cadre:

> The first step on the road to power is the shattering discovery that only you and people like you can make a difference.[55]

Crucially, the perception of incipient momentum helped activists to overcome setbacks. When thirty-eight RCP candidates received a total of just 2,298 votes – a paltry average of sixty-one – in the local elections of May 1986, national organizer Ann Burton admitted that the 'disappointing' results highlighted the 'gap' between reality and the party's much-vaunted hopes of displacing the Labour Party within twelve months.[56] Nevertheless, the leadership maintained that while the pace of change was frustrating, the direction remained vital. Writing in the party's theoretical journal, Mike Freeman averred that the 'decay of Labourism' underscored the 'tremendous potential' of independent class politics. For the first time since the Second World War, Freeman asserted, it was possible to 'win a real hearing for anti-capitalist ideas'.[57]

---

52 'New General Secretary', *tns*, January 1984.
53 'Stepping out', *tns*, August 1984.
54 With fewer responsibilities than full members, supporters constituted a second circle of party activists. They were primarily expected to sell papers and attend party events. 'Supporters speaking', *tns*, 28 February 1986.
55 Frank Richards, 'The road to power', *tns*, 8 August 1986.
56 Among the dismal results in May 1986, the party's stronger performances came in areas where the RCP had established branches and undertaken anti-racist activism. In Bradford, for example, three candidates won 158 votes in total. Richard Ardern won 139 in Handsworth in inner-city Birmingham, while Yasmin Arnould won 101 in the south London borough of Lambeth. Ann Burton, 'Summing up the elections', *tns*, 16 May 1986.
57 Freeman, 'The road to power', 74.

'We must be prepared to put our lives on the line'

Alongside espousing 'unconditional support' for 'Irish freedom', militant anti-racism was a campaigning priority throughout the RCP's first decade. Founding East London Workers Against Racism (ELWAR) as a front group in 1979, the RCT elaborated its strategic rationale: in parallel with the organization's position on Ireland, radical anti-racism was integral to the struggle against social-chauvinism in the working class.[58] Revolutionary opposition to racism, the Tendency's founders asserted, would arraign the nationalism and reformism which pervaded the labour movement. By the time the RCT became the RCP in May 1981, a national conference had mooted replicating ELWAR's work in provincial cities across Britain.[59]

With a distinct anti-capitalist dynamic, WAR activities were consistently geared to challenge workers' illusions in the state. When trade unionists implored the government to restrict the movement of labour, capital, and goods, Frank Richards asserted, they implicitly confirmed their statism.[60] Confronting working-class economic nationalism and the 'respectable face of racism' in the labour movement, cadres exhorted workers to identify their independent class interests.[61] Echoing the party's interventions on Ireland, WAR fulminated against a 'patriotic' trade union bureaucracy which encouraged workers to define themselves by their nationality rather than by their class.[62]

ELWAR mobilised in a society scarred by virulent racism. Between 1976 and 1981, thirty-six racist murders were recorded in Britain, with most occurring in east London and the Midlands.[63] In the Greater London Council (GLC) elections of May 1977, the far-right National Front won 119,060 votes (5.3 percent), with its strongest performances in safe Labour wards in east and north London. Publishing his history of the organisation the same year, *Guardian* journalist Martin Walker predicted that the Front would soon overtake the Liberals as the third-largest party in Britain.[64] Hostility to immigration was not the preserve

---

58 ELWAR constituted the RCT's first, localized anti-racist organization. As the RCP developed through the 1980s, the wider Workers Against Racism (WAR) umbrella established networks in several provincial cities, most notably in Bradford, Birmingham, Coventry and Manchester.
59 'the next step conference', *tns*, March 1981.
60 Richards, *Under a National Flag*, 2, 16, 18.
61 *Racial Oppression*, 2.
62 Workers Against Racism, *Cleansing Our Ranks: A Platform for Anti-racist Trade Unionists* (London: Junius, December 1981), 6.
63 Vincent Latour, 'Between consensus, consolidation and crisis: Immigration and integration in 1970s Britain', *Revue Française de Civilisation Britannique*, 22 (2017), doi.org/10.4000/rfcb.1719, paragraph 27.
64 Martin Walker, *The National Front* (London: Fontana, 1977).

of extremists, but percolated the political mainstream. In January 1978, Leader of the Opposition Margaret Thatcher told Granada Television's *World in Action* that Britons were 'really rather afraid that this country might be rather swamped by people with a different culture'.[65]

In this febrile atmosphere, ELWAR activists offered immigrants and minorities physical defence against assault and arson. Patrolling estates where racist attacks abounded, especially in Tower Hamlets and Hackney, ELWAR guarded besieged families. Workers' defence activities were intended both to isolate the racist minority, and to exemplify the solidarity of unified workers. Cadres undertook training in martial arts and self-defence, and organised overnight vigils in trouble hotspots. 'We must be prepared to put our lives on the line for this', Judy Harrison told a 70-strong ELWAR meeting in 1980. 'You have to meet violence with violence where it is necessary, and it must be organised'.[66] Rob Killick, who moved to London in 1979, remembers harrowing experiences during ELWAR's street patrols:

> The idea that British society's racist now – trust me: in the late seventies, early eighties, you had little kids being attacked in the street and all this kind of stuff. It was pretty bad.[67]

Having lived on Brixton's Railton Road in the 1970s, James Woudhuysen similarly contrasts the virulent racism of that era with politics today:

> Although I was never involved in the [Brixton] riots, the atmosphere and the general feeling then was one hundred percent different from what it is now . . . It was in the atmosphere. It really *was* the atmosphere, you know. Racism was just *there* in the air, in a way that it's just not now.[68]

ELWAR escalated their patrols after twenty-eight-year-old Parveen Khan and her three children were murdered in a racist firebombing in Walthamstow in July 1981. Subsequently, activists camped in the homes of families who suffered attacks. Speaking in 1982, Charles Longford explained the group's methods on the streets:

> We are looking for groups of boys hanging around in the area. Normally when they see us they disperse, but there have been confrontations. What we try to do

---

65 Margaret Thatcher Foundation: 'TV Interview for Granada *World in Action*', 27 January 1978. Available at margaretthatcher.org/document/103485 (accessed 7 June 2022).
66 Lucy Hodges, 'White vigilantes protecting black families', *Times*, 1 December 1980.
67 Rob Killick, 20 August 2020.
68 James Woudhuysen, 7 December 2022.

is take out ringleaders. It can become very nasty. There was an occasion when one of our group was very nearly stabbed.[69]

By January 1982, ELWAR had become the subject of parliamentary consternation, when Conservative backbencher Nicholas Winterton unsuccessfully entreated Home Secretary William Whitelaw to proscribe the 'vigilante group'.[70]

As former ELWAR activist Norman Lewis remembers, defence work in difficult circumstances articulated the party's vision of working-class independence:

> People were physically under attack and we organised to defend them. We used to go over there, organise the people on the estate who were against racism, to oppose and isolate those racists in or outside the estate who were coming in. We had some hairy, hairy moments. Some real physical confrontations with some very nasty people, even people wielding knives. We'd organise patrols. We were on call twenty-four hours a day. Getting called at three in the morning would mean going to east London to help a family who'd had a brick through the window, or had petrol set alight through their front door. We got a whole load of people involved in patrols and a willingness to physically defend the victims of racism. This was aimed not only to provide physical defence for people who really needed it. It also demonstrated what working-class independence was in practice: not calling the police or the state to do it, or anybody other than ourselves. ELWAR aimed to give practical shape to what working-class independence meant.[71]

Accentuating their own revolutionary dynamic, cadres disdained left-wing anti-racists whose focus on the fascist fringe, they argued, failed to tackle nationalism in the labour movement. The Anti-Nazi League (ANL) originated in 1977, when members of the SWP and Labour leftists instituted a broad organization to oppose the ascendant National Front. By the following summer, the ANL enjoyed the support of more than 40,000 radicals.[72] Winning endorsements from some fifty local Labour Party branches, the ANL distributed nationwide 1.7 million leaflets, 300,000 stickers, 90,000 posters and 25,000 badges. Attracting support from numerous popular musicians, the organization also coordinated major music carnivals in Victoria Park and Brockwell Park in 1978.[73] Imploring workers to

---

69 Shyama Perera, 'Vigilantes move against racism', *Guardian*, 18 January 1982.
70 Hansard: House of Commons, 29 January 1982, Volume 16.
71 Norman Lewis, 16 February 2021.
72 Nigel Copsey, 'Meeting the challenge of contemporary British fascism? The Labour Party's response to the National Front and the British National Party', in Nigel Copsey and David Renton (eds), *British Fascism, the Labour Movement and the State* (Basingstoke: Palgrave Macmillan, 2005), 188.
73 Michael Higgs, 'From the street to the state: Making anti-fascism anti-racist in 1970s Britain', *Race & Class*, 58 (2016): 75.

unify to isolate the National Front, the ANL gained significant traction in the labour movement, counting among its affiliates some twenty-five trades councils and dozens of union branches.[74]

As far as ELWAR activists were concerned, the ANL treated fascism as the domain of fringe extremists and therefore erroneously divorced fascism from its class character.[75] Fascism, Frank Richards asserted, was not an aberration from bourgeois democracy, but 'the political form through which the bourgeoisie attempts to resolve intense class conflict'.[76] Instead, alongside waging a mass grassroots campaign, the ANL looked to the state to help to extirpate racism. For instance, after rioting in St Pauls in April 1980 – when a police raid sparked unrest in an area marked by heightened racial tension – the Bristol ANL demanded a 'public enquiry' as well as an independent trade union investigation.[77] RCT cadres warned that failing to locate fascism specifically in the capitalist crisis perpetuated a liberal delusion that racism could be ameliorated without a revolutionary challenge to capitalism.[78]

Accusing the ANL of fixating myopically upon a supposed 'Nazi' fringe, RCP cadres prioritized combating the nationalism and social-chauvinism which pervaded the trade union movement. Especially before the general election of 1979, ANL activists specifically devoted their energies to picketing fascist meetings and warning voters against the 'Nazi' Front. In Preston, as many as 300 ANL supporters mobilized mass pickets and leafleting campaigns against the Front: 'We just want to underline that people should avoid the Front like a plague', the local organizer told the *Lancashire Evening Post*.[79] By contrast, the RCT's founding milieu criticized the ANL's 'narrow anti-fascism': anti-immigrant prejudices, Frank Richards asserted, were not limited to the ranks of the National Front but were lamentably 'widespread' in the labour movement.[80]

While physical defence established ELWAR's profile in embattled communities, strategists implored supporters to take their vanguardist anti-racism into the

---

74 David Renton, 'Guarding the barricades: Working-class anti-fascism, 1974-1979', in Copsey and Renton (eds), *British Fascism*, 145.
75 National Organisation of Revolutionary Communist Students, *Higher Education: Fight the Cuts – Defend Overseas Students* (London: Revolutionary Communist Tendency, 1979), 4.
76 Richards, *Under a National Flag*, 4.
77 Bristol Anti-Nazi League, *Defend St Pauls!* (Bristol: Bristol Anti-Nazi League, 1980).
78 *Racial Oppression*, 22. Developing similar themes in the late 1980s, Paul Gilroy criticized the ANL for mobilizing nationalist sentiment. By castigating British fascists as 'sham patriots' staining an essentially tolerant nation, Gilroy argued, the ANL implied that racism was a marginal political aberration which the state could police. Paul Gilroy, *There ain't No Black in the Union Jack: The Cultural Politics of Race and Nation* (London: Routledge, 2002 [first edition 1987]), 71, 194–5.
79 'Campaign will call for Front boycott', *Lancashire Evening Post*, 9 April 1979.
80 Richards, *Under a National Flag*, 16.

trade unions. Exhorting sympathizers to 'fight racism in the labour movement', ELWAR organizers suggested template resolutions for activists to lobby their workplace or union branch. Epitomizing the RCP's critique of left reformism and nationalism, the proposed motions invited workers' organizations to oppose all immigration controls, resist deportations and 'bring out [their] members to defend black people when they're attacked'.[81] ELWAR's intensive fly-posting operation on the ground positioned anti-racism as the 'central political issue around which East London workers must unite'.[82]

The experience of the Saddique family in Stratford illustrated the extent of the torment which many Asian families had endured in ELWAR's terrain. In 1982, the Saddiques bought a shop in the East End, but daily racist attacks prevented them from operating their business. The teenage Nasreen Saddique witnessed members of the National Front physically attacking her father, mother and brother and daubing their terraced house with racist abuse. After persistent vandalism, the windows were permanently boarded. Nasreen Saddique told journalists that the police had not offered meaningful help.[83] Newham Rights Centre introduced the Saddiques to ELWAR. Interviewed in 2018, Nasreen Saddique recalled how ELWAR activists 'stayed with us, early evening until one, two in the morning, depending on the situation on the night'. The police rebuked the Saddiques for accepting ELWAR's help.[84] Meanwhile, in Tower Hamlets, ELWAR activists supporting a Bangladeshi single father and his three children canvassed 500 homes on the Glamis estate. According to organizer Keith Tompson, cadres met 'more than 300 anti-racists', of whom thirty joined later meetings to coordinate defence.[85]

Circumnavigating the police was a core tenet of the RCP's anti-statist class politics. When rioting erupted in Brixton in April 1981, WAR instituted its second London branch, identifying the police as aggressors to be resisted: 'The police

---

81 East London Workers Against Racism, *Our Flag Stays Red* (Revolutionary Communist Pamphlets, No. 9, April 1981), 14.
82 Working Class Movement Library (hereafter, WCML): Fascism Box 4: *East London Workers Against Racism* (n.d. [1982]).
83 Nick Davies, 'Asians attacked by police, says witness', *Guardian*, 9 December 1983.
84 'Nasreen Saddique – "Anne Frank with a telephone"', *Journey To Justice*. Available at jtojhumanrights.org.uk/local-stories/local-stories-posts/nasreen-saddique-anne-frank-with-a-telephone/ (accessed 15 October 2021). To highlight the Saddiques' plight, ELWAR also invited radical journalist John Pilger to visit the family. It was to be the beginning of an enduring friendship: in a series of articles for the *Daily Mirror* and the *Independent*, Pilger publicized the Saddiques' torment.
85 Keith Tompson, *Under Siege: Racism and Violence in Britain Today* (London: Penguin, 1988), xiii, 140.

are not a neutral force that can be made accountable to workers'.[86] Attributing the Brixton disturbances to 'systematic police harassment', South London Workers Against Racism (SOLWAR) helped fifteen Black youths, charged with riotous behaviour, to sue the police and 'turn the tables on the state'.[87] Similarly, in July 1981, when more than 1,000 Manchester youths besieged a police station in Moss Side, WAR activists hailed what they termed independent opposition to repression. Encouraging this incipient anti-statism, Manchester WAR activist Denise Smith exhorted Black youths to expel the police from Moss Side permanently.[88] When disorder resumed in Brixton in 1982, three leading RCP cadres hijacked a police-community liaison meeting and congratulated local rebels for their 'response to incessant police harassment'. Turning his back on the police chair, Farekh Afzal hailed those who had rejected the authorities and reasserted the 'right of black people to fight back against the police'.[89]

Despite the profile and boldness of their community defence, WAR activists met with suspicion within some embattled minorities. WAR's critique of the police chimed with leftists in immigrant communities: at WAR's national conference in July 1981, for example, a representative of the Indian Workers' Association praised cadres for publicizing police harassment.[90] But community groups were often more wary of the RCP's wider revolutionary programme, especially after ELWAR started distributing Bengali-language flyers in 1981. Bangladeshi organizations in east London, for instance, failed to produce the promised support for an ELWAR march.[91] Despite their presence in Brixton during the unrest of 1981 and 1982, WAR activists were largely unable to draw local people into the party orbit. In March 1982, when SOLWAR organized a public meeting to discuss police harassment, RCP activists comprised more than half of the participants, and only nine members of Brixton's Black community

---

86 South London Workers Against Racism, *Police out of Brixton!* (Revolutionary Communist Pamphlets, No. 10, April 1981), 6.
87 WCML: Fascism Box 4: South London Workers Against Racism, *Put the Police in the Dock!* (n.d. [1981]).
88 Lucy Hodges, 'Left at riots – to help people', *Times*, 10 July 1981.
89 Timmins, 'Brixton blacks question police demolition role'; Stephen Cook, 'Group denies agitators to blame for riot', *Guardian*, 4 November 1982.
90 UPI0000015545: 'Special Branch report on a national conference of the Revolutionary Communist Party titled "Workers Defence Takes Off"', 19 August 1981. Available at ucpi.org.uk/publications/special-branch-report-on-a-national-conference-of-the-revolutionary-communist-party-titled-workers-defence-takes-off/ (accessed 12 July 2021).
91 UPI0000015249: 'Special Branch report on a public meeting held by East London Workers Against Racism in support of their candidate in the Greater London Council elections', 29 April 1981. Available at ucpi.org.uk/publications/special-branch-report-on-a-public-meeting-held-by-east-london-workers-against-racism-in-support-of-their-candidate-in-the-greater-london-council-elections/ (accessed 12 July 2021).

attended.⁹² Some seven years after ELWAR began campaigning in east London, the anti-racist Newham Monitoring Project accused leftists of exaggerating their significance for their own ends. Sunder Kangesan, a former race relations officer, dismissed WAR: 'We do not have anything to do with them . . . they just make up stories about race attack victims'.⁹³ Other leftists deliberately disaggregated ELWAR's defence work from the specific politics of the RCP: Winston Carr of *Socialist Newsletter*, for example, lauded ELWAR's 'vitally necessary' vigilantism but lamented its 'self-imposed sectarian isolation from organised Labour'.⁹⁴

The RCP's firmest connections in minority communities stemmed from direct engagements with victims of racist attacks. WAR mobilized in Coventry, for example, in 1981, when racists murdered twenty-year-old student Satnam Singh Gill. Coventry Workers Against Racism (COVWAR) galvanized local students, militants and unemployed youth for protest demonstrations.⁹⁵ The organization also regularly assisted those who had suffered police brutality. When a Black youth was assaulted in custody in October 1981, COVWAR liaised with the victim's family and organized pickets at police premises.⁹⁶ The RCP leadership remained concerned, however, that the demands of defence might lead cadres to identify physical work as an end in itself. Briefing the party conference of 1982, Frank Richards reasserted that anti-racist activism must persistently be oriented to expose nationalism and reformism on the left.⁹⁷

Anti-deportation campaigns enabled WAR to take avowedly vanguardist politics into broader milieux encompassing the left, the labour movement and ethnic minority communities. Activists forged strong connections with families facing an ordeal. At a public meeting launching three ELWAR candidates' campaigns for the GLC elections of 1981, for example, a Filipino worker spoke from the floor to thank ELWAR effusively for their support in her own struggle.⁹⁸

---

92 UPI0000017977: 'Special Branch report on a public meeting of the South London Workers Against Racism discussing the police', 31 March 1982. Available at https://www.ucpi.org.uk/publications/special-branch-report-on-a-public-meeting-of-the-south-london-workers-against-racism-discussing-the-police/ (accessed 12 July 2021).
93 '"We just want more members"', *Telegraph & Argus*, 13 June 1986.
94 Winston Carr, 'Racist Attacks', *Socialist Newsletter: Journal of the Socialist Labour Group*, 12 (January 1981).
95 Warwick Digital Archive: UWA/PUB/S/HB/15/1: 'Links with the Outside World', *University of Warwick Students' Union Handbook! 1981-1982* (Coventry: Warwick University Students' Union, 1981).
96 Richard Jones, 'RCS Meeting', *Warwick Boar*, 21 October 1981.
97 *Building the new leadership:* RCP conference bulletin (1982).
98 UPI0000016193. 'Special Branch report on a public meeting of the East London Workers Against Racism including talks by Fran Eden and Joan Lamont on fascism and immigration', 28 January 1981. Available at ucpi.org.uk/publications/special-branch-report-on-a-public-meeting-of-the-east-london-workers-against-racism-including-talks-by-fran-eden-and-joan-lamont-on-fascism-and-immigration/ (accessed 2 June 2021).

Featuring prominently in high-profile cases, cadres amplified their revolutionary opposition to *all* immigration controls. WAR's activity during the Afia Begum Defence Campaign constituted a case in point. A young Bangladeshi immigrant living in London with a newborn baby, Afia Begum was widowed in March 1982 when her husband, Abdul Hamid – who held a legal right to permanent residence in the UK – died in a fire. Declaring that Hamid's death invalidated Begum's entry permit, the Home Office ordered Begum's deportation.[99] Begum's case became a cause célèbre: seventy Members of Parliament, including leading Labour parliamentarians such as Tony Benn and Michael Foot, argued that Begum had the right to remain.

During protracted disputes until Begum's eventual deportation in June 1984, WAR activists challenged sympathizers to oppose *all* immigration controls. When Begum campaign supporter Tony Benn addressed a WAR meeting in 1982, RCP cadre Farekh Afzal publicly exhorted the leading Labour leftist to oppose in parliament all residency controls.[100] Cultivating class independence sometimes entailed defying reformist instincts among the minority communities. At an ELWAR rally in 1982, for example, Judy Harrison confronted a Bengali councillor in Tower Hamlets who endorsed the RCP's critique of 'racist housing policies' but suggested that some immigration laws were necessary.[101]

Cadres confronted leftists and trade unionists who supported Begum on liberal grounds but failed to repudiate on principle immigration controls. Initiating a grassroots group of Asian women – the so-called 'sari squad' – RCP cadre Para Mullan played a leading role in the Afia Begum Defence Campaign. As well as coordinating public meetings and demonstrations attracting media attention,[102] the 'sari squad' produced a video and travelled to the European Parliament in Strasbourg to publicize Begum's plight.[103] Mullan remembers the campaign as a momentous experience articulating a keystone principle:

---

99 Joan Phillips, 'No more deportations!', *tns*, July 1983.
100 UPI0000019003: 'Special Branch report on a public meeting of Workers Against Racism and the Greater London Council's Committee for Women to discuss the forthcoming deportation of Afia Begum', 19 April 1983.
101 The disagreement swiftly devolved into a dispute between ELWAR and the councillor in relation to control of the Begum campaign's funds. UPI0000018684: 'Special Branch report on a public meeting of the East London Workers Against Racism discussing the forthcoming deportation of Afia Begum', 5 October 1982. Available at ucpi.org.uk/publications/special-branch-report-on-a-public-meeting-of-the-east-london-workers-against-racism-discussing-the-forthcoming-deportation-of-afia-begum/ (accessed 12 July 2021).
102 'Brittan protest: Four bound over', *Westminster & Pimlico News*, 26 August 1983.
103 *Right to be Here: A Campaigning Guide to the Immigration Laws* (London: GLC Anti-Deportation Working Group, 1985), 71; 'Defend Afia Begum!', *tns*, October 1983.

I formed a squad of fifteen or so Asian women. [We] called ourselves the 'sari squad' and we went around the country and internationally publicising her plight. We wore saris and inevitably caused a stir wherever we went. One of those activities was chaining ourselves to the railings outside the Home Office. . . . We were arrested and thrown into jail for one night. The jail guards were very amused to see Asian women in saris spending a night in jail. They had never seen anything like this before. We also took a tour to Europe, campaigned in Amsterdam, in Germany, and spoke at the European Parliament in Strasbourg. . . . Our opposition to all immigration controls was made very clearly via all these channels.[104]

Reflecting its localized character and limited organizational resources, the RCP's anti-racist activism won greater support at the grassroots union branch level than in the labour movement leadership. In east London, members of the National Union of Teachers (NUT), for example, distributed ELWAR's news-sheets and joined demonstrations against racist attacks. But when ELWAR supporters moved the NUT's national conference to oppose all immigration controls, the motion was rejected out of hand.[105] In Bradford and Leeds, meanwhile, activists called in vain for public sector employees to boycott 'race checks', which policed eligibility for welfare payments and healthcare.[106] Manchester WAR's campaign in the health service gained greater traction, however. Escalating an initial boycott at Wythenshawe Hospital,[107] WAR activists successfully mandated the National Union of Public Employees (NUPE) to oppose the checks.[108]

Generating significant publicity throughout the 1980s, the RCP's anti-deportation campaigns highlighted exemplary cases to challenge British workers to assert independence from the state. When George Roucou, a shop steward in the Union of Construction, Allied Trades and Technicians (UCATT), was threatened with deportation, WAR activist Charles Longford, alongside UCATT organizer Billy Gill, organized Roucou's defence campaign.[109] Roucou also won support from the Civil and Public Services Association and the students' union

---

104 Para Mullan interview with the author, 13 December 2021.
105 'Teachers' next step', *tns*, February 1981.
106 'Wreck the checks!', *tns*, February 1982; Scott Smedley, 'Racial Checks Picket', *Leeds Student*, 3 December 1982; West Yorkshire Archive Service, Bradford WYB339/4/9/4: Revolutionary Communist Party, *Vote Revolutionary Communist Party* (Bradford: Revolutionary Communist Party, 1986).
107 Workers Against Racism, *Cleansing Our Ranks*, 10.
108 Charles Longford, 'Cleansing our ranks', *tns*, December 1982.
109 Roucou settled and married in Manchester after arriving from the Seychelles in 1975. In 1979, the Home Office lost Roucou's passport and directed him to apply for a replacement. But Roucou was subsequently informed that because the Seychelles had gained independence in 1976, he had lost his right to stay in the UK.

at Manchester University.¹¹⁰ As part of a packed itinerary, Longford took the campaign into trade union organizations in Birmingham, Bristol, Liverpool and London, convening more than 100 shopfloor meetings in the early weeks of 1987. To isolate and confront racists in the labour movement, at every meeting, Manchester WAR organizers held a vote on whether Roucou should be supported.¹¹¹

The intensive activity peaked on 6 February 1987, when more than 1,500 demonstrators, on a one-day strike, marched through Manchester city centre demanding that Roucou be allowed to stay. In a feat of inter-organizational cooperation, WAR rallied workers from Roucou's own direct works department, as well as up to 800 from the General, Municipal, Boilermakers and Allied Trades Union and public sector unions such as NALGO and NUPE.¹¹² UCATT's Manchester shop stewards council pledged full support.¹¹³ When the appeal court finally dismissed the deportation case in April 1987, the judge commended the campaign organizers. Roucou's legal representative also wrote to thank the organization:

> The contribution made by WAR members in developing the campaign's contacts with trade unions and in the labour movement and in terms of pure hard work has been enormous and is deeply appreciated.¹¹⁴

For Longford, the verdict – a 'great victory for George and his family' – had amplified in the labour movement the challenge to immigration controls.¹¹⁵ Manchester RCP activist Karen Guldberg, meanwhile, heralded a broader working-class challenge to the state: 'We may have won this fight, but we have a war to win.'¹¹⁶

However, WAR's involvement with campaigns involving trade unionists aroused the suspicion of labour movement organizers. Despite the RCP's tactical resourcefulness, moderate officials insisted that revolutionary participation discredited anti-deportation struggles. In 1986, WAR activists in Leeds mobilized in support of Rose Alaso, who, alongside her eight-year-old son Brian, was threatened with deportation to Uganda. When WAR convened meetings

---

110 Mary Ann Molloy, 'Roucou campaign continues', *Mancunion*, 29 January 1987.
111 Workers Against Racism, *Racist Attacks – Racist Deportations – Racist Police – Who Can Help?* (Manchester: Manchester Workers Against Racism, n.d. [c.1991]).
112 'Workers fight deportation threat!', *WAR News: Workers Against Racism Bulletin*, March 1987.
113 'A sinister development', *Workers Press: Weekly Paper of the Workers Revolutionary Party*, 24 January 1987.
114 Tompson, *Under siege*, 147.
115 'Staying power!', *Daily Mirror*, 9 April 1987.
116 Karent [sic] Guldberg, 'Roucou to stay!', *Mancunion*, 1 May 1987.

at the TUC's Brighton conference, Alaso's union told her to choose WAR or NALGO running her campaign. NALGO official John Fitches even informed the police that his union dissociated itself from WAR.[117] The RCP front received a marginal degree of support among grassroots activists, with approximately 1,000 individual or branch affiliates nationwide.[118]

Senior trade union officials were justified in identifying the RCP's anti-racist campaigns as an attack upon the labour movement bureaucracy. Challenging workers to act independently, WAR campaigns indicted the unions for promulgating the idea of a national interest and thereby encouraging class collaboration. Addressing a public anti-racist meeting in 1981, a COVWAR activist asserted that labour movement demands for economic protectionism and immigration controls emboldened 'acceptable' racism.[119] COVWAR cadres Inez Landa and Helen Simons similarly attributed fascism among working-class youth to 'decades of chauvinist ideology propagated by the leadership of the labour movement'.[120]

The strategic imperative of galvanizing class opposition to nationalism in the labour movement underpinned WAR's Workers March Against Racism in September 1982. Over four days, more than 400 activists proceeded from east London's Brick Lane to the TUC conference in Brighton. Pitted broadly against 'fascist attacks, police brutality, [and] racist pass laws', the march drew support from more than 200 trade union branches and trades councils as well as Labour leftists such as Tony Benn, Paul Boateng and Ken Livingstone.[121] Before the march, speakers at WAR regional day schools included pioneering activists such as Jayaben Desai, who had famously combatted both iron-fisted management and reactionary union leaders during the strike at Grunwick in the late 1970s.[122]

---

117 Pat Roberts, 'Bureaucrats call cops on WAR', *tns*, 19 September 1986.
118 '"We just want more members"'. Despite its organizational development, WAR's affiliates represented only 0.1 per cent of UK trade union members in 1986 (1,000 of 9,995,000 unionists). Jeremy Waddington, 'Trade union membership in Britain, 1980–1987: unemployment and restructuring', *British Journal of Industrial Relations*, 30 (1992): 290.
119 'Stand firm against racism', *Earlsdon Echo*, 7 July 1981.
120 Coventry Workers Against Racism, *Ghost Town* (Revolutionary Communist Pamphlets, No. 11, October 1981), 11.
121 Workers March Against Racism flyer (n.d. [1982]). Copy in author's possession.
122 'United we stand', *tns*, June 1982. A photo-developing business in the north-west London suburb of Willesden, Grunwick employed approximately 500 staff. Asian women, the majority of whom had arrived in Britain from Kenya and Uganda, formed the majority of employees in the mail order department. When working conditions deteriorated in the summer of 1976, Jayaben Desai and five colleagues commenced a strike which attracted considerable attention on the left and in the media over the following two years. In 1977, protesting the perceived lack of action by their union (the Association of Professional, Executive, Clerical and Computer Staff), Desai and three comrades initiated a hunger strike on the steps of the TUC headquarters in London. The union's right-wing leadership promptly suspended the strikers. 'If the strike is defeated', said Desai, 'we want to point

Seeking sponsorship for the march, party activists implored trade unionists to join them in challenging nationalist illusions in the state.

Intervening in industrial disputes involving migrant workers and ethnic minorities sharpened WAR's critique of nationalism in the trade unions. When thirty-eight Black workers at the Heathfield factory in Slough began a strike over a pay dispute in November 1982, WAR organized support for the pickets. First, thirty-one (white) workers belonging to the Society of Graphical and Allied Trades refused to join the strike. Second, the General and Municipal Workers' Union announced unceremoniously that they had settled with the government's arbitration body on the strikers' behalf. Urging workers to write letters of condemnation to the unions, WAR denounced officials for patronizing workers and conspiring with management. Farekh Afzal's scathing assessment of the union's 'sell-out' and 'inability to defend its members' echoed the strikers' own statement at the dispute's abrupt termination: 'The defeat at Heathfield is a disgrace to the whole trade union movement'.[123]

Mobilizing during a strike among twenty-one Asian textile workers at Aire Valley Yarns in Farsley in 1983, the Leeds RCP similarly railed against the tactics and strategy of the TGWU. Protesting against their hours and conditions, workers were on strike for ten weeks after their leader, Liaquat Ali, was summarily dismissed – ostensibly for attempting to unionize his colleagues. For revolutionary vanguardists, the dispute in west Yorkshire epitomized the labour movement's reformism. While the RCP pushed for mass pickets and a solidarity campaign blacking Aire Valley Yarns goods, the TGWU's regional organizers referred the case to an industrial tribunal – where a member of the management told Ali 'whatever the results . . . you will not be employed by this company'.[124] Negotiating a return to work for eighteen of the strikers – excluding Ali and two colleagues – the TGWU pledged a three-month moratorium on industrial action.[125] For Leeds RCP cadres Rob Knight and Inez Landa, Aire Valley Yarns mirrored disputes at Grunwick and Heathfield, where 'militant Asian workers were sold out by the official trade union leaders', and 'racist divisions within the working class' were 'deepened'.[126]

Cadres lambasted left-wing demands for state authorities to police racism. In 1976, for example, responding to the rise of the National Front, the CPGB

the finger in the right direction – at the TUC'. Robert Aimes, 'Starving for action', *Workers' Action*, 26 November 1977.
123 Farehk [sic] Afzal, 'Heathfield – a bitter defeat', *tns*, January 1983.
124 'Asian textile strike', *Socialist Action*, 10 June 1983.
125 'TGWU sellout', *Black Flag*, 15 July 1983.
126 Rob Knight and Inez Landa, 'Up against the wall', *tns*, July 1983.

Executive Committee had implored the government to ban 'all racist activity' and 'strengthen the Race Relations Act against incitement to race hatred'.[127] For revolutionary vanguardists, such calls perpetuated reformist illusions in 'state machinery'.[128] When leftists at Leeds University complained in 1982 that the police had failed to tackle racist violence, WAR activist John Kilminster told a students' union debate that the state could play no progressive role: only a unified working class could fight racism and advance its own class interests.[129] WAR national organizer Keith Tompson fulminated against the readiness of 'the left' to 'hand over the job of fighting racism to the British establishment'.[130]

The controversy at the Polytechnic of North London (PNL) surrounding National Front organizer Patrick Harrington highlighted the RCP's strategic differences from the left on anti-racism. From May 1984, some 350 PNL students, including a large contingent from the Socialist Worker Student Society, defied a High Court injunction and picketed the college to prevent Harrington, a third-year philosophy student, from entering.[131] For the following seven months, the stand-off attracted mass pickets from student activists and significant attention on the radical left. For the Spartacists, for instance, barring Harrington – a 'direct threat to the safety of every black, Asian, Irish, immigrant, Jewish, gay and socialist student and worker' – constituted an imperative 'defence . . . against race terror'.[132] On the Labour left, meanwhile, the *Socialist Organiser* grouping exhorted 'the whole labour movement' to support the student protests.[133]

By contrast, RCP cadres regarded the campaign against Harrington as typical of a misguided penchant for selective anti-racism. Focusing solely upon the extremism of the marginal Front, RCP activists argued, diverted attention from the more pervasive problem of nationalism in the labour movement. Campaigning against the 'idiot' Harrington, Kirk Williams opined, distracted from the 'issues of real concern' such as

> discriminatory fees, passport checks and deportations. . . . The threat to black students comes not from the feeble remnants of the National Front but from the British state.[134]

---

127 Evan Smith, *British Communism and the Politics of Race* (Leiden: Brill, 2018), 158, 182–3.
128 Richards, *Under a National Flag*, 18.
129 Adam LeBor, 'Armchair War', *Leeds Student*, 12 November 1982.
130 Workers Against Racism, *The Roots of Racism* (London: Junius, 1985), 72.
131 Cath Christenson, 'Students stop Nazi at college', *Socialist Worker*, 5 May 1984.
132 'Drive fascist Harrington off NLP!', *Workers Hammer*, October 1984.
133 'Police defend Nazi leader', *Socialist Organiser*, 24 May 1984.
134 Kirk Williams, 'Fight racism, not idiots', *tns*, October 1984.

For vanguardists, the protests against Harrington divorced anti-racism from the struggle for a holistic class politics.

As the RCP grew beyond its initial bases in the capital and Canterbury, Coventry and Manchester, WAR expanded its activities in provincial cities. Within two years of the advent of its branch in Bradford in 1984, organizers could call upon a network of approximately 150 WAR supporters to coordinate workers' defence patrols in Girlington, Heaton and Scholemoor, where racist attacks upon Bangladeshis and Pakistanis were especially commonplace. By 1986, the Bradford RCP sold on average 500 copies of *the next step* each week.[135]

Developing its front group tactics, Bradford WAR combined defence work with demonstrations propagating the party's politics. After repeatedly suffering racist attacks on the Haworth Road estate, Asian families invited WAR activists into their properties to keep guard.[136] Simultaneously, cadres mobilized around the local labour movement and religious groups to raise the party's class opposition to all immigration controls. In June 1986, organizing a mass march against racist attacks, the Bradford RCP drew support from members of regional trades union branches and the Bradford Council of Churches.[137] Kirk Leech, Bradford branch organizer in the mid-1980s, remembers the period as a testament to the party's organizational energy and commitment:

> Racism in west Yorkshire was a significant political and social problem. We grew very quickly. Bradford is a small city, but in the rush hour we could have twenty-five people plus selling the weekly *the next step*. We carried out a lot of activity against racism, highlighting its politically divisive nature, exposing labour movement complicity, taking on the racists. We organised workers' defence, physically confronting them alongside local white people who recognised the need to stand up. I was arrested twice. We stayed overnight in Asian families' houses to defend them, accompanied their kids to school through hostile areas. We organised a march through the city of near two thousand people. . . . This period was for me personally pivotal: it had a profound influence on me, confirming that I could make a difference, and that the RCP had the ideas and opportunity to make a big impact.[138]

Mirroring its critique of the ANL, the RCP's assessment of the Anti-Apartheid Movement (AAM) excoriated left-wing affinities with the state. By the mid-1980s, the AAM comprised approximately 7,500 members, who amplified its calls for

---

135 Sian James, 'Shock troops in the race war', *Telegraph & Argus*, 13 June 1986.
136 David Lewis, 'Family driven out by racist attacks', *Telegraph & Argus*, 5 May 1986.
137 'Marchers protest at race attacks', *Telegraph & Argus*, 16 June 1986.
138 Kirk Leech, 7 September 2020.

consumers to boycott South African goods and for the British government to impose United Nations–mandated sanctions and embargos against Pretoria.[139] In 1981, the AAM launched its 'Isolate Apartheid South Africa' campaign, imploring Western governments to levy economic sanctions.[140] The AAM enjoyed considerable support among the labour movement hierarchy: the TUC conference of September 1981, for example, unanimously endorsed the sanctions lobby.[141] For RCP cadres, the AAM's orientation towards the government misguidedly implied that British imperialism could play a progressive role in South Africa.[142] Manchester University RCP activists Mary Ann Molloy and Lynn Revell, for example, castigated leftists who perpetuated an 'illusion' by imploring the British ruling class to contravene its economic interests and oppose apartheid from an 'ethical' standpoint.[143]

Because building class opposition to British imperialism was the vanguardist priority, party theoreticians repudiated the AAM's emphasis upon state action against the apartheid regime. Instead, the RCP leadership envisioned developing revolutionary opposition to British imperialism at home. Like RCP strategists, Alex Callinicos of the SWP called for 'independent working-class action' in Britain against apartheid, hailing, for example, dockers blacking goods bound for South Africa. Callinicos, however, held that '*any* action against the apartheid regime' was 'to be welcomed'.[144] Reviewing the SWP veteran's writings on apartheid, founding RCP cadre Sabena Norton insisted that whereas the SWP would tail spontaneous anti-apartheid sentiment, the RCP challenged workers to confront their own ruling class on a consistent, anti-imperialist basis.[145]

Concomitantly, at the tactical level, cadres championed direct action against the British ruling class. In Newcastle, for example, where Northern Engineering Industries produced turbine generators for export to Johannesburg, RCP supporters convened factory gate meetings, imploring workers to sabotage production and strike against 'apartheid's British backers'.[146] When fifty Glasgow student radicals disrupted a recruitment presentation by Marconi – suppliers

---

139 Gavin Brown, 'Anti-apartheid solidarity in the perspectives and practices of the British far left in the 1970s and 1980s', in Smith and Worley (eds), *Waiting for the Revolution*, 67–8.
140 'Isolate South Africa! Sanctions now!', *Anti-Apartheid News*, April 1981.
141 *Isolate Apartheid: Report of the Anti-Apartheid Movement Trade Union Conference Held on November 27, 1982* (London: Anti-Apartheid Movement, 1983), 22.
142 Charles Longford, *South Africa: Black Blood on British Hands* (London: Junius, 1985), 60–1.
143 Mary Ann Molloy and Lynn Revell, R.C.P.S.S., 'An end to token gestures', *Mancunion*, 30 October 1985.
144 Alex Callinicos, *South Africa: The Road to Revolution* (London: Socialist Workers Party, 1985), 37–8.
145 Sabena Norton, 'Socialism begins at home', *tns*, 4 October 1985.
146 'Action against apartheid', *tns*, 11 October 1985.

of radar and military equipment to Pretoria – RCP cadre Frank McElhinney applauded the 'successful disruption' as a direct challenge to British capitalist interests in South Africa.[147] Cadres took their calls for 'direct action' into mainstream anti-apartheid milieux: in 1985, for instance, Leeds RCP activists on an NUS anti-apartheid demonstration challenged the AAM's strategy.[148] Prioritizing a critique of British capitalism, activists encouraged workers in the transport and telecommunications sectors, for example, to pool information and sabotage South Africa's supply chains.[149]

As this chapter has shown, through the early years of the RCP, a hardcore of approximately 100 revolutionaries challenged British workers to jettison the nationalism and reformism, which cadres abhorred on the left and in the labour movement. Campaigning energetically for 'Irish freedom' and against racism, activists aspired to build a vanguard defined by theoretical and programmatic clarity. The tactical use of elections cast in sharp relief the disjuncture between the scale of the RCP's ambitions and the degree of its influence. Far from being discouraged, however, cadres regarded these setbacks as momentary reverses, which merely confirmed the necessity of their challenge and the distinction of their critique. Considering themselves equipped with the requisite ideological independence through the mid-1980s, activists remained determined to supplant the 'dead hand' of labourism. As the following chapter demonstrates, during the miners' strike of 1984 and 1985, the RCP intensified its challenge to the reformist traditions of the British left and the labour movement.

---

147 Frank McElhinney, Revolutionary Communist Society, 'Anti-apartheid: Actions speak louder than words', *Glasgow University Guardian*, 5 December 1985.
148 'Letters', *Leeds Student*, 1 November 1985.
149 Longford, *South Africa*, 67.

3

From the miners' strike to 'moral panics', c.1984–9

Although the RCP was still a relatively small revolutionary party, by the mid-1980s its committed members could draw encouragement from several years of frenetic activity, most prominently on Ireland and anti-racism.[1] By 1986, WAR boasted twelve branches in London and twenty-five more across Britain's provincial towns and cities.[2] Concurrently, students formed a substantial proportion of the RCP's recruits: in the mid-1980s, the party claimed some 1,000 supporters across its student societies at forty-five universities and polytechnics in England and Scotland.[3] Interviewed in 1989, Frank Richards testified that students and graduates comprised 60 per cent of the RCP's membership.[4] As Kirk Leech recalls, the RCP tended to enthuse radical students more immediately than workers and trade unionists:

> In one or two places we had a bit of support, but we were never active or powerful within trade unions. . . . In the north-east, for some reason, we always got a good following amongst the trades councils on Ireland. So we used to get their banners, and some members, to come on the IFM demonstrations. But other than that we weren't really involved so much in the local trade union movement at all. We were pretty much outside of it. So probably my experience would be more young students, petit-bourgeoisie.[5]

Striking, propagandistic interventions in cause célèbres established a profile for the party's critique of the labour movement. Activists readily bore the barbs

1 At this juncture, the RCP's membership of between 100 and 200, supplemented by perhaps 1,000 supporters, paled in comparison to the Militant tendency's 7,000 and the SWP's 4,000. The WRP, meanwhile, claimed 9,000 members, until it imploded into several factions in 1985, after Aileen Jennings, a former secretary to party leader Gerry Healy, accused Healy of sexually abusing dozens of women. Kelly, *Contemporary Trotskyism*, 40, 46.
2 'What we stand for', *WAR News: Workers Against Racism Bulletin*, March 1987.
3 'RCP student supporters' groups', *tns*, September 1984; Alastair Dalton, 'Reds in the dark', *Student: Edinburgh University Student Newspaper*, 17 October 1985.
4 Adam LeBor, 'Distinguishing Marx from perestroika', *Independent*, 5 April 1989.
5 Kirk Leech, 7 September 2020.

which underlined their heretical status on the left. Revelling in their alterity, cadres perceived in hostile environments confirmation that they were developing a genuine alternative, as Ann Furedi recalls:

> We were going right the way back to basics to build something that was absolutely, completely different and challenging. When it came to developing positions and propaganda around it, it came from a different perspective, I think. . . . What that meant was that right from the very beginning, you were never part of the crowd, in a sense. . . . That, in some ways, had a profound toughening up effect on people because you really are in a position where you know, before you open your mouth, that what you said was not going to be popular.[6]

British radicals routinely portrayed the RCP as contrarian, elitist or wedded to idealistic abstraction, far removed from the class struggle. Discussing with BBC journalists the early stirrings of the IFM in 1982, for instance, CPGB West Midlands organizer Tony McNally dismissed the 'provocative group' determined to 'incite hostility'. 'No responsible section of the labour and trade union movement', McNally warned, should have 'anything to do with it'.[7] A correspondent of the CPGB's factional paper *The Leninist* similarly interpreted the RCP's programmatic independence as 'congenital sectarianism'.[8] A more explicitly pro-Soviet *Leninist* reader listed the assorted faults of the 'anglo-centric, publicity seeking, middle class . . . arrogant and stupid' party.[9]

For their part, RCP cadres asserted that theoretical lucidity, combined with an iconoclastic method, could develop a transformative vanguard. Evoking the ferment of the late 1970s and 1980s, Alan Hudson – formerly an RCP organizer in east London, Manchester and Sheffield – reconstructs the pervasive sense of revolutionary possibility:

> Irrespective of the fact that there isn't a vanguard, irrespective of the fact that it's a huge task, you are operating in a period of incredible flux.[10]

Another former leading activist similarly evaluates cadres' sense of their historical agency and responsibility:

---

6   Ann Furedi, 7 October 2021.
7   'Youth for Irish freedom', *tns*, May 1982.
8   Geraldine Duffy, 'Noble Platitudes', *Leninist*, August 1985. *The Leninist* first appeared in 1981 as the factional paper of the self-styled Provisional Central Committee of the CPGB. Opposing the CPGB's Eurocommunist direction, from 1985 this milieu criticized Gorbachev's reforms in the Soviet Union.
9   Dermot Minkin, 'RCP', *Leninist*, November 1985.
10 Alan Hudson interview with the author, 22 October 2021.

> Though there was a recognition of the immensity of the task, it did not seem outlandish to believe in the late 1970s and even at the start of the 1980s that there was some basis for building an independent, alternative tradition to that of the reformist radical left.[11] [. . .]
>
> I think it's much more difficult to understand that now, to comprehend that any group of people could have thought that was possible. Obviously, at that time, it was another world. . . . Internationally, everything that was going on, the anti-imperialist movement, Vietnam, everything that came out of that, then this upsurge of strikes and radicalism in the 1970s. And then the eighties, all the big strikes and Thatcherism. . . . It didn't seem that crazy, actually. . . . I think we did know that would be a very, very long shot. . . . I think we were always quite realistic about that. . . . The task was seen as a necessary one, but I don't think anybody was under any illusions about how hard it was going to be.[12]

The vanguard's vital role – stimulating, transforming and leading class politics – animated cadres dedicated to changing the world. Linda Murdoch remembers joining the RCP in the mid-1980s, invigorated by its world-historical tasks:

> It wasn't like, *we as the party politicise the working class*. It wasn't like that. But we had a role to play in doing that, a crucial role. It's not going to happen without us. We had to expose the state for what it was so the working class can become politicised itself. It was a vanguard that did that. So that was the direction of travel.[13]

Fused with cadres' camaraderie and cohesion, the perception of formal and strategic independence propelled activists throughout the 1980s. Decades after declaring the demise of vanguardism and class politics, veterans still recall the sensation of campaigning to overcome the past defeats of the working class:

> We were aware that we were doing things which were quite unique and distinct. I was obviously a more senior member by the eighties, so involved in recruiting people and so on. . . . We felt we were engaged in something historic in a way.[14]

In this small, disciplined revolutionary group, the collective pursuit of momentous objectives largely transcended the scale of the tasks or the adversity of circumstances. In veterans' life-history testimonies today, the party network's defining role provides a constant theme: the subjective sense of belonging has survived the vicissitudes of political life. Furthermore, adducing the continual

---

11 Joan Hoey to the author, 7 August 2022.
12 Joan Hoey, 6 August 2022.
13 Linda Murdoch, 21 December 2021.
14 Phil Mullan, 11 March 2021.

adversity of objective circumstances, activists underline the long-standing camaraderie which harmonizes past and present political conviction through profoundly altered circumstances. Ann Furedi, who served as the RCP's national organizer from the mid-1980s, remembers

> a very confident sense . . . that this was going to be something absolutely big time. It didn't matter if there weren't very many of you at that particular time. . . . I think, for me, it gave me a place in the world. It sort of situated me in something.[15]

Beginning with the party's engagement with the miners' strike of 1984 and 1985, this chapter examines how vanguardist strategy navigated a struggle in the labour movement and the working class. Sustaining its critique of trade union class collaborationism, throughout the strike the RCP repudiated capitalist realism of the National Union of Mineworkers (NUM). Pleading the mining industry's economic viability, cadres asserted, could only condemn workers to the vicissitudes of capitalism. The strike and its defeat, it is argued, highlighted a growing disjuncture between the RCP's theoretical and programmatic endeavour and its overall failure to supplant labourism.

The chapter proceeds to scrutinize cadres' analysis of 'moral panics' in the late 1980s. Accordingly, it charts the embryonic critiques of a supposed crisis of class subjectivities. While activists remained dedicated to cultivating revolutionary politics in the working class, by the end of the 1980s, they increasingly admitted that the vanguardist campaign for independent class politics was failing to gain traction. Cadres' analyses of 'moral authoritarianism' called workers' attention to the machinations of a conservative ruling class determined to fragment the working class and marginalize radical alternatives.

'Universally condemned by the British left'

In 1974, during a period of increased industrial unrest, Harold Wilson's Labour Party returned to government. With the National Coal Board (NCB) and the NUM, Wilson swiftly agreed the Plan for Coal, ending the miners' strike of 1974. Signatories to the corporatist arrangement committed to develop new mines, implement new technologies and extend the lifespan of existing collieries. NUM officials celebrated proposals for some 42 million tonnes of new

---

15 Ann Furedi, 7 October 2021.

mining capacity.[16] On the miners' union executive, the ascendant left hailed the production increase as a victory for 'king coal'.[17]

A decade after the Plan for Coal was agreed, the NCB announced that the agreement would be terminated. In March 1984, NCB officials declared that twenty collieries would close in the following twelve months: 20,000 workers would be made redundant. By 6 March, when the miners' strike formally began, many pits had already seen unofficial industrial action in solidarity with those threatened with closure. The Scotland and Yorkshire Area NUM members commenced a strike, and on 12 March, with approximately half of Britain's 184,000 miners out, NUM president Arthur Scargill called for a total nationwide stoppage.

At this early juncture, miners throughout Yorkshire, Kent, Scotland and South Wales solidly supported the strike, while most across Nottinghamshire, Derbyshire, Leicestershire and Staffordshire continued to work. Henry Richardson, the left-wing leader of the Notts miners, implored men in his area to join the strike. Rather than holding a national ballot on strike action, Scargill and the leftists among the NUM leadership encouraged militant 'flying pickets' to travel to the East Midlands to persuade their fellow miners to walk out. By 19 March, however, area ballots in the coalfields of the Midlands, north-east and north-west indicated within the NUM considerable opposition to the strike.[18]

Few aspects of the RCP's history have generated such controversy as the party's engagement with the miners' strike of 1984 and 1985. Throughout the dispute, RCP strategists called for the NUM to hold a national ballot on industrial action. Branding cadres 'scabs' and 'traitors', rival leftists accused the RCP of undermining the strike. For propagandists in the WRP, for example, the RCP's stance was 'no different from Thatcher's'.[19] Coining an epithet for the 'Ray Chadburn Party', the Spartacists condemned the RCP's 'strike-breaking line'.[20] Alex Callinicos of the SWP caustically claimed that RCP cadres 'actually agree[d]' with the Thatcher government and the NCB chief Ian McGregor.[21]

---

16   Jonathan Winterton, 'The 1984-85 miners' strike and technological change', *British Journal of the History of Science*, 26 (1993): 5–6.
17   Bill Message, 'The miners and the Labour government', *International Socialism*, September 1976.
18   Francis Beckett and David Hencke, *Marching to the Fault Line: The Miners' Strike and the Battle for Industrial Britain* (London: Constable, 2009), 53–64.
19   *News Line*, 19 April 1984.
20   'RCP: Ray Chadburn Party', *Spartacist Britain*, April 1984. Ray Chadburn was the president of the Nottinghamshire miners, the majority of whom broke with the NUM during and after the strike.
21   *Socialist Review*, May 1984.

Fulminating against the RCP's 'monstrous' calls for a ballot, the *Leninist* charged the party with providing 'excuses for blacklegging'.[22]

Long after the strike ended in 1985, hostile leftists positioned the RCP's position during the strike as a byword for its wider unorthodoxy. For Bob Pennington of *Socialist Outlook*, the call for a ballot – which 'would have disrupted the strike and given one group of workers the right to vote another sections' [*sic*] jobs away' – typified the RCP's 'ultra-left' and 'sectarian' contrarianism.[23] A decade after the strike, the Spartacists adduced the party taking 'the line of the coal bosses and the scabs' as evidence of its 'sinister' agenda.[24] After the RCP dissolved in the 1990s, left-wing militants in Red Action equated the RCP's calls for a ballot and the anti-strike position of 'the entire right wing press'.[25] On the strike's twentieth anniversary, *weekly worker* correspondent Ian Donovan invoked the RCP's 'sensationalist ballot mongering' to signal its supposed disingenuousness:

> This cavalier disregard for the consciousness and interests of striking miners revealed something of the real nature of the RCP as an odd, middle-class grouping that really was rather out of place in a working class struggle. It provided a glimpse of what the RCP was to become, as it gradually abandoned the working class and socialism entirely.[26]

For years before the strike, RCP cadres had argued that the NUM's strategy exemplified the errors of collaborationist trade unionism. Party activists argued that the Plan subjugated workers' independent class interests to the dictates of capitalism. In 1981, when Scargill lauded the British industry's success despite foreign imports and competition, RCP cadre Pat Roberts scorned the Yorkshire leader's 'nationalist ramblings'. Identifying with the national economy, Roberts averred, meant that Scargill could celebrate only a 'victory for the industry, not for the working class'.[27] A union which made miners responsible for sustaining a profitable industry, Frank Richards declared, could not represent workers' independent class interests.[28]

For revolutionaries seeking to explode working-class illusions in the state, the strike presented a crucial dynamic. Cadres asserted that if miners repudiated

---

22 Marshall, 'The Revolutionary Communist Party'.
23 Bob Pennington, 'The RCP – an infantile disorder', *Socialist Outlook*, May–June 1987.
24 'Sinister RCP defends fascists', *Workers Hammer: Newspaper of the Spartacist League*, January–February 1994.
25 'The rise and fall of the Ray Chadwick Party', *Red Action: The Bi-Monthly Bulletin of the Organisation Red Action*, December 1998–January 1999. Presumably the headline was intended to refer to Ray Chadburn.
26 Ian Donovan, 'Pickets, ballots and workers' defence', *weekly worker*, 18 March 2004.
27 Pat Roberts, 'Scargill is to blame', *tns*, February 1982.
28 Frank Richards, *The Miners' Next Step* (London: Junius, 1984), 29.

conciliation with the bosses, the dispute could crucially undermine labourism. Addressing a public meeting in Bradford in May 1984, RCP general secretary Kate Marshall extolled 'open warfare between the working class and the capitalist system'.[29] Activists prepared to intensify their cadre-training in mining communities. In his keynote speech to the Preparing for Power conference of July 1984, Frank Richards reported enthusiastically that workers were losing respect for the government, police, employers and collaborationist union leaders. Most pertinently, Richards asserted, the strike had 'discredited' left-wing penchants for nationalization, statism and trade union collaboration with bosses. Conditions were ripening, the RCP leader concluded, for a vanguard to supersede the strictures of labourism:

> Things are now running in the RCP's favour . . . never have the objective conditions been better for building a revolutionary party.[30]

The call for a ballot reflected the party's conviction that only a mass campaign for strike action could assert and ultimately strengthen the miners' strategic hand. From March 1984, the RCP advocated rank-and-file control of the dispute, on a national basis transcending the union's federalized character.[31] Cadres exhorted miners to unify in command of their campaign, independent of the union bureaucracy. The strike's uneven development during the spring of 1984 informed the party's calls for a national ballot. When pits remained open across the Midlands, most notably in the Nottinghamshire coalfield, RCP activists asserted that a 'national focus' was required for 'all-out stoppage'.[32]

The RCP's position on the ballot prompted SWP theoretician Alex Callinicos to reprise his charges of idealistic abstraction. From this perspective, RCP strategists' theoretical preoccupations obscured the 'concrete needs' of the class struggle. For Callinicos, the demand for a ballot epitomized a 'sect' which indulged in 'abstract theorising'. While RCP cadres promoted a ballot to establish clarity and unity through contestation, Callinicos dismissed this 'ludicrous' position which, he intimated, would divide the miners still further and 'might well' result in defeat.[33]

---

29 Revolutionary Communist Party, *Can There Be a Revolution in Britain?* (1984). Copy in author's possession.
30 'Preparing for power 1984', *tns*, August 1984.
31 Mike Freeman, 'Fighting divisions', *tns*, April 1984.
32 'Unity must be won', *the miners' next step: Revolutionary Communist Party strike special* (n.d. [April 1984]).
33 Alex Callinicos, 'Pickets and ballots', *Socialist Review*, May 1984.

Although the party attained pariah status on the left, its strategic demand for a ballot to strengthen the strike was not entirely unique: on 9 April 1984, Labour Party leader Neil Kinnock had telephoned Scargill, imploring the NUM president to hold a national vote on strike action. Until the miners gave formal majority support for industrial action, Kinnock argued, Thatcher and her allies could readily dismiss the strikers as unrepresentative.[34]

Developing their established critique of labourism, RCP ideologues condemned the NUM's record of collaboration since nationalization in 1947. Cadres averred that a reformist union bureaucracy, perpetuating workers' illusions in a 'national interest', constituted an obstacle to independent class politics. Assuming responsibility for the industry's profitability, the argument ran, the Plan for Coal's enthusiasts in the NUM divided workers by region.[35] Miners who considered themselves competing with other areas, Frank Richards argued, could not mobilize as a class. For Richards, the refusal of most Notts miners to join the strike stemmed from the sectionalism of the NUM strategy.[36] Rejecting collaborationist unionism, RCP cadres repudiated the NUM's capitalist realism. According to one senior activist, Scargill's emphasis upon the industry's economic viability was 'dangerous nonsense', which conceded the terms of the debate to the capitalist class. Only an uncompromising campaign for miners' 'economic needs', 'irrespective' of the NCB's plight, could advance class struggle.[37]

RCP cadres were among an array of radicals – including members of the SWP, WRP, the Spartacist League and others – mobilizing in the coalfields in 1984 and 1985. Like many leftists, RCP cadres joined picket lines, raised funds for striking miners and organized demonstrations at police stations where arrested strikers were detained. While cadres refused to contribute to committees under the aegis of the Labour Party or NUM, they independently collected money and food, and liaised directly with miners.[38] Within the first three weeks of the strike, the party raised £775 in donations.[39]

Exhorting miners to strengthen their solidarity connections, cadres organized meetings between miners and industrial workers in Bradford, Manchester and

---

34 Beckett and Hencke, *Marching to the Fault Line*, 75–6.
35 'It's them against us', *the miners' next step: Revolutionary Communist Party strike special* (n.d. [April 1984]).
36 Richards, *The Miners' Next Step*, 13, 40.
37 Helen Swift, 'Seven questions for Arthur Scargill', tns, October 1984.
38 'RCP reply: "Unfair criticism"', *Workers Press*, 22 November 1986.
39 'Supporting the miners', *the miners' next step: Revolutionary Communist Party strike special* (n.d. [April 1984]).

London.[40] Party demonstrations repeatedly indicted the labour movement for the perceived shortcomings of secondary action. When union leaders gathered to discuss the strike in November 1984, for example, cadres heckled Electrical, Electronic, Telecommunications and Plumbing Union leader Terry Duffy and hanged an effigy of TUC secretary Norman Willis.[41] RCP activists were not alone in imploring workers from related sectors to ally with the miners. The SWP, for instance, repeatedly urged steelworkers, for instance, to curtail supplies. At a rally at Skegness, six weeks into the strike, SWP Central Committee member Chris Harman asserted that secondary action held the key to the strike's success: 'the picketing isn't heavy enough, the blacking isn't adequate'.[42] Within the coalfields, however, RCP activists asserted unflinchingly that without galvanizing their own number, the miners were doomed to failure: until all miners were out on an unequivocal demand for the right to work, cadres insisted, appeals for solidarity from other industrial sectors would lack heft.

Not for the first time, the RCP's interventions were distinguished by the degree to which they confronted the prevailing tactics and strategies of the labour movement. Especially in Yorkshire and Derbyshire, cadres took their criticisms of NUM strategy into picket line discussions and public meetings in miners' welfares.[43] Positioning the ballot as a strategic imperative, party vanguardists welcomed a battle of ideas to win miners to revolutionary politics. Where other leftists feared that a ballot would divide the miners and undermine the strike, RCP theoreticians championed a nationwide vote precisely to clarify miners' independent interests.[44] Activists clearly understood their pariah status among radicals: Pat Roberts acknowledged that the party's position on the strike had been 'universally condemned by the British left'.[45]

The critique of the NUM strategy provoked significant hostility among miners. Especially in militant areas such as south Yorkshire, miners routinely argued that a ballot would derail the strike. A month into the strike, when RCP cadre Bob Radcliffe told Hatfield Miners Welfare that a national vote would galvanize the miners, 'bollocks to the ballot' was the meeting's overwhelming response.[46] At a coordinating meeting in Dunscroft, miners' wives were similarly unequivocal,

---

40 'Striking out', *tns*, June 1984.
41 'Abuse greets TUC at pit talks', *Reading Evening Post*, 28 November 1984.
42 Chris Harman, 'Class struggle hots up', *Socialist Review*, May 1984.
43 'Supporting the miners'.
44 Dave Hayes, 'Thirty Years On: The Socialist Workers Party and the Great Miners' Strike', *International Socialism*, 142 (Spring 2014): 27–56.
45 Pat Roberts, 'The fight for a national strike', *tns*, June 1984.
46 'RCP: Ray Chadburn Party'.

telling an RCP cadre: 'We're not going to ballot on our livelihoods!'⁴⁷ An RCP cadre in Yorkshire in the mid-1980s, John Gillott recalled 'some hairy moments . . . when we were criticising the NUM and Scargill':

> From the point of view of many of those older miners, you're like some young kid coming and telling them what's what and they didn't necessarily care for it. . . . You were in at the deep end, I suppose. You'd be sent on your own to somewhere like Doncaster and expected to go into a packed meeting and stand up and make an intervention which not many people were going to like.⁴⁸

Recalling working-class opposition to the party's attacks on reformism and nationalism, Joan Hoey remembered how the strike tested cadres' convictions in the Yorkshire coalfield. In miners' welfares and on picket lines, contradicting Scargillite orthodoxy and arguing for the ballot

> was hard to do, and there was a lot of questioning of it within the party. . . . A lot of people . . . were quite wary of it, so there was a lot of debate. . . . You're in that situation, you're with these miners and there's always the pressure to just accommodate. . . . It was a lot of pressure on you to kind of water down what you were saying on the ballot, because you just got such flak and hostility. . . . You are, of necessity, all the time putting forward positions . . . which are the complete contradistinction to the kind of instinctive reformist positions: it's a pressure. . . . You were out on a limb, basically.⁴⁹

The contemporary writings of David Douglass, a militant on the Doncaster NUM strike committee and a representative of the Yorkshire NUM executive in 1984, valuably distinguish between the lucidity of the RCP's critique and its limited ability to supplant miners' loyalty to the union. Writing in a personal capacity three months into the strike, Douglass scorned leftists 'invading the pit villages . . . dispensing their tablets of gold to the untutored masses'. But Douglass reserved particular remarks for RCP cadres, who influenced a minority of miners with

> some success because they are friendly people and can mix (which is rare on the left) because they raised large sums of money and because they got stuck into the picket line along with the miners.⁵⁰

---

47 'Women organise for strike victory', *Spartacist Britain*, April 1984.
48 John Gillott, 6 October 2020.
49 Joan Hoey, 6 August 2022.
50 North of England Institute of Mining and Mechanical Engineers: Dave Douglass Archive: Miners' Strike Box 1: David Douglass, *Bores under the Floor: A Brief Guide to the Wave of 'left' Groups and Newspapers Currently Invading the Pit Villages* (June 1984).

But the RCP's interventions on strategy, Douglass opined, alienated most miners, who perceived the demand for a ballot as an attack on the strike itself:

> Putting forward such anti strike calls has already got them kicked out of many Welfares in Doncaster and has led them to be attacked on demonstrations.[51]

Workers who opposed the strike were equally wary of external intervention. Calling for a return to work, one Mansfield miner epitomized the animosity towards leftist 'agitators . . . people who have hardly seen the outside of a pit let alone the inside'.[52]

In parallel with their experiences of electoral experiments, cadres found that their liaisons with miners broadly reaffirmed the difficulties of overriding workers' defensive loyalties to their traditional methods and institutions. In Pontefract, for example, where the RCP campaigned persistently, the party recruited several miners. But as Alan Hudson, then the party's organizer in Sheffield, recalls, progressing beyond this 'foothold' and winning workers to a revolutionary critique of labourism proved more elusive:

> There was a gap between [miners'] total commitment and their faith in their own leadership, particularly in Yorkshire. So I think what we discovered quite soon was that it was very easy to get accepted if you did things which supported them in a physical way, like collecting food and money. That was fine. . . . But if you made any political challenge it immediately became very difficult.[53]

In the summer of 1984, surveying the early months of the strike, Frank Richards admitted:

> Most miners remained unconvinced by our approach. . . . The dead weight of the traditions of collaboration and sectionalism have left their marks.[54]

By 3 March 1985, when an NUM delegate conference voted to return to work, the RCP had unequivocally declared the strike defeated.[55] Party theoreticians' bleak verdict diverged considerably from the more sanguine assessments of the radical left. For example, when the strike ended, the Militant tendency lauded the miners who

---

51 Ibid.
52 Jon Ham, 'Trendies cannot fool the miners', *Nottingham Evening Post*, 20 April 1984.
53 Alan Hudson, 22 October 2021.
54 Richards, *The Miners' Next Step*, 44.
55 WCML: Miners' Strike Box 2: Revolutionary Communist Party, *Our Day Will Come: The End of the Miners' Strike* (n.d. [1985]).

revived the best traditions from the past and ushered in a new future for the British trade union movement . . . [and] brought class politics back on the agenda. . . . Their fighting spirit and self-sacrifice can lay the basis for a campaign to drive the Tories from office.[56]

Similarly, addressing the NUM's annual conference in July 1985, Scargill refused to regard the strike as a reverse:

> Let no-one talk to me about defeat or setbacks. . . . We should stand confident and proud of what we have achieved, proclaiming the positive aspects of the dispute, and the most important victory of all – the struggle itself. Within our union and our communities, the strike brought forth revolutionary changes.[57]

While leftists hailed the miners' endurance as a template for future struggle, the RCP proclaimed a historic reverse for the working class.[58] Whereas union officials defended their strategic approach, RCP cadres argued that the strike's defeat confirmed the dead end of collaborationism and nationalism. For *the next step*'s editorial board, accepting the NCB's 5.2 per cent pay offer in April 1985 marked the NUM leadership's 'final admission of unconditional surrender'.[59]

Having declared the strike's failure, the RCP cadres maintained that vanguardism remained both imperative and feasible – but averred that objective conditions had become more adverse. From this perspective, defeating the miners significantly advanced the Thatcher government's coordinated attacks upon organized labour. *the next step*'s editorial warned of a 'dangerous state of fragmentation and demoralisation in the coalfields'.[60]

Simultaneously, reviewing the strike as a damning indictment of left reformism, cadres reasserted the necessity of a vanguardist alternative. For Mike Freeman, the emboldened capitalist offensive redoubled the importance of convincing workers to jettison 'the bureaucratic strategy that . . . led the strike to defeat'.[61] Similarly, Frank Richards delineated the 'great scope' for revolutionary politics to overcome discredited business unionism.[62] Examining the strike for the RCP's theoretical journal in 1986, Freeman concluded that a 'working class challenge' was more vital than ever.[63]

---

56 'Demand amnesty', *Militant: The Marxist Paper for Labour and Youth*, 8 March 1985.
57 'Arthur Scargill – 1985 NUM Conference Speech'. Available at ukpol.co.uk/arthur-scargill-1985-num-conference-speech/ (accessed 13 June 2022).
58 'The only honourable settlement', *Yorkshire miners' next step: strike bulletin* (March 1985).
59 'Unfinished business', *tns*, 19 April 1985.
60 Ibid.
61 Mike Freeman, *Our Day Will Come: The Miners' Fight for Jobs* (London: Junius, 1985), 8.
62 Frank Richards, 'The party of the future', *tns*, 19 April 1985.
63 Freeman, 'The road to power', 38.

Defying considerable hostility to advocate the ballot had tested activists' commitment to their position and occasioned a rare schism in the party. In the strike's latter stages, a cadre cell – including, most prominently, Fran Eden, Judy Harrison, Tony Allen and Gareth Evans – argued that prioritizing the ballot had prevented the party from intervening more directly to maximize its influence and recruitment in the coalfields. The intra-party dispute peaked with a series of debates during the annual conference of 1985, when approximately ten dissenters – known to the majority as the 'red herrings' – left the organization. Acknowledging the 'big loss' to the party, a former Political Committee cadre recalled the red herrings accusing RCP strategists of having failed to 'get their hands dirty' during the strike.[64] For Eden, Harrison and their comrades who left the RCP, the party's strategy had lapsed into doctrinaire idealism. It was neither the first nor the last time that critics would charge the RCP leadership with sacrificing practical impact on the altar of theoretical preoccupation.

Today, the miners' strike features in activist retrospectives primarily as a pivotal moment reducing revolutionary possibilities. Surveying subsequent events, veterans of the party routinely position the miners' defeat as a threshold which rendered vanguardism increasingly vain. Especially when narrated retrospectively, remembering the miners' strike as an epochal rupture substantiates cadres' claims to unsentimental prescience. For activists who later declared that class politics were in abeyance, the events of 1984 and 1985 marked the beginning of the denouement:

> I think in the seventies, there was definitely a sense that there was a possibility that things could move and that there could be a new left-wing working-class movement. . . . After the defeat of the miners' strike I stopped personally believing that there was going to be any real change.[65]

After the strike, vying to engage more immediately with workers amid escalating industrial conflict, party strategists reconfigured *the next step* as a weekly newspaper. Polemicizing around unfolding events, the new format was especially conducive to engaging prospective recruits in conversation during street sales. Like many other supporters of the organization, Jon Bryan, a Newcastle Polytechnic student in the late 1980s, first encountered the RCP when he bought a copy of the newspaper:

---

64 Joan Hoey, 6 August 2022.
65 Rob Killick, 20 August 2020.

> When they were selling papers, they didn't just sell you a paper like a newsagent, but they tried to engage you. I think the RCP were maybe a bit more persistent, a bit more interested. *Do you want to come to a meeting?* They wanted you to take *the next step* – in every sense.[66]

The party's holistic theoretical rigour and strategic vision continued to inspire recruits. Interviewed in 1989, Oxford graduate and *Living Marxism* marketing manager Suke Karey remembered joining the RCP two years earlier:

> In three years at Oxford the RCP was the first thing that forced me to challenge my ideas and think things through. I went to a meeting called 'What is Marxism?' and found it incredibly stimulating. Complicated ideas were presented clearly and with a high level of discussion afterwards. For the first time I felt I had a role in politics. Outside the RCP I felt a lack of confidence, but the party gives you a framework and constantly sets new challenges. . . . We take ourselves seriously in terms of changing the world.[67]

Continually campaigning in mining communities after the end of the strike, RCP cadres vowed to renew their revolutionary challenge. The Union of Democratic Mineworkers (UDM) formed during the strike in 1985, when 72 per cent of the Notts miners, disenchanted with the NUM's militancy, voted to secede.[68] By its peak in March 1986, the UDM could count 28,000 members. RCP activists campaigned against the incipient union as it mobilized in Durham, Leicestershire and south Derbyshire. Eschewing the NUM and UDM alike, cadres maintained their calls for miners to forge an independent, national union around a revolutionary programme.[69] Polemicizing against the labourist bureaucracy remained the cornerstone of the party's politics: tellingly, a correspondent of the CPGB's theoretical magazine could rail against the RCP's 'hypercritical . . . classical Trotskyist contempt for trade union leadership'.[70]

In mining communities which had experienced severe repression, cadres attempted to harness spontaneous anti-statism into a more holistic revolutionary politics. RCP activists remained active in Yorkshire and the East Midlands throughout 1985 and 1986. Rallying support for jailed miners formed the focal point for these campaigns against the authorities. Mobilizing in solidarity

---

66 Jon Bryan interview with the author, 15 March 2021.
67 LeBor, 'Distinguishing Marx from perestroika'.
68 David Howell, 'Defiant dominoes: Working miners and the 1984–5 strike', in Ben Jackson and Robert Saunders (eds), *Making Thatcher's Britain* (Cambridge: Cambridge University Press, 2012), 160.
69 Freeman, *Our Day Will Come*.
70 John Kelly, 'Assessing the strike', *Marxism Today*, June 1985.

with the 'Shirebrook Ten' – miners jailed for burning working miners' buses – cadres invited support for the 'class war' activists.[71] When Pontefract miner and RCP supporter Keith Hammond was arrested in February 1986, the party coordinated street demonstrations and directed local community campaigns against the police.[72]

Advocating independence from the NUM, the RCP urged miners to repudiate negotiations with employers over pay deals and production quotas. In November 1985, when the Yorkshire NUM board voted to accept an incentive scheme, party supporters condemned 'divisive' collaboration with the NCB. For cadres who saw the strike's defeat as a setback for revolutionary politics, area agreements with bosses could only entrench regional atomization.[73] When Yorkshire miners' leader Jack Taylor commended to workers the official colliery review procedures, RCP activists implored miners to reject outright redundancies and pit closures.[74] Exhorting workers to shun the NUM, UDM and 'cosy' collaborationism alike, Yorkshire RCP organizer Joan Phillips recapitulated the mantra of the radical pamphlet *The Miners' Next Step* (1912), which had rejected liberal liaisons with industry leaders:[75]

> The old policy of interest between employers and ourselves should be abolished, and a policy of open hostility installed.[76]

Both theoretically and practically, cadres sharply differentiated the reformism of union leadership (or, more pejoratively, 'bureaucracy') and the revolutionary potential of the rank-and-file. Such distinctions were not unique to the RCP. For example, even before joining the RCP in the mid-1980s, Linda Murdoch had chaired a NALGO shop stewards committee in Glasgow, in which she assimilated a 'great education' in 'how the union leaders were really there to stifle any trade union independence'.[77] But vanguardist cadres aspired to *transform* unionized workers' spontaneous forms of militancy, giving a revolutionary lead: to this end, activists concentrated upon establishing 'contacts' among radical

---

71 RCP, *Free the Shirebrook 10!* (n.d. [1985]).
72 *Police State Comes to Pontefract* (RCP press release, 24 February 1986). Copy in author's possession.
73 *The Miners' Next Step*, 28 November 1985.
74 *The Miners' Next Step*, 24 January 1986.
75 Putatively authored by the radical Rhondda miner Noah Ablett, *The Miners' Next Step* renounced the conciliatory methods of the colliers' leaders in the Welsh coal strike of 1898 and promulgated instead a combative, syndicalist trade unionism to empower the rank-and-file. Ben Curtis, *The South Wales Miners, 1964-1985* (Cardiff: University of Wales Press, 2013), 2–3.
76 Joan Phillips, 'The miners one year on: our day will come', *tns*, 14 March 1986.
77 Linda Murdoch, 21 December 2021.

Figure 3 Members of *the next step* editorial board at a party in London given for Joan Phillips on her appointment as the RCP's Yorkshire organizer, 1986 (left to right: Andy Clarkson, Mike Fitzpatrick, Mick Hume and Joan Phillips). Credit: Joan Hoey.

workers. A former RCP supporter who later became a senior trade union official reflected on the modus operandi:

> There were parts of the working class that were more active than others. . . . It was . . . *let's get in there and try and influence that and see if we can direct it in a particular way*. It was about not necessarily accepting the immediate trade union consciousness.[78]

Correspondingly, when Linda Murdoch joined the RCP in Glasgow, she was 'encouraged to be in the unions and talk to people . . . to politicise individuals'.[79]

The extent to which individual activists established a cachet within a particular trade union significantly informed their degree of success in developing a compelling profile for the party's politics. Especially in lower-profile industrial disputes – where the role of the vanguard was less apparent – cadres who lacked kudos in a union branch struggled to polarize debates among workers, let alone win activists to the vanguard. In such instances, activists might marginally raise a strike's profile or generate additional funds but would ultimately play a peripheral role. For example, in South Shields in 1985, the predominantly female garment workers at Contracts Ltd, a subsidiary of French Connection,

---

78 Jon Bryan, 15 March 2021.
79 Linda Murdoch, 21 December 2021.

commenced a strike over working conditions and union recognition. RCP activists on Tyneside enjoined workers to support the strikers. Overall, however, cadres struggled to make a distinct or discernible impact, besides joining pickets and organizing a one-day demonstration outside city centre shops which stocked French Connection clothes.[80]

When their connections with industrial disputes were more tangential, cadres especially struggled to overcome the institutional animus of union hierarchies. Wary of even ephemeral challenges to their legitimacy, union organizers warned members against engaging with external agitators. In 1987, for instance, when forty-seven workers at HFW Plastics in Gateshead were sacked after a pay dispute,[81] employees began a strike and called for 'physical support' on a heavily policed picket line.[82] However, local officials belonging to the Society of Graphical and Allied Trades publicly shunned the support of Newcastle RCP organizer Kirk Williams, who had raised funds and joined the picket line.[83] A former party organizer in London, Manchester and Newcastle similarly reflected on their experiences of the labour movement:

> I always found the trade union work slightly more difficult. . . . It wasn't always obvious to me how things should be done. . . . It's not so obvious always what you can deliver. . . . You're not [for example] a health worker or a shipyard worker. . . . Mainly we were just keeping people sweet and friendly so that their signature was on a list if you were doing something more broadly about health workers. . . . A lot of it is being nice to people who, whether they understand the RCP project or not, sort of think that they're in a relationship with the project and we need to keep them on board and we need to support them.[84]

Cadres exerted greater influence upon unionized labour in cases where they had pre-existing links to union milieux as shop stewards or regional representatives. In Greater Manchester, for example, Dave Hallsworth served as the secretary of Tameside Trades Council in the 1980s. In west London, John Fitzpatrick chaired NALGO's Hammersmith branch. RCP activists maximized their profile when they accentuated specific campaigns with a clear strategic link to the vanguardist project. As a NUPE shop steward, for instance, Para Mullan exhorted the national

---

80 Sarah Gear, 'In the right gear', *Courier: Newcastle University Students' Newspaper*, 21 November 1985; Claire Foster, 'Strike in South Shields', *tns*, 22 November 1985.
81 Although the HFW Plastics were ostensibly sacked for refusing compulsory overtime, they had spent four years in dispute with management over a pay freeze. 'Students deny paid picket', *Palatinate: The Durham Student Newspaper*, 18 June 1987.
82 'Police attack plastics workers', *Workers News: Paper of the Workers International League*, July 1987.
83 'Keep out of our strike warning', *Newcastle Evening Chronicle*, 19 May 1987.
84 Former RCP member interview with the author, November 2021.

congress to support Afia Begum's campaign against deportation and to oppose all immigration controls. Occasioning rare instances of explicit accord with union activists, these single-issue campaigns brought the party considerable publicity. But cadres remained wary lest their interventions on such causes obscure their overarching objectives. Since the threat of deportations aroused opposition and moral outrage among liberals as well as leftists, RCP activists were at pains to stress the connection to their strategic imperative: building a revolutionary working-class movement.

'Moral authoritarianism' and the AIDS crisis

After the miners' strike, RCP theoreticians forecast an intensified capitalist offensive. With Thatcher's government fortified, the argument ran, the ruling class would escalate its assault upon working-class living standards. In this analysis, it was increasingly crucial for revolutionaries to train a vanguard. The party retained its campaigning emphases on Ireland and anti-racism as the issues which most starkly illuminated the distinction between reformist and revolutionary politics.

However, in the latter half of the 1980s, strategists also identified 'moral authoritarianism' as an increasingly salient line of the ruling-class attack. Activists argued that by propagating inflammatory and divisive social conservatism, the bourgeoisie demonized and marginalized radical challenges to authority. Writing in 1985, RCP general secretary Kate Marshall posited that capitalism's moralistic defenders sought a reactionary consensus to counter social conflict.[85] When *the next step*'s editorial board surveyed readers in 1986, combating repressive moralism ranked as their third priority, behind only the party's long-standing work on Ireland and anti-racism.[86]

Leading RCP cadres committed to expose the perceived class character of oppressive moralism. Published in 1988, Joan Phillips's keynote critique identified 'moral panics' as bourgeois pretexts for the state to extend its coercive

---

85 Kate Marshall, *Moral Panics and Victorian Values: Women and the Family in Thatcher's Britain* (London: Junius, 1985), 29, 35.
86 Some 256 readers – of whom three quarters were party members or supporters – responded to the mail survey. More than half of the respondents considered the fight against racism and nationalism as the party's most important task, while 34 per cent pointed specifically to campaigning on Ireland. Alongside advocating for women's freedom and gay rights, combatting moral panics emerged as the next important struggle. Kate Marshall, 'Readers' survey results', *tns*, 16 January 1987.

apparatus.[87] Designed to elucidate oppression's specific roots in capitalism, campaigns against moral authoritarianism were intended to impel class independence. An RCP activist at Newcastle University pithily summarized the strategic rationale:

> Without being able to challenge bourgeois ideology the working class will never be able to fight for the basic necessities which are denied to women, blacks and gays.[88]

Concomitantly, cadres asserted that only a unified proletarian movement, acting holistically *as a class*, could defy a ruling class which demonized social and political unorthodoxy: there could be no question of fighting, for instance, for women's rights, or gay rights, in isolation. Writing in the party's theoretical journal, Kate Marshall warned that 'sectional preoccupations' could only derail a cohesive class movement.[89] As far as vanguardists were concerned, politics divorced from the clarificatory categories of class struggle degenerated into bourgeois reformism. Recapitulating the point in 1990, Frank Furedi expounded the requirement for revolutionaries to situate each political problem in 'the totality within which it belongs. The concept of *totality* is central to Marxist theory'.[90]

Persistently locating moral authoritarianism in a broader repressive agenda, activists asserted that fighting social conservatism necessitated a consistent class analysis. In 1985, for example, when the right-wing Ulster Unionist Party MP Enoch Powell introduced the Unborn Children (Protection) Bill to parliament, the bill's liberal opponents noted that its proposed ban on human embryo research portended restricting access to abortion. The Birth Control Campaign implored Powell's opponents to lobby their MPs or the Prime Minister.[91] RCP cadres, by contrast, situated the bill in a concerted conservative defence of the family. Inviting students to join the party's demonstrations in Westminster, Leeds RCP organizer John Gillott distinguished revolutionary anti-capitalism from liberal opposition to moralism.[92]

---

87 Joan Phillips, *Policing the Family: Social Control in Thatcher's Britain* (London: Junius, 1988), 61, 74, 103, *passim*.
88 Sarah Gear – R.C.P., 'Women's oppression – answered or not?', *Courier: Newcastle University Students' Newspaper*, 13 February 1986.
89 Kate Marshall, 'Picking up the fragments', *Confrontation*, 2 (Summer 1987): 119.
90 Frank Furedi introduction to Franz Jakubowski, *Ideology and Superstructure in Historical Materialism* (London: Pluto Press, 1990), x–xi.
91 Wellcome Collection SA/BCC/D/89: Birth Control Campaign, *A Guide to Enoch Powell's Unborn Children (Protection) Bill: Why This Bill Should Be Opposed*, 1985. Available online at wellcomecollection.org/works/g57ngdfv (accessed 31 August 2021).
92 John Gillott, 'Capitalism and gays', *Leeds Student*, 3 May 1985.

Seizing upon the cause célèbres of social politics, activists persistently oriented their analyses in a critique of class forces. Picketing an address by the conservative activist Mary Whitehouse at Leeds University in 1986, RCP supporters propounded access to abortion and twenty-four-hour nurseries as components of the 'real freedom' which revolutionaries envisioned.[93] Similarly, joining National Abortion Campaign demonstrations against the Alton Bill in 1988, cadres stipulated that feminist demands for reproductive control must be oriented in revolutionary class politics.[94] An RCP supporter at Warwick University urged feminists to identify capitalist social relations as the root of a system which consigned working-class women 'to the role of domestic slaves and breeders'.[95]

Maintaining that the bourgeoisie contrived moral panics to fragment the working class and to stigmatize dissent, RCP theoreticians expounded thoroughgoing ideological independence from authority. Party propaganda warned workers that to justify draconian governance and atomize the populace, the ruling class exaggerated the amount of heinous crime. The RCP's programme for the general election of 1987, for example, declared that right-wing politicians and the press afforded child abuse 'inordinate' publicity, to generate a

> climate of tension and anxiety which leads people to distrust one another and instead put their faith in the authorities.[96]

Without repudiating entirely authorities' interference in private life, cadres argued, the working class could not develop its independence. Kate Marshall warned that workers who advocated strengthening the police, censorship or the judicial system could only entrench the forces of reaction.[97]

The British government's public health campaign during the AIDS crisis elicited particular hostility from RCP cadres, who perceived moral authoritarianism in the official messaging. By July 1985, 110 people had died of HIV/AIDS in the UK, and Chief Medical Officer Donald Acheson estimated that as many as 10,000 people were infected.[98] From 1986, Secretary of State

---

93 Rachel Smith, 'Mary, Mary, never contrary', *Leeds Student*, 31 January 1986.
94 Introduced to the Commons in 1987, Liberal MP David Alton's Abortion Amendment Bill proposed to reduce from twenty-eight to eighteen weeks the period in which a woman could access abortion. The bill failed in parliament at its third reading.
95 Justin Flude, Fight the Alton Bill Campaign/Revolutionary Communist Party, 'Robinson Crusoe?', *Mercury: Newspaper of Warwick University Students Union*, 20 January 1988.
96 Revolutionary Communist Party, *The Red Front: A Platform for Working Class Unity* (London: Junius, 1987), 30.
97 Kate Marshall, 'Repression won't stop rape', *tns*, 21 March 1986.
98 Jon Agar, *Science Policy under Thatcher* (London: UCL Press, 2019), 123.

for Health and Social Services Norman Fowler oversaw a mass information campaign under the slogan 'don't die of ignorance'. Information broadcasts warned ominously of a 'threat to us all'. Distributed to every UK household in January 1987, the government leaflet warned that 'depending on their behaviour ... any man or woman' could acquire the virus.[99]

Accusing the government of exaggerating the risk of infection beyond the most vulnerable cohorts, RCP cadres fulminated against what they regarded as a moralistic, repressive campaign. From this perspective, authorities counselling sexual abstinence encouraged and exacerbated established societal prejudices. As Adam Burgess has noted, some two-thirds of respondents to the British Social Attitudes survey in 1988 wanted public information to castigate 'morally reprehensible' sexual practices; almost one-third considered AIDS a 'punishment' for declining moral standards.[100] For Jenny Graham, a paediatrician and RCP activist in Glasgow, the government's emphasis upon 'safe sex' contributed to a ruling-class 'moral crusade' propagating 'conservative values'.[101] West London RCP cadre Eve Anderson averred that the authorities 'seized on the AIDS issue' to advocate restraint and conformity and to 'stir up greater hatred against homosexuals'.[102]

Situating 'moral authoritarianism' firmly in bourgeois rule, members of the RCP positioned gay liberation firmly within vanguardist class struggle. Distributing propaganda at a gay rights conference in London in July 1987, RCP activists intervened in workshop debates to promote their 'fighting charter'. Cadres stipulated that campaigns for equal rights could only advance meaningfully through a class struggle which fundamentally challenged the state.[103] In the same vein, standing as the RCP's candidate in the Vauxhall by-election of 1989, veteran gay rights activist Don Milligan asserted that

> independent actions and organisations of lesbians and gay men are important, but they are no substitute for wider political objectives.[104]

---

99 Wellcome Collection Dd 8934684 HSSH J0306 AR: Department of Health and Social Security, *AIDS: Don't Die of Ignorance* (London: Her Majesty's Stationery Office, 1986). Available online at wellcomecollection.org/works/kx943x59 (accessed 31 August 2021).
100 Adam Burgess, 'The development of risk politics in the UK: Thatcher's "remarkable" but forgotten "Don't Die of Ignorance" AIDS campaign', *Health, Risk & Society*, 19 (2017): 233.
101 Jenny Graham, 'Capitalism is sick too', *tns*, 16 January 1987.
102 Eve Anderson, Revolutionary Communist Party, Shepherds Bush Road, Hammersmith, 'Fight for gay rights', *Fulham Chronicle*, 22 January 1987.
103 Ian Dunn, 'Fiasco in London', *Gay Scotland*, July 1987.
104 Jan Milligan, 'The equal-rights candidate', *The Pink Paper*, 10 June 1989.

Figure 4 RCP activists during a demonstration in London on 9 January 1988 against Section 28 of the Local Government Act, which stipulated that a local authority could 'not intentionally promote homosexuality' or 'promote the teaching . . . of the acceptability of homosexuality'. Credit: Pandora Kay-Kreizman/*the next step*.

Repudiating the public health campaign as a government attempt to promote 'national hysteria' and to inculcate conservatism in the populace, Milligan and Michael Fitzpatrick led the RCP's critique. Gay men and intravenous drug users, they asserted in 1987, faced the most acute risk: beyond those 'fairly clearly defined groups . . . HIV infection is not at present a serious health problem'.[105] Identifying the spread of the disease among gay and bisexual men as a consequence of iniquitous oppression, the RCP cadres castigated the

> climate of guilt, secrecy and fear that surrounds much homosexual activity in Britain [and] creates the conditions in which the Aids virus can flourish.[106]

Concurrently, Fitzpatrick and Milligan indicted the left and the gay liberation movement for echoing the government's safe sex mantra. In a hostile review of an SWP pamphlet which declared that 'everyone who is sexually active is at risk', Milligan chided socialists who endorsed the state's calls for restraint.[107] Leftists presenting

---

105 Michael Fitzpatrick and Don Milligan, *The Truth about the Aids Panic* (London: Junius, 1987), 29–30, 36.
106 Ibid., 34.
107 Duncan Blackie and Ian Taylor, *AIDS: The Socialist View* (London: Socialist Workers Party, 1987), 3–4.

the epidemic as a threat throughout society, Milligan contended, were attempting to shield the gay community from stigma – but in doing so they abandoned an overarching fight for liberation, independent of the state.[108] Gay rights activists who followed the government's line on abstemiousness, Fitzpatrick and Milligan opined, erroneously portrayed the state as a potentially progressive agent.[109]

While the RCP's position on AIDS reflected its strategic opposition to state interference in private life, other leftists more defensively prioritized averting a homophobic backlash. RCP activists stressed the inordinate danger to gay men precisely to challenge the social roots of homosexuals' oppression. Conversely, most British radicals feared that accentuating the rate of infection among gay men gave succour to homophobic bigotry. The physician and SWP activist Dave Widgery, for example, emphasized that AIDS was 'no more a gay disease than German measles is German'.[110] The Spartacists, meanwhile, accused the RCP of propagating 'reactionary prejudices' and 'the dangerous and imbecilic line that AIDS is some sort of "gay plague"'.[111] For socialists who regarded the AIDS crisis as a matter of unparalleled urgency, the RCP's anti-statist position appeared doctrinaire and even dangerous. A correspondent to *Workers' Liberty*, George Davey Smith, archly caricatured Fitzpatrick and Milligan:

> Once the structures of capitalist society are smashed, AIDS ... will instantly and automatically disappear. So long as you vote for your Red Front candidate, you can forget about AIDS and safe sex.[112]

As Lucy Robinson has noted, the RCP's position on AIDS sparked a furore among gay liberation activists, who accused the party of downplaying the epidemic's severity and undermining a pressing public health response.[113] For campaigners who advocated safe sex awareness, Fitzpatrick and Milligan propagated abstract dogma. Ridiculing *The Truth about the Aids Panic*, one hostile reviewer dismissed the notion that the 'liberation of the worker' would 'check the spread of AIDS'.[114] Other gay rights activists charged the RCP with diverting attention from the immediate priority of minimizing the spread of the virus.[115] At a Pride rally in

---

108 Don Milligan, '"Too little too late"', *tns*, 3 April 1987.
109 Fitzpatrick and Milligan, *The Truth about the Aids Panic*, 51.
110 Dave Widgery, 'AIDS and the New Puritanism', *Socialist Worker Review*, July–August 1986.
111 'AIDS tragedy in Thatcher's Britain', *Workers Hammer: Monthly Paper of the Spartacist League*, February 1989.
112 George Davey Smith, 'How not to fight AIDS', *Workers' Liberty*, June 1987.
113 Robinson, *Gay Men and the Left*, 177–8.
114 Ruth Walker, 'The truth about the AIDS pamphlet', *Gay Scotland*, May 1987.
115 Anna McGovern, 'Take Edward's advice', *The Pink Paper*, 2 February 1992; Geoff Woodford, 'Revolutionary', *The Pink Paper*, 9 February 1992; Keith Flett, 'Unusual positions', *The Pink Paper*, 16 February 1992.

London's Kennington Park in June 1990, thirty protesters from OutRage! – a new, militant gay rights organization[116] – zapped the RCP stall. Branding cadres 'murderers', demonstrators directed chants against Fitzpatrick, Milligan, and their comrades: 'people are dying while the RCP keeps lying'.[117] For OutRage! co-founder Simon Watney, RCP activists

> care little or nothing about the grim realities of the international epidemic, beyond ways in which they can exploit it to their own imagined political ends.[118]

Revisiting their pamphlet in the early 1990s, Fitzpatrick and Milligan lamented especially the gay liberation movement's affinity with the state-sponsored safe sex campaign. From the vanguardist perspective at the turn of the decade, a perceived lack of ideological independence in the gay rights movement mirrored a broader nadir of radical politics. Although Milligan accepted that safe sex campaigns had 'saved people from disease and death', he nevertheless criticized gay rights activists who attempted to 'counter' homophobic 'bigotry' by denying that gay men faced particular risk.[119] In 1992, Milligan – who had left the RCP in February 1990, but still considered himself a 'communist'[120] – suggested that the 'repressive hypothesis' of *The Truth about the Aids Panic* was 'flawed' by overstatement. He did not, however, wish to 'disown' the pamphlet's 'basic arguments', situating the government response to the epidemic in an intensifying moral authoritarianism.[121]

Similarly, for Fitzpatrick, who retained his position in the leadership of the RCP until it dissolved, the gay liberation movement's support for the government's initiatives reflected an atmosphere of political conformism in the early 1990s. Writing in 1992, Fitzpatrick posited that the gay movement's 'misguided' attempts to avert homophobia had generated a stultifying alliance with the 'medical establishment' and bolstered the government's 'moral crusade ... promoting sexual and moral conformity'.[122] Tracing a broader crisis of political contestation, Fitzpatrick lambasted leftists and gay rights campaigners who he considered to have propagated conservative hostility towards 'permissiveness'

---

116 Founded in May 1990 after the homophobic murder of London actor Michael Boothe, OutRage! undertook civil disobedience and direct action to publicize and combat homophobic discrimination. Ian Lucas, *OutRage! An Oral History* (London: Cassell, 1998).
117 'Pride Zap', *The Pink Paper*, 7 July 1990.
118 Simon Watney, 'Misleading nonsense', *The Pink Paper*, 28 July 1990.
119 'Reflections on the Aids panic', *Living Marxism*, January 1990.
120 'And another thing', *The Pink Paper*, 21 February 1993.
121 Don Milligan, *Sex-Life: A Critical Commentary on the History of Sexuality* (London: Pluto Press, 1992), 91–2, 147 n. 2.
122 Michael Fitzpatrick, 'Aids risk and the scare war', *Guardian*, 10 April 1992.

across society as a whole.¹²³ Scorning radicals who had acquiesced in government campaigns 'enforcing sexual morality', a London RCP supporter complained that the left had made the vanguardist struggle for revolutionary independence 'more difficult'.¹²⁴

'Young, angry, thinking people'

Reviewing its progress in the late 1980s, the leadership of the RCP delineated the scale of the tasks ahead. Reporting to the party conference of December 1986, the Political Committee juxtaposed the organization's internal vitality and the 'difficult' external conditions. According to the leadership, cadres' campaigns had established a 'solid reputation' for the RCP, which was in a 'stronger position' than ever. Simultaneously, the capitalist offensive had advanced, and the working class appeared demoralized. At this conjuncture, Frank Richards told activists, the party-building project was progressing 'behind schedule'. It behoved the RCP to 'develop' its 'active relationship with the working class'.¹²⁵

The general election of June 1987 underlined the disjuncture between the scope of the party's ambitions and the degree of its influence. Standing fourteen candidates under the banner of the Red Front,¹²⁶ RCP strategists intended to use the election to elevate their challenge to the Labour Party and reformism.¹²⁷ The campaign developed the themes of Kate Marshall's candidacy in the Greenwich by-election of February 1987, when the RCP veteran had exhorted voters to reject capitalist realism and instead to 'join our movement to build a party that is really fighting for a change'.¹²⁸ The Red Front's programme bullishly reiterated an inspired vision of revolutionary transformation:

> There is no reason why people should not enjoy a prosperous and worthwhile life. . . . We live in an age of scientific breakthroughs in information technology and medicine which show the tremendous potential for social progress.¹²⁹

---

123 Michael Fitzpatrick, 'Aids panic in disarray', *Living Marxism*, July 1992; Michael Fitzpatrick, 'The dangers of healthy living', *Living Marxism*, September 1992.
124 Julie Nevan, 'Last word on revolution', *The Pink Paper*, 23 February 1992.
125 Frank Richards, 'The future is in our hands', *tns*, 5 December 1986.
126 The Red Front also drew support from the minute Revolutionary Democratic Group, alongside left-wing militants in Red Action, who welcomed Red Front candidacies as an outlet for workers to 'stand up and show what they think'. 'Vote Red Front', *Red Action*, June 1987.
127 Karen Guldberg, 'When the time comes to fight', *Mancunion*, 9 June 1987.
128 Working Class Movement Library, Salford: *Fighting for a Change! Vote Kate Marshall* (London: Junius, n.d. [1987]).
129 Revolutionary Communist Party, *The Red Front*, 12–13.

While party strategists did not envisage their candidates significantly impacting national electoral arithmetic, they pitted the Red Front as a fight back against 'the capitalist state' and 'its repressive forces in society'.[130] Not for the first time during election campaigns, cadres relished the chance to amplify their vanguardist challenge. Embracing the opportunity for additional publicity, activists hoped to supplant working-class labourism. Running a high-profile campaign in Hammersmith, for example, lawyer John Fitzpatrick toured the constituency in a loaned Land Rover bedecked with red banners. Interviewed a fortnight before polling day, Fitzpatrick enthused about public engagement:

> There is a real response to the views we are putting across. We are making some headway in breaking people away from the Labour Party.[131]

However, after the Red Front's fourteen candidates realized only 3,177 votes in total, superseding the Labour Party appeared more as a theoretical necessity than an attainable objective. Senior members of the RCP acknowledged that their positions had gained little traction in the working class. Reviewing the election, *the next step* editor Mike Freeman admitted that the Red Front had been 'unable to make the national impact in the election we had originally intended'.[132] In the absence of 'coherent class politics', Frank Richards told the Preparing for Power conference of 1987, it was 'inevitable' that workers would experience 'passivity and resignation': it remained for the RCP to reconstitute 'an *authentic* Marxism' in the working class.[133]

If the election underscored the quantitative limits of the RCP's impact, however, party veterans asserted that their *qualitative* distinction could impact working-class politics. For cadres who perceived their task as reinvigorating a moribund revolutionary tradition, the lack of popular support did not invalidate the project; rather, it impelled the party anew to sharpen its challenge to the working class. Writing shortly after the election, Richards and Freeman regarded the conjuncture as 'more of an opportunity than a problem'.[134]

Imbued with an enduring sense of ideological distinction, cadres remained determined to win workers to a revolutionary alternative. Setbacks did not incline activists to modify their approach or ideas but instead fortified their resolve to transform class politics. Whereas SWP theoretician Alex Callinicos

---

130 *Stand Up Fight Back: Vote Red Front* (1987).
131 'Red John's revolution woos voters', *Hammersmith & Shepherds Bush Gazette*, 28 May 1987.
132 Mike Freeman, 'Editorial: Taking on Labourism', *Confrontation*, 2 (Summer 1987): 3.
133 Frank Richards, '"Teach the truth"', *tns*, 7 August 1987.
134 Frank Richards and Mike Freeman, 'The third Thatcher term', *Confrontation*, 4 (Summer 1988): 140–1.

intimated that radicals should 'focus on the consciousness and combativity of workers themselves',[135] the RCP's theoretical journal vowed to renew its 'political struggle against Labourism'.[136] In July 1987, activists spent two days of their week-long summer school assessing the balance of class forces. In his keynote address, Richards insisted that with a stagnant left 'in abject retreat', theoretical acuity and organizational dynamism equipped cadres with a compelling challenge to the working class.[137]

Insisting that vanguardism remained feasible, party theoreticians eschewed left-wing suggestions that the conjuncture required radicals to modify their aims and methods. Coining his thesis of 'Thatcherism' from the late 1970s, for instance, the cultural theorist Stuart Hall held that the Tory ascendancy had decisively shifted British politics to the right, defining a new 'common sense', which championed rugged individualism and undermined collectivism.[138] Elaborating in the CPGB's journal *Marxism Today*, Hall declared that Thatcherism had pervaded the working class and its institutions and 'fundamentally changed the political rules of the game'.[139] For RCP strategists, by contrast, working-class Conservatism reflected not the mystical allure of the new right but indicted the ideological and strategic weakness of the left. Reviewing the Tories' third successive election victory, Mike Freeman highlighted labourism's 'programmatic defects', rather than the advance of what Hall termed Thatcherism's 'authoritarian populism'.[140] For another member of the Political Committee, Joan Phillips, the idea that Thatcherism was 'mesmerising' the working class merely evaded the left's political bankruptcy.[141] The corollary of the RCP's critique was that independent revolutionary politics could yet present, in the words of WAR organizer Keith Tompson, a 'credible opposition to Mrs Thatcher'.[142]

As well as attracting new supporters on university and polytechnic campuses, through the mid-1980s the RCP also recruited a minority of its new members from wider left milieux. Activists who had experienced other radical organizations especially noted the RCP's self-proclaimed ideological independence and organizational élan. An erstwhile member of the CPGB, Gordon Lee joined the RCP in Edinburgh in 1985, hailing this 'party of the future ... completely

---

135 Alex Callinicos, 'Looking for alternatives to reformism', *International Socialism*, Winter 1987, 116.
136 Linda Ryan, 'Labour or The Red Front?', 7–30, *Confrontation*, 2 (Summer 1987): 25.
137 'The battle for the nineties'. Preparing for Power flyer (1987).
138 H. F. Pimlott, *Wars of Position? Marxism Today, Cultural Politics and the Remaking of the Left Press, 1979–1990* (Leiden: Brill, 2022), 119.
139 Stuart Hall, 'Thatcherism – a new stage?', *Marxism Today*, February 1980.
140 Mike Freeman, 'The decline and fall of British Labourism', *Confrontation*, 4 (Summer 1988): 36–7.
141 Joan Phillips, 'The missing link', *Living Marxism*, December 1988.
142 Tompson, *Under Siege*, 153.

independent of reformism'.[143] Activists' self-assured commitment and emphasis upon the primacy of ideas could overcome leftists' initial reservations. Until meeting the RCP through relatives in the party in Glasgow, Linda Murdoch, a disillusioned former member of the WRP, was reluctant to join another organization:

> I used to go to the odd [RCP] meeting. I used to go to supporters' meetings, but I wouldn't pay any money [laughs]. I just refused. . . . I remember sitting in these meetings thinking: I want to say something, I want to say something. I went to one and it was just fascinating. . . . The real difference was they *explained* oppression. . . . And then I remember going to the bar one Friday evening, after one of these meetings, and they were handing out *the next step* for people to sell the next day. And I got so fed up, I went, *give me some of them, I'll sell them!* [laughs] [. . .] And that was the start of it. I went out and sold *the next step*. My first sale was at Hillhead tube in Glasgow. I remember it vividly.[144]

The party leadership's decision to launch Living Marxism in 1988 reflected its determination to assert to a wider audience the working class as an agent of history. Maintaining the maximal aspirations which had always defined the RCP, the monthly magazine's first editorial ideated 'liberation through social revolution' overthrowing the 'capitalist system . . . which hangs as a dead weight around the neck of humanity'.[145] With an initial print run of 15,000, editor Mick Hume pitted *Living Marxism* as an 'intellectual alternative' for 'young, angry, thinking people'.[146] The review challenged the reader to 'understand how the world works – so that you can help to change it'.[147] Within two years, *Living Marxism* had some 6,000 subscribers.[148] Remarkably for the outlet of a small revolutionary party, *Living Marxism* established a distribution deal with national retailer WHSmith. By 1991, the magazine had even achieved the peculiar prominence of appearing in ITV's long-running soap opera *Coronation Street*.[149]

By the end of the 1980s, among vanguardists who were increasingly conscious of the party's marginality, there was a tendency to idealize the very concept

---

143 'Pure sect', *Leninist*, October 1985.
144 Linda Murdoch, 21 December 2021.
145 'The living and the dead', *Living Marxism*, November 1988.
146 Adam LeBor, 'Marx wars', *Guardian*, 16 January 1989. The magazine's title implicitly referenced that of the *International Council Correspondence* under Paul Mattick's editorship between 1938 and 1942.
147 'Living Marxism', *Living Marxism*, November 1988.
148 Information from former RCP supporter.
149 Mavis Wilton, 'Look sharp and think on', *Living Marxism*, March 1991. Mavis Wilton was not, in fact, an RCP cadre, but the fictional co-proprietor of the *Coronation Street* newsagent's shop which stocked the magazine.

of human agency. Dedicated activists had forged a dynamic organization which revelled in its heretical status on the left. Cadres still aspired to develop a vanguard capable of leading the dictatorship of the proletariat. But as they struggled, without major advance, to win workers to independent revolutionary politics, activists were left to champion more abstractly the transformative potential of the subaltern subject. For example, in 1989, on the bicentennial of the French Revolution, Frank Richards contributed a feature to *Living Marxism*: Marxists would not, he averred, identify with its 'bourgeois politics'. But in the absence of a proletarian vanguard at the turn of the 1990s, Richards lauded the revolution's subjective essence: 'it is men and women who make history. Nothing in society is natural or permanent'.[150] As the following chapter demonstrates, this radical humanism, hitherto implicit in RCP politics, became an increasingly visible bedrock for the organization in the 1990s, as the vanguardist project entered its critical phase.

150 Frank Richards, 'Vive la revolution!', *Living Marxism*, July 1989.

4

'The empire strikes back'

Anti-imperialism and the Gulf, the Balkans and Ireland, c. 1989–95

By the end of the 1980s, the RCP's vanguard-building strategy was almost a decade old. The organization could count between 100 and 200 dedicated members as well as a wider network of several hundred supporters. Persistent campaigning on 'the Irish war' and militant anti-racism had raised the party's profile. Additionally, its controversial interventions during the miners' strike and the AIDS crisis had established the RCP as a distinct and divisive critique on the British left.

As the previous chapters have demonstrated, there was a significant disjuncture between the brio of the party's campaigns and their limited ability to develop a vanguard in the working class. Full-time RCP activists were proficient organizers of high-profile events. By the late 1980s, the IFM's August march, for example, attracted thousands of demonstrators. With a substantial readership, *Living Marxism* gained a reputation as a lively, polemical outlet. Yet in its cardinal task – training a revolutionary vanguard in the working class – the organization proceeded inchmeal. The low level of support for Red Front candidates in the general election of 1987 confirmed the gulf between the party's ambition and its progress.

At the turn of the 1990s, however, the leadership of the RCP assessed the disintegration of the Soviet Union, its attendant global upheaval and an altered balance of class forces in Britain. Declaring the epochal defeat of the working class, cadres attempted to redefine revolutionary anti-capitalism. Lamenting an age of diminished subjectivity, theoreticians aspired to reinstate popular belief in humanity's history-making capacity. First and foremost, they committed to establishing foundationally the *possibility* of a revolutionary alternative.

Tracing the evolution of the RCP from vanguardism to dissolution, this chapter analyses how the party navigated what cadres called the world-historical defeat of the working class. Scrutinizing activists' assessments of developments in the USSR and Eastern Europe, the Middle East, Ireland, South Africa and beyond, it examines how theoreticians attempted to formulate a new anti-capitalism after class struggle. In so doing, it explains why, by the eve of its dissolution in the mid-1990s, the RCP propagated a radical humanist politics which both maintained and modified the party's core precepts.

'The left . . . no longer exists'[1]

Through 1989, the crises of communist regimes in East Germany, Czechoslovakia and Romania enthused RCP cadres who celebrated the collapse of 'Stalinism'. Theoreticians who had long regarded the Soviet Union as the acme of counter-revolution welcomed the malaise of its satellites.[2] In the summer of 1989, the RCP convened at Eastbourne to discuss the popular protests against the regimes in Central and Eastern Europe. Contributing to a sanguine party symposium, Frank Richards hailed Stalinism's decline, which removed 'an historic barrier to the self-emancipation of the international working class'.[3] When the Berlin Wall fell in November 1989, *the next step* editor Joan Phillips declared that the post-war order's 'prolonged period of capitalist stability' was 'reaching an end'.[4]

For the RCP leadership, this moment of international instability created space for revolutionary politics. Moreover, while the vanguardist task remained formidable, its exponents were no longer burdened by unwanted association with Stalinism's spectre. Formulating its theses in November 1989, the Political Committee anticipated a short-term fillip for Western liberal democracy but resolved that Stalinism's demise enabled Marxists to 'recreate' a 'communist tradition'.[5] Theoreticians admitted that gaining traction in the 'disoriented'

---

1 Frank Richards, 'Midnight in the century', *Living Marxism*, December 1990.
2 Frank Furedi's analysis of the USSR drew especially upon Glasgow University economist Hillel Ticktin's critique. Like Ticktin, Furedi concluded that the Soviet Union was neither a planned nor a capitalist formation but a backward economy under the haphazard rule of a bureaucratic elite. The Stalinist bureaucracy, Furedi asserted, had reversed the Bolsheviks' revolutionary advance by the turn of the 1930s. Frank Füredi, *The Soviet Union Demystified: A Materialist Analysis* (London: Junius, 1986), *passim*, see especially 33; Hillel Ticktin, 'The class structure of the USSR and the elite', *Critique*, 9 (1978): 37–61.
3 Frank Richards, 'Theses on Stalinism in the Gorbachev period', *Confrontation*, 5 (Summer 1989): 110.
4 Joan Phillips, 'The German crisis', *tns*, 17 November 1989.
5 'Clearing the way for communism', *Living Marxism*, January 1990.

working class remained a titanic endeavour. But cadres asserted that the atrophy of Stalinism and labourism in Eastern and Western Europe, respectively, had 'cleared the decks' for revolutionary politics.[6]

However, for strategists who positioned themselves in a historic struggle for revolutionary ideas, the decay of Stalinism did not automatically represent an advance: it remained for cadres to train a movement in the working class in Britain. Political Committee representative Mick Hume, for example, sharply distinguished the largely peaceful transitions to democracy in Hungary and Poland from the proletarian revolution which the RCP aspired to lead.[7] Through 1990, party theoreticians were increasingly dismayed not only by the halting progress of vanguardism but by what they considered a more profound dearth of appetite for political transformation. Cadres complained that the denouement of the Cold War fastened many workers in the belief that an alternative social system neither could nor should be countenanced. In the summer of 1990, the key theme of Preparing for Power addressed society's 'climate of pessimism and irrationality'.[8] Writing at the end of the year, another member of the Political Committee opined that while Stalinism's crisis created an opportunity for Marxism to emerge as a 'living force', across Europe the left was in its greatest disarray since the revolutions of 1848.[9]

Declaring a deeper crisis of appetite for social transformation, RCP activists accentuated the fundamental humanist tenets which had underpinned their revolutionary ideas. Vanguardist class politics could not convince workers who discounted social transformation as neither feasible nor desirable. Consequently, theoreticians espoused a 'new Enlightenment' to elevate the 'values of liberation, of experimentation and of progress'.[10] At this juncture, cadres vied to reinvigorate belief in humanity's transformative potential as a basis for reanimating revolutionary politics. Invoking the Enlightenment to assert the 'possibility of social progress',[11] activists upheld the human potential to overcome a 'profound sense of pessimism' and remake the world.[12]

The RCP's revolutionary credo drew heavily upon Marxism's Enlightenment foundations. Where the Enlightenment philosophes of the eighteenth century adumbrated the subject's capacity for reasoned reflection, Marx's theory of

---

6   'Marxism for our times', *tns*, 2 February 1990.
7   Mick Hume, '"How can you call yourself a Marxist?"', *Living Marxism*, March 1990.
8   'For a new Enlightenment', *tns*, 15 June 1990.
9   Robert Knight, *Stalinism in Crisis* (London: Pluto Press, 1991), 7, 47–8, 140, 166, 190–1.
10 'For a new Enlightenment'.
11 James Heartfield, 'Postmodern, ante-Enlightenment', *Living Marxism*, June 1990.
12 Frank Füredi, 'Out of the dark, into the light', *Living Marxism*, July 1990.

history further specified that social transformation would pivot upon *class subjectivity*.[13] Tapping these Enlightenment themes at the turn of the 1990s, the party's radical humanism remained moored explicitly to revolutionary politics. Cadres trumpeted human agency not as an abstraction but as a precursor to reinvigorating radicalism. When Cambridge leftist Gareth Stedman Jones argued in 1990 that Leninist vanguardism 'no longer' held 'meaning as a political project',[14] Mike Freeman repudiated this 'abandonment of Marxism' and reasserted the historical imperative of class revolution.[15]

By the end of 1990, however, the leadership of the RCP declared that the subjective decline of class politics had severely undermined revolutionary vanguardism. In November 1990, the Political Committee announced that the organization was 'not in a position to implement the ambitious programme of party-building that we embraced following the launch of the RCP in 1981'. Envisioning a period of internal consolidation, the leadership set activists the formidable challenge of forging a new 'anti-capitalist critique' to 'promote the reconstitution of the working class'.[16] After more than a decade as the organization's main propaganda outlet, *the next step* became a four-page weekly bulletin, geared primarily towards party members and supporters. Meanwhile, one group of rival leftists delighted in the 'demise' of the RCP's 'silly mass party strutting'.[17]

From the party's foundation, cadres had consistently acknowledged that winning workers to their position was ineluctably difficult. Nevertheless, activists who saw themselves undertaking a historically vital task remained motivated in what they perceived to be a phase of political flux. By the end of 1990, however, theoreticians reassessed their vanguardist strategy. A struggle for revolutionary ideas could advance only to the extent that it convinced workers: by this juncture, cadres increasingly believed that the working class had suffered a significant subjective defeat. Discussed serially in *Living Marxism*, Frank Richards's keynote essay 'Midnight in the Century' précised the Political Committee's diagnosis: 'for the time being at least, the working class has no political existence'. Richards's seminal intervention articulated the leadership's view that while workers might identify with their class in a descriptive, sociological sense, few would position

13 Kai Nielsen, 'Marx and the Enlightenment project', *Critical Review*, 2 (1988): 59–75.
14 Assessing the collapse of Stalinism, Stedman Jones argued that Marx was 'far more successful in evoking the power of capitalism than in demonstrating in any conclusive fashion why it had to come to an end'. Gareth Stedman Jones, 'Marx after Marxism', *Marxism Today*, February 1990.
15 Mike Freeman, 'Marxism lives', *Living Marxism*, April 1990.
16 'The RCP and the election', *tns*, 9 November 1990.
17 *Leninist*, 6 December 1990.

the working class as a cohesive, transformative political actor.[18] Revisiting his argument some three decades later, Frank Furedi recalls how perceiving diminished class subjectivities prompted RCP strategists to review their project and methods:

> With the end of the Cold War, you had not just the defeat of Stalinism and the whole Soviet bloc, but somehow the whole left-wing project was now extremely feeble and called into question. . . . You had a situation where people's sense of class . . . had become relatively unimportant. Insofar as it was important, it more or less had the character of a lifestyle – you know: *I'm working class and this is what working class people do* – rather than anything to do with a particular political orientation towards the world. And this is the point at which it becomes very clear that the classical political categories with which you made sense of life were becoming pretty much irrelevant and not particularly useful. I think for that reason one drew the conclusion that all the hopes that were invested previously in transforming society and creating this . . . liberating kind of life was somehow off the agenda. The sense of agency had become extremely feeble.[19]

Since RCP activists had always drawn inspiration from their perceived world-historical tasks, suspending the vanguardist project raised serious questions about the organization's future. The leadership directed cadres to formulate a new anti-capitalist politics. In practice, however, internal consolidation marked a significant strategic adjustment. For some sections of the rank-and-file, a more foundational struggle for 'Enlightenment values' represented a retreat from the RCP's compelling revolutionary programme. Noting a 'fairly rapid drop-out rate' in *Living Marxism* readers' groups in 1990, for example, one London supporter regretted that party events had ceased to address how to 'build an independent working class movement'.[20]

While the turn from vanguardism prompted protracted internal debate, the RCP maintained its organizational profile and panache. Although future strategy required clarification, the party maintained strident interventions exhorting independence from the state. The Gulf War provided a focal point for party activities. When a US-led coalition waged war on Iraq – after Saddam Hussein's regime had invaded Kuwait – the RCP's calls for 'victory to the Iraqi people' garnered attention on the left: *Living Marxism*'s January 1991 issue achieved

18 Richards, 'Midnight in the century'.
19 Frank Furedi interview with the author, 12 February 2021.
20 Alan Denehy, 'Has the RCP gone far enough?', *tns*, 7 December 1990.

record sales, and forty-nine new supporters joined the organization in February 1991 alone.[21]

Cohering younger activists who emphasized their ideological independence from reformism, the party's student organizations also remained hubs of activity. RCS activity peaked at the PNL, where three activists were elected to the students' union executive for the 1990/1991 academic year.[22] Kirk Leech, who organized the party's campaigns at PNL, remembered it as a 'strange place', where the Harrington saga several years earlier had engendered 'a pretty febrile atmosphere of protests and campaigns':

> Lots of left-wingers who had lost their jobs or had been blacklisted in employment, or kicked out, ended up doing degrees. Full of WRP, SWP, Militant – lots of people.[23]

With echoes of the party's engagements with the labour movement, tactical interventions on student-specific issues were geared to expound the party's independent aspirations. Mobilizing in support of expelled students, for example, Claire Foster and Elli Lee swiftly coordinated the biggest general meeting in the PNL union's history. Although they lost an intra-left argument on tactics, Foster and Lee celebrated 'most importantly' having 'demonstrated the possibility of organising around our politics'.[24] Simultaneously, RCS representatives persistently mirrored the party's wider positions, exhorting students to repudiate collaboration with authority both at the polytechnic and beyond. Observing the NUS conference in Blackpool at Easter 1991, one reporter noted the three RCS delegates from PNL addressing every possible motion and 'relating everything to the Gulf conflict'.[25]

Insofar as the party leadership delineated new objectives after the supposed defeat of the working class, theoreticians vowed to combat the reaction of the post–Cold War West. After a pyrrhic victory over Stalinism, cadres argued, the West was further beset by financial slump. *the next step*'s editorial posited in 1992 that without the 'ideological glue' of anti-Soviet sentiment, Western

---

21 'Building on our anti-war activities', *tns*, 22 February 1991; 'The supporters' drive: Progress so far', *tns*, 1 March 1991.
22 On separate PNL sites, Claire Foster and Paula McNamara were elected to vice-president positions, winning 168 of 428 votes cast and 141 of 293 cast, respectively. Julie Nurrish was elected as publicity officer, receiving 357 ballots and defeating the Socialist Worker Student Society candidate by four votes. 'Victorious night for Far left in the shape of the RCP and their allies', *fuse: Magazine of the Students Union of the Polytechnic of North London*, 215 (n.d. [c. March 1990]).
23 Kirk Leech, 7 September 2020.
24 Claire Foster and Elli Lee, 'Fighting scab student unionism', *tns*, 23 November 1990.
25 Clare Cook, 'Seven go mad in Blackpool: Reportback from NUS conference', *Fused: Magazine of PNLSU Executive*, 4 (June 1991).

liberal democracy had lost its cohesion.[26] For discontented revolutionaries, the malaise of the West had a severely deleterious impact upon political subjectivity: a flagging capitalist order inculcated in the populace a pervasive sense that no alternative system was available.

The Political Committee asserted that in this bleak conjuncture, it was incumbent upon revolutionaries to rejuvenate the concept of social transformation. Cleaving to their materialist analysis, cadres continually positioned class conflict as the paramount motor of history. Only the working class, Mick Hume stipulated in 1991, could effect its own emancipation – so it behoved radicals to reconstitute that class as a conscious political actor.[27] But how would cadres reanimate workers who did not, for the most part, identify their class as a historical agent? Sceptical activists feared that propagandistic calls to arms risked degenerating into hollow abstraction. A veteran of the RCP for a decade, Dave Chandler warned that with 'future forms of the class struggle ... indeterminate', repeating the mantras of class revolution would likely confuse and generate 'passivity': a 'new collective approach to social emancipation' was required.[28]

In this disorienting context, strategists identified as their most pressing task reasserting the *capacity* of the working class to identify its own interests and act independently to transform its circumstances. These radical humanist precepts mainly took the form of arraigning the supposed inertia and conservatism of Western politics. Evoking the need to restore the human subject as the author of social transformation, the opening weekend of the RCP's annual conference in 1991 was devoted to 'fighting the fear of the future' and establishing 'the meaning of progress in an age of reaction'.[29] Identifying an 'intellectual malaise' percolating leftists and conservatives alike, Frank Richards's keynote speech declared that elevating the human subject's historical agency constituted the 'principal task facing Marxist theory towards the year 2000'.[30] Theoreticians repudiated the American political scientist Francis Fukuyama's argument that Western liberal democracy was triumphant at the end of the Cold War.[31] Eschewing capitalist realism, RCP activists espoused a visionary politics, which reimagined the human subject

26 'Why the Tories are in crisis', *tns*, 21 October 1992.
27 'Casting more light on "Midnight in the Century"', *Living Marxism*, April 1991; Mick Hume, 'Whatever happened to the working class?', *Living Marxism*, May 1991.
28 Dave Chandler, 'Midnight in the Century', *Living Marxism*, November 1991.
29 RCP, *Towards 2000: Revolutionary Ideas for the Nineties* (1991).
30 Frank Richards, 'Realising the human potential', *Living Marxism*, September 1991.
31 First elaborated in 1989, Fukuyama's seminal thesis posited that the Cold War's denouement marked 'the end point of mankind's ideological evolution and the universalisation of Western

and its radical potentiality. Rejecting the 'end of history', Frank Furedi expounded instead a new politics affording 'a decisive role to the subjective factor, to the potential for human action'.[32]

Perceptions of a new conjuncture prompted strategic and tactical modification. In the 1980s, the RCP strategists emphasized issues which they considered germane to clarifying workers' class interests; in the early 1990s, cadres campaigned more eclectically to uphold the wider assertion that humanity could radically change society. This revolutionary humanism remained, in Freeden's terms, the core concept, while the party sought a post-vanguardist strategy. On occasion, conceptualizing such an alternative took nebulous forms: seeking to stimulate ideological independence against the status quo, activists necessarily espoused more abstract critiques. A student RCP supporter at Warwick University, for example, complained broadly that 'all critical opposition to existing conditions has been sacrificed on the altar of capitalist realism'.[33] The RCS pitch to Warwick students in 1992 resembled that of a debating society or philosophical think tank as much as that of a revolutionary organization:

> We live in a society bereft of ideas. Every western leader has proclaimed the 'triumph of capitalism'. Yet they have no idea of how to deal with the problems of their own system from mass unemployment to starvation in the Third World ... Join the *Living Marxism* Society and participate in developing the ideas that will help us to shape the future.[34]

The party's eight candidates in the general election of April 1992 similarly pitted themselves capaciously against 'the dull conformism of the present'. The RCP maintained its maximalist anti-capitalism – 'we refuse to accept the inevitability of scarcity and inequality' – in post-vanguardist, ideational terms: a vote for the RCP constituted a 'positive statement of faith in the future ... and the potential of collective action'.[35]

---

liberal democracy as the final form of human government'. Francis Fukuyama, 'The end of history?', *The National Interest*, 16 (1989): 4.
32 Frank Furedi, *Mythical Past, Elusive Future: History and Society in an Anxious Age* (London: Pluto Press, 1992), 70, 220, 239.
33 Sean McAlinden, 'Student politics are crap', *Warwick Boar*, 29 October 1991.
34 Warwick Digital Collections: UWA/PUB/S/HB/30/1. *Warwick Life '92* (Coventry: Warwick University Students' Union, 1992).
35 Revolutionary Communist Party, *Break Out of the Grey: Election Manifesto of the Revolutionary Communist Party* (London: Junius, n.d. [1992]).

'The moral rearmament of imperialism'

Anti-imperialist opposition to the Western campaign during the Gulf War of 1990 and 1991 dominated the RCP's early attempts to reanimate anti-capitalism in the new political phase. Recalling the party's erstwhile vanguardism, propaganda implored British workers to take sides against their government. Cadres hoped that building opposition to the state's intervention in the Middle East would initiate more thoroughgoing revolutionary independence in the British working class.

Until President George H. W. Bush's administration and the British government escalated their military involvement in the Gulf, the RCP took no sides in the local conflict between Iraq and Kuwait. When Iraqi forces invaded Kuwait on 2 August 1990, Kenan Malik identified Saddam Hussein's as a 'vicious, despotic regime' but contended that Iraq was merely 'a fairly typical backward capitalist country'.[36] Holding no brief for either of the two states, *the next step*'s editorial characterized the Iraqi invasion as a 'cynical gamble' for 'regional power' and Kuwait's claims to nationhood as 'an absurdity. . . . It is an oilfield with a flag'.[37]

Cadres' contempt for the regimes in Baghdad and Kuwait City reflected their interpretation of both states as the products of Western imperialism. For Mick Hume, Iraq and Kuwait were 'Meccano-kit countries . . . illegitimate states', born of imperialist meddling and ruled by 'Western-approved despots'.[38] The party's avowedly anti-imperialist assessment of the Gulf crisis indicted Western powers for exacerbating ethnic and religious divisions in the region. In a series of 'Red Lectures' in the autumn of 1990, for instance, the Newcastle RCS attributed carving the Middle East into 'artificial statelets' to the 'crimes' of governments in Washington, Westminster and Paris after the First World War.[39]

For strategists lamenting the decline of class subjectivities in Britain, the Gulf War presented a vital opportunity to stimulate popular opposition to Western intervention. When the Bush administration and Thatcher government threatened Iraq militarily, the RCP leadership recapitulated its orthodox anti-imperialism, comparable to its position during the Falklands War almost a decade earlier. Calling for the 'victory of the Middle Eastern masses over imperialism', Mick Hume's *Living Marxism* editorial defended Iraq against

---

36 Kenan Malik, 'The RCP and the Gulf crisis', *tns*, 7 September 1990.
37 'Take sides with the Iraqi people', *tns*, 18 January 1991.
38 Mick Hume, 'Hands off the Gulf!', *Living Marxism*, September 1990.
39 'Geoff Kidder, of the Revolutionary Communist Students, on the Gulf War', *Courier: Newcastle University Student Newspaper*, 4 October 1990.

'Western aggression'.[40] By highlighting Western depredation, cadres sought to instil in the populace ideological independence against the state. When the UN Security Council ordered Iraq to withdraw from Kuwait, Kirsten Cale castigated the Western powers for whom grandstanding in the Gulf represented a 'convenient pretext' to claim global hegemony.[41] Campaigning on the Gulf War during NUS executive elections in 1991, RCP candidates exhorted students to reject Western governments' claims to legitimacy.[42]

Locating the UN coalition's campaign in the Gulf in the West's bid to dominate the post–Cold War order, cadres stipulated that only outright anti-imperialism could reinvigorate class independence in Britain. Maintaining the Leninist distinction between oppressor and oppressed nations,[43] theoreticians maintained that opposing imperialism was the strategic priority – irrespective of the politics and programme of the 'oppressed' – that is, the Iraqi – regime. When defeated Iraqi forces retreated from Kuwait in March 1991, Rob Knight reiterated that the RCP 'had no illusions in Saddam Hussein ... an unexceptional third world dictator'.[44] Eve Anderson similarly condemned Hussein's 'repugnant' persecution of the Kurds and called for Kurdish self-determination.[45] The RCP's calls for 'victory to the Iraqi people' signified not sympathy for Hussein but cardinal opposition to emboldened Western imperialism. When the coalition's ground troops entered Iraqi-occupied Kuwait in February 1991, the RCP organized demonstrations at the US embassy in London. James Heartfield told the gathered press that the Western allies were the 'real butchers' in the Middle East.[46]

RCP strategists evaluated opposition to the Gulf War by the degree to which it fundamentally challenged Western regimes. In January 1991, as the coalition intensified its attacks upon Iraqi forces, 500 RCP members and supporters convened in London to discuss the war. The conference resolved that until workers explicitly demanded the defeat of British imperialism, they could not clarify or consistently act in their class interests: failing to espouse 'victory to the Iraqi people' allowed

40 Hume, 'Hands off the Gulf!'.
41 Kirsten Cale, 'Drawing lines in the sand', *Living Marxism*, December 1990. On 29 November 1990, UN Security Council Resolution 678 ordered Iraqi forces to leave Kuwait by 15 January 1991. When Hussein's regime failed to withdraw, a US-led UN coalition launched aerial and naval bombardment, followed by ground troops in February 1991.
42 Revolutionary Communist Students, *Peace in the Gulf! Western Forces Out!* (London: Revolutionary Communist Party, 1991).
43 See Chapter 1.
44 Rob Knight, 'Who gave the West the licence to kill?', *Living Marxism*, April 1991.
45 Eve Anderson, 'The secret of Saddam's success', *Living Marxism*, January 1991.
46 'Allies branded "real butchers"', *Aberdeen Press & Journal*, 27 February 1991.

the ruling class to obscure class divisions and engender a 'we're all in it together' spirit. So long as people accept that their interests are the same as those of the 'nation' they will find it difficult to challenge the capitalist class in any sphere – economic, political or military.[47]

From this perspective, pacifist or liberal complaints about the coalition signally failed to combat popular illusions in the state. Concomitantly, cadres arraigned leftists who criticized the West's conduct rather than its political content. Alongside sections of the Labour left and the SWP, the Campaign for Nuclear Disarmament (CND) formed the Committee to Stop War in the Gulf (CSWG), which advocated UN sanctions against Iraq. Addressing a 20,000-strong rally in Hyde Park in February 1991, CND chair Bruce Kent said that his organization backed British service personnel but sought an immediate cessation of hostilities. Labour left-winger Tony Benn, meanwhile, called for a ceasefire lest continued conflict galvanize an Arab revolt against the West.[48] For RCP cadres, the CSWG's stance perpetuated chauvinistic illusions in the British state. Calling for Western sanctions, *the next step* stipulated, could only 'bolster Western interference' in the region.[49] Mike Freeman explicitly distinguished the CND's demands, for Iraqi withdrawal and Western troops' safe return, from the RCP's calls for 'US and British defeat'.[50]

The RCP's calls for the defeat of the UN coalition caused acute controversy on the British left.[51] On the one hand, the party's short-lived campaigning group, the Hands Off The Middle East Committee (HOME), drew support from the RCG and the fringe Workers International League, which insisted that calling for an Iraqi victory over Western imperialism did not constitute 'capitulating to Iraqi nationalism'.[52] Conversely, for radicals who hoped more immediately for a revolution *within* Iraq, the RCP was unduly lenient towards Hussein's regime, which had deployed chemical weapons against the Kurds.[53] For example, in September 1990, after initial cooperation, the *Leninist* faction withdrew from the HOME, protesting the RCP's 'Iraq-defencist' position.[54] RCG theoreticians,

---

47 'Avoiding the issues won't stop the war' and 'The consensus for war', *tns*, 1 February 1991.
48 Angella Johnson, 'Police seek absentee after rally speech', *Guardian*, 4 February 1991.
49 'Peace in the Gulf: Western forces out', *tns*, 1 February 1991.
50 Mike Freeman, 'CND's alternative imperialism', *Living Marxism*, March 1991.
51 For an overview of British leftist responses to the Gulf War, see Evan Smith, 'How the first Gulf War shaped the British left', *Red Pepper*, 11 March 2021. Available at redpepper.org.uk/how-the-first-gulf-war-shaped-the-british-left/ (accessed 14 March 2021).
52 Graham Fenwick and Richard Price, 'US and Britain hold Middle East hostage', *Workers News: Paper of the Workers International League*, December 1990–January 1991.
53 Charles Tripp, *A History of Iraq* (Cambridge: Cambridge University Press, 2014), 236.
54 National Committee, Communist Party of Great Britain (*The Leninist*), 'Statement', *Leninist*, 5 October 1990.

meanwhile, endorsed the HOME's anti-imperialism but accentuated more sharply demands for self-determination for the Kurds and the Middle East's national minorities.[55]

After defeated Iraqi forces accepted a ceasefire on 28 February 1991, RCP cadres were left to lament popular support in the West for Operation Desert Storm. A MORI poll published on 27 January, shortly after air strikes on Iraq began, indicated substantial public sympathy with the Conservative government: some 61 per cent of respondents expressed satisfaction with John Major's handling of the crisis – outstripping even Thatcher's zenith (59 per cent) after victory in the Falklands in 1982.[56] Concurrently, in the United States, President Bush enjoyed an unprecedented popularity rating of 89 per cent.[57] Cadres' hopes of animating opposition to Western imperialism appeared especially forlorn. 'Western victory in the Gulf War', the party leadership averred,

> has led to a moral rearmament of imperialism. Many people, even on the left, now accept the idea of the superiority of Western culture and way of life.[58]

Organizing a national party conference in November 1991, Penny Robson implored supporters to challenge the 'right-wing offensive', which positioned the West as the world's rightful political hegemon.[59] Delineating an unpropitious balance of forces, the conference committed the RCP to challenge popular support for the Western capitalist powers.

Cadres also perceived the 'moral rearmament of imperialism' propelling Yugoslavia's disintegration and ethno-national wars in the 1990s. By recognizing seceding republics and subsequently intervening militarily in the resulting wars, the argument ran, Western elites provoked conflict in the Balkans. With echoes of the Gulf campaign, RCP cadres fulminated particularly against the degree of popular enthusiasm, not least among leftists and liberals, for Western military deployment in Bosnia from 1992. From the mid-1990s, press acclaim for NATO's campaign against the Bosnian Serbs became the focal point of the party's critique.

---

55 Eddie Abrahams and David Reed, 'Oil imperialism and the class struggle', *Fight Racism! Fight Imperialism!* 97 (September–November 1990); 'Stop the Gulf War', *Fight Racism! Fight Imperialism!* 99 (February–March 1991).
56 Alexander MacLeod, 'Britain's major wins highest approval since Churchill', *Christian Science Monitor*, 30 January 1991.
57 Brian Lai and Dan Reiter, 'Rally 'round the Union Jack? Public opinion and the use of force in the United Kingdom, 1948–2001', *International Studies Quarterly*, 49 (2005): 257.
58 'The silent race war', *tns*, 20 September 1991.
59 Penny Robson, 'The silent race war', *Living Marxism*, November 1991.

Before the Soviet Union collapsed, RCP activists broadly attributed Yugoslavia's political ructions to rivalries between the republics' rival Stalinist regimes.[60] For correspondents to *the next step*, Slobodan Milošević – who became leader of the Serbian League of Communists in 1986 – was a typically nationalist functionary, concerned principally with maximizing Serbia's power within the federated Yugoslavia. In Kosovo, vowing to support Serbs mistreated by the Albanian majority, Milošević reduced Kosovo's provincial autonomy, sparking strikes and protests among the Kosovo Albanians.[61] In 1989, defending ethnic Albanians' rights, RCP cadre Russell Osborne condemned Milošević's 'chauvinist tirades' and the 'Serbian reign of terror', which had 'unleashed a pogrom'.[62]

When rival nationalisms flared in the Balkans in the early 1990s, theoreticians regarded all Stalinist leaderships as equally toxic, reactionary forces, pitting Yugoslav workers in mutual conflict. When Croatia and Slovenia unilaterally declared independence in June 1991, the party's Balkans specialist, Joan Phillips, lamented the

> explosion of nationalism in Yugoslavia . . . the product of a fight for survival between bureaucrats who are all as bad as each other.[63]

At this juncture, the RCP favoured an 'all-Balkans federation': the 'retrograde step' of Yugoslavian 'fragmentation' would 'confuse and obscure the struggle between working class people and the bureaucracy by pitting one national group against another'.[64] Meanwhile, by the spring of 1992, Bosnia had descended into internecine war, with violent clashes between the republic's Serb, Croat and Muslim populations. Earlier indictments of Milošević notwithstanding, when the Western media demanded military action against the Serbs, RCP analysts rejected the suggestion that the Serbs posed a unique threat. By November 1991, noting the 'Western media['s] . . . increasingly anti-Serbian position', *the next step*'s editorial board decided to 'moderate its initial hostility to Serbia': in Bosnia,

---

60 Ben Brack, RCS, 'Hands off Serbia!', *fuse*, 220 (December 1991). Until 1991, Yugoslavia comprised a federation of six republics: Bosnia and Herzegovina, Croatia, Macedonia, Montenegro, Serbia and Slovenia. Serbia also included the autonomous provinces of Kosovo and Vojvodina.
61 During Yugoslavia's constitutional reforms between 1967 and 1974, Kosovo and Vojvodina were granted a degree of provincial autonomy within Serbia. During the 1960s and 1970s, the ethnic Albanian proportion of Kosovo's population steadily increased. By the early 1980s, ethnic Albanians comprised some 77.4 per cent of the Kosovan populace, and Serbs only 14.9 per cent. Nebojša Vladisavljević, 'Nationalism, social movement theory and the grassroots movement of Kosovo Serbs, 1985-1988', *Europe-Asia Studies*, 54 (2002): 777.
62 Russell Osborne, 'Pogrom in Kosovo', *tns*, 10 March 1989; Russell Osborne, 'Bloodbath in Kosovo', *tns*, 7 April 1989.
63 Joan Phillips, 'The dangers of secession', *Living Marxism*, August 1991.
64 Ibid.

Croats and Serbs alike were 'guilty of sectarian atrocities'.⁶⁵ But the Croatian and Slovenian declarations of independence, cadres argued, had significantly exacerbated regional tensions. Repudiating prospective NATO intervention, the party's 'Hands off Serbia!' slogan identified imperialism as a seismic threat to Yugoslavia.⁶⁶

Challenging liberal interventionism, RCP cadres asserted that while Milošević presided over a noxious nationalist regime, Serbia was not uniquely culpable for the conflict engulfing the Balkans from 1992. The party's internal bulletin characterized Milošević as a 'brutal, self-seeking politician', whose forces had 'certainly been responsible for many atrocities in the region'. But members and supporters were told that Serb leaders' virulent nationalism was not without parallel: leaders of all of Yugoslavia's republics had 'manipulated ethnic divisions for political ends'.⁶⁷ Western intervention, cadres contended, could only worsen such a volatile situation.

Accentuating multipartite responsibility for Yugoslavia's violent disintegration bolstered the party's anti-imperialist position. Whereas advocates of Western intervention positioned the Serbs as the principal aggressors, RCP cadres stressed the mutuality of antagonism between Bosnia's Serbs, Croats and Muslims. In November 1991, when the left-leaning *New Statesman and Society* called for military action against the Serbs,⁶⁸ the RCP rejected the 'depiction of Croatia as innocent victim' which underpinned ostensibly humanitarian demands for an armed strategy.⁶⁹

Delineating the 'moral rearmament of imperialism', analysts charged global powers – most notably Washington and the European Community – with fighting self-aggrandizing proxy conflicts in the Balkans.⁷⁰ By January 1992, the EC declared that Croatia and Slovenia were legitimate sovereign nations. For RCP cadres, by recognizing secessions, the United States and reunified Germany had exacerbated instability and abetted local nationalists. For Joan Phillips, Germany's pivotal support for Croatian separatism made 'all-out civil war between Croatia and Serbia inevitable'.⁷¹ Endorsing Croatian independence,

---

65 'Hands off Serbia!', *tns*, 8 November 1991.
66 'Yugoslavia: Explaining the issues', *tns*, 22 November 1991.
67 'Targeting Serbia', *tns*, 5 June 1992.
68 Imploring John Major's government to 'stand up and fight' for 'Croatia and freedom', David Marshland called for the British to forge a military alliance with Croatia, demand a Serbian ceasefire within seven days and launch air strikes against the Serbs if no such cessation was forthcoming: 'only war will stop this war'. *New Statesman and Society*, 1 November 1991.
69 'Hands off Serbia!'.
70 Joan Hoey, 'Policy without principle: The U.S. "Great Game" in Bosnia', *The Nation*, 30 January 1995.
71 Joan Phillips, 'Who lit the Yugo powder-keg?', *Living Marxism*, January 1993.

Andy Clarkson argued, enabled Western capitalism to dominate a fragmented Eastern Europe.[72]

After NATO deployed a 'peacekeeping force' in Bosnia in 1992, activists amplified their conviction that external interference in the Balkans had profoundly worsened regional instability. From the vantage point of 1993, with NATO involvement in Bosnia increasing, RCP supporter Paul Flewers averred that Western support for Croatian and Slovenian independence had transformed the Balkans from a site of competing local nationalisms to an arena of major international conflict.[73] The US recognition of Bosnia and Herzegovina as an independent state from April 1992, Wystan Massey contended, typified the 'cynical games of one-upmanship' among Western powers 'desperate to establish their credentials as world leaders'.[74]

For RCP cadres, in Bosnia as in the Gulf, Western governments bereft of a galvanizing anti-Soviet crusade sought purpose and power in foreign policy. Where once Western leaders had rallied against the Soviet menace, they now asserted authority by militating against Saddam Hussein and Slobodan Milošević. For governments in Washington, Westminster, Paris and Berlin, Joan Phillips argued, the spurious pretext of 'international peacekeeping' – contributing troops to NATO's forces in Bosnia – conveniently diverted public attention from 'slump, scandals and sleaze' at home.[75] In the Balkans, meanwhile, jaded former communists cynically deployed chauvinist demagoguery. In Serbia and Croatia, respectively, Phillips contended, Milošević and Franjo Tuđman represented 'former Stalinist bureaucrats who have embraced nationalism to save their own skins'.[76]

In their attempts to counteract supposed media distortion, leading cadres produced highly provocative coverage of the Balkan wars. Challenging portrayals of the Serbs as the sole, or chief, aggressors, in 1993 *Living Marxism* coordinated a photographic exhibition in London and Birmingham, titled 'A selective silence'. Defying a government ban, the exhibition graphically depicted atrocities against Serbs in Bosnia.[77] The front cover of the magazine's March

---

72 Andy Clarkson, 'Support Croatia?', *Living Marxism*, March 1992.
73 Paul Flewers, 'Yugoslavia: How the West *has* won', *Living Marxism*, October 1993.
74 Wystan Massey, 'Aid farce is merely self promotion', *Hammersmith & Shepherds Bush Gazette*, 21 May 1993.
75 Joan Phillips, 'Where peace means war', *Living Marxism*, April 1994.
76 Joan Phillips quoted in 'Letters', *London Review of Books*, 19 August 1993.
77 After seeing the images in Belgrade's Museum of Applied Arts, *Living Marxism* assistant editor Joan Phillips liaised with art historian and film-maker Bojana Isaković to bring the exhibition to Britain. Under the terms of UN sanctions against Serbia, the Department for Trade and Industry proscribed the photographs from display. David Pallister, 'Serb show defies ministry', *Guardian*, 25 February 1993.

1993 issue featured the severed heads of Serbs killed and mutilated in the war. Insisting that the RCP took no side in the war, Joan Phillips positioned 'A selective silence' as a vital corrective to skewed Western narratives. Publicizing the banned photographs, Phillips argued, would 'draw attention to the fact that people are being told only one side of the story about the war in Yugoslavia'.[78] The party's polemical engagement would later envelop the organization, but in 1993 the trade magazine of the British press 'congratulated' *Living Marxism* for questioning the familiar portrayals of culpability and victimhood.[79]

Members of the RCP repeatedly asserted that they held no brief for Milošević: 'a brutal, self-serving politician' leading a regime 'responsible for many civilian deaths in Bosnia'.[80] But for some Balkans analysts, especially on the British left, *Living Marxism* correspondents served as Serb apologists. Writing as a Cambridge undergraduate, Attila Hoare characterized the RCP magazine as 'little better than a propaganda sheet for right-wing Serbian nationalism' peddling 'anti-Croat' untruths.[81] Hoare subsequently claimed that Belgrade had funded *Living Marxism*'s controversial exhibition to discredit the Bosnian Muslims and Croats.[82]

On the British left, refusing to single out the Serbs as perpetrators was not entirely unique to the RCP. The SWP, for example, similarly castigated Serb and Croat leaders alike and outright opposed external intervention. In its distaste for moralistic Western commentary, senior SWP activist Duncan Blackie's analysis would not have appeared out of place in a contemporary *Living Marxism* editorial:

> Many who brand the Serbs as the sole aggressors will now admit . . . that the Croatian leadership has been culpable too . . . it is quite wrong to portray the war in Bosnia as the struggle of the oppressed against oppressors.[83]

Blackie's position bore considerable resemblance, for example, to Mick Hume characterizing the Yugoslav conflict as

---

78 Joan Phillips, 'Breaking the selective silence', *Living Marxism*, April 1993.
79 The *UK Press Gazette* opined that while the truth of the Yugoslav conflict was 'no more likely' to be found in *Living Marxism* than elsewhere, the magazine's critical position promised to 'contribute to a more balanced view of the conflict'. 'Balkan balance and terror', *UK Press Gazette*, 8 March 1993.
80 Eddie Veale, '"White niggers" of the new world order', *Living Marxism*, July 1992.
81 'Letters', *London Review of Books*, 9 September 1993. After graduating in 1994, Marko Attila Hoare assisted Workers' Aid to Bosnia, a voluntary coalition of leftists, trade unionists and refugees coordinating food parcels and financial assistance to Bosnia. Hoare subsequently completed his doctorate at Yale and gained recognition as an authority on the history and politics of the Balkans.
82 Attila Hoare, 'On Bosnia and the left', *Against the Current*, July–August 1995.
83 Duncan Blackie, 'War without end?', *Socialist Review*, July–August 1995.

a squalid civil war between self-serving nationalist regimes, in which no side can claim to be fighting for right or justice.[84]

However, for those leftists who regarded the Serbs as supremely culpable for the conflict, the RCP's stance represented an unconscionable apologia for a regime perpetrating ethnic cleansing against Bosnia's Muslim and Croat populations.[85] Defending Bosnia against Serbia's 'fascist . . . war of aggression', the WRP, for example, coordinated food convoys to Tuzla as part of the Workers' Aid for Bosnia campaign.[86] For one WRP supporter, the exhibition 'A selective silence' had confirmed that the RCP were 'the principal cheer leaders for the Serb Chetniks'.[87] Another WRP veteran, Charlie Pottins, went further still, drawing parallels between *Living Marxism* and the 'Holocaust revisionism of the far Right's David Irving'.[88]

As far as RCP cadres were concerned, liberal and left-wing support for UN and NATO intervention in the Balkans indicated imperialism's continual recrudescence. Portraying a deteriorating balance of forces in the 1990s, RCP theoreticians reproached radicals who implored their government to play a progressive role in Bosnia. Not only had the working class ceased to constitute a political actor, but popular illusions in the state were gaining momentum. In April 1993, when a *New Statesman and Society* editorial called for increased military action against the Serbs, Mike Freeman scorned 'former radicals' imploring a 'government they once opposed to act on their behalf'.[89]

Living Marxism's most contentious coverage was yet to come. In the summer of 1995, in the war's deadliest atrocity, Bosnian Serb forces massacred more than

---

84 Mick Hume, 'Would you believe them?', *Living Marxism*, September 1995.
85 For an academic account positioning the RCP among 'Serbophiles' in an 'ideological alliance between the far right and the far left', see Daniele Conversi, 'Moral relativism and equidistance in British attitudes to the war in the former Yugoslavia', in Thomas Cushman and Stjepan G. Meštrović (eds), *This Time We Knew: Western Responses to Genocide in Bosnia* (New York: New York University Press, 1996), 244–81.
86 *Workers Press* Editorial Board, 'Halt fascism in Bosnia', *Workers Press*, 8 July 1995.
87 Tom Carter, 'The "bloody awful" RCP', *Workers Press*, 9 September 1995.
88 Charlie Pottins, '"Horror stories"', *Workers Press*, 4 November 1995. In 1995, David Irving – a British historian of Nazi Germany – wrote to Penguin Books demanding that the publisher withdraw from circulation Deborah Lipstadt's book *Denying the Holocaust: The Growing Assault on Truth and Memory* (1993). Dorot Professor of Modern Jewish History and Holocaust Studies at Emory University, Lipstadt had ranked Irving among 'the most dangerous spokespersons for Holocaust denial'. After Penguin refused to withdraw Lipstadt's book, Irving issued a defamation writ. At the conclusion of the subsequent trial in 2000, Justice Gray ruled in Lipstadt's favour, and concluded that Irving was 'an active Holocaust denier . . . anti-semitic and racist'. Wendie Ellen Schneider, 'Past imperfect: Irving v Penguin Books Ltd., No. 1996-I-1113, 2000 WL 362478 (Q. B. Apr. 11), appeal denied (Dec. 18, 2000)', *Yale Law Journal*, 110 (2001): 1533. See also Richard J. Evans, *Telling Lies about Hitler: The Holocaust, History and the David Irving Trial* (London: Verso, 2002).
89 Mike Freeman, 'Left, right, left, right', *Living Marxism*, June 1993.

8,000 Muslim prisoners at Srebrenica.[90] Several months later, in a pseudonymous article in *Living Marxism*, 'Linda Ryan' went beyond refusing to condemn the Serbs in isolation and disputed the scale of the killing. There was 'no hard evidence', Ryan averred, 'that 3,000, let alone 8,000, Bosnian Muslims were massacred in Srebrenica'.[91] The controversy surrounding Ryan's erroneous claims would not be the last in *Living Marxism*'s prolonged engagement with the Balkans.

Identifying recrudescent imperialism as a defining feature of the post–Cold War order, the RCP launched a new front group, the Campaign Against Militarism (CAM), in November 1992. Formulated at a 1,000-strong conference in London, CAM's manifesto held that chauvinist support for Western interventionism in the developing world represented the 'dominant political outlook'.[92] With echoes of the party's established front organizations, most notably the IFM and WAR, the leadership of the RCP intended the CAM to propagate key party positions among wider milieux. Activities would agitate against popular acquiescence in the West's global grandstanding. Demonstrations, exhibitions and propaganda were geared to counteract the 'weakness' of 'anti-imperialist' politics in the West.[93] During a television appearance in 1995, CAM organizer Kate Margam eschewed pacifism and attributed the worsening conflict in the Balkans to the interference of 'foreign powers': 'there wasn't a war there before those countries got involved'.[94] The organization's uncompromising anti-imperialism was not lost on British pacifists, who regarded the front group as a dangerous misnomer: 'The RCP have as much in common with the peace movement as wolves have with vegetarianism'.[95]

Becoming a focal point for party activists through 1993, the CAM retained the party's long-standing strategic assertion that workers could not act independently in their class interests if they identified with their nation and its capitalist rulers. Writing from Newcastle, Ian Abley held that a movement opposing militarism could draw radicals into a more thoroughgoing critique of the capitalist slump and its social context.[96] In this respect, the CAM's struggle against Western interventionism articulated a fundamentally anti-capitalist conviction:

---

90 The UN's International Criminal Tribunal for the former Yugoslavia (ICTY) later presented evidence 'beyond reasonable doubt' that Bosnian Serbs had executed between 7,000 and 8,000 Bosnian Muslims in a calculated, genocidal operation. For an overview of the ICTY investigation, see 'Facts about Srebrenica'. Available at icty.org/x/file/Outreach/view_from_hague/jit_srebrenica_en.pdf (accessed 2 February 2022).
91 Linda Ryan, 'What's in a mass grave?', *Living Marxism*, March 1996.
92 'A manifesto against militarism', *Living Marxism*, October 1992.
93 Mike Freeman, *The Empire Strikes Back: Why We Need a New Anti-War Movement* (London: Junius, 1993), 31–3, 37, 39, 54–5.
94 Kate Margam quoted in *The James Whale Show*, 4 August 1995.
95 Ross Bradshaw, 'Campaign against militarism but beware of imitations', *Peace News*, August 1993.
96 Ian Abley, '"Peace" excuse does not fool us', *Newcastle Journal*, 17 June 1993.

> Whether in Mogadishu or Millwall, our problems arise from a capitalist system that is running out of control and has to employ ever more barbaric methods to try to stem the chaos.[97]

However, the CAM's class dimension was seldom so explicit. Perceiving their anti-imperialism as a minority interest in a populace which broadly endorsed Western intervention, activists positioned independence from authority as the most pressing prerequisite for transformative politics.

For cadres who lamented the 'moral rearmament of imperialism', the immediate priority was to combat popular affinities with the state. *the next step* editor Kenan Malik averred in 1992 that ascendant Western chauvinism since the Gulf War had marginalized the revolutionary challenge:

> The West has become the force for good and for change while anti-imperialist forces have become the menace that needs sorting out.... The New World Order is a moral and ideological triumph for the West.[98]

The Warwick RCS similarly vowed to challenge assumptions of Western hegemony and rectitude:

> The rise of militarism, as the accepted outlook in Western countries, is the biggest problem we face today. Every political commentator agrees on one thing – the West should intervene more in the affairs of the Third World and the former Eastern Europe.... The West is the cause of the problem in these parts of the world and so cannot be the solution.[99]

By the mid-1990s, among RCP cadres who harboured residual hopes of reanimating anti-capitalist politics, the 'moral rearmament of imperialism' represented a further obstacle.[100]

'A historic defeat for the liberation movement'

For activists who railed against Western interventionism, from the late 1980s, the trajectory of liberation movements in Palestine, South Africa and, latterly, Ireland compounded the conviction that radical anti-imperialism was receding

---

97 'The race against barbarism', *tns*, 15 October 1993.
98 'The Bishu massacre and the New World Order', *tns*, 18 September 1992.
99 Warwick Digital Collections: UWA/PUB/S/HB/26/1. *Warwick Life '93* (Coventry: Warwick University Students' Union, 1993).
100 Frank Furedi, *The New Ideology of Imperialism: Renewing the Moral Imperative* (London: Pluto Press, 1994), 99, 107–8, *passim*.

worldwide. RCP cadres had always positioned the Irish conflict as a pivotal issue for revolutionary politics in Britain. But radicals compromising with their powerful adversaries in Africa and the Middle East nevertheless represented significant and disquieting features of the post–Cold War world. Cadres asserted that negotiated settlements with imperialism could only buttress an undynamic capitalist order. By August 1991, the leadership's invitation for the annual London IFM march had acquired particular urgency. The Irish conflict had attained additional importance since 'national liberation movements that advanced in the seventies and eighties are now on the defensive'.[101] Standing against Secretary of State for Northern Ireland Peter Brooke in the general election of April 1992, IFM organiser Alex Farrell reasserted the revolutionary imperative of backing unconditionally republicanism's 'mortal threat to our rulers and their "United Kingdom"'.[102]

Cadres who abhorred the 'moral rearmament of imperialism' in Britain deplored liberation movements diluting their demands. RCP theoreticians already regarded the African National Congress (ANC) and Palestine Liberation Organisation (PLO) as petty-bourgeois nationalists rather than revolutionary anti-capitalists. The party's South Africa analysts, for example, repeatedly warned that although the ANC built its struggle on the commitment of the Black working class, its leaders would ultimately settle for a stake in governing a capitalist South Africa.[103] Middle East specialist Daniel Nassim similarly exhorted militant Palestinian workers and peasants to 'break their links with the Arab bourgeoisie' and to establish a revolutionary working-class movement to 'defeat Zionism'.[104] Cognisant of the political limitations of the ANC and the PLO, the RCP endorsed their respective struggles to the extent that they implicitly challenged 'imperialist' regimes.

However, when cadres perceived these movements adopting more conciliatory positions towards their adversaries, they charted a shifting global balance of forces. In this analysis, developments in Palestine and South Africa marginalized revolutionary politics, providing respite for a crisis-ridden imperialist order. After the PLO accepted United Nations (UN) resolutions 242 and 338 in 1988 – recognizing Israel and seeking a two-state solution – Nassim lambasted the

---

101 'Challenge Britain's colonial war', *Living Marxism*, August 1991.
102 Linen Hall Library, Belfast: Northern Ireland Political Collection: Irish in Britain Box 1: Irish Freedom Movement, *Standing for Irish Freedom against Peter Brooke* (London: Irish Freedom Movement, 1992).
103 'Struggle in South Africa: The African National Congress', *tns*, 9 August 1985; Charles Longford, 'Botha's kiss of death', *tns*, 23 August 1985.
104 Daniel Nassim, 'Occupied Palestine: Twenty years of war', *tns*, 5 June 1987.

movement's 'steady drift to the right'.[105] Similarly, in 1990, when the newly unbanned ANC entered negotiations with the Pretoria regime, the RCP Political Committee warned that a compromise with capitalism would produce a 'neo-colonial' South Africa.[106] Contrasting the militant potential of the Black working class and the perceived reformism of its leadership, Jenny Graham concluded in the spring of 1990 that it was 'difficult . . . not to feel pessimistic about the chances of a concerted working class challenge to the strategy of the ANC'.[107] When the ANC's deputy spokesman in Britain, Billy Mafethal, decried 'terrorism' and dissociated his organization from the Irish republican movement, a leading RCP correspondent scorned Mafethal's diplomatic overtures.[108]

For activists who aspired to the revolutionary overthrow of the Western order, modi vivendi in South Africa and the Middle East consolidated the influence of imperialism. Cadres who had always fulminated against the perceived reformism of the anti-apartheid movement averred that the transition to democracy stabilized South Africa for the capitalism class. When the ANC proposed a multi-party coalition government, Charles Longford scorned a retreat from the 'democratic principle at the heart of the liberation struggle'.[109] In 1994, Mandela became the country's first Black president, leading a 'government of national unity' in which the erstwhile premier, F. W. de Klerk of the National Party, served as deputy. Visiting South Africa the following year, Longford asserted that the Black working class which had sustained the ANC's struggle had been 'removed from the political map' in the 'new' South Africa. Charging the liberation movement with class collaboration, Longford lamented that South Africa's capitalist structures remained intact.[110]

As far as party analysts were concerned, the Israeli–Palestinian peace process further consolidated imperialist hegemony in the new world order. From this critical perspective, two-state solutions yielded only sectional gains for the PLO without challenging the Israeli regime or its Western backers. In September 1993, PLO chairman Yasser Arafat and Israeli prime minister Yitzhak Rabin signed the first Oslo Accords, forming a basis for bilateral negotiations in which signatories recognized their 'mutual legitimate and political rights'.

105 Daniel Nassim, 'When did the PLO sell out?', *tns*, 16 June 1989.
106 'Where is South Africa going?', *tns*, 16 March 1990.
107 Jenny Graham, *The End of Apartheid? South Africa in the 1990s* (London: Junius, 1990), 38–9.
108 Interviewed by the *Irish News* in February 1990, Mafethal claimed that the ANC 'has nothing and never has had anything to do with the IRA', and that claims to the contrary left ANC leaders 'very concerned'. Eddie Veale, 'The price of diplomacy: ANC spokesman attacks IRA', *Irish Freedom: Bulletin of the Irish Freedom Movement*, May–June 1990.
109 Charles Longford, 'Freedom indefinitely postponed', *Living Marxism*, February 1993.
110 Charles Longford, 'Power to which people?', *Living Marxism*, April 1995.

The Declaration called for land in the West Bank and Gaza to be transferred gradually from Israeli to Palestinian authority, but negotiations on longer-term issues pertaining, inter alia, to borders, security, settlement, refugees and the critical question of Jerusalem, were to begin only two years after Israel withdrew from Jericho and the Gaza Strip.[111] Arafat subsequently implored Palestinians in the 'occupied territories' to renounce 'violence and terrorism'.[112] Reviewing the interim arrangements, RCP veteran Mark Ryan argued that the Palestinians had gained only attenuated autonomy in Jericho and the densely populated Gaza Strip.[113] The Palestinian left castigated Oslo for failing to delineate Palestinian statehood and territory.[114] For the intellectual Edward Said, the agreements represented an 'instrument of Palestinian surrender, a Palestinian Versailles'.[115] RCP cadre Eve Anderson similarly opined that Arafat and his comrades had renounced their struggle against Israel, marking 'the defeat of the PLO as a liberation movement'.[116]

Simultaneously, through the early 1990s, the strategic reorientation of the Irish republican movement significantly compounded the RCP's sombre assessments of the 'moral rearmament of imperialism'. 'Unconditional support' for republicanism's existential challenge to the British state was a mainstay of the party's strategy throughout the 1980s. For revolutionaries training a vanguard, it was vital for British workers to clarify and act upon their class interests by taking sides against their imperialist rulers. Especially after the ANC opened negotiations with Pretoria, and the Western coalition's war in Iraq received widespread approval in Britain, RCP theoreticians regarded the Irish republican struggle as an enduring emblem of anti-imperialism. Advertising the annual London IFM march in August 1991, party leaders elevated 'the Irish war' still further, since national liberation movements from the Middle East to southern Africa and Central America were 'now on the defensive'.[117] In 1992, reviewing a debate on Northern Ireland between Mick Hume and veteran Labour leftist Tony Benn, one radical observer could cast Hume as a 'captain of young Roundheads' to Benn's 'Digger preacher', divided politically but sharing excessive hubris: 'Both

---

111 Geoffrey R. Watson, *The Oslo Accords* (Oxford: Oxford University Press, 2000), 41.
112 Clare Fermont, 'Bookwatch: *Palestine* and the Middle East "Peace Process"', *International Socialism*, 72 (September 1996): 122.
113 Mark Ryan, *War and Peace in Ireland: Britain and the IRA in the New World Order* (London: Pluto Press, 1994), 40.
114 Grace Wermenbol, *A Tale of Two Narratives: The Holocaust, the Nakba, and the Israeli-Palestinian Battle of Memories* (Cambridge: Cambridge University Press, 2021), 30.
115 Edward Said, 'The morning after', *London Review of Books*, 21 October 1993.
116 Eve Anderson, 'Illusory peace', *Living Marxism*, October 1993.
117 'Challenge Britain's colonial war'.

seem to think that one day the mass of people will suddenly turn to them'.[118] Addressing the RCP's Towards 2000 conference later that year, IFM organizer Alex Farrell identified the republican movement as 'one of the few national liberation forces in the world still fighting'. Another veteran, Phil Murphy, told the meeting that Ireland had 'won a new relevance because it represents one of the few active anti-imperialist struggles'.[119] Declaring the Irish conflict's 'new importance', IFM leaders Eve Anderson, Fiona Foster and Kevin Kelly extolled the defiant republican campaign:

> The fight for Irish freedom should serve as an inspiration to anti-capitalists. It demonstrates that it is still possible to mount a challenge against the new imperialism.[120]

However, by the end of 1992, RCP cadres argued that the republican movement, too, had succumbed to resurgent imperialism. Damning indictments of a movement capitulating to Western diplomacy reflected two key reassessments within the RCP. First, and most saliently, cadres averred that Sinn Féin's new strategy of negotiations failed to challenge British imperialism. Second, they opined that anti-Irish prejudice was no longer a major obstacle to revolutionary politics in Britain – thus eliminating the party's established rationale for refusing to criticize republicans. Endorsed by the *ard fheis* (annual conference) in 1992, Sinn Féin's policy document *Towards a Lasting Peace in Ireland* envisioned a 'national democracy' and invited the British government, UN and EEC to find a 'peaceful resolution' to the conflict.[121] Writing in the movement's newspaper after more than two decades of 'armed struggle', senior Provisional Martin McGuinness applauded his colleague Gerry Adams 'ask[ing] the British prime minister to initiate a peace process'.[122]

For RCP theoreticians who had always endorsed the republican challenge to the British state, *Towards a Lasting Peace* indicated that the movement had admitted that its attempts to overthrow British imperialism were defeated. Republicans seeking a settlement insisted, of course, that Irish unification remained attainable through an inclusive peace process. In July 1994, for

---

118 Mike Belbin, 'Difference theory', *Troops Out: Magazine of the Troops Out Movement* 15, no. 5 (July–August 1992).
119 'The Irish war in the new world order', *Irish Freedom: Bulletin of the Irish Freedom Movement*, Autumn 1992.
120 'The new propaganda offensive', *Irish Freedom: Bulletin of the Irish Freedom Movement*, Autumn 1992.
121 Sinn Féin, *Towards a Lasting Peace in Ireland* (Dublin: Sinn Féin, 1992).
122 'Adams brings peace plan to Number 10', *An Phoblacht/Republican News*, 26 March 1992.

example, a seminal Sinn Féin conference in Letterkenny, County Donegal congratulated the leadership and

> reiterate[d] the membership's confidence that the Ard Chomhairle [party executive] will bring the national peace project to a successful conclusion.[123]

But for RCP activists who had endorsed republicanism only to the extent that it fundamentally threatened the state, Sinn Féin's overtures to supranational institutions were deplorable. *the next step*'s editorial told supporters that parleying with Westminster could lead Sinn Féin only into compromise and reformism, following 'ominous' precedents in South Africa and Palestine, where

> reactionary regimes, solidly backed by the West, are now in a position to dictate terms to corrupted and enfeebled liberation movements.[124]

Historically, party activists had tactically limited their public complaints about republicanism's ambiguous politics. In a climate of general hostility towards the IRA, the argument ran, criticizing republicans could only exacerbate national chauvinism. While muting their misgivings, RCP activists had always identified the republican movement as a classically petit-bourgeois liberation movement seeking a transfer of national power, rather than a class revolution. Propounding 'Irish freedom', the RCP championed republicanism's anti-imperialist content, rather than its particular political and tactical forms. Once activists believed that the republican movement had ceased to threaten British imperialism, they castigated a leadership milieu seeking a negotiated settlement. Writing in 1993, Eve Anderson contrasted the 'determined practical activity' of the republican grassroots, and the movement's

> shapelessness at the level of politics and ideas. . . . The republican movement has always been loose and amorphous politically.[125]

Similarly, *the next step* editor Kenan Malik delineated the party's long-standing critique of pan-class nationalism:

> We have always disagreed with the political programme and strategy of the republican movement – just as we have disagreed with the programme and strategy of every petit-bourgeois liberation movement across the globe.[126]

---

123 *The Starry Plough/An Camchéachta*, Autumn 1994.
124 'Irish liberation struggle in jeopardy', *tns*, 20 November 1992.
125 Eve Anderson, 'Who's influencing whom?', *Irish Freedom: Bulletin of the Irish Freedom Movement*, Winter 1993.
126 'The response to Warrington', *tns*, 2 April 1993.

RCP strategists interpreted Sinn Féin's response to the Downing Street Declaration of December 1993 as confirmation of republican leaders' illusions in diplomacy. Agreed by the Westminster and Dublin governments as a foundation for peace talks in Northern Ireland, the Declaration stipulated that Northern Ireland's constitutional status could only change by majority votes in both jurisdictions on the island of Ireland. Upholding this principle of consent – by which Northern Ireland's unionist majority retained an effective veto on Irish unification – the Declaration self-evidently contradicted republican orthodoxy, which held that the entire island of Ireland was the sole unit for national self-determination.[127] Yet through the winter of 1993 into 1994, republican activists discussed the Declaration in depth. Although IRA prisoners rejected the document – a 'masterpiece of ambiguity', in the words of former Sinn Féin Director of Publicity Danny Morrison[128] – they remained convinced that peace talks would yet generate a more auspicious moment.[129] Meanwhile, Sinn Féin's leadership instituted a 'peace commission', detailing eight leading party officials to study some 228 activists' written responses to the Declaration. While the commission recorded considerable frustration with the Declaration's terms on unionist consent, the overall tenor suggested that a 'peace process was possible'.[130]

Sinn Féin's modified methods, seeking multi-party talks with the Westminster and Dublin governments, prompted RCP theoreticians to obituarize the republican challenge to the state. That republicans could even contemplate a constructive response to the Downing Street Declaration dismayed Eve Anderson: the Provisional leadership, Anderson averred, was 'making concessions unthinkable a few years ago'.[131] For RCP activists, when republican militants invited international institutions to arbitrate on the Northern Ireland conflict, they forfeited their challenge to imperialism. Condemning Gerry Adams's 'evident desperation to be involved in talks with Britain', Mick Kennedy

---

127 During talks with the constitutional nationalist Social Democratic and Labour Party (SDLP) in 1988, for example, the Sinn Féin hierarchy had reaffirmed the principle that 'self-determination' referred to the 'Irish people as a whole'. Sinn Féin Publicity Department, 'Sinn Féin Document No.2' (19 May 1988), in *The Sinn Féin-SDLP Talks, January–September 1988* (Dublin: Sinn Féin, 1989).
128 'Morrison: Why we haven't said "Yes"', *Irish Press*, 25 February 1994.
129 'H-Block Submission to Sinn Féin Peace Commission', *The Captive Voice/An Glór Gafa*, Summer 1994. For intra-republican analyses of the Downing Street Declaration, see Jack Hepworth, *'The age-old struggle': Irish Republicanism from the Battle of the Bogside to the Belfast Agreement, 1969–1998* (Liverpool: Liverpool University Press, 2021), 71–81; Jack Hepworth, '"Progress will not occur if we continually adopt positions of principle": Irish republican prisoners and strategic reorientation, c. 1976-1998', *Irish Political Studies*, 37 (2022).
130 *The Starry Plough/An Camchéachta*, Autumn 1994.
131 Anderson, 'Who's influencing whom?'.

criticized republican strategists for seeking assistance from the EEC and UN, institutions at 'the cutting edge of the new imperialism'.[132]

For vanguardists who had instrumentalized the republican dynamic to polarize and animate British workers, suing for a peace settlement marked Sinn Féin's capitulation in the new world order. Once republicans demanded inclusion in all-party talks with the British government, IFM activists could no longer herald a mortal threat to the state. When even republicans seemed to consider Westminster a neutral arbiter, Fiona Foster asked a party conference in 1993, how could British radicals articulate anti-imperialist politics?[133] An activist who joined the IFM at this juncture conveys the malaise which soon pervaded the milieu:

> I hadn't been involved in the Irish Freedom Movement when it was at its height. And so I came to this when these questions were being asked. . . . I think for some people it must have been shattering. People who had spent their entire lives, political lives, absolutely involved in something as intensely as this, and then having to re-think.[134]

In the winter of 1993, when the TOM invited British radicals to contribute to the annual Bloody Sunday commemoration, RCP and RCG representatives withdrew from the organizing committee. Whereas the TOM's annual general meeting confidently held that British withdrawal was 'achievable within one year',[135] the RCP and RCG insisted that the nascent peace process represented a reverse for anti-imperialism.[136]

By August 1994, when the IRA declared a ceasefire to 'enhance the democratic peace process',[137] RCP activists had declared the historic defeat of Irish republicanism. The contrast between republican strategists' bullish pragmatism and RCP cadres' jeremiads magnified the party's perception of anti-imperialism's decline. Throughout republican ranks, militants positioned the ceasefire as a step forward on a constitutional path towards Irish unification. The IRA statement announcing the cessation declared that 'advances made by nationalists and for their democratic position' had created an 'opportunity to secure a just and lasting settlement'.[138] In west Belfast, celebratory rallies thronged the streets.

---

132 Mick Kennedy, 'Republicans under pressure', *Living Marxism*, February 1993.
133 'Lifting the lid', *Irish Freedom: Bulletin of the Irish Freedom Movement*, August 1993.
134 Former RCP supporter and IFM activist interview with the author, November 2021.
135 Christine Gare, 'Working for peace: TOM AGM', *Troops Out*, July–August 1993.
136 Pam Robinson, 'TOM and the Bloody Sunday Organising Committee', *Fight Racism! Fight Imperialism!* 116 (December 1993–January 1994).
137 'Seize the moment for peace', *An Phoblacht/Republican News*, 1 September 1994.
138 Ibid.

The mothers of two long-serving IRA prisoners were among thousands of republicans lining the Falls Road. They were witnessing 'history being made', one told a local newspaper. 'I thought I'd never see the day', said another. 'We've won and we'll go down in history'.[139]

By contrast, for RCP cadres, republicans' negotiating strategy confirmed anti-imperialism's epochal recession. By 1994, IFM organizers perceived imperialism morally rearmed not only in relation to the Gulf or the Balkans but in the conflict which had preoccupied the party so acutely throughout its lifespan. As editor of the IFM's journal, Fiona Foster devoted the magazine's final issue to

> showing that the current peace process is a sham . . . it cannot deliver the peace with justice that Irish nationalists have struggled for over the past 25 years.[140]

Shortly before disbanding, the IFM formally endorsed a veteran activist's book-length analysis of republican reorientation. In *War and Peace in Ireland* (1994), Mark Ryan argued that Sinn Féin strategists were following the PLO and ANC into regressive settlements with imperialism.[141] Even before the IRA called its ceasefire, another IFM veteran had delivered a crushing verdict:

> What the IRA has failed to win on the field of battle, Sinn Fein has no chance of winning at the negotiating table. There is no avoiding the grim reality that the 'peace process' represents a historic defeat for the liberation movement.[142]

---

139 'Ceasefire', *Andersonstown News*, 3 September 1994.
140 *Irish Freedom: Bulletin of the Irish Freedom Movement*, Summer 1994.
141 Ryan, *War and Peace in Ireland*, *passim*, especially 39, 71, 74.
142 'Ireland since the Downing Street declaration', *Irish Freedom: Bulletin of the Irish Freedom Movement*, Summer 1994.

5

'Class politics cannot be rebuilt, regenerated or rescued'

Reorientation and renewal, c. 1993–2000

After 1990, when Frank Richards declared 'for the first time this century capitalism faces neither intellectual nor practical alternatives', the RCP's tasks changed.[1] Previously, cadres campaigned to build a revolutionary vanguard in the working class. However, from the early 1990s, with no immediate prospect of forging such a movement, the party aspired to develop a novel anti-capitalist critique. Following Richards's assertion that the working class had ceased to constitute a self-conscious political agent, revolutionaries committed to formulating a new emancipatory politics.

Rejecting the Fukuyamian orthodoxy which accentuated liberal democracy's global hegemony in the early 1990s,[2] party theoreticians upheld the possibility of an alternative to capitalism and especially to its prevailing liberal forms. Activists continued to envision superseding capitalism with a human-centred alternative. In this imagined future, human ingenuity, mastering nature and technology, would liberate all from want. Cadres retained the striking ideals which had always inspired their commitment. Introducing an edition of *The Communist Manifesto* in the year that the party disbanded, Mick Hume highlighted how Marx and Engels envisioned a revolution not to reverse but to extend radically capitalism's 'achievements',

---

1 Richards, 'Midnight in the century'.
2 Revisiting his thesis in 1992, Fukuyama nuanced his original position, reframing the 'end of history' more as an inquiry than as a declaration. Nevertheless, while Fukuyama did not discount the possibility of future authoritarian challenges to liberal democracy, he maintained that the global conjuncture of the early 1990s witnessed 'a complete absence of coherent *theoretical* alternatives': Fukuyama could still narrate a 'current liberal revolution . . . something like a Universal History of mankind in the direction of liberal democracy'. Francis Fukuyama, *The End of History and the Last Man* (New York: The Free Press, 1992), 39–70, 137, 235.

overcoming nature for the good of humanity, through the rapid development of industry, science, agriculture and telecommunications.[3]

Concurrently, party theoreticians perceived an increasingly adverse conjuncture. Not only had class politics lost subjective traction at the turn of the decade, they argued; in the new world order, even the concept of humanity's transformative *potential* appeared discredited. For ideologues who had envisioned a revolution, these diagnoses had profound strategic consequences throughout the 1990s. From the turn of the decade, considering class politics suspended, they attempted to inculcate in the populace ideological independence from the state and authority. By the mid-1990s, perceiving a more foundational struggle for political subjectivity, activists vowed to assert fundamentally the history-making potential of the human subject.

Scrutinizing the final years of the RCP, this chapter examines how the party milieu transitioned from revolutionary vanguardism to bedrock campaigns to exalt the human subject. Straddling the RCP's dissolution and the network's first post-party activities, it analyses strategic and tactical shifts. Until the early 1990s, the organization accentuated key campaigns on 'the Irish war' and racism to clarify class interests. Later, in an attempt to instil an ethos of radical humanism, activists seized upon a more diverse range of political controversies. Positioning humanity as the subjective agent, rather than the passive object, of history, into the mid-1990s activists employed eclectic tactics which primarily rejected the state and authority.

The party network's strategic review gave rise to evolving organizational forms. By 1996, with class politics in abeyance and activists campaigning principally against the 'diminution of the subject', members of the RCP consensually dissolved the party. Activists resolved to maintain contact as friends and colleagues pursuing professional and political interests. From 1997, the party's erstwhile monthly review, *Living Marxism*, rebranded simply as *LM*, became the focal point for the post-party network. After ITN sued *LM* for libel in relation to the magazine's first issue, the legal defence case galvanized the former RCP network anew.

This chapter begins by assessing how, after declaring the nadir of class consciousness, the RCP attempted to forge a new anti-capitalist politics. Tracing especially the CAM's diffuse attacks upon state authoritarianism, it reviews the party's retreat into elemental radical humanism. Probing the RCP's dissolution, the following section analyses the pervasive themes of the first post-party activities. Most notably, activists fulminated against a paradigmatic 'culture of fear' which

---

3   Mick Hume introduction to Karl Marx and Frederick Engels, *The Communist Manifesto* (London: Junius/*Living Marxism*, 1996), xii–xiii.

corroded the historic potential of the human subject. The chapter concludes with the libel verdict which condemned *LM* to closure but inadvertently reinvigorated the former party network at the turn of the millennium.

'Rescuing the subject'

After declaring class politics moribund at the turn of the 1990s, the RCP leadership delineated a more fundamentally humanist radicalism. If the British working class would not identify its historical agency, revolutionaries must expound both the possibility and the necessity of a political alternative. Determined to defy an adverse balance of forces, RCP members and supporters stipulated, pace Francis Fukuyama, that the end of the Cold War did not mark the 'end of history'. Repudiating capitalist realism, activists attempted to inculcate among workers a sense of ideological independence from the state.

Following Frank Richards's assessment in 'Midnight in the Century', RCP cadres asserted that class politics were, at least temporarily, in abeyance. Simultaneously, activists maintained that humanity retained the essential ingenuity to effect political transformation. To uphold Skinner's historiographical maxim on the principle of temporal specificity, it must be noted that cadres had not mapped a thoroughgoing strategic transformation: on the contrary, with vanguardism suspended, there was a considerable disjuncture between the clarity of the party's emancipatory vision and the increasing haziness of its methods. Urging voters to 'break out of the grey', the RCP's eight candidates in the general election of 1992 retained the party's core anti-capitalism, idealizing an alternative 'system that frees people from exploitation . . . and allows everybody the opportunity to develop their talents'. But in the absence of class subjectivity, the party's principles were inevitably more clarion than its programme. Since building a revolutionary movement was not imminently plausible, candidates invited support more generally for 'the *potential* of collective action . . . to take the imaginative leap from the dull conformism of the present'.[4]

---

[4] The RCP's candidates in April 1992 were Ben Brent (Bristol West), Theresa Clifford (Sheffield Hallam), Helene Gold (Glasgow Hillhead), Susannah Hill (Vauxhall), Pam Lawrence (Manchester Gorton), Kenan Malik (Birmingham Selly Oak), Wystan Massey (Hornsey and Wood Green) and Keith Tompson (Oxford East). Additionally, Nigel Lewis stood on a WAR ticket in Holborn and St Pancras, while Alex Farrell represented the IFM in the City of London and Westminster South – the parliamentary constituency of Peter Brooke, Secretary of State for Northern Ireland. The ten candidates won a total of 985 votes. Revolutionary Communist Party, *Break Out of the Grey*. Italics added.

Championing humanity's *capacity* to supersede capitalism marked a partial retreat for the RCP in the early 1990s. Theoreticians averred that the downturn of radical subjectivity forced revolutionaries to adapt. Cadres who had formerly positioned themselves as the vanguard 'party of the future' now stressed more fundamental principles. Anticipating the general election, RCS activists Khalid Deverill and Dominic Wood positioned the party candidates 'attempt[ing] to put real political issues back onto the election agenda' to avert 'terminal boredom and political cynicism'.[5] The leadership appealed for new recruits to assert more foundationally humanity's revolutionary potential. In April 1992, the Political Committee asserted that its election campaigns were designed

> to win as many supporters as possible to the party, and it is by that criterion that we will evaluate our performance.[6]

Standing on an IFM ticket, Alex Farrell candidly prioritized raising the party's profile. 'To be honest', Farrell told an Irish diaspora newspaper,

> canvassing is not the basis of our campaign. We'd regard it as a successful campaign if we got national publicity and no votes.[7]

While class vanguardism was no longer on the agenda, the RCP's idealistic anti-capitalism continued to pique interest: during three weeks of campaigning before the general election of 1992, 200 new supporters joined the party. Futuristically expounding 'the human potential', party theoreticians pledged to equip independent thinkers to challenge mainstream political consensus:

> Our aim is to attract those with the highest aspirations and the fiercest drive for a better life, and provide them with the intellectual and organisational weapons necessary to meet those aspirations.[8]

As its public meetings, day schools and *Living Marxism* readers' groups continued apace, the party further developed its reputation for intellectual and organizational panache. In the spring of 1993, party organizers reported that nearly 3,000 people had attended a packed programme of events in the first three months of the year.[9] Newcomers relished the prospect of honing a revolutionary alternative to the straitened horizons of contemporary politics. An activist who

---

5   *Fuse – Election Special* (n.d. [c. March 1992]).
6   'The RCP and the election', *tns*, 6 March 1992.
7   'Irish Freedom candidate stands against Peter Brooke', *The Irish People*, 4 April 1992.
8   'The RCP and the election', *tns*, 1 May 1992.
9   'Perspectives for party work', *tns*, 2 April 1993.

Figure 5 Irish Freedom Movement activists at a rally for their candidate, Alex Farrell, who stood in the City of London and Westminster South constituency against Peter Brooke, Secretary of State for Northern Ireland, in the general election of April 1992. Credit: ANL/Shutterstock.

became involved with the party as a supporter in the early 1990s reflects on the RCP's appeal:

> I think the most attractive thing was the willingness to listen to and discuss and kind of engage with ideas that were unorthodox, about all kinds of things. So for someone who felt, look, things are changing in the world . . . the certainties, if they ever existed really that strongly, can't exist today . . . all the things that seemed certain have become uncertain . . . there was a sort of rigour and a questioning which I liked . . . Yeah, that attracted me, the being unorthodox, questioning, and being able to . . . engage with ideas that are outside of a particular left or right framework.[10]

Paradoxically, while the party undertook strategic review in a supposedly conservative political climate, many new supporters and members joined the organization. Kirk Leech, who spent more than a decade in the party, juxtaposed the tight-knit milieu which he joined and the membership turnover of the 1990s:

> When I joined [in 1982] I was number thirty or number forty or something. If anybody left the party it was big news. . . . It was like a club: you knew everybody.

10 Former RCP supporter and IFM activist interview with the author, November 2021.

But in the nineties, when I was on the PC, we opened up and people would join the party and leave, and sometimes you wouldn't know who they were.[11]

In his history of British Trotskyism, John Kelly suggests that by 1995, on the eve of its dissolution, the RCP claimed 380 members and between 1,100 and 1,200 supporters and contacts.[12] While it is impossible to verify the precise figures, the rise of *Living Marxism* and the party's turn to more accessible, high-profile campaigns certainly propelled the RCP's rising public prominence, as Mike Fitzpatrick recalls:

> One of the interesting features of the 1990s was that whereas left-wing movements declined in numbers, our membership actually increased, I think because of the strength of *Living Marxism*. . . . It achieved a degree of recognition and impact. . . . The world of the left was disintegrating. Our own political direction was uncertain. But in terms of the narrow organisational development, we attracted a lot of dynamic young people, many of whom are making successful careers for themselves today. So it was a strange period really.[13]

With class politics suspended, veterans of the RCP underlined the radical humanist precepts which had always undergirded their project. Among revolutionaries who repudiated the capitalist realism of the new world order, uplifting the agency of the subject was a prerequisite for renewing emancipatory politics. In 1993, Kirsten Cale organized a *Living Marxism* conference reasserting the necessity of major ideological contestation.[14] For the magazine's editor, Mick Hume, reanimating combative debate was integral to 'furthering the cause of human liberation'.[15]

For the younger generation of activists, the party that they joined in the early 1990s had already resolved that class politics were in indefinite abeyance, and committed to a more basic campaign to uphold the human potential to remake the world. Dolan Cummings recalls joining the RCP in 1992:

> By the time I joined, nobody was any under any illusions that we were fomenting revolution, or that we were meaningfully a communist party. So it was slightly odd. It felt realistic. It didn't feel like student politics, playing at it. . . . The summer conference at the time was Towards 2000 . . . I was told the conference used to be called Preparing for Power. Yeah, that just seemed like a world apart.

---

11 Kirk Leech, 7 September 2020.
12 Kelly, *Contemporary Trotskyism*, 38, 120.
13 Mike Fitzpatrick, 22 August 2020.
14 Maurice Chittenden, 'PC or not PC. . . . that was 1993's burning question', *Sunday Times*, 26 December 1993.
15 Mick Hume, 'Let's get serious', *Living Marxism*, January 1994.

By the time I joined . . . there was no question that we were preparing for power. So of course we changed that. *Towards 2000*: suitably vague, forward-looking. I remember we were always kind of around the milieu with other left-wing groups . . . and I remember someone pointing at us saying, *look at them, 'Towards 2000': they think they've got to wait til 2000 when the revolution comes*. And they were laughing. I mean, I don't want to kind of pooh-pooh all that, because it was good that people were idealistic. But our perspective then was very much that that's not what we were about; it was about trying to preserve some sort of idea of political agency. I mean, it was quite vague sometimes, but we were dealing with some very concrete political issues.[16]

Throughout the 1980s, the party's vanguardist strategy posited 'the Irish war' and anti-racism as the most salient controversies through which workers would clarify and act upon their class interests. Once the Political Committee declared that vanguardism was no longer appropriate, party strategy evolved. Rather than exposing and igniting class conflict, activities were designed more basically to exemplify ideological independence from the ruling class and the authorities more broadly. The core modus operandi – polarizing debates to clarify the issues – endured. But by the mid-1990s, to exhort rudimentary belief in the human capacity to challenge authority, cadres agitated around an ever-wider range of political furores. In 1993, the organization's internal bulletin directed activists to engage energetically with an array of political fora to oppose militarism, racism and repression:

> Only through getting people to disagree with us will we be able to enter into the kind of political discussion necessary.[17]

As the party mobilized more catholically to challenge the establishment, its most enduring front groups, the IFM and WAR, gradually became more peripheral. The IFM eventually wound up in 1994, while WAR's activities also waned. Whereas in the 1980s the RCP's anti-racism persistently posited workers' *class* interests, occasional spikes of WAR activity in the early 1990s were intended more generally to stimulate popular independence from repression and authoritarianism. For RCP cadres, official regulation was no substitute for grassroots anti-racism. In 1993, for example, when the Metropolitan Police banned British National Party (BNP) demonstrations in Brick Lane, WAR protested the proscription. It was 'much better', said WAR activist Sharmini Singh, for a committed public to oppose the BNP by

16 Dolan Cummings interview with the author, 17 February 2021.
17 'Breaking the ban', *tns*, 16 February 1993.

deal[ing] with this problem ourselves. . . . Accepting the police's right to tell people where they can and cannot stand, what they can and cannot say, is a recipe for disaster.[18]

Similarly, standing for ELWAR in a council election in Tower Hamlets the following year, Mukith Miah positioned anti-racism as an organic expression of political solidarity: 'When it comes to fighting racism, we can't trust the police or the council – it's up to us.'[19]

Seizing upon a plethora of emerging political controversies, in the mid-1990s the CAM attempted to invigorate elementary independence from authority, especially upon young people. The party's youngest front group repudiated not only the 'moral rearmament of imperialism' but also repression at home. In 1994, when the Conservatives' Criminal Justice and Public Order Bill passed the House of Commons, the CAM coordinated demonstrations.[20] Following Home Secretary Michael Howard's pledge to the Conservative Party conference of October 1993 to 'crack down on crime', the bill developed Howard's 'twenty-seven-point plan', strengthening police powers and classifying additional criminal offences.[21] Theoretically, the party front continued to situate militarism and authoritarianism firmly in a 'capitalist system that is running out of control'.[22] Leading RCP cadres upheld the Leninist critique of the state. Introducing an edition of *The State and Revolution* in 1994, James Heartfield maintained that Lenin's

> insights into the state's ultimately coercive nature, into the superficiality of parliamentary power and into the bureaucratic exercise of power . . . are strikingly confirmed in our own times.[23]

In practice, CAM protests often took a libertarian form which chimed, superficially at least, with generalized anti-government sentiment, not least among students. In October 1994, for example, the local Labour MP and some 300 people, including many from Falmouth College of Arts, joined a CAM march in Cornwall against the legislation.[24]

---

18 Edward Gorman, 'Anti-racist groups defend rights of BNP', *Times*, 29 September 1993.
19 '"It's up to us"', *Living Marxism*, May 1994.
20 *The Criminal Justice and Public Order Bill: The Control of Young People* (Campaign Against Militarism briefing, No. 8, May 1994).
21 Francesca Klug, Keir Starmer and Stuart Weir, 'Civil liberties and the parliamentary watchdog: The passage of the Criminal Justice and Public Order Act 1994', *Parliamentary Affairs*, 49 (1996): 536–49, at 540.
22 'The race against barbarism'.
23 James Heartfield introduction to V. I. Lenin, *The State and Revolution: The Marxist Theory of the State and the Tasks of the Proletariat in the Revolution* (London: Junius, 1994), xviii.
24 '"Kill the bill" march attracts 300', *Falmouth Packet*, 20 October 1994.

Party theoreticians insisted that a populace which did not resist state encroachment in public and private life would neither envisage nor enact social transformation. Activities articulating a capacious imperative – the need to resist authority and to envision an alternative society – took disparate forms. Latching on to transient controversies, in the space of three months in 1993, the CAM protested against licensing restrictions in Glasgow nightclubs,[25] police roadblocks reducing vehicular access to central London[26] and the Royal Edinburgh Military Tattoo.[27]

Reviewing its campaigns at the end of 1993, the Political Committee called for activists to intensify their heterogeneous interventions. Jettisoning an earlier, 'over-organised style of work', the leadership exhorted organizers to respond rapidly to controversies which enabled the 'ambitious' party to propagate its hostility towards officialdom.[28] Arraigning passivity towards the state, activists' libertarian initiatives spanned a multitude of issues. When Oxford City Chamber of Commerce installed security cameras in the city centre in 1994, for example, history undergraduate Cronain O'Kelly implored his fellow students to oppose the 'infringement' of 'personal privacy'. For O'Kelly, the specific case underlined the broader need to challenge authoritarianism:

> Our fear of crime is blinding us to the potential loss of freedom we will endure if these developments are not checked. The government is more than happy to stick its nose into our classrooms, bedrooms and other areas of our private lives. We can't let them get away with taking away our rights.[29]

Reflecting today, former RCP supporter Paul Flewers suggests that the 'strange' combination of party activities concealed a deeper intellectual malaise in the 1990s:

> The party reacted [to 'Midnight in the century'] in a strange sort of way. It got really furiously active on things, as if to compensate subconsciously for this admittedly implicit theoretical shift, which basically puts the whole Marxist project in jeopardy. To drive any doubts about that out of your mind, trying to get really involved in activities.[30]

---

25 'Nightclub curfew protest', *Herald*, 29 September 1993.
26 'Protesters plan action over City checkpoints', *Independent*, 5 July 1993; Richard Duce, 'City beats roadblock disruption', *Times*, 6 July 1993.
27 Erlend Clouston, 'Tourists get a glimpse of MacChismo', *Guardian*, 19 August 1993.
28 'Perspectives for 1994', *tns*, 7 January 1994.
29 Cronain O'Kelly, 'Camera alert', *Cherwell*, 11 February 1994.
30 Paul Flewers interview with the author, 3 November 2021.

Similarly, Tim Martin – a veteran supporter who served on the party's publication productions team in the early 1980s – argues retrospectively that 'Midnight in the century' dismissed class struggle prematurely. Reconstructing the moment, Martin asserts that the vanguard party still had a historical role to play:

> Stalinism is down and out. Labourism is on the back foot. You know, our main political camps of opponents are on the defensive: we should be pushing ahead. You know, I still think we should have found ways to do that . . . Frank's thesis, 'Midnight in the century', basically says the working class is not, in the short term, a vehicle for agency that we can deploy, relate to, motivate, you know. I'm drawing out the logic of that argument. But the question was: *so what, then?* . . . Many of us who differed from where some of the leading comrades like Frank have ended up now have all said, *mea culpa, we should have realised earlier than we did shifts that were taking place.*[31]

Highlighting perceived ruptures in the organization's political trajectory, these dissenting narratives deliberately highlight their subjective discomposure to underline their disaffection towards the RCP's afterlives. Rhetorical self-rebuke – 'we should have realised earlier than we did' – implicitly casts the post-party initiatives as infidelities besmirching a revolutionary tradition.

The party's revolutionary Marxism was always inherently a specific form of radical humanism. During the RCP's vanguardist period, these humanist underpinnings were almost entirely implicit but nonetheless integral. The ideal of working-class liberation rested upon the subject as the agent of its own emancipation. These revolutionary dialectics categorically identified class struggle as the motor of history: as Alan Harding argued in 1991, whereas bourgeois thinkers trumpeted human progress in general, Marxists distinctly envisioned the dictatorship of the proletariat. Nevertheless, Harding maintained, the revolutionary project rested upon an 'optimistic outlook', championing the subject's capacity to struggle for its own 'liberation'.[32]

As former RCP activists campaigned more foundationally against diminished subjectivity from the mid-1990s, their project's radical humanist underpinnings became more explicit. By the millennium, inveighing against pervasive degraded views of humans' ability to make history, the ex-RCP network espoused 'Enlightenment' values. These invocations were best understood with reference to Jonathan Israel's valuable distinction between moderate and radical Enlightenments. For Israel, the key radical Enlightenment thinkers in England

---

31 Tim Martin interview with the author, 1 December 2021.
32 Alan Harding, 'The idea of progress', *Living Marxism*, May 1991.

– most notably Tom Paine and Mary Wollstonecraft – crucially echoed Baruch Spinoza in elevating human reason, freedom of thought and expression, and democracy. Inasmuch as continental radicals – including Condorcet, Diderot and d'Holbach – expounded egalitarian universalism, RCP theoreticians had built their own revolutionary politics upon a similarly positive orientation towards the subjective agent of history.[33] Diderot's concept of human reason as the origin of all knowledge, for example – championing what Vincenzo Ferrone aptly terms the 'triumph of the individual' – provided a humanist basis for the revolutionaries and communists of the nineteenth century.[34] Since historical materialism appropriated and developed such radical humanism, it followed that after the RCP declared class politics subjectively defeated in the 1990s, the ex-party network could fall back upon these key humanist precepts and principles.

After the leadership declared class vanguardism suspended, cadres fell back upon the humanist core of their politics. Through the mid-1990s, theoreticians maintained their original critique – in essence, that capitalism could not maximize society's productive potential for the benefit of all – and sought an anti-capitalist alternative. But having pronounced class politics in abeyance, these radical anti-capitalists pinpointed a political context which was increasingly averse to any transformative project. Concomitantly, theoreticians delineated a more fundamental struggle to restore the human subject as an agent of history. In a keynote *Living Marxism* essay in 1995, the long-standing leader of the RCP asserted that in a 'peculiarly conservative and fear-ridden climate', it was crucial to 'rescue the subject, to insist . . . that people can stand up for themselves and make a difference to their circumstances'. Furedi stressed that championing subjectivity was not inherently progressive, but in a 'peculiarly conservative and fear-ridden climate', expounding its potential represented the 'precondition' for reconstituting a 'human-centred' political project.[35] As radical humanists, former RCP cadres fulminated, inter alia, against a perceived culture of fear and a reduced political realm. Challenging these developments defined the milieu's engagements between the party's twilight years in the mid-1990s and the millennium. By the turn of the millennium, radical humanists proclaimed universalism ('the subject') rather than the particular historical agency of the working class.

---

33   Jonathan Israel, *A Revolution of the Mind: Radical Enlightenment and the Intellectual Origins of Modern Democracy* (Princeton: Princeton University Press, 2010), 10–11, 19–21, 56–7, 72.
34   Vincenzo Ferrone, *The Enlightenment: History of an Idea* (Princeton: Princeton University Press, 2015), 109–10.
35   Frank Füredi, 'Rescuing the subject', *Living Marxism*, November 1995.

Transposing the RCP's perennial emphasis upon the primacy of ideas, the militant defence of subjectivity took multiple forms from the mid-1990s. Primarily, activists combined Enlightenment assertions of the human capacity for reason and knowledge and Marx's history-making subject. With class struggle in abeyance, however, the result was a radical humanism which increasingly subsumed class distinctions. *Living Marxism* science correspondents John Gillott and Manjit Kumar, for example, lauded the human potential to innovate, overcome natural challenges and improve living standards.[36] Similarly, upholding humans' ability to differentiate and evaluate contrasting ideas, the RCP leadership scorned relativism as a barrier to critical thinking.[37] Meeting in December 1994, the Political Committee aspired to reinvigorate ideological contestation: 'if all opinions are equally valid, then ignorance and insight are of equal value'.[38]

From the foundation of the party, cadres had regarded the notion of freedom under capitalism as an oxymoron. Capitalist social relations, theoreticians stipulated, gave the appearance of personal autonomy but ultimately condemned workers to a struggle for survival.[39] Following Georg Lukács, cadres considered individual freedoms under capitalism as inherently 'corrupt and corrupting ... unilateral privilege based on the unfreedom of others'.[40] Only a class revolution could maximize and marshal society's productive forces for collective benefit, securing true freedom.[41]

However, from the mid-1990s, with no imminent prospect of a revolution for 'real' liberation from want, activists espoused more disaggregated campaigns for 'freedom'. Railing against what they perceived as a mood of anti-political disengagement, RCP cadres trumpeted the emancipatory aspirations which continued to inspire them. Imploring radicals to reclaim the ideal of 'freedom', James Heartfield reminded the *LM* summer school of 1997 that the party network had always regarded independence from the state as a 'precondition' for 'any kind of progressive social change'.[42] The former RCP milieu had not reduced its ambitions to attenuated individual autonomy within the framework

---

36 John Gillott and Manjit Kumar, *Science and the Retreat from Reason* (London: Merlin Press, 1995), 147, 250.
37 Price, 'Raving Marxism'.
38 Pat Roberts, 'Problems of the new political cycle', *Living Marxism*, February 1995.
39 Mike Freeman, 'Whose freedom?', *Living Marxism*, December 1988. For another leading cadre's polemical critique of bourgeois freedom, see also *Fighting for a Change! Vote Kate Marshall*. Copy in author's possession.
40 Lukács, *History and Class Consciousness*, 315.
41 Füredi, *Soviet Union Demystified*, 9.
42 James Heartfield, 'Who made freedom a dirty word?', *LM*, June 1997.

of bourgeois democracy. Rather, in non-revolutionary circumstances, their libertarian campaigns were conceived tactically to initiate critical analyses of the state and officialdom.

To reinvigorate in the populace an independent orientation against authority, cadres redoubled their emphasis upon freedom of expression. For party strategists, struggles against repression were a bedrock for developing a political alternative. Accordingly, activists agitated widely against what one leading cadre called 'puritanical censoriousness'.[43] In 1993, for example, members of the RCP protested against the convictions connected to Operation Spanner, a high-profile police investigation into sadomasochistic activity. In December 1990, sixteen men had been convicted of assault and sentenced to terms of imprisonment of up to fifty-four months: the court rejected the defence's argument that the activity was consensual. After five of the defendants unsuccessfully appealed their case in 1993, the Birmingham RCP convened a provocative exhibition at their Angle Gallery. Risking breaching obscenity laws, the 'Sex Crimes' installation challenged the state's right to invade private life. More than 400 people had visited the exhibition on its opening day.[44] When landlords evicted the Angle Gallery from the premises, party supporters defied the order, commencing a ten-week sit-in.[45]

Although RCP activities in the mid-1990s took more diffuse forms to elevate more fundamental political ideals, their contents, in part, echoed long-standing assaults upon national chauvinism. Additionally, new stunt tactics upheld the old imperative of critical independence from the state. In 1994, for instance, on the fiftieth anniversary of D-Day, the Angle Gallery hosted an exhibition subverting what organizer Ceri Dingle termed 'nauseating celebration' and 'pornography for patriots'.[46] Similarly, from August 1994, the CAM's year of events ('No More Hiroshimas') corralled popular opposition to 'global militarisation' and 'imperialist intervention'.[47] By comparison to the party's vanguardist period, however, the class dimensions were much less explicit. Instead, activities were positioned as a rudimentary challenge to authority. Fighting 'all forms of legal, social and political restraints', Frank Richards averred, was the first task for visionaries who idealized 'the further development of the human potential'.[48]

---

43 Ann Bradley, 'Spanner and screw', *Living Marxism*, May 1993.
44 Phil Smith, 'Left-wing slant to the Angle', *Birmingham Daily Post*, 18 August 1993.
45 Philip Smith, 'Censorship row gallery digs in', *Birmingham Daily Post*, 5 October 1993.
46 Paula Whittingham, 'Gallery to stage D-Day "antidote"', *Sandwell Evening Mail*, 13 May 1994.
47 'No more Hiroshimas', *Living Marxism*, September 1994.
48 Frank Richards, 'There is an alternative', *Living Marxism*, August 1994.

Based upon such broad premises, RCP campaigns against authoritarianism and censorship gained particular traction in universities. As Evan Smith has noted, freedom of speech was a perennial commitment both of the RCP and its post-party networks.[49] But in the mid-1990s, anti-censorship activism acquired specific strategic significance. In the absence of meaningful political contestation, activists expounded *Living Marxism*'s strapline: 'ban nothing, question everything'.[50] Evan Smith has highlighted the case of the Glasgow RCS, which initiated a campaign against censorship in 1995.[51] Glasgow RCS supporters positioned freedom of speech not as an end in itself but as a precondition for a rumbustious political culture required to renew revolutionary politics. '[O]pen and free' argument, Emily Young opined, was integral to 'clarification and debate'.[52] The 'essential' importance of free speech, Liz Frayn concurred, resided in facilitating the 'space to create a real political alternative'.[53] Similarly, writing as an RCP supporter at Sussex University, Jennie Bristow regarded free speech as paramount for a critical citizenry 'deciding our own course of action independent of official interference'.[54]

Inveighing against a perceived culture of anodyne politics, cadres intensified their anti-censorship campaigns in the mid-1990s. Especially on university campuses, radicals argued that 'no platform' policies entrenched political passivity. Abhorring conformism in a circumscribed political realm, RCP activists sought more ideological contestation, not less. In 1996, when Edinburgh University students endorsed the Anti-Nazi League's calls for psychology lecturer Chris Brand, a self-professed 'scientific racist', to be sacked, Helene Guldberg repudiated the demands:

> We cannot deal with arguments we find objectionable by sweeping them under the carpet. It is only by bringing such ideas out into the open that they can be exposed and demolished.[55]

For Guldberg, clamorous calls for Brand's dismissal signified a greater problem: a 'suffocatingly censorious' political climate, in which unorthodoxies of all

---

49 Smith, *No Platform*, 8, 30, 120, 181.
50 Jennie Bristow, 'Stand up for free speech', *Living Marxism*, January 1996.
51 In 1995, the Queen Margaret Union at Glasgow University refused to affiliate the RCS, since the latter's 'ban nothing' position contradicted the union's 'no platform' restrictions on racists, sexists and homophobes. In January 1996, the RCS forced the union to convene an extraordinary general meeting, where a large majority voted for the RCS to be affiliated. Smith, *No platform*, 197; Stephen Rixon, 'Whose rights?', *Glasgow University Guardian*, 31 January 1996.
52 Emily Young, 'P.C. or free?', *Glasgow University Guardian*, 6 November 1995.
53 Liz Frayne [sic], 'Hypothetical horrors', *Glasgow University Guardian*, 31 January 1996.
54 Jennie Bristow, 'Free speech on campus', *Living Marxism*, October 1995.
55 Helene Guldberg, 'Why ban racist Brand?', *Living Marxism*, June 1996.

stripes were liable to official silencing.⁵⁶ RCP supporters aspired instead to an emboldened, combative public sphere. Jenny Jarvie of the Glasgow RCS idealized 'a climate where important issues can be debated'.⁵⁷ Similarly, in August 1996, when fifty ANL demonstrators forced a debate between Brand and RCP veteran Kenan Malik to be cancelled, Malik 'condemn[ed]' the 'attempt to suppress free speech'.⁵⁸ Without open disputation, RCP activists asserted, there could be no prospect of clarifying or fighting for a radical political alternative.

The network's paradigmatic campaigns against diminished subjectivity also pivoted upon challenging a prevailing 'culture of fear'. Theoreticians contended that until a critical mass identified the social system, and not humanity itself, as the root of its problems, there could be no meaningful challenge to that system. Railing against the 'fear' and 'historical pessimism of our times', Alan Hudson asserted that 'experimentation and exploration' were essential for 'human progress'.⁵⁹ Adam Burgess, meanwhile, invoked the supreme confidence of the eighteenth-century Enlightenment philosophes who expounded the 'possibilities of man and his inexorable progress'.⁶⁰ The 'culture of fear', Frank Furedi averred, was an inherently conservative force impeding a meaningful collective challenge to the status quo.⁶¹

A populace preoccupied with its own vulnerability, activists argued, could not countenance an alternative. *Living Marxism*'s July 1996 conference began with a weekend of events 'challenging the victim culture': Ann Bradley's session addressed the imperative of reconstituting the active subject, while Frank Furedi convened a course promoting 'humanism'.⁶² For the magazine's editor, Mick Hume, the priority was to supplant precautionary principles and reimagine 'people as problem-solvers rather than risk-avoiders'.⁶³ Revisiting *The Communist Manifesto*, Hume scorned the 'pessimistic mood' of the mid-1990s, which portrayed 'atomised, powerless individuals' incapable of acting collectively to transform their world.⁶⁴ Theorizing the 'alienated sensibility' of

56 Helene Guldberg, 'Who's the cleverest of us all?', *Guardian*, 1 May 1996.
57 Dani Garavelli, 'Students protest on race author's rights', *Scotsman*, 17 May 1996.
58 Until ANL pickets forced the cancellation, Malik and the science writer Marek Kohn were due to debate Brand at the Cyberia internet café in Edinburgh. Jubilant ANL activist Keir McKechnie celebrated having 'denied Brand the platform that he so desperately seeks'. Robert McNeil, 'Police call off Brand debate after protests from anti-Nazis', *Scotsman*, 23 August 1996.
59 Alan Hudson introduction to Frederick Engels, *Socialism: Utopian and Scientific* (London: Junius, 1996), vii, xliii.
60 Adam Burgess, *Divided Europe: The New Domination of the East* (London: Pluto Press, 1997), 87.
61 Frank Furedi, *Culture of Fear: Risk-Taking and the Morality of Low Expectation* (London: Cassell, 1997).
62 'Challenging the victim culture', *Living Marxism*, July–August 1996.
63 Mick Hume, 'Forget poverty, let's talk about the real issues', *Living Marxism*, July–August 1996.
64 Mick Hume introduction to Marx and Engels, *Communist Manifesto*, xv, xxi–xxii.

the late twentieth century, Andrew Calcutt inveighed against a political zeitgeist which cast human beings as atomized individuals, helpless and passive, and unable to act collectively, less still to effect social transformation.[65]

Fulminating against societal fragmentation, cadres also regarded identity politics as innately divisive and conservative. With echoes of Jürgen Habermas's analysis, RCP veterans highlighted how the 'new social movements' emanating from the New Left diverged from the class categories of earlier political contestation.[66] During their vanguardist phase, cadres lambasted identity politics for deviating from paramount class distinctions: writing at the dawn of the 1990s, a member of the Political Committee castigated these 'petit-bourgeois . . . individualistic preoccupations'.[67] By the mid-1990s, activists scorned identity politics less in terms of class per se and more generally as a barrier to social transformation. As far as party veterans were concerned, accentuating the particular and the immutable rendered the subject an atomized object of history. 'Anti-humanist . . . celebration of "identity" – as a child, or a black woman, or a gay man', Frank Furedi warned, 'means emphasising who you are rather than what you could be'.[68] For Mick Hume, meanwhile, identitarianism epitomized the diminished, inert subject in an epoch of reaction:

> 'identity' politics . . . amounts to little more than reconciling yourself to what you are stuck with, and celebrating the powerlessness of the individual in capitalist society.[69]

Veterans of the RCP similarly castigated environmentalism as a facet of the politics of diminished subjectivity. Those who lamented humanity's impact upon nature, former cadres asserted, epitomized societal misanthropy. Cadres had always dismissed the suggestion that humans should defer to 'natural' limits upon production. Recalling *The Communist Manifesto*'s qualified praise for the industrial revolutions harnessing resources – albeit inefficiently and inequitably – RCP cadres had similarly envisioned revolutionizing production for universal

---

65 Andrew Calcutt, *Arrested Development: Pop Culture and the Erosion of Adulthood* (London: Bloomsbury, 1998), *passim*. See especially 23, 107–8, 241.
66 Writing in 1981, the German philosopher Jürgen Habermas offered a taxonomy of 'new social movements' emerging from the global cycle of protest of the late 1960s. For Habermas, the 'new' environmental, feminist and youth movements, for example, departed from the 'old' capital-labour struggles and prioritized instead questions of culture, lifestyle and identity. Jürgen Habermas, 'New social movements', *Telos*, 49 (1981): 33–7.
67 Knight, *Stalinism in Crisis*, 164.
68 Frank Füredi, 'PC – the philosophy of low expectations', *Living Marxism*, December 1993.
69 Mick Hume, 'A revolutionary project for our times', *Living Marxism*, July–August 1995.

benefit.[70] Aspiring to a social revolution to supersede capitalism's constraints, Frank Richards castigated 'profoundly conservative' environmentalists who sought only 'survival'.[71] Especially during their vanguardist phase, the party milieu regarded environmentalism as a pessimistic vogue among 'intellectuals who have lost faith in the prospects for a revolutionary transformation of society'.[72]

Throughout the mid-1990s, the RCP's erstwhile exponents located environmentalist politics in a wider regressive zeitgeist. Accusing green activists of propagating anti-humanism, veterans of the party drew upon Marx's early critique of 'primitive communism'. For Aidan Campbell, environmentalists represented a 'profoundly conservative and reactionary force' whose calls for restraint in production and development reflected 'the general primitivist sentiments of our times'.[73] *Living Marxism*'s science correspondents, John Gillott and Manjit Kumar, accentuated the progressive potential of rational scientific inquiry. Repudiating the 'fatalism' of those who abnegated experimentation, Gillott and Kumar averred that upholding the scientific method meant reinstating the human capacity for rational, reasoned action.[74]

Although the RCP disbanded in 1996, veterans retained a radical humanist commitment to the transformative potential of scientific advancement and technological innovation. But these positions became mired in renewed rancour in 1997, when Furedi and Gillott appeared as talking heads on a controversial documentary broadcast on Channel 4. Polemicizing against environmentalism, *Against Nature* cast green politics as irrational and misanthropic and caused major controversy. The following year, for example, the Independent Television Commission watchdog ordered Channel 4 to apologize for distorting, by selective editing, the views of four leading conservationists.[75] Frank Furedi's contributions elaborated themes from his book *Population and Development* (1997), which scorned ecologists' 'Malthusian world view' of 'every human being' as a 'potential

---

70 For Karl Marx and Frederick Engels, capitalist production could neither maximize productive potential nor avoid profound environmental damage. Nevertheless, *The Communist Manifesto* acknowledged how industrialization had transformed humanity's relationship with the natural environment. Marx and Engels, *Communist Manifesto*, 17–18.
71 Frank Richards, 'Red and Green won't go', *Living Marxism*, October 1989.
72 *Preparing for Power: Revolutionary Communist Party Summer School 1989*, 13.
73 For Marx, 'crude' primitive communism, far from envisioning universal emancipation, promoted a 'return to the *unnatural* simplicity of the *poor*, unrefined man who has no needs and who has not even reached the stage of private property, let alone gone beyond it'. Karl Marx, 'Economic and philosophical manuscripts' (1844). Marx, *Early Writings*, 346; Aidan Campbell, *Western Primitivism: African Ethnicity – A Study in Cultural Relations* (London: Cassell, 1997), 217, 222–6.
74 Gillott and Kumar, *Science and the Retreat from Reason*, 33, 218.
75 Paul McCann, 'Channel 4 told to apologise to Greens', *Independent*, 2 April 1998.

polluter'. Recapitulating the revolutionary critique of environmentalist 'fatalism', Furedi attacked the 'limited view of human potential' and asserted that scientific development could overcome crises of production.[76] When the environmental activist George Monbiot denounced the RCP contributors to *Against Nature* as a 'tiny group of cranks' who blithely asserted that climate change was 'nothing to worry about',[77] Furedi accused Monbiot of 'low-life' ad hominem attacks. As a 'libertarian humanist', the ex-RCP leader regarded apocalyptic green politics as an anti-humanist component of a 'general Culture of Fear that prevails in society'.[78]

'No easy solutions'

Perhaps paradoxically, diagnosing a diminished political sphere in the mid-1990s strengthened RCP activists' perception of their own independence. While cadres perceived an increasingly adverse external conjuncture, for the most part, the organization remained unified: some 97 per cent of respondents to a supporters' survey in 1993 endorsed the party's 'theory and ideas'.[79] A pervasive sense of intellectual distinction endured, too: in an organization whose members had always especially stressed ideational acuity, the leadership remained confident that the 'clarity of the RCP's analysis allows us decisively to enter contemporary political debate'.[80]

In a supposedly dormant political realm, reasserting the human potential imbued cadres with a heightened sense of ideological alterity. When activists reviewed the party's direction in 1995, Fiona Foster's contributions especially highlighted the profound perspicacity which many veterans located in their milieu. The RCP, Foster wrote, informed her 'framework for understanding the world . . . there but for the grace of the RCP go I'. On the one hand, Foster implicitly asserted that the revolutionary project was forlorn: without a critical mass in society, the party had experienced increasing isolation. Simultaneously, Foster's remarkable testimony captured an unstinting, if abstract, belief in the human potential to change the world. Moreover, contrasting her dynamic network to 'the kind of morose and depressive and fatalistic attitudes which

---

76 Frank Furedi, *Population and Development: A Critical Introduction* (Cambridge: Polity Press, 1997), 149, 151, 161.
77 George Monbiot, 'The revolution has been televised', *Guardian*, 18 December 1997.
78 'For nature and against labels', *Guardian*, 19 December 1997.
79 'The RCP and you', *tns*, 19 March 1993.
80 'Reportback from the Political Committee', *tns*, 14 May 1993.

permeate the world of our workmates and families', the veteran activist evinced an almost messianic commitment to arming

> people with a new set of faculties ... to give people a life ... to go out there and save people from this level of unhappiness, confusion and cynicism ... I do feel that being one of the few people in the world who can really understand imposes a certain burden and definite isolation.[81]

By this juncture, the subjective perception of organizational distinction was indivisible from the party's objective marginality. Activists throughout the strata of the RCP warned that the post-vanguardist party was in danger of lapsing into an entirely negative critique. The Political Committee's report of January 1994 declared the party's difficulties:

> While we are often very good at knocking down our opponents' arguments we are less prepared to make our own case sound convincing.[82]

Here lay the tension between the party's emphasis upon transformational ideas and its assessment of diminished subjectivity. Without a singular programmatic focus, calls for a new Enlightenment risked evaporating into abstraction.

From the party's foundation, RCP cadres had stressed the humanist bedrock of their revolutionary politics. RCP theoreticians had always drawn overtly upon Marxism's Enlightenment antecedents. As Vincenzo Ferrone has percipiently argued, Marx borrowed from and transcended Hegelian idealism: historical materialism specified class conflict as the key motor of history and the working class as the revolutionary agent.[83] Drawing upon Hegel's Enlightenment dialectics, Marx's praxis stressed the active dimension of the subject. Adumbrating class consciousness, Marx asserted that workers' conceptual lives were not reducible to principles of individual psychology but were rooted in social relations of production. Marx upheld Hegel's 'idealism' insofar as it configured human perception and contemplation as active processes. But in his 'Theses on Feuerbach', Marx further underlined subjectivity's transformative 'practical' implications:

> It is men who change circumstances. ... The philosophers have only *interpreted* the world, in various ways; the point is to change it.[84]

---

81   Fiona Foster, 'Contribution to OTAM' (n.d. [c. 1995]). Copy in author's possession.
82   'Perspectives for 1994'.
83   Ferrone, *Enlightenment*, 23.
84   Marx, *Early Writings*, 422–3.

RCP cadres hailed the Enlightenment emphasis upon the subject's intellect and idealism. But by the mid-1990s, the party's ultimate determination to transform the world – 'the point is to change it' – was liable to be lost in negative broadsides against a pre-political age. Activists lamenting diminished subjectivity faced a similar dilemma to that which preoccupied the Enlightenment philosophes of the late eighteenth century: Was the subject to be championed in terms of its ontological capacity for reason, or, more radically, as a transformative agent of history? For example, Immanuel Kant's essay 'What Is Enlightenment?' – first published in 1784 – railed against paternalistic officialdom and implored readers to employ their reason to overcome intellectual immaturity. However, while Kant seminally expounded the subject's capacity for independent, rational reason and self-understanding, his political implications were more ambiguous: troubled by questions of moral agency, Kant bridled at justifications for resisting despotism.[85]

For some supporters, a party retreating into radical humanist principles – asserting the potential for transformation rather than building the movement per se – was shorn of its raison d'être. Such activists were dissatisfied with the party's ongoing search for a new anti-capitalism. *Living Marxism* editor Mick Hume admitted in 1994 that correspondents to the magazine increasingly demanded a specific strategic programme.[86] Addressing an internal debate in 1995, Ben Brack averred that the party's 'lack of political direction' had generated 'a deep sense [of] demoralisation' in the ranks. 'Blandly' espousing human reason and rationality 'in seeming abstraction', Brack opined, represented a 'lack of progress in constructing an alternative to the status quo'.[87] *Living Marxism* readers in Brighton and Oxford, meanwhile, charged the organization with failing to delineate a cohesive radical methodology.[88] Cancelling his subscription to the magazine in 1996, one former supporter charged the RCP network with regressing from a revolutionary critique into 'hysterical' pleas 'for "bourgeois liberty", as Marx would have termed it'.[89] Echoing the influential German Marxist Karl Korsch, these dissenters implied that solely negative critique marked a regression from Marxism's active, transformative core.[90]

---

85 Immanuel Kant, *An Answer to the Question: 'What Is Enlightenment?'* (London: Penguin, 2009), 1–11.
86 'Negative Marxism', *Living Marxism*, March 1994.
87 *Our Tasks and Methods: Discussion No. 1* (n.d. [c.1995]). Copy in author's possession.
88 'Negative Marxism'; David R. Clarke, 'What alternative?', *Living Marxism*, September 1994.
89 Dave Richards, 'So farewell then. . .', *Living Marxism*, December 1996–January 1997.
90 Upholding the unity of theory and practice, Korsch asserted that Marx's theory of history provided an inherently dynamic analytical lens, not for 'contemplative enjoyment of the existing world but

Further from the organization's hierarchy, a network of supporters grew disillusioned with what they regarded as an intellectual and strategic impasse. For these activists, the RCP's post-vanguard phase had produced only a conceptional emphasis upon undifferentiated, classless 'human potential'. As one of their number recalls, discontent surfaced internally in 1993 and 1994, when the party leadership organized a series of meetings for supporters:

> People who'd been on the edge of the party for years were asked where they thought the party was going. . . . Various people, long-time supporters . . . got up, and we were denouncing the way the party was going, furiously. The upshot was we just dropped out. I was going to write something and then I thought, *why bother? This party's had it. Why waste my time?* I always remember that meeting. They were shocked, the party people there. But we all dropped out, because we thought, *well we're not going to shift these guys*. It wasn't members, it was supporters. . . . After what happened at the forum, I wouldn't be surprised if [the leaders] were glad to see the back of us. We were of no use to them with our old-hat Marxism.[91]

Moving from revolutionary vanguardism towards broader, ostensibly more popular campaigns appealed less to one former activist, who perceived a growing

> sense of routinism, a shift away from the vanguard-building issues of gender, race, and Ireland, towards what I considered to be more liberal, opportunist, and less clarificatory issues around peace and free speech and these sorts of things.[92]

In the summer of 1995, the RCP convened national conferences to debate the party's direction. To stimulate the discussion, cadres returned to one of their foundational documents, *Our Tasks and Methods*. Senior cadres largely reiterated their commitment to a struggle for subjectivity in an age of reaction. The declining class consciousness which Frank Richards had adumbrated in 1990, they argued, had precipitated the further diminution of the subject. Summarizing the first round of discussions, party veteran Pam Lawrence declared that after the 'suspension of class struggle', there were 'no easy solutions' for revolutionaries in a society which generally saw 'all problems . . . resulting from humans themselves rather than [from] the social system'. Almost two decades after the RCT adopted *Our Tasks and Methods*, a more junior activist, Cronain O'Kelly, contrasted the political flux and possibilities

---

its active transformation'. Karl Korsch, 'Why I am a Marxist' (1934), in *Three Essays on Marxism* (London: Pluto Press, 1971), 61.
91 Paul Flewers, 3 November 2021.
92 Former RCP member interview with the author, November 2021.

of the 1970s and a 'period of what appears to be unparalleled reaction' in the mid-1990s. Eschewing voluntaristic responses to such adverse conditions, discussants identified as their key task fundamentally championing the human potential to remake the world. In the prevailing conditions, Hilary Salt opined, it was 'impossible' to espouse an 'objective need' for change or to position the working class as its agent: the first imperative was to elevate the subject and the 'possibility of changing society'.[93]

Members overwhelmingly wished to sustain what they considered a unique political and philosophical tradition. Concurrently, many regarded the party itself as an obsolete, even anachronistic, form. For Frank Furedi, *Living Marxism* had established itself as a bulwark against depoliticization and diminished subjectivity. But the RCP, Furedi declared, had been 'too unsystematic' and failed to overcome 'disjointed forms of consciousness'. Positioning his milieu in an essentially defensive struggle for radical humanism, Furedi also lambasted deteriorating standards of debate within the organization:

> At present there is a philistine tendency to discuss without preparation and reflection. . . . Most discussions are too reactive and too tactical.[94]

Pithily summarizing the debate which precipitated the RCP's dissolution, Dolan Cummings narrates the post-party transition as necessary to preserve and reanimate its ideological distinction:

> It was those kind of discussions . . . *if we want to maintain this tradition we're going to have to find a different way of doing it*. And there was a recognition that the party structure wasn't really appropriate to the opportunities that were available.[95]

Especially for long-standing cadres, adverse external conditions made it increasingly essential to uphold fundamental principles via different political forms, as Phil Mullan recalls:

> We had this thing which nobody wanted to just ditch and throw out: we had this camaraderie, this collective intellectual framework and this collective intellectual coherence. It seemed the natural thing to do for us to say, *well, that organisational form is becoming more and more of a barrier . . . to pursue the independence of thinking and the battle of ideas which has always been part of our*

---

93 *Our Tasks and Methods: Discussion No. 1* (n.d. [c. 1995]).
94 Ibid.
95 Dolan Cummings, 17 February 2021.

tradition.... We were in this pre-political phase: that was a phrase I remember from the 1990s.⁹⁶

From this perspective, the organizational transition was not the obverse of political survival but rather its vital corollary. As Alan Hudson reflects, the vestiges of a vanguardist party were not necessarily apt for the foundational task of reasserting humanity's history-making potential:

> You couldn't find a form of organisation specifically able to address that problem. You don't need a party in that sense to do that. But you do need an intellectual and coherent tradition.⁹⁷

In 1996, after a series of internal meetings, members of the RCP voted, by an overwhelming majority, to disband the party. Frank Furedi later remembered the decision provoking among members

> a kind of combination of a little bit of shock with relief, you know. People felt that this was the time to do it. I was actually quite surprised by the lack of opposition to it.... I think many of us felt that we had lost our dynamic or no longer had that kind of mojo that we had beforehand.... We felt that there was a kind of insurmountable chasm between us and the world outside which you couldn't just voluntaristically minimise or resolve.⁹⁸

Although closing the organization after fifteen years was a momentous decision, it prompted many former activists to pursue their politics through looser contacts with old comrades. Kirk Leech remembers the transition as both jarring and crucial for veterans to renew their critical analyses:

> In the end I think we worked out we needed to do it. A lot of us struggled to find our way. But we took the decision, you know, and I remember the office got cleaned out, we burned all this stuff, and we got rid of loads of things without any kind of emotion.... People went off and organised their own, often individual projects. Some, *spiked* and whatever, became quite successful. Other things and some people just disappeared from political and public life.⁹⁹

Several activists swiftly launched grassroots campaign groups to pursue their special interests. Organizing small-scale public events and authoring press polemics, some of these libertarian initiatives were rather ephemeral. For example, from 1996, under the flag of Families For Freedom, Tiffany Jenkins,

96 Phil Mullan, 11 March 2021.
97 Alan Hudson, 22 October 2021.
98 Frank Furedi, 12 February 2021.
99 Kirk Leech, 7 September 2020.

Kate Moorcock and Bernadette Whelan wrote to national newspapers, arguing that overprotecting children stultified their experiential development.[100] Meanwhile, Carlton Brick and Duleep Allirajah founded the Libero network to

> campaign for freedom in football and . . . give two fingers to the increasingly intrusive regulation of the game, on and off the pitch.[101]

Writing on the eve of the RCP's dissolution, a former member of the party recapitulated the radical humanist core of the milieu's Marxism:

> capitalism constrains [the individual's] creativity and abilities, not only by forcing the mass of people to struggle to survive, but also by making a personality creative only in so far that it is commercially realisable.[102]

The same year, *Living Marxism* published *The Point Is to Change It: A Manifesto for a World Fit for People*. The text represented the party's closing statement. Introducing the book, Mick Hume reiterated cadres' abiding anti-capitalist critique:

> We are no less fervent than ever in our rejection of capitalist exploitation, our criticism of a society which puts profit before human needs, or our opposition to the system of global imperialism that condemns millions to misery.

But for revolutionaries who aspired to a world transformed, the manifesto declared, the most immediate problem was 'the diminished role of *subjectivity*'. For contributors to the ongoing magazine, therefore, the first priority was asserting the 'human potential to change things for the better'.[103]

Reflecting on the end of the RCP more than twenty-five years later, veterans form two broad positions. For the majority, including most of the erstwhile leadership, dissolving the party was a necessary response to changed objective circumstances. With hindsight of the party milieu's complex but enduring trajectory, these retrospectives assert that dropping an outdated organizational form was imperative for activists to maintain their political 'tradition'. For Norman Lewis, deciding to disband was

---

100 Bernadette Whelan, 'Wheen under the whip', *Guardian*, 5 November 1996; Kate Moorcock, 'Put your trust in Santa Claus', *Independent*, 19 November 1996; Tiffany Jenkins, 'Age of anxiety', *Independent*, 27 October 1997.
101 'Cry freedom', *Observer*, 22 December 1996.
102 Suke Wolton, 'Afterword: On the problem of anti-humanism', in Suke Wolton (ed.), *Marxism, Mysticism and Modern Theory* (Basingstoke: Macmillan, 1996), 176.
103 LM, *The Point Is to Change It: A Manifesto for a World Fit for People* (London: Junius, 1996), xii, 67, 102.

the difference between clinging on to the past and understanding that the world had changed. We never simply repeated the politics and theory of the left. We had always developed an independent intellectual tradition, but which now had to be adapted to circumstances beyond our control. We had lost, basically. And what was left was to understand the impact that this was going to have on subjectivity, on politics. It was adapting to change, not dogmatism. We now had to fight for the humanist impulses underpinning everything we had attempted to do but in new ways, even though none of us had any idea what that would mean in practice.

Far from terminating the party's politics, Lewis argues, disbanding the RCP enabled the network to

> continue and develop the ideas in terms of how politics and class interests and society were going to change and move forward. This is a really important point for me because it is exactly the point that attracted me to the RCP in the first place: the fact that it wasn't just a superficial repetition of what had happened in the past. . . . This was a real attempt to engage with reality and to change reality in circumstances, as Karl Marx once said, not of our own making. It's a point so many deliberately misinterpret. We were not conspiring to take over any institutions through stealth. Instead, we became a network of individuals, bound by our common experience of politics and intellectual commitment who now had to navigate a new world.[104]

Mike Fitzpatrick similarly recalls former cadres committing to maintain informal connections and develop their politics in a post-party era:

> When we finally wound up the RCP in 1996 some said we should have done this sooner. But we felt that we owed something to the people who had become engaged in the party and had joined with us in this process of transformation, and we couldn't just abandon our legacy. There was a bit of pig-headedness about that, but pig-headedness was quite important to our whole project right from the beginning. [. . .] It was a shift from challenging the labour movement to challenging wider society and to engaging with wider society – and in some respects it's a pity we didn't make that move earlier, actually. There was this cliché about the dead hand of labourism. And the dead hand of labourism was a real force in British political life and to some extent it held its dead hand over us, because we remained part of its shell for longer than we should have.[105]

---

104 Norman Lewis, 16 February 2021.
105 Mike Fitzpatrick, 22 August 2020.

Conversely, for a cohort of disillusioned former RCP supporters, the dissolution was the coup de grâce for an organization beset by internal malaise. Whereas most members of the RCP pointed to objective forces frustrating the revolutionary project, these dissenters largely attributed the party's defeat to its internal reorientation. Once the party leadership abandoned class vanguardism in the early 1990s, these former supporters argue, the RCP was bound to degenerate into classless abstraction. For one of the critical number, veteran south London supporter Paul Flewers, the end of the RCP signalled not only adverse external conditions but the intellectual bankruptcy of formerly incisive theoreticians:

> The last party thing I went to was the '97 summer school, about the time the party dissolved. It was pathetic. It was tiny: it was only about three days long. But what really shocked me was the decline in the theoretical quality, the intellectual quality. I hadn't been to a party meeting for a year or so. And I thought, *what has happened to these people?* It was like the whole lot of them had been lobotomised. People who were intelligent were now coming out with banalities.[106]

Depicting a dramatic disjuncture, Flewers casts his erstwhile comrades signally departing from their independent revolutionary theory and practice. Having already started to drift from the party by the mid-1990s, Flewers and other disenchanted supporters did not protest the decision to disband.

By May 1997, when Tony Blair led the Labour Party back into government after seventeen years of Conservative rule, the erstwhile leaders of the RCP had performed the final obsequies for class politics. 'Social change', Mick Hume lamented, was 'off the agenda'.[107] The concept of class revolution, Frank Füredi declared, could not be 'reinvented, rebuilt, reinvigorated or rescued'.[108] For revolutionaries who remained unreconciled to the status quo, it was crucial to reanimate first principles, asserting the human capacity to change the world.

'Ban nothing, question everything'

After the RCP disbanded, many of the friends and comrades who had formed its inner circle vowed to maintain contact, pursuing their own political and

---

106 Paul Flewers, 3 November 2021.
107 Mick Hume, 'Thou shalt not', *LM*, June 1997.
108 Frank Füredi, 'Class politics cannot be rebuilt, regenerated or rescued today', *LM*, May 1997.

professional initiatives. Through their individual activities and their magazine – rebadged simply as *LM* in 1997 – they resolved to propagate a radical humanist politics. For its co-publisher Claire Fox, *LM* systematically challenged a depoliticized climate in the late 1990s:

> I really loved the idea of *LM*. We'd got to a point where we'd got a readership, a subscription, a subscriber base, all these great writers. No party. Also, at this point, you could say we were going beyond left and right with some seriousness. How would we maintain a network of these individuals?[109]

Cohering the former RCP network into its post-party phase, the rebranded magazine synthesized activists' opposition to diminished subjectivity. Inasmuch as it was designed to confront contemporary orthodoxies in relation, for example, to the culture of fear, the magazine was intended to court controversy. From 1997, however, *LM* was at the centre of a dispute of an exceptional order of notoriety.

ITN's libel case against *LM* originated in February 1997, when the first issue of the rebranded magazine carried an article titled 'The Picture That Fooled the World'.[110] Written by freelancer Thomas Deichmann, the polemic had originally been published in the fringe left-wing German magazine *Novo Argumente* – of which Deichmann was the founding editor-in-chief. The photographic 'picture' in question dated from August 1992, during the early stages of the Bosnian War. It depicted Fikret Alić, an emaciated Bosnian Muslim, behind a barbed wire fence at the Bosnian Serbs' Trnopolje internment camp. The infamous image of Alić appeared on the front pages of the *Daily Mirror* and *Daily Star*, adjacent to headlines drawing explicit parallels with the Holocaust.[111] In subsequent reportage imploring the West to act against the Serbs, the photograph became a visual refrain.

More than four years later, *LM* asserted that ITN journalists Penny Marshall and Ian Williams had misrepresented the situation at Trnopolje. Alić and his fellow Bosnian Muslims, Thomas Deichmann alleged, were

---

109 Claire Fox, 1 September 2020.
110 Thomas Deichmann, 'The picture that fooled the world', *LM*, February 1997. For a detailed academic analysis examining and contextualizing the legal case, see Campbell, 'Atrocity, memory, photography, part 1'; Campbell, 'Atrocity, memory, photography: part 2'. For a more partisan but nevertheless valuable overview of the ITN team's coverage and the subsequent trial, see Stewart Purvis and Jeff Hulbert, *When Reporters Cross the Line: The Heroes, the Villains, the Hackers and the Spies* (London: Biteback, 2013), 1–39.
111 'Belsen 92: The picture that shames the world', *Daily Mirror*, 7 August 1992; 'Belsen 1992', *Daily Star*, 7 August 1992.

not imprisoned behind a barbed wire fence.... It was not a prison, and certainly not a 'concentration camp', but a collection centre for refugees, many of whom went there seeking safety and could leave again if they wished.[112]

In their assertions to the contrary, Deichmann argued, the reporters had distorted reality and contributed to an anti-Serb media chorus. When *LM* refused to pulp every copy of the magazine and pay damages, ITN issued writs for libel against editor Mick Hume and publisher Helene Guldberg.[113] *LM* responded belligerently, demanding that ITN's team be stripped of prestigious awards won for their coverage of the Bosnian War.[114]

Deichmann's article sat firmly within *Living Marxism* correspondents' critique of the 'journalism of attachment'.[115] Between 1992 and 1995, RCP veterans routinely charged journalists including Martin Bell and Roy Gutman with producing emotive, partisan reports in the Balkans. As far as *Living Marxism* writers such as Joan Phillips were concerned, impassioned coverage reduced the war to moralistic binaries. Reports portraying the Bosnian Serbs as uniquely malevolent, the argument ran, bolstered the Western appetite for military intervention.[116] For Mick Hume, exponents of 'attachment' were a 'menace to good journalism'. When 'crusading' war reporters depicted 'exclusively moral struggles in which Right fights Wrong', the *LM* editor asserted, they simultaneously obscured complex causality and justified Western

---

112 Deichmann, 'The picture that fooled the world'. As David Campbell's forensic analyses have demonstrated, in court in 2000, Deichmann and Hume modified the article's emphases. Under cross-examination, Hume told the court that there had 'never been any question in my opinion or in the article that I published that this [Trnopolje] camp was anything other than a grim place at which there were beatings, there were killings and there were rapes. There has never been any question of that. We have never argued contrary to that'. Revisiting his article, Deichmann told Court 14: 'I do not say that they at the time were able to leave and there – you know, there were fences, there were guards, which we have seen here, armed guards'. Hume's and Deichmann's cardinal distinction was between Trnopolje and the Nazi concentration camps of the 1930s and 1940s. Hume testified that the article's 'primary purpose was not to enter a discussion about what this camp was, it was about what the camp was not, a Nazi-style concentration camp, which the world took it to be on the strength of those ITN reports. It is about what the camp was not. It was not a Nazi-style concentration camp'. Similarly, Deichmann told the court that Trnopolje might have been 'awful', but was not 'a place like Auschwitz and Belsen where mass extermination is taking place'. Campbell, 'Atrocity, memory, photography, part 1', 24; Campbell, 'Atrocity, memory, photography, part 2', 147.
113 Vanessa Thorpe, 'ITN "may sue over article"', *Independent on Sunday*, 26 January 1997.
114 *LM Demands that ITN News Team Is Stripped of Awards*. LM press release, 10 February 1997. Copy in author's possession.
115 Eschewing dispassionate 'bystander' reportage, veteran war correspondent Martin Bell coined the 'journalism of attachment' to signify commentary which 'cares as well as knows', accentuating the most personal and tragic dimensions of human experience in conflict. Greg McLaughlin, *The War Correspondent* (London: Pluto Press, 2002), 43.
116 See, for example, Joan Phillips, 'The invention of a Holocaust', *Living Marxism*, September 1992; Joan Phillips, 'Gutman: Still guilty', *Living Marxism*, August 1993.

intervention.[117] In 1994, several RCP veterans formed the London International Research Exchange as one of their milieu's first non-party organizational offshoots. Promoting 'critical journalism and research', the new group's first major project critiqued contemporary war reportage.[118]

Especially after ITN issued its writ in 1997, *LM* writers insisted that they did not take sides in the Balkans but absolutely opposed Western intervention – and what they regarded as contributory anti-Serb media bias. When *LM* published Deichmann's interview with Bosnian Serb leader Radovan Karadžić – who was indicted in 1995 by the International Tribunal at The Hague, for genocide and crimes against humanity – Hume maintained that his magazine did 'not carry a torch [for] Serbian nationalists'; rather, *LM* sought to destabilize portrayals of the conflict as 'Good v[ersus] Evil'.[119] Replying to a critic in the *London Review of Books*, Hume similarly reiterated that his magazine harboured no illusions in the Serbian leadership.[120] Taking the stand in Court 14 in 2000, Hume reasserted his 'non-partisan' position on the Balkans' local conflicts:

> I had never taken any side in the war in Yugoslavia and nor had my magazine ever taken any side ... my interest in writing about it wasn't to do with the local conflict itself so much as ... [in] the discussion of that conflict.[121]

Defending the article throughout the legal proceedings, *LM*'s representatives positioned Deichmann's piece as a vital rejoinder to a media campaign which demonized the Serbs. For *LM*'s supporters, ITN's accusations epitomized a narrow, censorious political sphere. When ITN editor-in-chief Richard Tait complained that Deichmann's article had besmirched his reporters' reputation,[122] Mick Hume retorted that Tait and his colleagues had become 'lost' in a 'moronic ... moral crusade over Bosnia'.[123] Shortly before the trial commenced, stressing

---

117 Mick Hume, *Whose War Is It Anyway? The Dangers of the Journalism of Attachment* (London: Informinc, 1997), 5, 8, 15, 25.
118 London International Research Exchange, *Journalists at War* (n.d. [1994]); London International Research Exchange flyer (n.d. [1995]). Copies in author's possession.
119 Mick Hume, 'Media monsters', *LM*, July–August 1997.
120 Hume specifically rebutted Michael Stewart's suggestion that 'the *Living Marxism* crowd... want us to believe that the camps of Omarska, Trnopolje and elsewhere are inventions of the world capitalist conspiracy against "socialist Yugoslavia"'. Michael Stewart, 'Atone and move forward', *London Review of Books*, 11 December 1997; Mick Hume, 'Socialist as Surbiton', *London Review of Books*, 1 January 1998.
121 Mick Hume quoted in Independent Television News (ITN), Penny Marshall and Ian Williams versus *Living Marxism* (*LM*), Michael (Mick) Hume and Helene Guldberg, 28 February–14 March 2000 (hereafter, ITN et al v. *LM* et al transcript). Day 8 AM transcript, 30, lines 19–33. Available at balkanwitness.glypx.com/LM-Trial-Transcript/transcript-day8-am.pdf (accessed 17 January 2022).
122 Richard Tait, 'We did not fool the world', *Spectator*, 24 May 1997.
123 Mick Hume, 'Faking the news?', *Spectator*, 31 May 1997.

Figure 6 Claire Fox (left) and Helene Guldberg (right) at the offices of *LM* magazine, 10 January 2000. Credit: Mark Chilvers/Independent/Alamy.

the multicausality of the Balkans conflicts, Claire Fox again invited *LM*'s adversaries to debate the issues publicly.[124] *LM* remained in print from 1997, while its few full-time staff coordinated their 'Off the Fence' campaign, seeking funds and high-profile support.

During the libel case, the former RCP network became the subject of still greater notoriety, especially among its critics on the left. The *Guardian* journalist Ed Vulliamy – who had been in Bosnia with Marshall and Williams in 1992 – cast *LM* as a 'tinpot Holocaust denier'.[125] For the environmentalist George Monbiot, the magazine's position on the Balkans indicated that *LM* had 'less in common with the left than with the fanatical right'.[126] Former Nottingham RCP activist Robert Leader, meanwhile, denounced his former comrades' trajectory, 'from calling themselves die-hard communists to espousing the virtues of the free market'.[127]

124 'Fight us on screen, not in the courts', *Independent*, 11 January 2000.
125 Ed Vulliamy, 'Poison in the well of history', *Guardian*, 15 March 2000. In addition to his contemporary journalism, Vulliamy later recorded his experiences of reporting from Bosnia and testifying at the International Criminal Court at The Hague. Ed Vulliamy, '"Neutrality" and the absence of reckoning: a journalist's account', *Journal of International Affairs*, 52 (1999): 603–20; Ed Vulliamy, *The War Is Dead, Long Live the War: Bosnia – the Reckoning* (London: Vintage, 2013).
126 Monbiot, 'Far left or far right?'.
127 '*Living Marxism* and the Serbs', *Guardian*, 17 March 2000; Robert Leader, 'Marxist manoeuvring', *Spectator*, 22 April 2000.

Conversely, *LM*'s free speech campaign yielded seemingly unlikely affinities. Taking the magazine's side in the legal case, conservative commentators Auberon Waugh and Toby Young were among the self-professed defenders of 'a free press and open debate'.[128] Meanwhile, right-wing historian David Starkey and former Tory MPs Matthew Parris and George Walden joined more than 150 noted writers sponsoring *LM*'s 'Off the Fence' campaign.[129] By the start of the trial in the spring of 2000, the Off the Fence campaign had raised £70,000 in donations.[130]

For veterans of the RCP, avowedly conservative libertarians' support for *LM* confirmed the transformed political landscape sketched in *The Point Is to Change It* (1996). In a constricted, censorious climate, the party's closing statement suggested, the first task – reanimating the public sphere – would stimulate thinkers of diverse political backgrounds. At the trial's conclusion, reviewing these 'strange alliances', Hume noted that right-wing defenders of free speech might not have seemed 'natural allies of a magazine that began life as *Living Marxism*'.[131] Temporarily, at least, radical anti-capitalists and conservatives alike sought fundamentally to stimulate political contestation. Their ultimate motives for piquing debate differed: *LM*'s conservative defenders broadly wished to establish a free-market consensus; by contrast, expounding humanity's history-making capacity, the former party network still ultimately aspired to supersede capitalism.

But in the peculiar circumstances of the libel trial, these curious bedfellows jointly fulminated against what they perceived as a narrow, intolerant political culture. Accordingly, seeking high-profile support and funds, *LM* organized Off the Fence activities around the broadest libertarian themes. Inviting support

---

128 'Press freedom', *Spectator*, 3 May 1997.
129 Prominent literary supporters of the 'Off the Fence' campaign included John Berger, William Boyd, Margaret Drabble, Doris Lessing, Blake Morrison, Paul Theroux, Colm Tóibín and Fay Weldon. Helene Guldberg and Claire Fox, 'Free Speech Appeal', *LM*, March 1998. More than a decade after the trial, BBC world affairs editor John Simpson and Fleet Street veteran Roy Greenslade recanted their support for *LM*. Apologizing in 2012 and 2013, respectively, Simpson and Greenslade said that while they had initially opposed the libel charges, they now considered ITN's case a justified, even necessary, defence of journalistic accuracy. 'It seemed to me at the time', Simpson reflected, 'that big, well-funded organisations should not put small magazines out of business; but it's clear that there were much bigger questions involved'. For his part, Greenslade had supported *LM* 'not because I thought it was correct in its assertions, but because I do not believe media organisations (or journalists) should use the libel law'. In hindsight, however, Greenslade justified ITN's case as the 'only way to prevent lies being spread about their journalism as the *LM* allegations gained credibility. . . . I hereby apologise to ITN's reporters and [Ed] Vulliamy for having offered to help *LM*'. 'John Simpson: I was on wrong side in Bosnia death camps libel trial', *Observer*, 22 April 2012; Roy Greenslade, 'Journalism books that tell it how it was, how it is and how it should be', *Guardian*, 11 September 2013.
130 Julia Hartley-Brewer, 'High stakes in battle over Serbian guilt', *Guardian*, 15 March 2000.
131 Mick Hume, 'It it's freedom you want, steer clear of the forces of liberalism', *Spectator*, 8 April 2000.

from public figures, activists from the revolutionary tradition framed a more generally accessible critique of censorship. Reprising RCP slogans on the 'right to be offensive' and the exhortation to 'ban nothing, question everything',[132] *LM*'s Free Speech Festival at the Institute of Contemporary Arts in 1998 hosted more than 150 speakers from the politics, media and arts sectors.[133] Delivering the keynote address, Professor Nadine Strossen, president of the American Civil Liberties Union, upheld absolute freedom of speech.[134] Public events in the late 1990s established the *LM* network's profile in London cultural circles. In 1999, for example, the 'Culture Wars' conference at Hammersmith's Riverside Studios attracted more than 1,000 people, including publishers, literary agents, writers, film-makers and academics.[135] Recalling the genesis of the Institute of Ideas in 2000, Claire Fox accentuates the iterative, even unexpected, dynamics of the initiative:

> It was going to be the University of Ideas, but we thought it sounded boring. We called it the Institute of Ideas. And it was a month of debate and each weekend there would be this day conference at the Royal Society, day conference at the Tate Modern. And there would be lots and lots of evening events throughout the country. . . . *LM* magazine was being sued for libel, all over the newspapers, people demonising us left, right, and centre, and yet for no apparent reason these organisations approached me and asked me whether I would work with them. So it was the Society of Arts, the Royal Shakespeare Company, Tate Modern in its new form, the Royal Institution, and the British Library, saying, *we really like your* LM *events, can we work with you?* [. . .] And I suddenly had this big crowd of people. Now that was phenomenal.[136]

Founding the Institute of Ideas, Fox pitched its 'Free Speech Wars' events as an oasis in a political desert, in which 'debate is too often sidelined in deference to consensus'.[137]

On 14 March 2000, Mr Justice Morland completed his summing up after a two-week trial at the High Court. Justice Morland repeatedly reminded

---

132 Revolutionary Communist Students organizations had organized around these demands since the early 1990s. See, for example, Revolutionary Communist Party, *The Right to Be Offensive* (London: Revolutionary Communist Party, 1993); 'The right to be offensive', *Living Marxism*, February 1994; 'The story continues. . .' and Robert Clough, Revolutionary Communist Students, 'Hopefully the last word on the great Sun debate', *Leeds Student*, 4 March 1994.
133 Claire Fox and Helene Guldberg, 'Free Speech Wars', *LM*, April 1998.
134 Jennie Bristow, 'Warrior fights for freer speech', *Times Higher Education Supplement*, 13 March 1998.
135 Claire Fox, 'Culture wars', *LM*, April 1999.
136 Claire Fox, 1 September 2020.
137 'An intellectual map for the twenty-first century', *Last Magazine*, Summer 2000.

jurors that the case hinged not upon whether Marshall and Williams had been 'inaccurate, unfair or misleading', but rather upon whether the defendants – upon whom was the burden of proof – had established that Marshall and Williams had 'deliberately' compiled misleading footage. Unless the jurors believed that Deichmann and Hume had proved such a case, they would find for the ITN journalists. On this basis, the jury unanimously decided that *LM* had libelled ITN and its reporters.[138] Addressing the press outside the court, Williams argued that the magazine had overstepped the boundaries of acceptable expression:

> There is absolutely no doubt that freedom of speech is essential to society. But the freedom to print lies masquerading as the truth, as *LM* did, is not.[139]

For the condemned magazine's fiercest adversaries, the verdict irrefutably confirmed *LM*'s malign agenda. The following year, after the International Criminal Tribunal for the Former Yugoslavia convicted Bosnian Serb general Radislav Krstić of genocide, Marko Attila Hoare positioned *LM* among Serb apologists and 'revisionists' who had 'repeatedly denied that a genocide had taken place'.[140]

The three-year legal case had profound ramifications for the former RCP cadres who ran *LM*. The court awarded ITN, Marshall and Williams total damages of £375,000 and further ordered *LM* to pay a £500,000 legal bill. As they prepared the magazine's final issue in the summer of 2000, Hume and Guldberg faced bankruptcy.[141] Standing outside the High Court after the decision, Hume denounced libel law as a 'disgrace to democracy'.[142]

Yet the adverse experience also intensified the magazine network's libertarian instincts. Having amplified their free speech fundamentalism during the late 1990s, activists entered the new millennium increasingly determined to confront what they considered a hollow, censorious political climate. For Guldberg, the libel case underlined the importance of freedom of expression for reinvigorating political contestation.[143] Within months, alongside the Campaign for Press and Broadcasting Freedom, the nascent Institute of Ideas had mobilized to build

---

138 Mr Justice Morland quoted in ITN et al v. *LM* et al transcript. Day 10 PM transcript, 41, lines 10–15, 55, lines 22–27; Day 11 AM transcript, 9, lines 27–32; 10, lines 1–5. Available at balkanwitness.glypx.com/LM-Trial-Transcript/transcript-day10-pm.pdf and balkanwitness.glypx.com/LM-Trial-Transcript/transcript-day11-am.pdf (accessed 12 July 2022).
139 Ian Williams quoted in 'ITN wins Bosnian war libel case', *BBC News*, 15 March 2000. Available at news.bbc.co.uk/1/hi/uk/677481.stm (accessed 8 November 2021).
140 Marko Attila Hoare, 'Genocide in the former Yugoslavia: A critique of left revisionism's denial', *Journal of Genocide Research*, 5 (2003): 543, 553–5.
141 Matt Wells, '*LM* closes after losing libel action', *Guardian*, 31 March 2000.
142 'Was *LM* bullied into oblivion. . .', *British Journalism Review*, 11 (2000): 40.
143 Helene Guldberg, 'Question and be damned', *Independent*, 21 March 2000.

opposition to the UK's 'plaintiff-friendly' libel laws.[144] As the legal academic David Campbell noted in 2002, the case's high media profile, combined with *LM*'s intensive campaigning, enabled the magazine's network to expound its politics to audiences 'well beyond their previous reach'.[145] Commenting upon the contrasting outcomes of the trial more than twenty years later, former activists remember how the *LM* defence case, defeated in the High Court, nevertheless galvanized its milieu:

> The irony is that nobody knows whether if we hadn't been sued for libel the RCP would have been a very, very small footnote . . . *LM* is sued for libel and that brought people back together. Those people who thought the party was over had a campaign. So the Revolutionary Communist Party, such as it was, had a new lease of life. Not as a party. But it meant that there was a focus of some understandable fury at this attempt to close down this magazine.[146]

Overtly contrasting their tribulations and the network's subsequent endurance, these retrospectives assert an ideological thread – braided through freedom of speech and renewed contestation – connecting considerably different political conjunctures and forms either side of the millennium.

In less than a decade, the activists who formerly comprised the RCP had declared the demise of class politics, disbanded their party and lost a major libel case, which forced their major organizational outlet to close. They perceived a bleak political conjuncture in which social transformation had been disregarded as neither possible nor desirable. Yet the majority of former members of the RCP maintained contact as old friends and comrades, organizing multifarious initiatives which developed their humanist, libertarian critique. The tasks which the network had identified during the 1990s – reinvigorating the subject as an agent of history – appeared increasingly herculean. But for activists who insisted that there must be an alternative, the challenge remained as compelling as it was imperative.

---

144 'A town named sue', *Free Press: Journal of the Campaign for Press and Broadcasting Freedom*, May–June 2000.
145 Campbell, 'Atrocity, memory, photography, part 2', 161.
146 Claire Fox, 1 September 2020.

6

'Encouraging the unsayable to be said'
spiked and the Institute of Ideas, *c.* 2000–2010

At the turn of the millennium, the core cadre which had constituted the RCP at its dissolution experimented with new organizational forms. Most notably, former *LM* editor Mick Hume launched the online magazine *spiked*, while Claire Fox established the Institute of Ideas. As many veterans of the party furthered their careers – not least in academe and the media – *spiked* and the IoI provided an outlet for activists to confront what they considered a deleteriously anodyne public sphere. Reflecting upon the first decade of the Institute of Ideas, Fox accentuated its record of 'encourag[ing] the unsayable to be said'.[1] Hume similarly championed *spiked* as a vital challenge to the 'edgeless blancmange' of mainstream politics in the 2000s.[2]

Through the first decade of the twenty-first century, the network's critique developed the political themes of the RCP's twilight years. Extending the campaign against diminished subjectivity, activists lamented an atomized public and a circumscribed political realm. *spiked* articles and Institute of Ideas events fulminated against trends which, veterans argued, typified the loss of popular belief in humanity's ability collectively to transform society.

On the one hand, ex-RCP activists retained the Marxist aspiration to a higher social plane. Lamenting the decline of radical politics, they remained resolutely opposed to a status quo which inhibited the development of the forces of production. Simultaneously, however, they stipulated that diminished subjectivity precluded not only class politics but even a more basic emancipatory agenda. In this specific conjuncture, then, former RCPers elucidated a peculiar variant of Marxism, which posited that class conflict was suspended but championed radical humanist first principles and yearned for a world transformed.

---

1 'Happy birthday: Claire Fox, 52', *Times*, 5 June 2012.
2 Mick Hume, 'Brighton bomb memories', *spiked*, 13 October 2009.

In an adverse conjuncture, former cadres' politics almost entirely took the form of negative critique. Declaring a historic nadir for even bedrock humanist precepts, activists suggested that it would be futile voluntarism to prescribe a specific political programme. Beyond a general commitment to reinvigorate public debate, their analysis left ex-RCPers largely criticizing prevailing ideas. This chapter examines how activists employing new organizational forms arraigned impediments to reinvigorating the human subject as an agent of history.

Proceeding through two sections, the chapter begins by assessing former RCP activists' analyses of what they considered a low ebb for political subjectivity. Scrutinizing their analyses of social atomization and the politics of fear, the first section orients the milieu's libertarianism in what veterans called a 'pre-political' era. The ex-RCP network, it is argued, formulated a particular brand of anti-statism, which posited independence from authority as a fundamental point of departure for any transformative politics.

The chapter's second section shifts the focus from activists' negative critiques of prevailing social trends. In so doing, it interrogates how, through these wilderness years, erstwhile RCP members imagined an alternative world. Veterans insisted that without a subjective force for social transformation, there could be no question of delineating a specific programme. Instead, retaining the Marxist aspiration to a higher social plane, activists formulated a syncretic radical humanism. The network had for long declared class politics moribund. But an enduring vision of a radical alternative – superseding capitalism and maximizing human fulfilment – continually underpinned their critical analyses throughout the 2000s.

'A prevailing climate of misanthropy'

As far as its supporters were concerned, *LM*'s defeat in the High Court reinforced the difficult imperative of contentious politics. Rather than recanting, the network's most influential figures remained determined to challenge what they considered anodyne consensus politics. Mick Hume – who had faced a legal bill of almost £1m in damages and costs[3] – insisted that *LM*'s 'spirit', as an 'independent voice of dissent and debate', remained 'alive and kicking'.[4]

---

3   Mick Hume, 'The day I faced being a £1m bankrupt', *Times*, 7 March 2005.
4   Mick Hume, 'The last of the iconoclasts?', *Times*, 23 June 2000.

Founding *spiked* and the Institute of Ideas, former RCP cadres positioned their network as a vital antidote to an ossified public realm. In their post-party activities and professional commitments alike, veterans railed against political paradigms which they regarded as impediments to a humanist renaissance. During its inaugural summer of public debates in 2000, the Institute of Ideas invited many former *LM* writers to discuss 'freedom and its limits' and 'the precautionary principle'.[5] Founding *spiked* in 2001, editor Hume promised a 'radical' forum challenging contemporary orthodoxies.[6] Promptly identifying a bête noire, the *Guardian* noted *spiked*'s 'contrarian-libertarian take on the world'.[7] Recalling *spiked*'s inauspicious beginnings, Claire Fox positions these post-party initiatives firmly in a sequence of maverick political outsiders:

> When the editorial team of *LM* magazine said, *we want to start* spiked, *an online magazine* – I was the kind of person who thought that an online magazine wouldn't work, you had to have a real magazine. And I never wanted to see a magazine again in my life because I'd just been through a libel case. I wasn't remotely interested in the editorial side of things. . . . I took no notice and basically said, *we've got this office: you can sit in the corner and get on.*[8]

Echoing *LM*'s flair for provocation, Institute of Ideas events swiftly piqued interest among the press and publishers: London house Hodder and Stoughton commissioned a series of short books modelled on Institute of Ideas debates.[9] Through the 2000s, the organization expanded its regular calendar of conferences and salons, attracting high-profile speakers from beyond the ex-party milieu. Concomitantly, the organization garnered increasing media attention. In October 2005, the Institute of Ideas convened its first Battle of Ideas, a festival of debates at the Royal College of Art.[10] The following year, the London *Times* co-hosted the Battle, which became the Institute's annual flagship event.[11]

In a new epoch which they defined by its dearth of debate, former RCP activists recapitulated the party's modus operandi, deliberately polarizing debates to clarify and demarcate allegiances. With mainstream politics hollowed into technocracy and triviality, they argued, reinstating rumbustious argument was crucial. For Alan Hudson, for example, all-encompassing political contestation

---

5 'An intellectual map for the twenty-first century', *LM*, April 2000.
6 'Radical voice', *Daily Telegraph*, 12 March 2001.
7 Mark Tran, 'Marx lives', *Guardian*, 12 February 2001.
8 Claire Fox, 1 September 2020.
9 'An intellectual map for the twenty-first century'.
10 Dolan Cummings, 'Introduction', in Dolan Cummings (ed.), *Debating Humanism* (Exeter: Societas, 2006), 1.
11 'Join the debate', *Times*, 12 October 2006.

was vital not 'to celebrate conflict for its own sake' but as a 'public function' stimulating critical debate.[12] Claire Fox, meanwhile, positioned the Institute of Ideas not as an introspective discussion forum but as a means to enliven a robust, evaluative political culture. Introducing a series of debates in 2002, Fox pitted the organization against 'current relativist orthodoxy [which] celebrates all views as equal as though there are no arguments to win'.[13]

Libertarianism became an increasingly important component of the network's politics in the 2000s. Superficially, ex-RCP activists' critiques resembled the impulses usually associated with Thatcherites and right-wingers rolling back the frontiers of the state.[14] Michael Fitzpatrick, for example, castigated the Blair government's public health agenda for invading private life with professional regulation.[15] But the former RCP network's libertarianism had a distinct character. Whereas conservative libertarians defended the capitalist market against state encroachment, *spiked* correspondents regarded big government as both a symptom and a cause of public passivity. Veterans of the party who castigated an enlarged state did so not to preserve the free market but to challenge its apparatus. Mick Hume, for example, abhorred the regulatory state as an obstacle to more profound efforts to 'change society'.[16] Whereas Thatcherites trumpeted the private individual's autonomy under capitalism, ex-RCP activists championed the agency of the subject as a precondition for revolutionary upheaval.

Perceiving a climate of degraded subjectivity, activists espoused freedoms from the state not as sectional ends in themselves but as foundational precursors to a more pugnacious political sphere. In the context of the early twenty-first century, the perennial emphasis upon freedom of speech acquired

---

12 Alan Hudson, 'Intellectuals for our times', *Critical Review of International Social and Political Philosophy*, 6 (2003): 47.
13 Institute of Ideas, *Compensation Crazy: Do We Blame and Claim Too Much?* (London: Hodder & Stoughton, 2002), viii.
14 Addressing the College of Europe in Bruges on 20 September 1988, Margaret Thatcher repudiated the centralizing tendency towards supranational federalism in the European Economic Community. Thatcher famously celebrated having 'successfully rolled back the frontiers of the state in Britain'. Charles Moore, *Margaret Thatcher: The Authorized Biography – Volume Three: Herself Alone* (London: Allen Lane, 2019), 149.
15 Michael Fitzpatrick, *The Tyranny of Health: Doctors and the Regulation of Lifestyle* (Abingdon: Routledge, 2000), 6. In 1998, Tony Blair's first government produced *Our Healthier Nation*, a Green Paper delineating a 'contract' by which 'the Government, local communities and individuals will join in partnership to improve all our health'. *Our Healthier Nation: A Contract for Health*. Presented to Parliament by the Secretary of State for Health by Command of Her Majesty, February 1998. Cm 3852 (London: The Stationery Office, 1998).
16 Mick Hume, 'Sick society', *New Statesman*, 23 October 2000.

special significance as a sine qua non for renewed contestation.[17] In 2003, for example, opposing Home Secretary David Blunkett's plans to increase police powers, Josie Appleton expounded a fundamental public challenge to official authoritarianism.[18] 'Challenging the government', Appleton later averred, was an active citizenry's 'civic duty'.[19]

Diagnosing a vapid political culture under New Labour, the ex-RCP milieu complained that even political dissent mainly took cynical, defeatist forms. For *spiked* correspondents, mass mobilization against the Iraq War constituted an 'anti-political' retreat rather than an overarching challenge to the establishment. During worldwide demonstrations on 15 February 2003, more than 1 million people protested in London against the US-led coalition's imminent invasion of Iraq.[20] The majority of British leftists hailed the anti-war movement as a seismic development. Hailing the unprecedented scale of the protests, the SWP – whose veterans were among the Stop the War Coalition's (StWC) founders in 2001 – intimated that the movement could topple the government.[21] By contrast, ex-RCP activists regarded the anti-war movement itself as a symptom of 'depoliticization', by which radicals withdrew from the political sphere, rather than vying to transform it. For Jennie Bristow, the StWC's 'not in my name' mantra demonstrated that the protests, though great in number, lacked ideological distinction. Disowning Western militarism, Bristow averred, did not amount to challenging it outright.[22] Furthermore, after Blair's government defied major public opposition and invaded Iraq, Mick Hume identified a pervasive 'sense of powerlessness and apathy' in British politics. Aspiring ultimately to 'far-reaching political change', Hume advocated more 'adversarial politics'.[23] For *spiked* columnist Brendan O'Neill, radicals intoning 'not in my name' typified 'a cynical mood and a sense of disengagement'.[24]

---

17 Tessa Mayes, *Restraint or Revelation? Free Speech and Privacy in a Confessional Age* (London: spiked, 2002), 44, 59.
18 Receiving royal assent on 20 November 2003, Blunkett's Criminal Justice Act expanded police powers of stop and search. It also removed the 'double jeopardy' clause, which hitherto prevented a defendant from being tried twice for the same offence. Josie Appleton, 'Blunkett's justice', *spiked*, 28 May 2003.
19 Josie Appleton, 'Citizens, do your duty', *Guardian*, 11 November 2009.
20 Joris Verhulst, 'February 15, 2003: The world says no to war', in Stefaan Walgrave and Dieter Rucht (eds), *The World Says No to War: Demonstrations against the War on Iraq* (Minneapolis: University of Minnesota Press, 2010), 7.
21 Andrew Stone, 'Anti-war demonstration: A day to change the world', *Socialist Review*, February 2003.
22 Jennie Bristow, 'The problem with the peace movement', *spiked*, 27 February 2003.
23 Mick Hume, 'The problem isn't that our political life is too brutal . . . it isn't brutal enough', *Times*, 29 July 2003.
24 Brendan O'Neill, 'Whatever happened to the anti-war movement?', *spiked*, 1 October 2003.

Bemoaning social fragmentation, ex-party activists negatively contrasted the conjuncture of the 2000s from their ideal of subaltern subjects identifying their interests and collectively supplanting authority. From this perspective, an atomized public encapsulated the subjective weakness of political agency. Concluding a detailed psephological study of Basildon, a bellwether constituency in Essex, Dennis Hayes and Alan Hudson drew an 'unpalatable message: Basildonians feel disengaged from and mistrustful of political and administrative institutions'. For Hayes and Hudson, Basildon captured in microcosm an increasingly fractured polity, where individuals lived in 'isolated relief, without much reference to each other'.[25]

In the 2000s, developing *LM*'s critique of a 'culture of fear', the ex-RCP network excoriated what they perceived as overwhelmingly misanthropic, reactionary political trends. In 2005, presenting a Channel 4 documentary on immigration, Kenan Malik exhorted citizens to repudiate 'fear . . . the principal language of politics' and to call boldly for open borders.[26] As subjectivity was diminished, the argument ran, human beings increasingly derived meaning not from their capacity to galvanize, reason and act but by accentuating their vulnerability. For instance, in his radical analysis of social work in early twenty-first-century Britain, Kenneth McLaughlin paradigmatically lamented how the subject's discursive degradation emboldened and empowered the authorities to intervene in private life.[27]

Asserting that a populace afflicted by mutual fear could not transform its circumstances, former cadres inveighed against distrust among British citizens. For Dolan Cummings, the rise of anti-social behaviour orders (ASBOs) in the early 2000s signalled the abject downturn of informal communitarian autonomy.[28] Increasing recourse to the state to resolve local disputes, Cummings opined, illustrated a 'culture of fear' which precluded mutual solidarities.[29]

25 Dennis Hayes and Alan Hudson, *Basildon: The Mood of the Nation* (London: Demos, 2001), 42, 46.
26 *Let 'em All In* (Channel 4, 7 March 2005).
27 Kenneth McLaughlin, *Social Work, Politics and Society: From Radicalism to Orthodoxy* (Bristol: Policy Press, 2008), 79.
28 Introduced in the Crime and Disorder Act of 1998, ASBOs were civil orders prohibiting an individual from behaving 'in a manner that caused or was likely to cause harassment, alarm or distress to one or more persons not of the same household as himself'. After a sharp increase in applications over the previous two years, by June 2005 courts in England and Wales had reported 6,497 ASBOs to the Home Office. *Crime and Disorder Act 1998 c. 37*, Part 1 Chapter 1, 2; Roger Matthews, Helen Easton, Daniel Briggs and Ken Pease, *Assessing the Use and Impact of Anti-Social Behaviour Orders* (Bristol: Policy Press, 2009), 1.
29 Dolan Cummings, 'Don't conform, break the rules', *New Statesman*, 27 September 2004; Dolan Cummings, 'Introduction', in Craig O'Malley and Stuart Waiton, *Who's Antisocial? New Labour and the Politics of Antisocial Behaviour* (Institute of Ideas Occasional Papers, No. 2, April 2005) (London: Academy of Ideas, 2005), 3.

Convening an Institute of Ideas debate in 2005, Cummings, Craig O'Malley and Stuart Waiton lambasted Labour MP Frank Field's assessment of anti-social behaviour as the 'greatest challenge facing government ... [a] new barbarism'.[30] For Waiton, Field's incendiary remarks negated communities' 'robust' potential to resolve their own problems.[31] For radical humanists around *spiked* and the Institute of Ideas, the enfeebled subject of the 2000s was anathema. For Frank Furedi, the pervasive sense of human incapacity perpetuated popular passivity and buttressed paternalistic authority.[32] Fulminating against the 'therapy culture' as an inherently conservative phenomenon, Furedi argued that a citizen routinely portrayed as frail and vulnerable was neither equipped nor inclined to challenge authority, less still to reimagine society.[33]

Critics accused Furedi and his old comrades of exhuming the rugged individualism historically associated with the Thatcherite assault upon post-war Keynesianism. For commentators who upheld a progressive political role for the state, the *spiked* network expounded a callous doctrine of self-reliance. According to one reviewer, former RCP activists bemoaning the ontologies of victimhood and vulnerability resembled 'crusty generals writing to the *Daily Telegraph*'.[34] The writer Blake Morrison accused Furedi of advocating uncomplaining stoicism and 'quietest machismo'.[35] In these analyses, erstwhile communists had converted to a reactionary creed.

Conversely, the *spiked* milieu asserted that elevating subjectivity was integral to empowering humanity en masse. Furedi directly counterposed his network's 'humanist' outlook – valourizing autonomy, reason and experimentation – against a prevailing mindset which defined the subject by its 'state of vulnerability'.[36] Ex-RCP activists insisted that they were not promoting subjective independence as an individualistic end but as a crucial step towards overcoming social atomization and enabling a transformative movement. During doctoral study under Furedi's supervision at the University of Kent, Munira Mirza situated the baleful 'therapeutic ethos' in 'loosening' societal connectivity. Mirza asserted that combating social fragmentation was

---

30 Frank Field, *Neighbours from Hell* (London: Politico, 2003).
31 Stuart Waiton, 'The politics of antisocial behaviour', in O'Malley and Waiton, *Who's Antisocial?*, 34.
32 Frank Furedi, 'Trivial pursuits?', *LM*, April 2000.
33 Frank Furedi, *Therapy Culture: Cultivating Vulnerability in an Uncertain Age* (London: Routledge, 2004), 196.
34 James Park, 'Who are we today?', *Psychotherapy and Politics International*, 6 (2008): 63–5.
35 Blake Morrison, 'Pull yourself together!', *Guardian*, 20 December 2003.
36 Frank Furedi, *Politics of Fear: Beyond Left and Right* (London: Continuum, 2005), 164.

integral to restoring belief in humanity's collective potential.[37] Through many of their political and professional commitments, associates of the *spiked* network continually underlined a progressive humanism. David Chandler, for example, left the RCP around 1990, but he later wrote for *LM* and contributed articles to *spiked* in the 2000s while advancing his international relations scholarship. In a monograph published in 2002, Chandler critically examined how major powers invoked 'humanitarianism' to justify military intervention in the developing world. Asserting smaller states' sovereignty, Chandler averred, required a

> new humanism, a positive approach to problem solving that makes the most of people's capacity for autonomy and collective rational decision-making.[38]

Analysing social breakdown, *spiked* correspondents also censured New Labour for espousing a multiculturalist politics which accentuated particularism. Emphasising ethnicity as a defining, immutable characteristic, ex-cadres asserted, essentialized differences and rehabilitated racial thinking. Aspiring to transcend such distinctions, party veterans considered the multicultural ethos a pernicious departure from universalism. For Frank Furedi and his colleagues, diversity was a facet of experience not to be reified but to be synthesized in collective human agency.[39] *spiked*'s diagnosis coincided with more openly liberal egalitarians who positioned universalism as the basis for progressive politics. In a seminal critique of multiculturalism published in 2001, for example, political philosopher Brian Barry positioned 'universalistic' rights as the bedrock for social equality of opportunity.[40]

Many among Furedi's milieu could recall first-hand militant anti-racist activities from the late 1970s, when WAR asserted that racism was antithetical to workers' class interests. A quarter of a century later, the network's opposition to racism revolved less around clarifying class politics and instead reflected a more elemental humanist disdain for discriminatory credos. Eschewing the fixed categories of identity politics, Furedi regarded political alliances based upon, inter alia, race, religion or sexuality as hallmarks of the 'new conservatism'.[41] Resurgent racial thinking, Josie Appleton lamented, could only 'ferment divisions'.[42]

---

37 Munira Mirza, 'The therapeutic state: Addressing the emotional needs of the citizen through the arts', *International Journal of Cultural Policy*, 11 (2005): 263.
38 David Chandler, *From Kosovo to Kabul and Beyond: Human Rights and International Intervention* (London: Pluto Press, 2002), 71, 84, 214-36.
39 Eileen Chanin, 'Interview with Frank Furedi', *Australian Quarterly*, 78 (2006): 34-5.
40 Brian Barry, *Culture and Equality: An Egalitarian Critique of Multiculturalism* (Cambridge: Polity, 2001), *passim*. See especially 292-328.
41 Frank Furedi, 'Towards a new enlightenment', *Last Magazine*, Summer 2000.
42 Josie Appleton, 'Not a black and white issue', *Architects' Journal*, 6 May 2004.

For *spiked* correspondents, the riots which scarred Oldham, Burnley, Bradford and Leeds in 2001 indicted official multiculturalism for exacerbating social disunity.[43] Trouble escalated in Oldham in May 2001, when rising racial tensions between white Oldhamers and the South Asian community erupted into fighting, clashes with police and attacks on property, predominantly in the Glodwick area of the town. Approximately 500 people were involved, and the cost of the resultant damage was estimated at £1.4m.[44] Several years later, Munira Mirza posited that the race relations policies of the 1990s had worsened inter-communal hostilities in her hometown. Authorities' persistent emphases upon 'diversity', Mirza argued, had further divided Oldham into 'ethnic camps', heightening inter-communal distrust.[45]

New Labour's review of the Oldham riots committed the government to encourage greater inter-communal dialogue.[46] Commissioned by Home Secretary David Blunkett, the Cantle Report exhorted politicians, police and community leaders to promote 'cross cultural contact' under an overarching 'concept of citizenship [which] would also place a higher value on cultural differences'.[47] But for *spiked* correspondent and journalist Bruno Waterfield, the strife which tore Oldham asunder represented the 'product' of 'multicultural policy'. When policymakers portrayed unbridgeable gulfs between ethnic groups, Waterfield averred, 'the possibility of finding social solidarities based on shared experience is weakened'.[48] For *spiked* commentators, New Labour would not overcome but would merely manage, and thereby reinforce, societal division.

Kenan Malik and Munira Mirza led *spiked*'s critique of multiculturalism in the 2000s.[49] For Malik, twenty-first-century multiculturalism epitomized radicals 'shamefully' jettisoning 'secular universalism' for 'ethnic particularism'.[50] Drawing explicitly upon the left-wing US historian Russell Jacoby's critique, the former *the next step* editor warned that multiculturalism implied that ethnic

---

43 Kenan Malik, 'The trouble with multiculturalism', *spiked*, 18 December 2001.
44 Paul Bagguley and Yasmin Hussain, *Riotous Citizens: Ethnic Conflict in Multicultural Britain* (Aldershot: Ashgate, 2008), 1, 45–8.
45 Munira Mirza, 'Deepening the divide', *Prospect*, October 2010.
46 Nam-Kook Kim, 'Deliberative multiculturalism in New Labour's Britain', *Citizenship Studies*, 15 (2011): 128.
47 *Community Cohesion: A Report of the Independent Review Team Chaired by Ted Cantle* (London: Home Office, 2001). See especially 10, 2.12 and 2.13.
48 Bruno Waterfield, 'Imposing "parallel lives"', *spiked*, 22 January 2003.
49 A veteran of the RCP and WAR, Malik served as the final editor of *the next step* until it discontinued in 1994. As an undergraduate at Mansfield College in the late 1990s, Mirza was involved with *LM* readers' groups in Oxford. She subsequently undertook doctoral study at the University of Kent under Frank Furedi's supervision. After working for the conservative Policy Exchange think tank, in 2008 Mirza became an adviser to the mayor of London, Boris Johnson.
50 Kenan Malik, 'Born in Bradford', *Prospect*, October 2005.

groups bore fixed, particular characteristics: eternalizing racial and ethnic difference was antithetical to progressive universalism.[51] Contrary to their paternalistic claims to protect minorities, Malik declared, multiculturalism's adherents expounded a 'profoundly anti-humanist' politics. Concentrating upon ethnic categories, he argued, simultaneously exaggerated communities' internal heterogeneity and precluded broader collective solidarities.[52]

A co-founder of the network's Manifesto Club in 2006, Mirza held that multiculturalism encouraged among minorities a regressive sense of peripherality and grievance: conceptualizing society in terms of racialized silos could only exacerbate atomization. Addressing an Institute of Ideas discussion in 2005, Mirza argued that cultural policies which purported to champion multicultural 'diversity' obscured universal values in artistic expression.[53] The following year, endorsing a manifesto against narrow 'communal' identity politics, Mirza contended that the principled objective of equality required a 'universalist approach'.[54]

To their detractors, the *spiked* correspondents muted minority voices and wilfully ignored enduring racial discrimination. When Malik extended his critique of multiculturalism in a book published in 2009,[55] Arun Kundnani of the Institute of Race Relations castigated Malik's trajectory from 'East End anti-racist to West End anti-multiculturalist'. Kundnani charged Malik with espousing assimilationist dogma, which positioned 'minority culture as a threat to superior values'.[56] By contrast, for Malik, Mirza and their colleagues, multiculturalism and identity politics were deplorable primarily as obstacles to the ideal of progressive universalism.[57] From this perspective, activists accentuating ethnic and racial differences cemented the societal divisions which attended diminished subjectivity. For Frank Furedi, political preoccupations with immutable characteristics precluded individuals independently formulating and collectively pursuing their ideas.[58]

---

51 Russell Jacoby, 'The myth of multiculturalism', *New Left Review*, November–December 1994, 125–6; Russell Jacoby, *The End of Utopia: Politics and Culture in an Age of Apathy* (New York: Basic Books, 1999), 29–66.
52 Kenan Malik, 'Universalism and difference in discourses of race', *Review of International Studies*, 26 (2000): 156, 168; Kenan Malik, 'Making a difference: Culture, race and social policy', *Patterns of Prejudice*, 39 (2005): 378.
53 Dolan Cummings, 'Round-table rumbles at the National', *New Theatre Quarterly*, 22 (2006): 96–8.
54 Munira Mirza, 'Diversity is divisive', *spiked*, 23 November 2006.
55 Kenan Malik, *From Fatwa to Jihad: The Rushdie Affair and Its Legacy* (London: Atlantic Books, 2009).
56 Arun Kundnani quoted in *Race & Class*, 51 (2010): 87–90.
57 Kenan Malik, 'Multiculturalism and the politics of identity', in Cummings (ed.), *Debating Humanism*, 56–7.
58 Frank Furedi, *On Tolerance: A Defence of Moral Independence* (London: Bloomsbury, 2011), 149–54.

Negative critiques of social fragmentation and political quiescence cemented the *spiked* network's damning assessments of diminished subjectivity. After declaring class politics suspended in the early 1990s, members of the party milieu had been turning to more foundational principles, broadly championing 'human potential', for more than a decade. Through the 2000s, however, they perceived even these fundamental humanist precepts to be lamentably unpopular. Phil Mullan reproached the 'mood of fatalism' which implied a widespread 'loss of faith in human capability and in the potential to learn and adapt'.[59] Contributing to an Institute of Ideas debate in 2005, Frank Furedi bemoaned a 'prevailing climate of misanthropy' which engendered 'intense scepticism regarding the desirability of change'.[60] Humanists perceived considerable antipathy even to their most basic attempts to elevate the very *concept* of the subject as an agent of history.

Throughout *spiked* opinion pieces, Institute of Ideas fora, media commentary and academic publications, a hardy milieu of former RCP members agreed that their attempts since the mid-1990s to 'rescue the subject' appeared increasingly forlorn. Reasserting humanity's history-making capacity – a prerequisite for a revolutionary project – now seemed a herculean task. In 2002, delineating 'subjectivity in denial', James Heartfield charted the corroded humanist premises of emancipatory politics. While Heartfield insisted that the subject retained its residual, powerful potential, he opined that the balance of forces had marginalized even the suggestion that humanity could tackle the major social problems of poverty, inequality and oppression.[61] During an Ideas for Freedom conference at the end of the 2000s, Neil Davenport summarized the network's bleak assessment of a '*pre*-political stage in human history'. For those 'upholding a belief' in 'emancipation', Davenport intoned, degraded human subjectivity represented a profound obstacle.[62]

'Let's replace capitalism with something even more dazzlingly cocky and human-centric'

Having declared class politics subjectively weak, rather than objectively flawed, the network's associates maintained that capitalism inhibited humanity's productive potential. While lamenting a lack of popular ardour for transformative politics,

---

59 Phil Mullan, *The Imaginary Time-Bomb: Why an Ageing Population is Not a Social Problem* (London: I. B. Tauris, 2000), 109, 215–16.
60 Frank Furedi, 'The legacy of humanism', in Cummings (ed.), *Debating Humanism*, 25.
61 James Heartfield, *The 'Death of the Subject' Explained* (Leicester: Perpetuity Press, 2002).
62 Neil Davenport, 'Whatever happened to the class struggle?', *spiked*, 3 December 2009.

conceptually, at least, theoreticians retained vivid ideals of a radical alternative. For activists who had once worked to build a revolutionary vanguard, a 'pre-political' society was deplorable. By their own admission, party veterans' ideas had not gained sufficient traction to gain a critical mass in society. In a critical review of former SWP activist Mark Steel's memoir, for instance, Mick Hume declared that the 'socialist project' had 'failed'.[63] Recognizing this failure did not, however, prevent the network from adumbrating radical humanist fundamentals in their post-party forms, media interventions and professional careers. Concurrently, newspaper editors and radio producers seeking unorthodox commentary increasingly invited contributions from Institute of Ideas and *spiked* associates, who routinely embraced the opportunity. Consequently, through the 2000s, the network attained a growing public profile. Meanwhile, in their professional lives, some former party organizers, doubtless drawing upon the intellectual and organizational rigour that they had honed in the RCP, progressed into senior positions in the private sector.

In the perceived absence of a subjective force to transform society, the network's politics tended towards philosophical idealism through the 2000s. Rather than expounding specific tactics, old comrades vociferously asserted humanity's potential to improve its lot. The result was a syncretic humanism which drew explicitly, if selectively, upon the network's Marxist tradition. Considering class struggle – the Marxian motor of history – in decline, *spiked* and Institute of Ideas associates accentuated more capaciously the seismic agency of the subject – with a timely emphasis upon the philosopher's caveat: 'not in circumstances of his choosing'.[64] Former RCP cadres maintained that in a climate of misanthropy, Marx's visionary humanism assumed ever greater importance. In 2001, for example, Mick Hume lamented that Marx's theory of class struggle had little 'direct relevance' to the political conjuncture. *spiked*'s founding editor insisted, however, that mainstream political torpor made all the more vital Marx's dialectical emphasis upon 'the history-making potential of humanity'.[65] Interviewed in 2008, Claire Fox identified the 'role of the human agency in change' as the philosopher's most topical and 'profound' insight.[66]

---

63 Mick Hume, 'Things didn't get better', *New Statesman*, 7 May 2001.
64 'Men make their own history, but they do not make it just as they please in circumstances they choose for themselves; rather they make it in present circumstances, given and inherited. Tradition from all the dead generations weighs like a nightmare on the brain of the living'. Marx, 'Eighteenth Brumaire', 32.
65 Mick Hume, 'A mouldering Marx', *New Statesman*, 14 January 2001.
66 Claire Fox quoted in 'The boot's on the other foot: Was the Left right after all?', *Times*, 21 October 2008.

Issued in supposedly adverse circumstances, these humanist precepts sometimes lapsed into abstraction. Former activists had not renounced the Marxist theory of history, nor had they disavowed the social salience of class. But when identifying a societal malaise, one-time proponents of proletarian revolution espoused classless, humanist universalism. Addressing an Institute of Ideas debate in 2001, Kenan Malik averred that upholding the quintessentially human 'capacity for conscious, rational dialogue and inquiry' was vital.[67] For party veterans resisting what they considered a misanthropic zeitgeist, it was paramount to assert the bedrock principles of independence, reason and collective action.[68] Writing in the mid-2000s, Frank Furedi declared that only a 'second Enlightenment', restoring en masse humanity's self-confidence to act upon the world, could overcome the 'sense of powerlessness'.[69]

Insisting that the nadir of contestation rendered 'left' and 'right' meaningless, former cadres often rejected shorthand political appellations. To the extent that ex-RCPers accepted labels in the 2000s, they usually asserted their tradition's fundamentally 'humanist' tenets, with a 'libertarian' emphasis upon independence from authority. Writing a column for the *Times* from 1999, Mick Hume adopted the mantle of a 'libertarian Marxist'.[70] Meanwhile, signalling an emancipatory resolve to reanimate subjectivity, Frank Furedi described himself as a 'libertarian humanist'. The term connoted the perceived adversity of the political climate: Furedi's 'main concern' was to combat 'the general Culture of Fear that prevails in society'.[71] Interviewed in the *Guardian* in 2005, Furedi reiterated his 'humanism' as a 'first-order idea' which undergirded a liberatory politics: 'we have to create a greater belief in human potential'.[72]

Upholding the materialist theory of history, former RCP activists continually considered class the cardinal category for social analysis. At the same time, they asserted that political subjectivities in twenty-first-century Britain did not, for the most part, configure class as a motor of history. For many British workers, the argument ran, class resonated more as a static sociological descriptor than as an active category connoting political agency. In their detailed local study,

---

67 Kenan Malik, *What Is It to Be Human? What Science Can and Cannot Tell Us* (London: Academy of Ideas, 2001), 27.
68 Frank Furedi, *Where Have All the Intellectuals Gone?* (London: Continuum, second edition 2006), 20.
69 Furedi, *Politics of Fear*, 90, 131, 168.
70 See, for example, Mick Hume, 'A bastion of rottenness and contempt for us all', *Times*, 19 June 2007.
71 'For nature and against labels'.
72 John Sutherland, 'Frank Furedi', *Guardian*, 19 December 2005. Furedi was more ambivalent about the 'libertarian' tag, lest it misleadingly imply a reactionary predilection for free-market capitalism. Simon Crompton, 'Kids' freedom fighter', *Times*, 26 July 2008.

for example, Dennis Hayes and Alan Hudson pithily concluded that while class informed Basildoners' 'cultural outlook', it did not 'define social and political views ... there is class without class struggle'.[73]

Veterans acknowledged that transitional changes under capitalism would always be suboptimal. Development would be volatile and inhibited, and its benefits would be unevenly distributed. In the absence of popular appetite for an alternative social system, however, *spiked* correspondents championed economic growth, both to maximize dynamism in the short term, and to raise expectations and demands for higher living standards. Hume simultaneously reaffirmed capitalism's inability to maximize society's productive potential and lambasted the subjective 'pessimism, cynicism, [and] fatalism', which compounded capitalism's objective flaws:

> Capitalism may well still be a restrictive system. Yet the pervasive culture of restraint, the over-anxious instinct to hold back, means that we are not even being allowed to test the system's limits ... if we were to raise our sights a little, we could be doing a lot better yet.[74]

The ex-RCP milieu had always aspired ultimately to supersede capitalism with a classless society in which maximized productive forces benefited all. Former cadres recalled *The Communist Manifesto*'s acknowledgement that capitalism had propelled industrial, agricultural and scientific progress.[75] In the 2000s, these concepts increasingly furnished abstract critiques. There was no prospect of the proletariat winning power, less still of it supplanting the state. But veterans retained their core ideal of a superior social system extending development and freeing all from want. Appointed to succeed Hume as *spiked* editor in 2007, former RCP activist Brendan O'Neill evoked this ideological lodestar:

> Marx wanted to destroy capitalism because he thought it didn't go far enough in remaking the world in man's image and organising society according to man's needs and desire. Today's sorry excuses for Marxists and anti-capitalists think

---

73 Hayes and Hudson, *Basildon*, 22.
74 Mick Hume, 'It is the best of times to be alive. Ever', *LM*, December 1999–January 2000.
75 Introducing an edition of *The Communist Manifesto* in the mid-1990s, Mick Hume highlighted how the authors were 'keen to uphold and even to celebrate the achievements of capitalism'. Marx and Engels famously acknowledged how rapidly the emergent bourgeoisie had revolutionized production and transformed humankind's mastery of nature: 'The bourgeoisie, during its rule of scarce 100 years, has created more massive and more colossal productive forces than have all preceding generations together. Subjection of nature's forces to man, machinery, application of chemistry to industry and agriculture, steam navigation, railways, electric telegraphs, clearing of whole continents for cultivation, canalisation of rivers, whole populations conjured out of the ground – what earlier century had even a presentiment that such productive forces slumbered in the lap of social labour?' Marx and Engels, *Communist Manifesto*, xii, 17–18.

capitalism has gone too far in its development of the forces of production and encouragement of consumerism. I'm with Marx. Let's replace capitalism with something even more dazzlingly cocky and human-centric.[76]

In their professional pursuits, *spiked* associates lionized innovation, especially in relation to science and technology. Championing human initiative and insight, they stressed the progressive potential of experimentation. Introducing their internet services company cScape in 2000, Rob Killick and Sandy Starr lauded the web's 'fantastic potential' to facilitate and enhance pioneers' 'ingenuity'.[77] Similarly, delivering the keynote address at a *spiked* conference in 2001, Phil Mullan, chief executive of Cybercafé Ltd, exhorted business leaders to maximize their 'productive use' of information technology.[78]

While acknowledging the turbulent and circumscribed character of capitalist development, the *spiked* network upheld experimentation as the sine qua non of neoteric politics. Veterans lamenting diminished subjectivity maintained a basically optimistic orientation towards humanity's ability to remake the world.[79] James Heartfield, for example, held that while hunger was endemic under capitalism, new agricultural techniques on larger tracts of land held the key to mitigating poverty in the developing world.[80] James Woudhuysen and Ian Abley, meanwhile, denounced New Labour's record on housebuilding but insisted that computer-aided design and mechanical construction could tackle the crisis.[81]

Adducing evidence of scientific and technological innovation, ex-RCP activists wrote effusively of humans' ability to enhance living standards. In a non-revolutionary context, such proclamations were intended to restore a principled belief in the possibility of progress. 'The fact is that people now are living longer, healthier and wealthier lives than ever before in human history', Mick Hume asserted at the turn of the century.[82] Railing against an 'age of cynicism and scepticism', Kenan Malik championed experimental science which had yielded 'new social and moral vistas' and 'helped transform material conditions'.[83] Similarly, former *Living Marxism* science correspondent John Gillott lauded

---

76 Brendan O'Neill, 'Help! I'm a Marxist who defends capitalism', *Spectator*, 1 December 2007.
77 Rob Killick and Sandy Starr, 'Freedom net', *Economic Affairs*, 20 (2000): 29–32.
78 Phil Mullan, 'Beyond the internet bubble', *spiked*, 25 October 2001.
79 'The politics of Furedi', *Policy*, 22 (2006): 47.
80 James Heartfield, 'The politics of food: Two cheers for agribusiness', *Review of Radical Political Economics*, 32 (2000): 317–30.
81 James Woudhuysen and Ian Abley, *Why Is Construction So Backward?* (Chichester: Wiley-Academy, 2004), 50; 'Constructive arguments', *Building Design*, 8 April 2004.
82 Hume, 'It is the best of times to be alive. Ever'.
83 Kenan Malik, 'Ethical odyssey', *RSA Journal*, February 2007, 52.

developments in green technology to reduce greenhouse gas emissions and 'manage, perhaps minimise, climate change'.[84]

As far as ex-RCP activists were concerned, the environmentalist economics of 'sustainable development' exacerbated capitalism's global inequities. In 2002, the UN Johannesburg World Summit on Sustainable Development committed signatory states to 'protect and manage' natural resources and to discontinue 'unsustainable patterns of production and consumption'.[85] Promoting 'environmental sustainability', the Johannesburg colloquium's premise held that humanity was living beyond the world's finite means, damaging biodiversity and depleting natural resources.[86] Conversely, during the Johannesburg conference, the charity WORLDwrite – which originated from CAM activities in 1994 – campaigned against the 'disastrous consequences of the sustainability mantra'.[87] For WORLDwrite's director, Ceri Dingle, the summit prevented even the imperfect gains of capitalist development from benefiting the developing world: 'Poverty is solved by making people wealthy, not by forcing humanity back into the primeval wilderness'.[88] When the UN General Assembly designated 2002 the International Year of Ecotourism – Deputy Secretary-General Louise Fréchette argued that tourism had precipitated 'irresponsible development' and 'indigenous cultures' being 'disrupted by the influx of foreign goods and cultural values'[89] – Kirk Leech told an Institute of Ideas forum that the gesture fetishized 'primitivism' and negated the imperative of worldwide industrial development.[90]

Especially when the most severe financial crisis for seven decades began in the late 2000s, the network's radical humanism predominantly took the form of broadsides against environmentalism and 'growth scepticism'. For *spiked* correspondents, 'growth scepticism' represented the economic parallel of diminished subjectivity. In Canada, for example, Professor Peter Victor argued that to 'make room for economic expansion in those countries where the need is greatest', the developed world should observe biophysical limits, rather than

---

84 John Gillott, 'Global warming – where's the consensus?', *spiked*, 22 May 2001.
85 *Plan of Implementation of the World Summit on Sustainable Development*, see especially 2, 13–36. Available at un.org/esa/sustdev/documents/WSSD_POI_PD/English/WSSD_PlanImpl.pdf (accessed 11 July 2022).
86 A. J. McMichael, C. D. Butler and Carl Folke, 'New visions for addressing sustainability', *Science*, 12 December 2003.
87 Ceri Dingle, 'Time to ditch the sustainababble', *spiked*, 29 August 2002.
88 Ceri Dingle, 'Summit for nothing', *Architects' Journal*, 5 September 2002.
89 *International Year of Ecotourism 2002 Launched at Headquarters Event*. UN press release ENV/DEV/607, 28 January 2002. Available at press.un.org/en/2002/envdev607.doc.htm (accessed 3 July 2022).
90 Kirk Leech, 'Enforced primitivism', in Institute of Ideas, *Ethical Tourism: Who Benefits?* (London: Hodder & Stoughton, 2002), 77.

pursuing perpetual economic growth.[91] For ex-RCP cadres, jettisoning growth meant further stultifying social development. For former *Living Marxism* economics correspondent Daniel Ben-Ami, this 'cowardly capitalism' worsened a deeply flawed social system. Rather than securitizing assets, Ben-Ami averred, extending production should be the priority: limited growth reinforced low political expectations.[92] Implicitly recalling Marx's qualified admiration for bourgeois development, Ben-Ami castigated growth scepticism for undermining 'humanity's capacity to increase its control over nature'.[93]

For the ex-RCP milieu, the anti-capitalism which flourished during the global financial crisis from 2007 typified a regressive politics of low expectations. For *spiked* correspondents, leftists' calls for financial restraint were antithetical to Marx's emancipatory vision of superseding capitalism. When radicals attributed the crisis to 'excessive' economic growth, production and borrowing, veterans of the RCP scorned these critics for decrying the developmental aspects of capitalist modes of production. For Furedi, anti-capitalists who asserted that 'capitalism develops far too much and far too fast . . . [with] destructive consequences for both the environment and for people' diverged entirely from his own critique of capitalism's inability to *maximize* the productive potential.[94] The twenty-first-century left, Furedi argued, disparaged capitalism's flawed but notable positive components. Addressing a Battle of Ideas debate in November 2008, Furedi censured 'small-minded criticism of capitalism':

> The things capitalism gets criticised for are its good bits. You know, the fact that capitalism does expand wealth, does have an imperative towards developing the forces of production. Capitalism has been able to create a globalised system where, to a considerable extent, we have prosperity. . . . There are no future-oriented movements attacking capitalism. The only movements against capitalism are backward-looking ones. . . . They are basically low-expectations critiques of capitalism and that, to me, is far worse than anything that capitalism does.[95]

For ex-party veteran Rob Killick, such anti-capitalism represented a reactionary inversion of Marxist emancipatory politics. Writing on his weblog, Killick argued

---

91 Peter Victor, *Managing without Growth: Slower by Design, Not Disaster* (Cheltenham: Edward Elgar Publishing, 2008), *passim*. See especially 23–38, 154–68.
92 Daniel Ben-Ami, *Cowardly Capitalism: The Myth of the Global Financial Casino* (Chichester: John Wiley & Sons, 2001), 6, 145, 153.
93 Daniel Ben-Ami, 'Growth is good', *spiked*, 2 March 2006.
94 Frank Furedi, 'What happened to radical humanism?', in Jonathan Pugh (ed.), *What Is Radical Politics Today?* (Basingstoke: Palgrave Macmillan, 2009), 27–8.
95 'Capitalism – what is it good for?' debate at Battle of Ideas, 1 November 2008. Available at youtube.com/watch?v=tmfEXOMcI7o (accessed 11 February 2022).

that calls for restraint in production and growth could only worsen capitalist inequities:

> Marx never rejected the economic growth that capitalism can bring. He understood that freedom from want was the basis of civilisation and that remains true today.[96]

During the recession, *spiked* correspondents continued to invoke the Marxist theory of crisis. Decades earlier, the RCP was founded upon a dialectical understanding of crisis theory, appreciating both capitalism's immanent tendency to break down and the countervailing forces which helped the system to survive.[97] A regular feature of RCP reading lists, the German-American revolutionary Paul Mattick drew heavily upon Henryk Grossman's analysis of the Marxist theory of crisis. Following Grossman, Mattick schematized the 'counteracting tendencies' by which capitalists palliated a crisis.[98] Grossman had delineated how capitalists could expand foreign trade, reduce variable capital costs or increase capital turnover: 'A tendency to breakdown, combined with countertendencies, amounts to a tendency to crisis with the conditions for renewed accumulation being created in crisis.'[99] For RCP cadres as for Mattick, it followed that the outcome of economic crisis was contingent upon political contestation: the system of production would not collapse automatically but could only be overthrown by the working class acting decisively on the historical stage.

Recapitulating these themes from 2007, *spiked* writers scorned liberals and radicals alike who asserted that Marx had 'forecast' the demise of capitalism. For RCP veterans, such claims falsely ascribed historical determinism to the philosopher and crucially obscured the salience of the subject. Marx was neither 'an anti-capitalist Nostradamus' nor a 'soothsayer', Mick Hume averred;[100] rather, the materialist dialectic configured a pivotal role for the active subject.[101] Brendan O'Neill reiterated that capitalism would not simply disintegrate under the weight

---

96 'Capitalism, anti-capitalism and the G20', 30 March 2009. Available at postrecession.wordpress.com/2009/03/30/capitalism-anti-capitalism-and-the-g20/ (accessed 8 January 2021).
97 In his analysis of capitalism's contradictions and tendency to crisis, Marx also delineated the 'counteracting' mechanisms by which capitalism mitigated the declining rate of profit. Karl Marx, *Capital: A Critique of Political Economy – Volume Three* (London: Penguin, 1991), 339–48.
98 Paul Mattick, 'The permanent crisis', *International Council Correspondence*, 1, no. 2 (November 1934); Paul Mattick, *Economic Crisis and Crisis Theory* (Abingdon: Routledge, 2015 [first edition 1974]), 121.
99 Henryk Grossman, *The Law of Accumulation and Breakdown of the Capitalist System: Being also a Theory of Crises* (London: Pluto Press, 1992), 95–6.
100 'The boot's on the other foot: Was the Left right after all?'.
101 Mick Hume, 'A Capital investment', *spiked*, 22 October 2008.

of its own contradictions: Marxism was not simply a 'prophecy of collapse' but a systematic critique asserting the 'role of human agency'.[102]

Concurrently, *spiked* associates railed against critics who attributed the crash to bankers' and consumers' profligacy. According to Rob Killick, the crisis confirmed Marx's wider premise: that capitalism was unable consistently and globally to develop the means of production.[103] For ex-RCP activists, isolating singular manifestations of capitalism failed to comprehend its holistic character. Fulminating against consumers' and financiers' 'idolatry' in 2008, the Archbishop of Canterbury, Rowan Williams, adduced Marx's theory of commodity fetishism.[104] Mick Hume retorted that demonizing 'the excesses of individuals' could only obscure capitalism's systemic contradictions.[105] For Hume and his colleagues, such calls for constraint epitomized a politics of low expectations. If expanding credit, borrowing and production caused catastrophe, austerity would be the bleak antidote. Writing in 2009, Daniel Ben-Ami elucidated the 'dangerous political consequences' of attributing the crisis to 'bankers' greed'. Ben-Ami warned that charging the financial sector with avarice would justify a prolonged period of sluggish market growth.[106]

For the economists among the former RCP milieu, the crisis itself primarily reflected a lack of dynamism pervading Western economies and the wider political culture. *spiked* correspondents attributed the crash not to the capital overaccumulation theorized most notably by Henryk Grossman but to declining productivity.[107] For veterans of the party, economic stagnation in the early twenty-first century mirrored a lack of confidence among the capitalist class. For James Heartfield, 'green' credos championing restraint in land cultivation and energy usage reflected a broader 'failure of capitalist Subjectivity'.[108] When progressives blamed the crisis upon reckless financiers, *spiked* writers reasserted that increased experimentation and productivity were integral to liberating humanity from hunger, poverty and menial work. For Daniel Ben-Ami, 'self-

---

102 Brendan O'Neill, 'This Marxist isn't laughing', *spiked*, 15 October 2008.
103 'Capitalism, anti-capitalism and the G20'.
104 Rowan Williams, 'Face it: Marx was partly right about capitalism', *Spectator*, 24 September 2008.
105 Mick Hume, 'There is (still) no alternative', *spiked*, 30 September 2008.
106 Daniel Ben-Ami, 'It's easy, and wrong, to blame "greedy" bankers for the meltdown', *Independent on Sunday*, 21 May 2009.
107 In the formative years of the RCP, its founders drew especially upon Grossman's theoretical work on capital accumulation. In his magnum opus, Grossman explained that when 'dead labour', such as technology or machines, replaced 'living labour' – the only source of new value – a crisis of overaccumulation ensued, causing investment to contract. The crisis of capitalism, then, originated intrinsically in the capitalist mode of production. Grossman, *Law of Accumulation*. See also 'Accumulation and breakdown', *tns*, May 1981.
108 James Heartfield, 'Living Marxism', *The Platypus Review*, 9 (December 2008). Available at platypus1917.org/2008/12/01/living-marxism/ (accessed 27 January 2022).

proclaimed radicals' who posited natural economic limits evinced a 'deeply conservative outlook', renouncing the pursuit of prosperity for all.[109]

As the global financial crash gave way to a deepening recession, former RCP cadres criticized anti-capitalists who called for greater regulation of the financial sector. For *spiked* associates, activists who decried speculative investments were recoiling from contestation rather than developing a meaningful emancipatory politics. Anticipating demonstrations at the G20 summit in London in April 2009, Rob Killick scorned anti-capitalists who posited no 'coherent alternative to capitalism', save advocating a 'permanent recession to combat global warming'.[110]

After taking power in May 2010, the Conservative-Liberal Democrat coalition government commenced an austerity programme. By October 2010, the coalition's spending review mapped an 'unavoidable deficit reduction plan' for £80 billion of savings through the parliamentary term.[111] At the beginning of a new decade, veterans of the RCP renewed their critiques of a supposedly straitened political sphere. Co-authoring a 'manifesto for innovation', James Woudhuysen, Martyn Perks and Norman Lewis arraigned a polity which had 'lost faith in progress and the future' and upheld the scientific and technological potential for 'radically new means of production'.[112] First, class politics had dissipated; second, the fundamental belief in human subjectivity had diminished. The result, Mick Hume complained, was a stultifying political realm in which not only was there 'no alternative', but contestation itself appeared circumscribed:

> Nobody is even asking the questions about what should come next or where our economy and society should be heading.[113]

A 'pre-political' epoch

In the first decade of the twenty-first century, a substantial network of former RCP activists maintained contact. Old comrades participated in Institute of Ideas events and contributed polemics to *spiked*. Other friends supported an array of post-party initiatives, usually campaigning around issues of interest to

---

109 Katherine Mangu-Ward, 'In defense of economic growth', *Reason*, December 2010.
110 'Capitalism, anti-capitalism and the G20'.
111 Simon Lee, 'No Plan B: The coalition agenda for cutting the deficit and rebalancing the economy', in Simon Lee and Matt Beech (eds), *The Cameron-Clegg Government: Coalition Politics in an Age of Austerity* (Basingstoke: Palgrave Macmillan, 2011), 63.
112 James Woudhuysen (ed.), *Big Potatoes: The London Manifesto for Innovation* (London: The Big Potatoes Group, 2010), 18, 25, 49.
113 Hume, 'There is (still) no alternative'.

veterans who deplored a crisis of subjectivity. Many former cadres continued to research and write, and a substantial number forged careers in the media and academe. The party no longer existed, but its leadership and middle-ranking cadre retained a self-consciously distinct political tradition.

Developing their diagnosis from the twilight years of the RCP, the network's central political theme in the 2000s concerned the perceived diminution of subjectivity. A widespread lack of belief in humanity's transformative potential, they argued, generated an anodyne political culture, characterized by low expectations, unwillingness to experiment and societal atomization. A fragmented populace which acquiesced unenthusiastically in the status quo was disinclined to imagine or enact an alternative.

Through the 2000s, the network's analyses largely took the form of negative critiques of prevailing political trends. Reasserting humanity's ability to remake the world and to overcome social, economic and environmental problems, ex-RCP activists fulminated against what they interpreted as the politics of bland managerialism and bureaucratic authoritarianism. The rise of officialdom was understood both to confirm and exacerbate the technocratic politics of an unchallenged, yet undynamic, state.

Seeking to reanimate political contestation through the 2000s, the former RCP milieu asserted first principles. Expounding a syncretic radical humanism, they reframed emancipatory tenets to challenge misanthropic ideas. In the supposed absence of radical subjectivity, activists fundamentally asserted humanity's history-making capability. Reiterating the capacity for reasoned, unified action, the milieu's humanist politics often took distinct libertarian forms. For capitalist libertarians, individual freedom possesses intrinsic value as an end in itself, pursued through private property rights, free-market economics and limited government.[114] In contrast from the libertarianism of conservative free-marketeers, former RCP activists exhorted subjective independence from the state and authority as a prerequisite for formulating an emancipatory political alternative to capitalism.

Class occupied a peculiar position in the network's analyses, featuring more as an interpretive lens than as an active category. On the one hand, ex-RCPers generally maintained a Marxist critique of social development, observing capitalism's internal contradictions and tendency to crisis. The essential Marxist aspiration to an alternative system of production, superseding class society

---

114 Martin van Hees, 'Freedom', in Matt Zwolinski and Benjamin Ferguson (eds), *The Routledge Companion to Libertarianism* (Abingdon: Routledge, 2022), 28.

and liberating all from want, underpinned veterans' analyses. Simultaneously, however, *spiked* correspondents depicted an era not only devoid of class politics, but amid a 'pre-political' crisis of radical subjectivity more broadly. Former RCP activists prioritized invigorating a collective sense of human capability. By definition, this universalist ethos did not distinguish according to class. Writing in 2002, Mick Hume dismissed as outmoded the political vocabulary of a previous era but reasserted a bedrock principle: 'I'm not a Trotskyist, but the idea of a human-centred morality is still central to all that I believe today'.[115]

---

[115] 'Mick Hume on Leon Trotsky's *Their Morals and Ours*', *New Statesman*, 2 December 2002.

7

From the 'demise of ideologies' to a 'people's decade', c. 2010–20

Throughout the early 2010s, the Academy of Ideas – formerly known as the Institute – convened a packed calendar of events, peaking each November with its flagship Battle of Ideas weekend festival. *spiked* remained a hive of online polemic, publishing articles and essays written not only by former RCP activists but increasingly by newcomers who admired the website's humanism and libertarianism. Meanwhile, many ex-RCPers continued to pursue successful careers in academe, the media and the private sector. Often, they maintained cordial contact with old comrades while developing professional and sometimes public profiles. Through *spiked*, Academy of Ideas events, media appearances and copious publications, the former party network maintained a distinct ideological tradition.

Politically, however, these were wilderness years for the radical humanists who had formerly belonged to the RCP. Developing earlier themes, they denounced what they perceived as a hollow, 'pre-political' culture characterized by diminished subjectivity and circumscribed contestation. To the extent that activists attained public prominence, they did so as unremitting critics of contemporary orthodoxies. Negative critiques spanned broadsides against technocratic governance, identity politics, statist labourism and environmentalism. Some three decades after the RCP formed, its erstwhile cadres had seldom been so profoundly disillusioned not only with objective forces but with the political landscape in toto.

In stark contrast, by the end of the 2010s, *spiked* editor Brendan O'Neill could celebrate a 'People's Decade' of 'peaceful, understated working-class revolt'.[1] For O'Neill and for many of his former comrades in the RCP, the defining moment was 23 June 2016, when 17,410,742 people – constituting a 51.9 per cent majority

---

1 Brendan O'Neill, 'The people's decade', *spiked*, 27 December 2019.

– voted for the UK to leave the European Union. Frank Furedi hailed the 'revolt' as an 'opportunity' to reignite 'real and substantial' political contestation.² *spiked* associates had ardently championed a Leave vote. Some ex-RCP cadres even stood as election candidates for the Brexit Party, which formed in November 2018, pressurizing Theresa May's Conservative government to fulfil the referendum result.

Analysing the ex-RCP network's engagement with the referendum and its aftermath, this chapter begins by analysing why veterans interpreted Brexit as a vital rebellion against technocratic politics. In doing so, it grounds the EU debate in the network's long-term radical humanist precepts. For theoreticians who had narrated the decline of subjectivity and contestation, the Brexit vote merited celebration most basically as a popular challenge to the status quo. Ex-RCP activists, it is argued, championed national 'sovereignty' as a core, if partial, component of reviving political disputation.

The chapter proceeds to examine how the former party milieu assessed the Black Lives Matter (BLM) protests which intensified worldwide sharply after the murder of George Floyd in Minneapolis in May 2020. Ex-RCP cadres' hostility towards critical race theory accentuated 'universal' humanist precepts and reasserted class – at least as a prism for social analysis – as the cardinal demographic category. Finally, scrutinizing *spiked*'s critique of the British government response to the Covid-19 pandemic, the chapter draws out tensions within the network. Former comrades did not unanimously share *spiked*'s libertarian opposition to lockdowns: the controversy occasioned a rare public dispute. Moreover, this analysis demonstrates the contrapuntal quality of veterans' contemporary political analyses. Many who celebrated Brexit as an expression of popular political independence later lamented widespread acquiescence in what *spiked* considered reactionary identity politics and authoritarian governance.

'Democracy: The unfinished revolution'³

Before the referendum of 2016, *spiked* correspondents lamenting societal dormancy essentially bemoaned the perceived decline of *collective* subjectivity. In a 'pre-political' age, they argued, the absence of meaningful contestation reflected and perpetuated societal fragmentation. Endorsing the Bulgarian intellectual

---

2   Frank Furedi, 'Revolt of the others', *spiked*, 30 June 2016.
3   Brendan O'Neill, 'Democracy: The unfinished revolution', *spiked*, 8 July 2019.

Ivan Krastev's damning assessment of contemporary protest movements since the global recession began in 2008, Tara McCormack arraigned the poverty of 'collective identity' in 'exit politics'.[4] Political dissent, McCormack argued, mostly constituted 'a cry of frustration', unable to 'challenge the status quo'.[5] Similarly, writing shortly after the general election of 2015, Ella Whelan of *spiked* charged the Labour Party with lacking a galvanizing ideology and imagination. Unifying citizens in a 'shared political outlook', Whelan averred, was crucial for any compelling attempt to 'change society'.[6]

Positioning the state as the obverse of citizens' autonomy, former RCP activists perceived bureaucratic authority dominating a circumscribed political realm in the 2010s. For veterans of the party, the officious, regulatory state, pervading public and private life, indicated a dismal popular inertia. For Josie Appleton, the ascendant 'busybody state' highlighted a 'weakening of civic life – a social fragmentation and mutual suspicion, and reduction of independence'.[7] In this phase of degraded subjectivity, ex-cadres regarded anti-statism as a cornerstone for rebuilding political dissent. In 2012, positioning herself in the 'Bolshevik' tradition's 'revolutionary struggle for freedom', Academy of Ideas director Claire Fox declared it 'dispiriting' to hear leftists employ 'libertarian' pejoratively.[8]

At this juncture, theoreticians considered the 'culture wars' a symptom of a vapid political sphere. Interminable controversies pertaining to sectional or identity-based concerns were taken as part of the 'pre-political' cul-de-sac. With major questions of social organization suspended, Frank Furedi argued, the 'culture wars' marked the 'demise of ideologies'.[9] Subsequently, to the dismay of a minority of their former comrades, several *spiked* correspondents engaged extensively in culture war disputes. A veteran who left the party around 1990 sharply distinguished the RCP's world-historical aspirations from *spiked*'s contemporary 'war on wokeness': 'I do not see the value of it . . . it's got nothing to do with building a vanguard'.[10] Although there is scope, then, for a degree of discomposure in activists' testimonies, these moderate criticisms of *spiked* implicitly uphold the party tradition against supposed deviation. Another

---

4 For Krastev, the protest movements, which emerged after the global recession of 2008, were 'a cry of frustration' with 'no interest in attempting an alternative to the existing forms of representation. . . . The protesters themselves have no suggestions, beyond acting out'. Ivan Krastev, *Democracy Disrupted: The Politics of Global Protest* (Philadelphia: University of Pennsylvania Press, 2014), 31.
5 Tara McCormack, 'The anti-politics of protest', *spiked*, 14 October 2016.
6 Ella Whelan, 'The left: From solidarity to pity', *spiked*, 21 May 2015.
7 Josie Appleton, *Officious: Rise of the Busybody State* (Winchester: Zero Books, 2015), 4, 105.
8 Claire Fox, '"I am happy to call myself a Bolshevik"', *spiked*, 16 May 2012.
9 Frank Furedi, *First World War: Still No End in Sight* (London: Bloomsbury, 2014), 241.
10 Former RCP member interview with the author, November 2021.

former member of the RCP similarly eschews the online magazine's 'culture warrior position':

> I don't really read *spiked* much anymore. I read an occasional article if it gets shared on social media or something, but I don't generally read it. Partly it was because I thought, *I know what they are going to say*, and then partly because it just started to irritate me.[11]

Identifying an acutely adverse conjuncture during the early 2010s, *spiked* associates were preoccupied with asserting the human capacity for independent reasoning and collective action. The breadth of these apologias signalled that the network was on the defensive, stipulating fundamental humanist premises. Marking the bicentenary of Thomas Paine's death, Brendan O'Neill lauded the American revolutionary's 'faith in human agency': for *spiked*'s editor, the belief that 'ordinary people' could comprehend and remake their world represented a conceptual oasis in 2010.[12] When the Leveson Report on the practices of the press recommended new restrictions, Mick Hume scorned the inquiry for undermining the public's critical faculties.[13]

During these wilderness years, the network galvanized around vague but stentorian aspirations to a renewed public sphere. Drawing upon the maverick American historian Christopher Lasch's concept of the 'minimal self', Jennie Bristow exhorted the millennial generation to aspire not merely to managing and mediating risk but to transforming society.[14] Claire Fox, meanwhile, implored the young adults of the early twenty-first century to reject the prevailing 'mood of fear and loathing' and 'shape the future as you want it. . . . History is yours for the making'.[15] Railing against a pervasive, 'degraded' view of the subject, Helene Guldberg asserted that upholding humanity's capacity to 'change society for the better' was the political priority for the 2010s.[16]

During its vanguardist phase in the 1980s, the RCP Political Committee regarded the UK's membership of the European Economic Community (EEC)

---

11 Former RCP member interview with the author, October 2021.
12 Brendan O'Neill, 'The common sense of Thomas Paine', *Guardian*, 17 November 2010.
13 Mick Hume, *There Is No Such Thing as a Free Press . . . and We Need One More Than Ever* (London: Societas, 2012); Mick Hume, 'Keep your nose out of the press', *English Journalism Review*, 24 (2013): 25.
14 Jennie Bristow, *The Sociology of Generations: New Directions and Challenges* (London: Palgrave Macmillan, 2016), 61. Lasch's concept of the 'minimal self' was grounded in a critique of corroded democracy in the mid-1980s. Analysing a rising 'professional and managerial class' employing a 'therapeutic mode of social control', Lasch posited that the 'exclusion of the public from political participation' was both a symptom and a cause of diminished subjectivity. Christopher Lasch, *The Minimal Self: Psychic Survival in Troubled Times* (London: Picador, 1984), 46–51.
15 Claire Fox, *'I Find That Offensive!'* (London: Biteback, 2016), 66–7, 178.
16 Helene Guldberg, *Just Another Ape?* (Exeter: Societas, 2010), *passim*. See especially 19, 150.

as a 'non-issue'.[17] Revolutionaries were not interested in choosing between 'different forms of capitalist domination'.[18] Through the mid-1990s, however, developments inside and outside the party prompted a reassessment of the European question. First, European institutions assumed more centralized authority. Founding the European Union (EU), the Maastricht Treaty of 1992 marked a 'new stage in the process of European integration'.[19] Second, the RCP's internal review – which culminated in its dissolution in 1996 – concluded that both revolutionary politics and subjective agency per se were in crisis. In this context, veterans saw supranational governance contributing to a narrowing domestic political sphere. Writing in the year the RCP disbanded, Jennie Bristow fulminated against European organizations as 'symbols of unaccountable power in an anti-democratic age'.[20]

By February 2016, when Prime Minister David Cameron announced that the referendum on the UK's membership of the EU would take place four months later, former RCP cadres had firmly identified Brussels as an instrument of anti-democratic technocracy. Since the turn of the century, *spiked* correspondents had opposed the EU's centripetal power dynamics. In December 2008, for example, when the EU directed the Irish electorate to vote again on the Lisbon Treaty – which 53.4 per cent of voters had rejected six months earlier – Josie Appleton's Manifesto Club published a satirical 'phrasebook' scorning Europhile antipathy to the referendum result.[21] Activists similarly lambasted the European 'troika' – comprising the European Commission, the European Central Bank and the International Monetary Fund – for insisting that the Dublin government implement an austerity programme to qualify for a financial bailout.[22] For James Heartfield, the EU epitomized an 'apolitical style of social administration', far

---

17 Joan Phillips, 'The new Europeans', *tns*, 26 May 1989.
18 '1992: What we think', *tns*, 5 May 1989.
19 John Major's government survived a substantial Tory rebellion and a vote of confidence before parliament ratified the Maastricht Treaty in 1993. The British delegation had secured an 'opt-out' from Maastricht's Social Chapter – which pertained to employment and welfare rights – and from plans for a single currency, but Conservative Eurosceptics nevertheless opposed an agreement which pledged intergovernmental cooperation on, inter alia, economic, foreign and judicial policy. Alwyn W. Turner, *A Classless Society: Britain in the 1990s* (London: Aurum Press, 2013), 142–60; *Treaty on European Union Including the Protocols and Final Act with Declarations* (London: Her Majesty's Stationery Office, 1994), *passim*, especially 80–6.
20 Jennie Bristow, 'Who's hiding behind Europe?', *Living Marxism*, July–August 1996.
21 Manifesto Club, *27 Ways to Say: No Doesn't Really Mean No* (London: Manifesto Club, 2008). The publication recalled earlier instances of EU intransigence, such as when the Irish electorate voted against the Nice Treaty in 2001, and French and Dutch voters rejected the revised European constitution in 2005.
22 Brendan O'Neill, 'The Republic of Ireland: Colonised by commissioners', *spiked*, 19 November 2010.

removed from 'popular democracy'.[23] In this schema, supranational technocracy was both a symptom and a cause of pre-political malaise.[24]

Asserting that European integration compounded circumscribed domestic politics, former RCP activists committed to defend 'national sovereignty'. For *spiked* associates, national independence was not an ideological terminus but rather a precondition for awakening a mature citizenry. In the late 1980s, when the RCP could still envision forging a revolutionary vanguard in the working class, cadres castigated Euroscepticism as a 'reactionary defence of national sovereignty'.[25] By the 2010s, having declared a 'pre-political' historic nadir, former party activists regarded such a defence of sovereignty not as reactionary but as a necessary foundation for reconstituting political subjectivity. Gauging vox populi in east London for a film project in 2012, WORLD write director Ceri Dingle insisted that most animosity towards Brussels arraigned the EU's 'contempt for democracy' and was 'clearly not fuelled by ignorance, parochialism or bigotry'.[26]

For the *spiked* milieu, leaving the EU was not necessarily sufficient to reanimate political life but would crucially remove a major obstacle to domestic contestation. When the referendum campaigns began in 2015, Phil Mullan asserted that leaving the trading bloc would not, alone, reinvigorate British politics. The former *Living Marxism* economics correspondent also acknowledged 'positive' European statutes upholding the free international movement of people, goods and services. Fundamentally, however, Mullan concluded, leaving the EU was imperative for 'democracy': EU membership precluded independent arguments for 'long overdue ... radically transformative' politics.[27] Claire Fox similarly considered Brexit crucial, albeit unable single-handedly to reinstate political contestation. After the UK finally left the EU, Fox acknowledged that sovereignty was not inherently democratic or progressive. Rather, she declared, Brexit opened new political possibilities: it was not 'a destination, but the beginning of a new democratic settlement'.[28] Likewise, for Alan Hudson, Brexit was a 'necessary' but 'insufficient' step towards mobilizing critical citizenship:

23 James Heartfield, 'Demobilising the nation: The decline of sovereignty in western Europe', *International Politics*, 46 (2009): 729.
24 James Heartfield, *The European Union and the End of Politics* (Winchester: Zero Books, 2012), 57, 270-1.
25 James Wood, 'A Marxist perspective on 1992', *Confrontation*, 5 (Summer 1989): 165.
26 Ceri Dingle, '"You can be a European and be against the EU"', *spiked*, 9 February 2012.
27 Phil Mullan, 'The real reason we should fight for a Brexit', *spiked*, 26 October 2015.
28 Claire Fox, *The Sovereign Subjects of History* (London: Academy of Ideas, 2021), 3, 8, 10.

Figure 7 Newly elected as a Member of the European Parliament, Claire Fox of the Brexit Party speaks on stage during the European election count at the Central Convention Complex, Manchester, 27 May 2019. Credit: Peter Byrne/PA Archive/PA Images.

> It was one battle in an ongoing struggle for the reinvigoration of democracy. I think it's slightly naive to hope or believe that it gives enough momentum in and of itself. More stimulation is needed and that's a real problem. Who are you stimulating and in what environments? That's the difficulty.[29]

Ex-RCP cadres' motivations for advocating a Leave vote largely diverged from those of conservative Eurosceptics. Defending 'national sovereignty' impelled both *spiked* correspondents and Thatcherites. For example, the Eurosceptic Conservative MEP Daniel Hannan, a founding member of the Vote Leave campaign, railed against the 'loss of sovereignty' inherent in the rise of supremacy in EU law.[30] But for ex-RCP Brexiteers, very different political ideas underpinned the principle of sovereignty. Whereas Vote Leave's calls to 'take back control' evinced reactionary economic isolationism and hostility to immigration, *spiked* Brexiteers promoted sovereignty as a precondition for upgrading domestic debate and developing an internationalist, humanist alternative.[31]

---

29 Alan Hudson, 22 October 2021.
30 Daniel Hannan, *Why Vote Leave* (London: Head of Zeus, 2016), 62–3.
31 Vote Leave accentuated the economic costs of EU membership – 'the EU costs us over £350 million a week' – and member states' inability to restrict immigration: 'A quarter of a million EU migrants

By the same premise, *spiked* shared radical left Eurosceptics' foundational animus to the EU's centralized power. For example, Costas Lapavitsas, an erstwhile member of Greece's anti-austerity Syriza administration in 2015, was a leading left advocate for Brexit, or 'Lexit'. Lapavitsas's critique of Brussels highlighted especially how the EU had imposed austerity economics upon member states after 2008 and would obstruct Keynesian and statist economic alternatives, such as major nationalization programmes.[32] However, whereas Lapavitsas and state socialists primarily arraigned the EU as a neoliberal vehicle for global capital, ex-RCP Brexiteers inveighed more fundamentally against corroded sovereignty.

Only a fringe minority of former RCP activists disavowed *spiked*'s position on the EU debate. Former Edinburgh activist Chris Gilligan, for example, charged his ex-comrades with exaggerating the progressive potential of leaving the EU. Blogging three months before the vote, Gilligan averred that a Brexit would neither 'reinvigorate democracy' nor 'popular sovereignty'. Advocating a Leave vote, Gilligan declared, could only bolster 'the elites' pretence' that EU membership, rather than overarching social relations, represented the preeminent political controversy.[33]

In contrast, for most ex-RCPers, the Brexit vote represented a seminal popular rebellion after more than two decades of degraded subjectivity and technocratic advance. From a long-term perspective, many veterans considered Brexit the first major political advance in a generation. For activists who had dissolved the vanguard party and inveighed against a pre-political era, the referendum result was 'the best thing that had happened for decades':

> [Brexit] was absolutely great. That was people sticking two fingers up. It was a long-delayed reaction to all those developments from the eighties onwards, where people recognised that they were not part of a debate about how things should be. They'd been completely excluded. And people said, *we've had enough of this*. A lot of people recognised the EU for what it was: a lot of unaccountable people making all sorts of decisions and talking down to us and lecturing us about what is best.[34]

---

come here every year. . . . This puts a big strain on public services like the NHS and schools'. Vote Leave, *Why Should We Vote Leave on 23 June?* (London: Vote Leave, 2016).
32 Costas Lapavitsas, *The Left Case against the EU* (Cambridge: Polity Press, 2018), 25–32, 113–41.
33 'Open letter on Brexit that spiked rejected', *Marxist Humanist Initiative*, 25 March 2016. Available at marxisthumanistinitiative.org/uk-news/open-letter-on-brexit-that-spiked-rejected.html (accessed 18 October 2021).
34 Former RCP member interview with the author, August 2021.

From this standpoint, the vote indicated that diminished subjectivity was reversible. Even veterans who had not hitherto regarded the EU as a major issue found a democratic essence in the Leave campaign. An activist who 'hadn't been very strongly committed to the position of Brexit' until 2016 recalled that militant Remainers' subsequent

> reaction . . . made me realise how right we were [to Leave] . . . I was so horrified by these demands for the second referendum. It just shows how little regard democracy was held in.[35]

Interpreting the referendum as a historic rebellion in defence of sovereignty, many among the ex-party milieu envisaged more thoroughgoing political reengagement. Addressing a keynote Battle of Ideas debate in 2019, Joan Hoey positioned 'democracy' as the 'pre-eminent political fault line'. Indicating 'realignment' in British politics, Hoey argued that Brexit exploded a generation of circumscribed politics: 'the status quo has been called into question and challenged'.[36]

Throughout the 2010s, the *spiked* network located rising populism across Europe in a wider assault upon elitist technocracy. Correspondents applauded these movements less for their particular forms than for their generally anti-elitist content. Ex-RCPers generally refrained from endorsing specific populists, instead championing their wider emphasis upon national sovereignty and hostility to unaccountable bureaucracy. In a floor speech at the Battle of Ideas in 2016, Joan Hoey positioned ascendant populism – whose leaders might 'not serve' their electorates well – as an indictment of 'failed . . . mainstream' politicians, who were 'completely disconnected from the people'.[37] For Frank Furedi, when the EU challenged member states' domestic policies, it corroded the political sphere. Highlighting Hungary's strained relationship with Brussels, Furedi contended that the EU's 'illiberal anti-populism' threatened democracy more gravely than did Viktor Orbán's right-wing government.[38] At a debate in London in 2017, Furedi held that the 'issues' with Orbán's Fidesz party – 'they're not exactly God's gift to liberal Enlightenment' – were secondary to the more

---

35 Former RCP activist interview, October 2021.
36 Joan Hoey quoted in 'After Brexit: The new political faultlines', Battle of Ideas, 2019. Available at youtube.com/watch?v=_h5I1FjCG7g2 (accessed 29 March 2022).
37 Joan Hoey quoted in 'The new populism', 2016. Available at youtube.com/watch?v=M1SorSO5Tac&t=3061s (accessed 28 January 2022).
38 Frank Furedi, *Populism and the European Culture Wars: The Conflict of Values between Hungary and the EU* (London: Routledge, 2017).

profound 'problem' of Brussels 'anti-populism', which would dilute political participation and accountability.[39]

Critiquing a pre-political epoch defined by lofty technocracy, ex-RCP activists positioned national sovereignty as a cornerstone of renascent democracy. Upholding national independence was not a parochial predilection but a crucial foundation for reanimating the demos. Eschewing the 'global' emancipatory frameworks of political philosophers Michael Hardt and Antonio Negri,[40] Frank Furedi argued that meaningful contestation required clearly demarcated boundaries.[41] In his keynote contribution at the Battle of Ideas in 2019, Furedi posited the nation state as the constitutive unit for a robust public sphere:

> I consider myself a man of the Enlightenment, universalistic outlook, which is very, very important to me. . . . But whether we like it or not . . . [the] nation is important . . . because up until now, there's no other framework in which you can have a situation where democracy can work. You cannot have a democratic society without a demos. And you cannot have a demos unless it's territorially bounded.[42]

By contrast, Furedi averred, empowering supranational institutions was

> regressive. . . . Because whoever runs the IMF, or the United Nations, or NATO . . . these are not people that are accountable to anybody. They might be wonderful people . . . but nobody elected them. They're not accountable to anybody.[43]

Similarly, distinguishing his position from 'insular and narrow-minded' nationalism, Phil Mullan espoused national sovereignty as 'not the opposite of internationalism' but rather 'its consort'. For Mullan, without national independence, citizens could not fight for the 'principles of democracy, reason,

---

39 'After Brexit: Reimagining Sovereignty – Gisela Stuart in conversation with Frank Furedi', 13 September 2017. Available at youtube.com/watch?v=fRf9K4RFd00 (accessed 7 April 2022).
40 In the first instalment of their major trilogy, Hardt and Negri conceptualized 'Empire' as a new form of sovereignty binding national *and* supranational institutions in the globalist epoch. Superseding the conventional imperialism which flowed from nation states, Empire had no fixed territory or boundaries. To challenge the new order, Hardt and Negri contended, it behoved radicals to formulate an alternative which similarly transcended the nation state. Revisiting their thesis in 2019, the post-Marxist theorists again criticized radicals who positioned national sovereignty as a 'defensive weapon against the predations of neoliberalism, multinational corporations and global elites'. Michael Hardt and Antonio Negri, *Empire* (Cambridge, MA: Harvard University Press, 2000); Michael Hardt and Antonio Negri, '*Empire*, twenty years on', *New Left Review*, 120 (November–December 2019).
41 Frank Furedi, *Why Borders Matter: Why Humanity Must Relearn the Art of Drawing Boundaries* (Abingdon: Routledge, 2021), 9, 57–8.
42 Frank Furedi quoted in 'Hungary: The bad boy of Europe?' Available at youtube.com/watch?v=U8u7StsG0uM (accessed 6 January 2022).
43 Ibid.

openness and progress'.⁴⁴ In a globalist context, Mick Hume told the Battle of Ideas in 2017, national sovereignty assumed additional importance as a prerequisite for renewing popular political participation:

> I'm an old Marxist internationalist and an anti-imperialist. I've always wanted to see an international brotherhood of humanity. But I've become increasingly aware of the importance of defending national sovereignty – particularly against the EU in our circumstances – as the absolute bedrock of democracy.⁴⁵

Although *spiked* Brexiteers stopped short of suggesting that Leave voters consciously articulated class politics, they perceived an acutely subaltern dimension in a rebellion against the 'elites'. When the Conservatives won the general election of December 2019 on a ticket of 'getting Brexit done', Brendan O'Neill hailed the

> sign that the people still wanted Brexit and that the working classes had finally broken from the Labour bureaucracy and asserted their political and moral independence.⁴⁶

Celebrating Brexit as a vital if inchoate expression of civic engagement, *spiked* correspondents regarded the vote as a salutary reminder of the

> residual power of the working class, even though it has no consciousness in itself as a class and no effective organisation.... It's not all bad news.⁴⁷

The *spiked* network characterized the Brexit vote primarily as a popular demand for political power. Downplaying the more sectional and reactionary facets of the Leave vote – such as opposition to immigration, for example – most ex-RCPers regarded the referendum as the emblem of an enlivened polity. In February 2020, former Brexit Party MEP Claire Fox addressed a conference in Stockport coordinated by Change Politics for Good, a pro-Brexit organization committed to elevating democracy. Recalling the Stockport meeting, Fox compared the referendum – when Leavers 'found their political voice as citizens' – to the radical historian Christopher Hill's famous depiction of ideological ferment during the 1650s interregnum: this seminal account of the seventeenth-century revolutionary underground vividly evoked a 'world turned upside down' amid a

---

44   Phil Mullan, *Beyond Confrontation: Globalists, Nationalists and their Discontents* (Bingley: Emerald Publishing, 2020), 23, 27.
45   Mick Hume quoted in 'What is ... democracy?' Available at youtube.com/watch?v=fn7EEaRdwK8 (accessed 27 October 2020).
46   Brendan O'Neill, 'The magnificence of Brexit', *spiked*, 31 January 2020.
47   Rob Killick interview with the author, 11 January 2021.

'fantastic outburst of energy, both physical and intellectual'.[48] Hill's depiction of 'glorious flux and intellectual excitement . . . overturning, questioning, revaluing . . . everything', Fox averred, was equally applicable to Brexit Britain.[49] Ascribing the Leave vote to a popular clamour for sovereignty, ex-RCP Brexiteers diverged from veterans of the SWP, for example, who hailed the referendum result broadly as a 'revolt against the establishment' while castigating the 'mainstream Leave campaign' as a 'disgusting mix of racism and reaction'.[50]

While some among the network acknowledged voters' heterogeneous motives, they insisted that the broader struggle for sovereignty defined the referendum result and its legacy. Denis Russell, for example, granted that some Leave voters had been primarily 'concerned with immigration – they could be quite right-wing with that'. But Russell maintained that the overall vote reflected a more positive democratic tendency.[51] Another former activist asserted that the 'vast majority' of Eurosceptics sought 'greater democratic control over our laws . . . immigration did come as part of the package . . . but that isn't *the* reason'.[52] Interviewed days after the referendum, Claire Fox positioned national sovereignty as an imperfect but vital vehicle for reanimating political contestation:

> Millions of people certainly voted Leave because of the immigration question. That saddens me, as I am a pro-immigration internationalist and I have advocated for an open borders policy for many years. But I also found it very galling to have to listen to the pro-EU open borders camp, proclaiming themselves as open borders, but then actually being advocates of 'Fortress Europe', those technocrats who try to stop African or Asian people from seeking asylum in Europe or in the UK. I do not think that the nation state per se is the ideal form of organizing, but neither is the European Union.[53]

As far as most former RCP activists were concerned, Brexit's significance resided not in specific policy minutiae but in activating totemically the *capacity* to transform domestic politics. Addressing a pro-Leave campaign group event

---

48 Christopher Hill, *The World Turned Upside Down: Radical Ideas during the English Revolution* (Harmondsworth: Penguin, 1991), 361 [first edition London: Maurice Temple Smith, 1972]).
49 Fox, *The Sovereign Subjects of History*, 1–2.
50 Charlie Kimber, 'Workers are right to reject Cameron's EU', *Socialist Worker*, 14 June 2016; 'Brexit vote was a revolt against the rich', *Socialist Worker*, 28 June 2016.
51 Regina Lavelle, 'Irish Brexiteers: "After the vote, I realised how undemocratic things have become"', *Irish Independent*, 4 May 2019.
52 Former RCP member interview with the author, October 2021.
53 Slawek Blich, 'Fox: I am on the Left and I want to exit', *Krytyka Politczna*, 30 June 2016. Available at politicalcritique.org/world/uk/2016/fox-i-am-on-the-left-and-i-want-to-exit/# (accessed 3 February 2022).

several weeks after the referendum, Kunle Olulode asserted that voters of diverse political perspectives had unified around the powerful principle of sovereignty.[54]

Since their support for Brexit asserted national sovereignty as a precondition for renewed contestation, several ex-RCP activists fulminated against any diluted settlement. For veterans who promulgated a threshold moment for political independence, only a total break from European institutions would suffice. When the UK and EU agreed a Brexit deal in December 2020, Jon Holbrook complained that the 479,000-word agreement legislated not only for trade but for 'broader issues of public policy'. A deal committing the UK to align with EU environmental, industrial, security and social policies, Holbrook argued, 'constrained' domestic democracy.[55]

From 2020, *spiked* correspondents inveighed against the Northern Ireland Protocol for attenuating the UK's withdrawal from the EU. Agreed by Westminster and Brussels to protect the EU single market and avoid a hard post-Brexit border on the island of Ireland, the Protocol demarcated a customs boundary in the Irish Sea. Cognizant of the symbiotic economic relationship between Ireland's two jurisdictions – in 2015, for example, Northern Ireland's £2.7 billion of goods exports to the Republic constituted 36 per cent of its total goods exports[56] – the Protocol's architects aimed principally to reduce friction in cross-border trade. To unionist politicians' considerable chagrin, the Protocol essentially kept Northern Ireland within the EU trading bloc. Unionists' prolonged protests against the Protocol culminated in February 2022, when Paul Givan – Democratic Unionist Party (DUP) leader and Northern Ireland First Minister – resigned, causing Northern Ireland's devolved Stormont Assembly to collapse. The historical irony of *spiked* correspondents and unionist grandees simultaneously opposing the Protocol was not lost on Brendan O'Neill, a veteran of the RCP and IFM.[57]

---

54 '"Immigration was used by both sides to exploit the working class vote" – Kunle Olulode', 14 July 2016. Available at youtube.com/watch?v=u6-pCetoASs (accessed 7 April 2022).
55 Jon Holbrook, 'Taking back control?', *Critic*, 29 December 2020. Available at thecritic.co.uk/taking-back-control/ (accessed 25 October 2021).
56 Nicholas Wright, 'Brexit and Ireland: Collateral damage?' in Benjamin Martill and Uta Staiger (eds), *Brexit and Beyond: Rethinking the Futures of Europe* (London: UCL Press, 2018), 111.
57 An inveterate supporter of Irish unification, O'Neill had lambasted the Good Friday Agreement of 1998 as a 'disgrace', by which the Irish republican leadership 'signed away everything they once stood for, accepting that there will not be a united Ireland'. Brendan O'Neill, 'A peace of nothing', *LM*, May 1998. More than two decades later, the *spiked* editor retained his aspirations for Irish unification but insisted that the UK's integrity and 'independence' from the EU came first: 'I say this as someone who has long wanted to see a United Ireland. But not this kind of United Ireland. Not an Ireland being increasingly united under the undemocratic purview of EU rule and against the wishes of both the Unionist electorate in Northern Ireland and the British people more broadly'. Brendan O'Neill, 'It's time to tear up the Northern Ireland Protocol', *spiked*, 8 April 2021.

But these curious political bedfellows' ultimate motivations for opposing the Protocol diverged: whereas unionists feared that the arrangement jeopardized Northern Ireland's constitutional position,[58] O'Neill and his colleagues fulminated primarily against 'a cynical dilution of Brexit'.[59] Pithily attesting Brexit's salience for 'democratic principle', Pauline Hadaway's critique of the Protocol positioned a clean break from the EU as a prerequisite for holistic political reassessment:

> For radical democrats, political power is not simply the power to change governments, but the power to change the way we are governed. This raises the possibility of making a choice between asserting the integrity of the UK or calling for Britain to signal its intention to make an orderly departure from Northern Ireland.[60]

'The dangers of the new anti-racism'

On 25 May 2020, in the US city of Minneapolis, George Floyd, a 46-year-old Black man, was arrested on suspicion of handling a counterfeit banknote. While Floyd was handcuffed, lying face down on the road, Derek Chauvin, a white police officer, knelt on Floyd's neck. Despite Floyd's protests, Chauvin maintained his position for nine minutes, killing Floyd. Some thirteen months later, Chauvin was convicted of second-degree unintentional murder and sentenced to twenty years and six months in prison. George Floyd's murder sparked protests worldwide against police brutality, coalescing around the international BLM movement through the summer of 2020.[61] Within three weeks of Floyd's death, Home Secretary Priti Patel announced that 210,000 people had joined more than 160 demonstrations across Britain.[62] In an especially well-documented protest in

---

58 Opposition to the Protocol dominated the two largest unionist parties' campaigns for Northern Ireland's Assembly elections in May 2022. The DUP identified the Protocol as 'an existential threat' to the union, while the Ulster Unionist Party agreed: 'Unionists cannot accept an internal border within the United Kingdom'. Democratic Unionist Party, *Our 5 Point Plan for Northern Ireland: Real Action on the Issues that Matter to You* (Belfast: Democratic Unionist Party, 2022); Ulster Unionist Party, *Build a Better Northern Ireland* (Belfast: Ulster Unionist Party, 2022).
59 O'Neill, 'It's time to tear up the Northern Ireland Protocol'.
60 Pauline Hadaway, 'Arlene Foster, Northern Ireland and a politics of permanent crisis', *spiked*, 30 April 2021.
61 Simultaneously a slogan, social media hashtag and proper noun, Black Lives Matter signifies a decentralized global organization, formed in 2013, comprising chapters worldwide. BLM strives to 'eradicate white supremacy' and achieve a 'world where Black lives are no longer systematically targeted for demise'. 'About Black Lives Matter'. Available at blacklivesmatter.com/about/ (accessed 12 March 2022).
62 Lizzie Dearden, 'Black Lives Matter: 210,000 people have joined UK protests and counter-demonstrations since George Floyd's death', *Independent*, 15 June 2020.

Bristol on 7 June, anti-racism protesters toppled and dumped in Bristol Harbour a statue of the seventeenth-century slave trader Edward Colston.

Throughout 2020, *spiked* correspondents inveighed vigorously against what they regarded as the deleterious advance of racialized identity politics. Ex-RCP activists especially lambasted the critical race theory which underpinned the BLM movement. Following theorists in the United States, adherents stipulated that racism was endemic throughout society and that white elites would only make concessions if doing so served their own interests.[63] BLM activists joining protests in Britain in 2020 denounced systemic racial discrimination and inequality.[64] RCP veterans' critiques of identity politics developed their hostile assessments of particularistic departures from universal humanist principles. Writing in the late 2010s, Frank Furedi excoriated identity politics as a 'consequence of the declining influence' of 'universalistic values'. Accentuating his ideals of humanity collectively transcending differences and transforming society, Furedi criticized identitarian emphases upon racialized particularities.[65]

For a *spiked* milieu which lionized race-blind universalism, BLM's critique of 'structural' racism and 'white privilege' rehabilitated divisive racial thinking. Writing in 2015, Brendan O'Neill positioned the contemporary 'myopic racial thinking' as a 'betrayal' of Martin Luther King's vision of a world in which all would be judged 'not by the colour of their skin but by the content of their character'.[66] After Floyd's murder, O'Neill posited that the 'wicked ideology' of 'racial collective guilt' was as invidious as the abhorrent prejudice that BLM opposed.[67] For the *spiked* editor, indicting white people en masse for racism served only to reify racial distinctions and exacerbate societal fragmentation. Writing for *spiked* in August 2020, Inaya Folarin Iman reproached the 'identitarian left' which would 're-essentialise the concept of "race"'. Championing instead

---

63 Originating in legal studies in the late 1980s, critical race theory emerged in militant polemics highlighting the limitations of liberal reforms since the 1960s. Early exponents, such as Kimberlé W. Crenshaw and Derrick Bell, questioned why economic, educational and legal inequalities persisted decades after civil rights legislation. For foundational critical race theory texts, see Kimberlé W. Crenshaw, 'Race, reform, and retrenchment: Transformation and legitimation in antidiscrimination law', *Harvard Law Review*, 101 (1988): 1331–87; Derrick Bell, 'Racial realism', *Connecticut Law Review*, 24 (1992): 363–79. For an overview of critical race theory's evolution, see Richard Delgado and Jean Stefancic (eds), *Critical Race Theory: An Introduction* (New York: New York University Press, 2017).
64 Remi Joseph-Salisbury, Laura Connelly and Peninah Wangari-Jones, '"The UK is not innocent": Black Lives Matter, policing and abolition in the UK', *Equality, Diversity and Inclusion*, 40 (2021): 22.
65 Frank Furedi, *What's Happened to the University? A Sociological Exploration of Its Infantilisation* (Abingdon: Routledge, 2017), 63.
66 Brendan O'Neill, 'College codes make "Color Blindness" a Microaggression', *Reason*, 5 August 2015.
67 Brendan O'Neill, 'I did not kill George Floyd', *spiked*, 3 June 2020.

'freedom, humanism and universalism', Iman launched the Equiano Project, a public forum to 'challenge identity politics' and 'reject racial essentialism'.[68]

Inverting BLM's race-conscious position, *spiked* correspondents followed a tradition of Marxist and humanist critiques of critical race theory.[69] While former cadres did not herald a return to class politics per se, they nevertheless insisted that inequalities and injustices derived primarily from social relations of class, rather than race or ethnicity. Questioned about 'white privilege' in 2018, Munira Mirza dismissed the 'ahistoric term', which 'doesn't mean anything really any more'. Mirza instead posited class relations as the cardinal social index:

> You can talk about white privilege in the context of 1950s Alabama, where being white had a material impact on your life ... it makes sense in that context, to an extent.... But today, it doesn't make sense.... I'm not sure a white, working-class guy who works in a factory, alongside Asian people – does he really have that much more of a privilege than the Asian people that he's working alongside? I don't think that it stands up as a meaningful term.[70]

For Alka Sehgal Cuthbert, the 'new anti-racism' of 2020 comprised 'reactionary, anti-human' ideas which occluded 'real class politics'. Cuthbert contended that attributing injustices chiefly to racial difference meant failing to challenge class hierarchies and their attendant inequities.[71] Similarly positioning class as the most salient social fault line, Kenan Malik advocated analysing class relations 'in a non-racialised sense'.[72]

As the head of the Number 10 Policy Unit, Munira Mirza oversaw the Commission on Race and Ethnic Disparities which Prime Minister Boris Johnson instituted in June 2020. Mirza's proximity to the commission – which was chaired by the distinguished educationalist Tony Sewell – prompted immediate reaction: Novara Media's Ash Sarkar branded Mirza a 'racial gatekeeper ... who gives political cover to ongoing injustice', while Shola Mos-Shogbamimu castigated a 'BROWN executioner to Delegitimize, Discredit & Deny #BlackLivesMatter'.[73]

---

68 Inaya Folarin Iman, 'Let's abolish race', *spiked*, 4 August 2020.
69 Paul Warmington, 'Critical race theory in England: Impact and opposition', *Identities*, 27 (2020): 24, 31.
70 Triggernometry, 'Munira Mirza on Multiculturalism, "Institutional Racism", "White Privilege" and Diversity', 9 December 2018. Available at youtube.com/watch?v=7ADPggwgJGQ (accessed 16 December 2020).
71 Alka Sehgal Cuthbert, *The Dangers of the New Anti-racism* (London: Academy of Ideas, 2020), 12, 16.
72 Kenan Malik, 'Being white won't hold boys back. Being working class just might', *Observer*, 18 October 2020.
73 Rakib Ehsan, 'Munira Mirza is the bigoted Left's worst nightmare', *Daily Telegraph*, 16 June 2020. For Mos-Shogbamimu's tweet, see twitter.com/sholamos1/status/1272785923483328512 (accessed 7 April 2022).

Flagging Mirza's 'dangerous appetite for iconoclasm and polarising rhetoric', the *Economist*, meanwhile, claimed that the former *spiked* columnist was unsuitable for an investigation into inequality:

> her passionate individualism offers few policy solutions to the problems of racism and limited opportunities available to black people.[74]

Published in March 2021, the commission's report rejected claims of systemic racism – 'we no longer see a Britain where the system is deliberately rigged against ethnic minorities' – and posited that inequities stemmed from endemic socioeconomic deprivation. While the Sewell report accepted that racism remained a 'force' in society – 'we do not believe that the UK is yet a post-racial system' – it drew furious denunciations.[75] The *Observer*'s editorial, for example, claimed that Sewell had 'reversed progress and betrayed black Britons'.[76] Some thirty-three trade union leaders, representing more than 5 million workers, urged the Prime Minister to reject the 'insulting' report, while TUC general secretary Frances O'Grady claimed that the commission 'denied the experience of black and minority ethnic workers'.[77]

Former RCP activists did not assess the Sewell report uniformly: veterans differed in the degree to which they perceived racial discrimination persisting in British society. Brendan O'Neill, for example, hailed Sewell's 'brave' report for eschewing the 'misanthropic conviction that Britain is a racist hellhole'.[78] For Kenan Malik, by contrast, the commission's 'polemical requirements' replaced 'one set of simplistic narratives with another'.[79] These differences aside, however, the former party milieu almost unanimously questioned the utility of categories such as 'institutional' or 'systemic' racism and called for a more fine-grained analysis. Castigating the 'either/or culture' which crudely dichotomized a complicated debate into pro- and anti-Sewell camps, Malik directed attention to the 'complex interplay of race, class, gender and geography'.[80] Similarly, Kunle Olulode – a former Red Front election candidate who served as a co-opted member of the commission – lamented that while its investigations had 'followed

---

74 Bagehot, 'Revolutionary conservative', *Economist*, 27 June 2020.
75 *Commission on Race and Ethnic Disparities: The Report* (March 2021), 9.
76 'The *Observer* view on the Sewell commission's race report', *Observer*, 4 April 2021.
77 Nosheen Iqbal, 'Downing Street race report is an insult to workers, say union leaders', *Observer*, 18 April 2021.
78 Brendan O'Neill, 'At last, the myth of "institutional racism" is collapsing', *spiked*, 31 March 2021.
79 Kenan Malik, 'Yes, we need a more nuanced debate about race. But this flawed report fails to deliver it', *Observer*, 4 April 2021.
80 Ibid.

the evidence honestly', the final report adduced evidence in a 'selective' fashion to posit 'assertive conclusions'. Consequently, Sewell provided

> no clear direction on what expectations of the role of public institutions and political leadership should be in tackling race and ethnic disparities.[81]

The resulting debate, Olulode complained, fuelled a binary dispute as to the existence of structural racism and lacked the requisite nuance for a matter of such import.[82]

'The lockdown has done untold damage'[83]

Having celebrated Brexit as a democratic advance against technocracy, many former RCP activists bemoaned perceived political regression during the Covid-19 pandemic from 2020. Above all, the *spiked* milieu criticized the British government's response to the crisis as a product of the precautionary 'culture of fear'. The transformed relationship between state and citizenry dismayed many veteran champions of critical independence from authority. The former party network was not entirely unified in its analysis: on the contrary, the pandemic provoked a rare public disagreement involving some leading former cadres. Nevertheless, a quarter of a century after the RCP dissolved, the Covid crisis cast in sharp relief ex-activists' political priorities.

When Boris Johnson's government imposed a lockdown on 23 March 2020, the ex-RCP milieu broadly considered extraordinary measures necessary to restrict the spread of Covid-19.[84] Until epidemiologists and medical professionals better understood the virus, they argued, it was sensible for the public to 'stay at home'. The day the lockdown began, *spiked* editor Brendan O'Neill averred that 'the vast majority of people accept there will be restrictions on their everyday freedoms in the next few months'.[85] Accepting the temporary

---

81 Nosheen Iqbal, 'Downing Street rewrote "independent" report on race, experts claim', *Observer*, 11 April 2021.
82 Kunle Olulode quoted in *Sky News*, 31 March 2021.
83 Brendan O'Neill, 'The lockdown has done untold damage to this country', *spiked*, 20 May 2020.
84 'You must stay at home', Johnson told the public during a televised address on 23 March 2020. Social mixing with persons beyond the household was not permitted. The prime minister declared that the 'only reasons' for leaving home were 'essential' shopping, 'essential' work, providing medical care for a vulnerable person or taking one form of exercise per day. Empowered to enforce compliance, police would disperse illicit gatherings. 'Prime Minister's statement on coronavirus (COVID-19): 23 March 2020'. Available at gov.uk/government/speeches/pm-address-to-the-nation-on-coronavirus-23-march-2020 (accessed 8 August 2022).
85 Brendan O'Neill, 'Dissent in a time of Covid', *spiked*, 23 March 2020.

suspension of freedoms followed the Prime Minister's suggestion that twelve weeks of special measures could 'turn the tide of this disease . . . we can send coronavirus packing'.[86]

Early in the lockdown, *spiked* correspondents lauded the social solidarity which flourished in community mutual aid networks. At a time of enforced isolation, former cadres hailed these altruistic initiatives. A fortnight into the lockdown, when 700,000 people volunteered to assist the National Health Service, while others delivered shopping and medicines to vulnerable neighbours, Brendan O'Neill hailed this 'social solidarity'. In April 2020, *spiked*'s republican editor even applauded the queen's televised speech – which praised the 'national spirit' and vowed 'we will meet again' – as 'surely her best ever'.[87]

However, the slew of restrictive laws, passed with minimal scrutiny or opposition, antagonized *spiked* supporters, who perceived big government corroding active citizenship. Within six months of the Coronavirus Act passing parliament in March 2020, the Conservatives had used 242 Statutory Instruments to expedite legislation.[88] The 342-page Coronavirus Act, meanwhile, passed parliament at breakneck speed, completing all Commons protocols in a single day and vastly expanding the government's emergency powers.[89]

spiked correspondents who considered it sensible to reduce social mixing resented these directives being imposed from above by legal statute. Castigating hyper-centralized decision-making, they warned that the government's response threatened the critical public sphere. By September 2020, more than a decade had passed since Kenan Malik had contributed to *spiked*, and his weekly *Observer* columns sometimes departed from the online magazine's partisan positions on the culture wars. Nevertheless, when the Coronavirus Act was due for renewal, Malik echoed *spiked* editorials and implored 'the left' to 'rediscover its old passion for liberty'. Differentiating his position from the lockdown scepticism of 'rightwing libertarians', the former editor of *the next step* did not oppose restrictions outright. Malik did, however, exhort the opposition to dissect emergency legislation more critically.[90]

---

86 Peter Walker, 'Boris Johnson: UK can turn tide of coronavirus in 12 weeks', *Guardian*, 20 March 2020.
87 Brendan O'Neill, 'Don't give in to fear', *spiked*, 7 April 2020.
88 Ronan Cormacain, *Parliamentary Scrutiny of Coronavirus Lockdown Regulations: A Rule of Law Analysis* (London: British Institute of International and Comparative Law, 2020), 5.
89 Julie Smith, 'COVID-19, Brexit and the United Kingdom – a year of uncertainty', *The Round Table*, 110 (2021): 63.
90 Kenan Malik, 'Where is the voice of the left as "libertarians" annexe the Covid-19 debate?', *Observer*, 27 September 2020.

To the extent that critical ex-cadres expounded an alternative response, they advocated a more targeted government policy, based upon voluntarism rather than compulsion. Elevated to the House of Lords as a non-affiliated peer in 2020, Claire Fox, now Baroness Fox of Buckley, was a panellist on the BBC's *Question Time* during the second national lockdown.[91] Ad hoc emergency measures by which 'freedoms' were 'arbitrarily' suspended, Fox argued, 'should at least be debated'. Refusing to trust public sensibility, and imposing restrictions without their consultation, corroded 'social solidarity'.[92] Within four weeks of Fox's *Question Time* appearance, Boris Johnson announced that the continual rise of infection rates left the government with no option but to tighten restrictions further. A less stringent approach, *spiked* columnists asserted, would mitigate the major health crisis while minimizing the incursion on citizens' freedoms. Throughout the pandemic, *spiked* amplified dissenters who championed a more discriminate governmental method. In 2021, for example, the online magazine published Martin Kulldorff and Jay Bhattacharya, two of the three authors – alongside Oxford epidemiologist Sunetra Gupta – of the Great Barrington Declaration of October 2020.[93] Criticizing the 'devastating effects' of lockdowns, Great Barrington called instead for 'Focused Protection' of the most vulnerable and at-risk groups while aiming for 'herd immunity among lower-risk groups'. Under these proposals, those who were not clinically vulnerable would 'immediately be allowed to resume life as normal'.[94]

Identifying social fragmentation as an exorbitant policy cost, many *spiked* correspondents fulminated against the atomizing impact of prolonged lockdowns. For activists who trumpeted collective understanding as a political imperative, siloing the population into households caused inestimable damage. Highlighting lockdowns' 'predictable harms', Jennie Bristow emphasized how enforced isolation eroded social solidarity. Public health campaigns which warned the young to obey the rules lest they 'kill granny', Bristow argued, exacerbated intergenerational divisions.[95] Similarly, *spiked* correspondents fulminated against the reconfigured relationship between citizen and authority.

---

91 When her appointment to the Lords was announced publicly in August 2020, Fox told the Academy of Ideas's newsletter that she was joining parliament's upper house to promote the Academy's 'values', including 'free speech (no ifs or buts), more public debate, arts and education for their own sake, and popular sovereignty'. Fox remained committed to abolishing the House of Lords. *Academy of Ideas Newsletter*, August 2020.
92 *Question Time* (BBC, 26 November 2020).
93 Martin Kulldorff and Jay Bhattacharya, 'The smear campaign against the Great Barrington Declaration', *spiked*, 2 August 2021.
94 'Great Barrington Declaration', 4 October 2020. Available at gbdeclaration.org/ (accessed 8 December 2021).
95 Jennie Bristow, *Growing Up in Lockdown* (London: Academy of Ideas, 2021), 3.

The author and film-maker Laura Dodsworth contributed several articles to *spiked* during the crisis. Charging the government with exacerbating fear among the populace, Dodsworth's book *A State of Fear* (2021) complained that by exaggerating risk to 'encourage compliance', the government had 'weaponised' fear and infantilized the public via a 'sinister form of control'.[96]

Especially during the second and third national lockdowns from November 2020, most *spiked* contributors situated the government's response to Covid in both a 'culture of fear' and ascendant technocracy.[97] From this perspective, enduring restrictions reinforced the hegemony of the precautionary principle and undemocratic rule by experts. For Jennie Bristow and Emma Gilland, for example, the Covid crisis had 'accelerated' pre-existing 'social atomisation'. In 'our modern "risk society"', Bristow and Gilland argued, popular apprehension reflected 'deeper cultural trends . . . a generalised sense of powerlessness and insecurity'.[98] For Josie Appleton, the ambit of the 'busybody state' had expanded during the pandemic, when regulatory authority 'turned against civic life in toto'.[99]

After the first lockdown gave way to milder measures in the summer of 2020, several *spiked* correspondents interpreted widespread support for restrictions as the hallmark of a submissive public. Those who had celebrated Brexit as a signal break with authority castigated what they perceived as a populace deferring to a rampant culture of fear. From this perspective, citizens surrendering their liberties indicated recrudescent passivity. Throughout the crisis, there was widespread enthusiasm for restrictions to safeguard public health and the NHS: three weeks into the lockdown, a survey of 1,131 members of the public indicated that 82 per cent agreed that the lockdown measures were necessary to avert national catastrophe.[100] When Boris Johnson announced a third national lockdown to begin in January 2021, a YouGov poll indicated that as many as 85 per cent of Britons supported the restrictions.

---

96 Laura Dodsworth, *A State of Fear: How the UK Government Weaponised Fear during the Covid-19 Pandemic* (London: Pinter & Martin, 2021), 192, 242–4.
97 A localized, three-tier system of restrictions began in England on 14 October 2020, before the second national lockdown was imposed from 5 November, effective until 2 December. On 6 January 2021, a third national lockdown commenced in England. Restrictions were gradually relaxed from April 2021, and most legal restrictions on social contact were removed on 19 July 2021.
98 Jennie Bristow and Emma Gilland, *The Corona Generation: Coming of Age in a Crisis* (Alresford: Zero Books, 2021), 27, 73.
99 Josie Appleton, *Toxic Sociality: Reflections on a Pandemic* (London: Academy of Ideas, 2022), 13.
100 Sofia Collignon, Iakovos Makropoulos and Wolfgang Rüdig, 'Consensus secured? Elite and public attitudes to "lockdown" measures to combat Covid-19 in England', *Journal of Elections, Public Opinion and Parties*, 31 (2021): 113–14.

Some 62 per cent 'strongly' backed the renewed lockdown, while 77 per cent of respondents averred that the government should already have tightened the rules.[101] Invoking Frank Furedi's critique in *How Fear Works* (2018),[102] Jennie Bristow complained that popular support for lockdowns demonstrated that the 'demand for protection' trumped the ideals of independence from authority.[103] In January 2021, on the eve of the third national lockdown, Norman Lewis argued that continued restrictions, despite vaccination roll-outs, corroborated a deeper societal malaise:

> Our society remains fixated on the dying, on the tragedy of the end of life, not on life's renewal or our victory over adversity.[104]

For *spiked* correspondents, the government's Covid policies had deplorably stymied the political realm which Brexit had enlivened. For some ex-RCPers, lockdowns themselves were less problematic than the paltriness of public debate which attended elite policy decisions. As the country emerged from lockdowns in 2021, Daniel Ben-Ami declared that the most 'urgent task' was to overcome social atomization and 'isolation'.[105] Restrictions were imposed in 'good faith', and the rules were largely followed in a spirit of 'heroic' communitarian altruism, Dolan Cummings averred. In the process, however, suspending civic and political life represented a significant cost: 'perhaps we also underestimated what we sacrificed'.[106] For Phil Mullan, meanwhile, the government's readiness to fortify capitalism during the crisis confirmed that the state underwrote a 'zombie economy... which staggers on without any prospect of rejuvenation'.[107]

Celebrating experimental science as a cornerstone of human progress, *spiked* correspondents distinguished sharply between the scientific advisers who counselled the government to impose restrictions and the pioneering immunologists who rapidly developed vaccines. For radical humanists, the former enjoyed inordinate executive influence upon policy, while the latter ingeniously equipped humanity to overcome the ordeal. Frank Furedi militated especially against widespread 'scientism': governmental and public acquiescence

---

101 Connor Ibbetson, 'Brits support new national lockdown', YouGov, 5 January 2021. Available at yougov.co.uk/topics/politics/articles-reports/2021/01/05/brits-support-national-lockdown-jan-2021 (accessed 10 August 2022).
102 Frank Furedi, *How Fear Works: Culture of Fear in the Twenty-First Century* (London: Bloomsbury Continuum, 2018).
103 Bristow, *Growing Up in Lockdown*, 14.
104 Norman Lewis, 'We cannot allow death to dominate our lives', *spiked*, 5 January 2021.
105 Daniel Ben-Ami, 'The origins of lockdown', *spiked*, 2 July 2021.
106 Dolan Cummings, *Taking Conscience Seriously* (London: Academy of Ideas, 2021), 8.
107 Phil Mullan, *Creative Destruction: How to Start an Economic Renaissance* (Bristol: Policy Press, 2017), 12, 167–83, 272; Mullan, *Beyond Confrontation*, 100.

in the directives of, for example, the Scientific Advisory Group for Emergencies. For Furedi, uncritical deference to 'The Science' epitomized technocratic rule, by which major political decisions were outsourced to unelected exponents of 'moral dogma'.[108] By contrast, *spiked* correspondents hailed the remarkable speed and success of vaccine design as the acme of human ingenuity. In November 2020, when Pfizer/BioNTech announced that trials indicated that its vaccine had 90 per cent efficacy, a *spiked* editorial celebrated the 'heroic effort' which promised to liberate humanity from the crisis.[109]

By 2021, however, *spiked*'s position on Covid occasioned a rare public disagreement among the former RCP milieu. Most notably, Mike Fitzpatrick – a founding RCT cadre who had served on the RCP's leadership throughout its lifespan – and John Gillott – who joined the RCP in the 1980s – accused *spiked* correspondents of underestimating Covid's consequences for public health and espousing libertarian dogma. As far as Fitzpatrick and Gillott were concerned, many of their former comrades had crudely interpreted the lockdowns as governmental authoritarianism exploiting the crisis to terrify the public into submission.[110] For decades, Fitzpatrick, a general practitioner, had criticized governments invoking health crises to justify repressive intervention in private lives.[111] So when Fitzpatrick arraigned *spiked*'s editorial in 2021, he asserted that Covid-19 represented a different magnitude of severity. In a podcast recorded in the spring of 2021, Fitzpatrick denounced the online magazine's 'rather dogmatic approach', which cast the virus as 'not really a big threat' and restrictions as 'a big fuss about not very much . . . promoting a culture of fear'.[112]

Charging the *spiked* milieu with misjudging the scale of Covid's threat to public health, Fitzpatrick and Gillott argued that some of their erstwhile comrades had

---

108 Frank Furedi, *100 Years of Identity Crisis: Culture War over Socialisation* (Berlin: De Gruyter, 2021), 4, 143.
109 'Humanity will beat the virus', *spiked*, 9 November 2020.
110 Fitzpatrick and Gillott implicitly concurred with the sociologist Sylvia Walby's bifocal analysis of the medical reality and the social construction of the pandemic: Walby arraigned those who singularly regarded government restrictions as a pretext for authoritarianism. Instead, Walby simultaneously acknowledged Covid's epidemiological gravity *and* directed critical attention to how the government 'attempted to control the narrative of the crisis' to legitimize their response. Sylvia Walby, 'The COVID pandemic and social theory: Social democracy and public health in the crisis', *European Journal of Social Theory*, 24 (2021): 23–4, 38.
111 In *The Truth about the AIDS Panic* (1987), co-authored with Don Milligan, Fitzpatrick contended that the Conservative government overstated the threat to the entire public to reinforce reactionary moralism. *The Tyranny of Health* (2000) charged New Labour with using the politics of public health to regulate private life. See Chapter 3 above.
112 The Marxist-Humanity Podcast: 'Episode 40 – COVID-19 Containment and the "Freedom-Loving" Backlash', 2 April 2021. Available at marxisthumanistinitiative.org/episode-40-covid-19-containment-and-the-freedom-loving-backlash?fbclid=IwAR3FJE72bXkq_YoU0F6JB-_crOD QWehW2t5rWhs-_3q2LQ4IHX-KhBl6GfQ (accessed 30 March 2022).

allowed reflexive anti-statism to dominate their analysis. Fitzpatrick contended that 'overwrought' *spiked* correspondents were reading the scientific evidence 'injudiciously' and 'virtue-signalling their love of freedom'.[113] Reviewing the crisis at the end of 2021, he suggested that libertarian lockdown sceptics lacked nuance:

> The virologists, microbiologists and infectious disease specialists (and the modellers!) have proven much more reliable than the sociologists, psychologists and political scientists. And if you don't understand the mathematics, put your faith in somebody who does.[114]

For Gillott, *spiked*'s editorial exaggerated valid critiques of domineering governance and the culture of fear:

> I think they've lost the plot a bit. [. . .] I regard Covid as an order of magnitude more dangerous than flu . . . and I think some of the analysis of it by the offshoots of *spiked* is just shockingly unscientific. . . . They're just obsessed with this idea that it's all about, you know, regulating lifestyle. Obviously there *is* fear out there that's probably irrational – there's probably a grain of truth to what they're saying. . . . I think obviously there *is* a heavy tendency towards regulating lifestyle. Government does use the science at times to do all these things. This is all true. . . . But then [*spiked*] just let it overwhelm their analysis on this issue. . . . I think their analysis is, to put it politely, very imbalanced. And very uninformed, a lot of it.[115]

In rancorous online exchanges, Gillott argued that Brendan O'Neill and his colleagues, by a 'striking failure' of judgement, 'underestimated the seriousness of Covid'.[116] The *spiked* editor counter-charged Gillott of 'actual lies, and wilful distortions'.[117] The acrimonious dispute did, at least, clarify the central interpretive difference among ex-RCP activists. With a degree of reticent support among old comrades, Fitzpatrick and Gillott regarded Covid as an unprecedented challenge necessitating an exceptional response. O'Neill and most *spiked* correspondents, by contrast, accentuated the dire implications of the crisis for 'freedom and

---

113 Michael Fitzpatrick, 'Why I became sceptical of the lockdown sceptics', *Medium*, 29 January 2021. Available at mike-93476.medium.com/why-i-became-sceptical-of-the-lockdown-sceptics-e8fb57dae68 (accessed 15 February 2021).
114 Michael Fitzpatrick, 'What, as a doctor, I've learnt in nearly two years of Covid', *Daily Telegraph*, 27 December 2021.
115 John Gillott, 6 October 2020. Emphasis in original.
116 John Gillott, '*spiked*-online and Covid', *Medium*, 8 February 2021. johngillott.medium.com/spiked-online-and-covid-c3f0d4f9d179 (accessed 15 February 2021).
117 Brendan O'Neill, 'More bad faith', *Medium*, 8 February 2021. medium.com/@burntoakboy/more-bad-faith-fa8686d17dbf (accessed 17 February 2021).

democracy'.[118] Whereas *spiked* located public support for restrictions in deferential, diminished subjectivity, Fitzpatrick and Gillott more sanguinely perceived a mature citizenry acting in altruistic solidarity. Those who lambasted the public for obeying restrictions, Gillott argued, 'belittled the communal spirit' of citizens modifying their behaviour to navigate a 'once in a generation' crisis.[119] Similarly, Fitzpatrick insisted that 'massive support' for lockdowns signified not 'contemptible rejection of freedom' but a rational response to a public health emergency.[120]

Such open disagreement seldom emerged within the former RCP network, but the extent of the breach should not be overstated. Especially in Fitzpatrick's case, the disagreement was largely confined to the Covid crisis. Even during the pandemic, he endorsed the milieu's key positions in relation, for example, to diminished subjectivity. Criticizing the decision of nine European states to pause the Oxford-AstraZeneca vaccine in March 2021,[121] Fitzpatrick continued to oppose the precautionary principle as 'a pernicious influence' in a 'wider culture of fear' which perpetuated the 'diminution of the whole concept of human subjectivity and its capacity to act in the world'.[122] Fitzpatrick also shared *spiked* columnists' distaste for 'woeful . . . cursory parliamentary scrutiny' of lockdown regulations: the absence of debate, the argument ran, demeaned democratic principles.[123] On the grounds of moral and bodily autonomy, he also opposed mandatory vaccination and vaccine passports.[124]

For many of the most vocal former RCP activists, the Covid crisis underlined the curious dynamics of political contestation at the dawn of the 2020s. For those who had envisioned transforming society decades earlier, an essential humanist precept endured: humanity had the capacity to act collectively to remake the world. Most recently, the Brexit mobilization had demonstrated, albeit inchoately, the residual potential of a mass struggle for political participation. Concurrently, the Covid experience reinforced the significant obstacles facing

---

118 Ibid.
119 Gillott, '*spiked*-online and Covid'.
120 Fitzpatrick, 'Why I became sceptical of the lockdown sceptics'.
121 During the first two weeks of March 2021, after reports of blood clots among patients who had received the Oxford-AstraZeneca vaccine, nine European states (Austria, Denmark, Estonia, Iceland, Italy, Latvia, Lithuania, Luxembourg and Norway) suspended the rollout, despite the European Medicines Agency insisting that the adverse evidence was negligible: only thirty incidents had been reported among more than five million people. Jacqui Wise, 'Covid-19: European countries suspend use of Oxford-AstraZeneca vaccine after reports of blood clots', *BMJ* (2021): 372, n.699, doi.org/10.1136/bmj.n699.
122 The Marxist-Humanity Podcast: 'Episode 40 – COVID-19 Containment and the "Freedom-Loving" Backlash'.
123 Fitzpatrick, 'Why I became sceptical of the lockdown sceptics'.
124 Fitzpatrick, 'What, as a doctor, I've learnt in nearly two years of Covid'.

those who aspired to an alternative. Ex-cadres warned that technocracy and social atomization placed democratic fundamentals in a parlous position. Furthermore, in the contemporary context of the culture wars, political forces which RCP veterans regarded as reactionary and divisive – epitomizing a culture of misanthropy, fear and low expectations – held considerable sway. Almost half a century since the founders of the RCT delineated their 'tasks and methods', exponents of its political tradition committed to a continual struggle to elevate the human subject as the author of its own destiny. Hailing a new, post-pandemic epoch, one veteran rhetorically evoked this ambitious orientation towards future political contestation: 'let's make some history'.[125]

'A better world is possible'[126]

By the turn of the 2020s, former RCP cadres and supporters formed three loosely defined milieux, differing by degrees of proximity to the central organizational offshoots of the party. Most former activists fit broadly into one of two concentric circles, comprising an *orthodox* core and a relatively remote *periphery*. By contrast, an avowedly dissenting *renegade* cohort lay definitely outside those concentric circles. These distinctions are entirely informal: veterans themselves have not actively schematized their network as such. Nevertheless, the differentiation contributes to the analysis of these activists' trajectories.

- The first, most *orthodox* cohort comprises especially those most closely connected to *spiked*, the Academy of Ideas or other post-party initiatives. Including several of the party's founders and former leaders, this largest group – including, most notably, Frank Furedi, Mick Hume, Claire Fox and Brendan O'Neill – wholly endorses the strategic trajectory from revolutionary vanguardism to radical humanism. The first priority in a pre-political age, they argue, is to restore the human subject as the agent of its own destiny. In keeping with the party tradition, the orthodox activists brook no concessions to those who they regard as their ideological opponents.
- Those belonging to the second milieu, at the *periphery* of the concentric circles, are considerably fewer in number, but they nevertheless include some former party organizers, such as Kenan Malik. Although in many

---

125 Fox, *The Sovereign Subjects of History*, 16.
126 Former RCP member interview with the author, August 2021.

instances these veterans have had little or no formal connection to the network since the 1990s, they do not generally disown their party past, nor have they departed significantly from their orthodox erstwhile comrades. They bear the intellectual imprint of the ideas and methods that they developed in the party. Some continue to attend the Battle of Ideas or occasionally contribute articles to *spiked*. Compared to the orthodox milieu, however, they are more ambivalent about some of the network's contemporary pronouncements, especially the belligerent engagement with present-day 'culture wars'.[127] Without organizing independently as a distinct group, those on the periphery tend not to engage with some of *spiked*'s more partisan, polarizing positions. They share the orthodox network's radical humanism, without necessarily enthusing about all of its forms. Seeking greater concord with interlocutors beyond the network's tradition, those on the periphery approach contemporary politics slightly less stridently.[128]

- Standing decidedly outside of those concentric circles, the third, openly *renegade*[129] cohort is by far the smallest, spanning those few ex-RCP activists who have publicly castigated the orthodox network's strategic and ideological journey, especially since the turn from revolutionary class vanguardism in the early 1990s. Including several long-standing RCP supporters – most prominently Paul Flewers and Tim Martin – the renegades accuse Furedi and his comrades of swapping revolutionary politics in the 1990s for reactionary credos and contrarianism. They argue that orthodox activists, especially in their post-party initiatives, have aligned with the adversaries of progressive politics. While largely upholding the party's path until 'Midnight in the Century' (1990), this milieu charges the former leadership of the RCP with turning not to a reduced version of their original objectives but to fundamentally different tasks.[130]

---

127 For example, a former member of the RCP who shared *spiked*'s assessments of Brexit and Covid-19 complained recently that the online magazine's culture wars polemics 'felt a bit like a betrayal of our political tradition at times. . . . The whole culture wars thing . . . being anti-woke, all that stuff – that isn't trying to understand the world'. From this perspective, in contrast from the transformative party project – 'the point is to change it' – negative critiques of cultural phenomena meant 'becoming part of a discussion that is going nowhere'. Former RCP member interview with the author, October 2021.

128 In his *Observer* column in 2018, one of the periphery's number, Kenan Malik, paradigmatically eschewed political dogma and doctrine: 'A modicum of certainty is a necessity; too much doubt can be disabling. Nevertheless, being a bit more uncomfortable in our views might be good for all of us.' Kenan Malik, 'We could all do with being a little less sure of ourselves', *Observer*, 16 December 2018.

129 'Renegade' is employed here semi-ironically, as the loaded term by which the most orthodox ex-RCP cadres refer to the few former activists who have openly dissented.

130 A veteran RCP supporter who finally left the network shortly after the party dissolved in 1996, Paul Flewers contrasts the RCP's revolutionary internationalism and *spiked*'s 'basically right-

Across the wider ex-RCP network, remarkable chiefly for its enduring togetherness throughout significant strategic review, this tripartite schema is illustrative. The boundaries of the orthodox and periphery milieux are especially blurred and dynamically porous: during specific controversies, individuals might appear to shift. In the network's recent disagreements in relation to Covid, for example, an important exponent, Mike Fitzpatrick, criticized *spiked*'s analysis. Overall, however, Fitzpatrick's broader politics remain closely aligned with the orthodox RCP tradition. Only the relatively small renegade cohort has departed sharply and irrevocably.

By the advent of the 2020s, most politically active former RCP activists – specifically the orthodox and periphery milieux outlined earlier – could trace a political tradition which had evolved considerably in form and strategy but maintained a radical humanist core. From the late 2010s, celebrating Brexit, critiquing identity politics and challenging lockdowns, the majority of ex-RCP cadres centrally upheld the capacity for humanity – acting idealistically, collectively and independent from the state and authority – to remake the world. By the 2020s, in the perceived absence of a subjective force for social change, the network's imagined 'alternative' was necessarily abstract, premised upon philosophical fundamentals rather than practical programmes. In outline, however, veterans continued to aspire to a world in which humanity maximized its resources and productive forces for universal benefit.

For nearly five decades, the ex-RCP network's fundamental, essentially humanist aspirations barely altered. In a review published in 2020, for example, veteran Phil Mullan tellingly positioned 'freedoms' and 'non-material values of autonomy and liberty' as the ideals which had made 'communism a worthy goal'.[131] But while the radical tenets endured, in contrast, activists entirely reassessed objective forces and subjective consciousness and concomitantly revised their own strategy. First, in the early 1990s, the party had declared the low ebb of class politics; second, from the mid-1990s, the network perceived a more fundamental crisis of subjectivity. Through the 2000s and early 2010s, the

---

wing' contemporary positions on, for example, 'sovereignty' and 'respecting borders'. 'All this stuff about freedom, *liberating the human potential*, an appeal to undifferentiated *people*', Flewers avers, is 'meaningless . . . so vague, so soggy, so unconvincing'. Flewers's hostility towards 'classless' humanism implicitly recalls the nineteenth-century Marxist critique of 'utopian socialists'. In contradistinction from their own 'scientific socialism', Marx and Engels argued, the 'utopians' evinced an essentially reactionary politics, seeking 'to improve the condition of every member of society, even that of the most favoured. Hence, they habitually appeal to society at large, without distinction of class; nay, by preference, to the ruling class'. Paul Flewers, 3 November 2021; Marx and Engels, *Communist Manifesto*, Chapter 3.

131 Phil Mullan, 'Fully Automated Vulgar Marxism', *spiked*, 7 January 2020.

diagnosis became graver still: veterans posited that even the concept of political contestation – with democracy cast as its most obvious form – was in a parlous position. As the milieu railed against the rise of technocracy – which was taken to epitomize a circumscribed public sphere – only Brexit provided partial relief.

From the 1990s, as the network's exponents delineated increasingly inauspicious political circumstances, ex-RCPers fell back upon a more foundational humanism. Today, activists invoking the revolutionary ideals which once inspired the RCP do so to substantiate a more basic humanism. Saluting Leon Trotsky in 2020, for example, Ella Whelan remarked broadly that the Bolshevik 'reminds us that there is always an alternative, always a future and always the potential to change it'.[132] From this perspective, the revolutionary communist Trotsky appeared relevant to the 2020s primarily as an Enlightenment philosophe ruminating on human agency.

132 Ella Whelan, 'The 21st century Bolshevik', *Critic*, October 2020.

'Pessimism of the intellect, optimism of the will'

The Revolutionary Communist Party and its curious afterlives

Veterans of the RCP are not entirely averse to acknowledging the peculiarity of their trajectories. Shortly after accepting a life peerage in the House of Lords, Claire Fox reflected candidly on an especially unusual political journey: 'I do actually have some sympathy with people who say: *you used to say this, now you say that*. It's a complicated story'.[1] But with the notable exceptions of Evan Smith's historical account and Michael Fitzpatrick's activist memoir, the RCP and its afterlives have seldom received detailed analysis. Instead, the organization appears intermittently in the historiography of modern Britain and Ireland, routinely referenced as a self-conscious aberration on the left. The RCP's historical positions in relation to the Northern Ireland conflict, the miners' strike and the AIDS crisis, for example, feature fleetingly in comprehensive subject-specific studies. In these accounts, the RCP's interventions are often footnoted curiosities, remarked upon for their unusualness.

Almost fifty years after the RCP's political forebears emerged from the British radical left, the organization's interventions and legacies remain enmeshed in controversy. Highlighting former cadres in senior positions in, for example, academe, the media and the private sector, critics frequently attribute malign motivations. For some leftists and commentators, either Frank Furedi and his comrades were never truly radical[2] or they converted to reactionary politics in the 1990s.[3] Analysing the RCP's free speech absolutism, Evan Smith positioned the party network's 'libertarian contrarianism chiming with right-wing discourses

---

1 Claire Fox, 1 September 2020.
2 'The rise and fall of the Ray Chadwick Party'.
3 According to Nick Cohen, after the Cold War ended, the RCP's 'wealthy but not very bright recruits' jettisoned 'ultra-left' communism and 'accepted market economics'. Nick Cohen, *What's Left? How the Left Lost Its Way* (London: Harper Perennial, 2007), 173–4.

on identity politics and "political correctness"'.[4] Other critics have depicted a contrarian milieu persistently undermining progressive politics.[5]

Some former RCP supporters concur that the network's trajectory since the party dissolved in the mid-1990s represents not a diminished version of the revolutionary project but an entirely different, reactionary agenda. Writing after *LM* closed in 2000, former Nottingham RCP supporter Robert Leader lambasted his 'ever-decreasing circle' of ex-comrades, who now propagated 'right-wing policies' and considered 'the market . . . a relatively progressive institution'.[6] A one-time RCP supporter who later joined the CPGB, Eddie Ford charted the party network's journey from 'extreme left to extreme right'.[7] Stripped of 'left-wing politics', Paul Flewers argues, the party's enduring hostility to statism and reformism left the rump of the organization to 'end up on the libertarian right'.[8]

Almost three decades since the RCP disbanded, many veterans today accentuate overarching ideological themes connecting their time in the party and their contemporary politics. First and foremost, they fundamentally uphold the human capacity collectively to transform the world. An 'alternative' society, organized for universal freedom, remains a beacon. The emphasis upon political 'independence' – especially from the state – has endured, as veteran Mike Fitzpatrick asserts:

> Independence is the key issue. Ideological independence and theoretical rigour and organisational discipline. I think they are the central principles that we tried to pursue all these years. And I think with some success.[9]

These enduring themes have traversed very different political contexts since the RCT emerged in the late 1970s. The organization emerged as a self-consciously upstart challenge to the left, whose influence it regarded as the baleful product of successive defeats. Repudiating reformism and Stalinism, the RCP vowed to develop an independent revolutionary vanguard. For their part, the Trotskyist left largely scorned the RCP, deploying 'idealist' pejoratively to imply that the primacy of ideas precluded the party from acting upon the world.

Until the early 1990s, cadres specifically expounded class vanguardism as a revolutionary strategy. Thereafter, the milieu pinpointed successive reverses for radical subjectivity. Correspondingly, their critiques predominantly arraigned

---

4 Smith, *No Platform*, 175.
5 Eddie Ford, 'Hitting the big time', *weekly worker*, 8 January 1998; Tran, 'Marx lives'.
6 Leader, 'Marxist manoeuvring'.
7 Eddie Ford, 'Farewell, *Living Marxism*', *weekly worker*, 12 July 2000.
8 Paul Flewers, 3 November 2021.
9 Mike Fitzpatrick, 22 August 2020.

perceived obstacles to an emancipatory project. The network's trajectory since the turn of the 1990s does not readily conform to Sebastian Berg's percipient tripartite taxonomy of radical responses to the end of the Cold War. RCP cadres neither carried on regardless, nor did they adopt reformism, nor did they entirely embrace what Berg terms 'post-Marxism'.[10] As we have seen, veterans perceived the mechanisms of class struggle as subjectively peripheral and therefore inappropriate. They did not, however, dispense with the Marxist essences of their critique.

Superficially at least, at the turn of the 1990s, party theoreticians echoed the diagnostic convictions of self-described 'post-Marxist' academics Ernesto Laclau and Chantal Mouffe: writing in the mid-1980s, Laclau and Mouffe asserted that with class subjectivities at a historic nadir, subaltern politics assumed increasingly disaggregated forms. Like the prominent Gramscian theorists, party cadres held that class conflict had largely ceased to propel radical politics. However, whereas Laclau and Mouffe implored leftists to formulate a 'radical and plural democracy' by embracing the 'new social movements' – such as environmental, feminist, and gay and lesbian rights organizations – the RCP leadership perceived a much deeper crisis of political subjectivity. While Laclau and Mouffe urged socialists to tap into diverse social 'antagonisms', RCP strategists declared that subjective agency was diminished and degraded in toto: from this perspective, a foundational return to first principles, reanimating a basic sense of the active subject, was a prerequisite for political renewal.[11]

Because its revolutionary politics especially emphasized the primacy of ideas, the RCP's erstwhile exponents could maintain a distinct and discernible ideological tradition after the party dissolved in 1996. After diagnosing crises of class politics and subsequently of subjectivity, the ex-RCP milieu prioritized the fundamental humanism which had always undergirded its idealistic interventions. In the case of the RCP, what Michael Freeden terms 'core concepts' – the revolutionary humanism which defined the organization from the outset – endured, while the 'peripheral' components – anchoring the 'core' in evolving historical contexts – modified significantly: the form and strategy of a democratic centralist vanguard gave way to a looser coterie of activists in campaign groups and public forums. From the 1990s, reasserting the history-making capacity of the human subject represented a less specific, yet crucial, iteration of the party's

---

10 Sebastian Berg, *Intellectual Radicalism after 1989: Crisis and Re-orientation in the British and American Left* (Bielefeld: Transcript Verlag, 2016), 21–2, 26.
11 Ernesto Laclau and Chantal Mouffe, *Hegemony and Socialist Strategy: Towards a Radical Democratic Politics* (London: Verso, 2014 [first edition 1985]), 133–77.

original objectives. The foundational humanist project, Frank Furedi admits, 'may not have been as ambitious as [the RCP's] beforehand. But it was still, and still remains, vitally important'.¹²

Decades after the RCP leadership declared class politics subjectively moribund, veterans continually assert the radical humanist basis of their critique. Forming the thematic bedrock of many veterans' subjective composure, the aspiration to human liberation remains vital for ex-RCP activists. But in a society with 'no sense of class', Para Mullan asserts, the priority is to uphold humanity's historic agency.¹³ For Brendan O'Neill, the radical humanist task is not to 'build a new socialist party' but to rejuvenate more generally the 'demeaned . . . values of reason, freedom, and progress'.¹⁴ Interviewed after being elected as a Brexit Party MEP in 2019, Claire Fox acknowledged a transformed global conjuncture – 'the past really is a different country' – while underlining ideological continuities:

> When I was in the RCP many moons ago . . . I was always a democrat, a supporter of liberty, agency and sovereignty, so I don't think I've travelled that far.¹⁵

Similarly, in a televised interview as a Brexit Party candidate in the general election of 2019, John Fitzpatrick underscored 'defence of democracy' as a 'consistent strand' in his 'political development' through the RCP, the trade union movement, legal advocacy and the Brexit Party.¹⁶

Today, from the vantage point of hindsight, many former cadres accentuate the defining humanism which has informed their politics for more than forty years. Elevating ideological and political independence, veterans formulating life histories stress their enduring themes:

> The pull-through for me is on the issue of democracy and freedom and free speech and open debate and ideas. . . . I think that's really where I started in the seventies, you know, was the desire to understand and to debate, to discuss, to learn, and then through that to try and change things.¹⁷

Similarly, for another former organizer, the RCP's humanist premises remain vital:

---

12 Frank Furedi, 12 February 2021.
13 Para Mullan, 13 December 2021.
14 Chris Mansour, 'Back to enlightenment values: An interview with Brendan O'Neill', *Platypus Review*, 103 (February 2018). Available at platypus1917.org/2018/02/03/back-enlightenment-values-interview-brendan-oneill/ (accessed 23 February 2021).
15 '"The Brexit Party is the start of a new politics"', *spiked*, 31 May 2019.
16 *Sunday Politics South East* (BBC, 27 October 2019).
17 Rob Killick, 20 August 2020.

> The key thing was the belief in the capacity of people to make a new world. . . . I think that's the core principle: human beings are not the problem; human beings are the solution to every problem.[18]

Commenting retrospectively, activists accentuate the humanist ethos which implicitly impelled the RCP and which motivates more explicitly its various offshoots. 'To some extent I would say even revolutionary communism was only a specific form of liberal humanism', Dolan Cummings avers.[19] For the late Helene Guldberg, RCP veterans' long-standing commitment to 'freedom, autonomy, equality and democracy' defined their 'positive impact in the public realm' in the 2020s.[20] Underscoring these continuities, veterans reviewing their trajectories simultaneously manage political and psychic composure while projecting themselves continuously as active agents of history.

Imbued with a sense of ideological distinction, many former activists credit their experiences in the RCP with invigorating their political and intellectual development. Veterans often attribute to their experiences in the party their readiness to question orthodoxies and to defy. A former organizer in Edinburgh and Manchester, Helene Guldberg remarked upon the 'immensely positive impact on my life' of 'learning to take ideas, analysis, reading and questioning seriously'.[21] Interviewed in 2013, Brendan O'Neill, who joined the RCP in the early 1990s, remembered his time in the party as 'a real hoot . . . because you were constantly thinking about the world and sharpening your mind'.[22] Even former activists disillusioned with the party's successors laud their education and experiences:

> I learned how to think politically in the RCP, learned how to read, research, and write political material. On a personal level, without my time as an RCP supporter, I very much doubt that I would have considered going to university, let alone going and getting a first-class BA in history, an MA, and then a PhD. . . . Not bad for someone booted out of school at sixteen as a duffer. I got a good grounding in Marxism in the RCP. I don't ever regret that.[23]

For many of its former exponents, the RCP's political independence shaped its ideological combativity and clarity. From the perspective of many former

---

18 Former RCP member interview with the author, August 2021.
19 Dolan Cummings, 17 February 2021.
20 Helene Guldberg to the author, 19 July 2021.
21 Ibid.
22 'Brendan O'Neill: What makes us human?' (BBC Radio 2, 9 October 2013). Available at bbc.co.uk/sounds/play/p01jhby6 (accessed 17 July 2021).
23 Paul Flewers, 3 November 2021.

activists, the organization's lucid emancipatory ideals inspired loyalty to the exacting demands of membership. Connecting RCP cadre-training to the milieu's ongoing capacity to critique contemporary orthodoxies, Linda Murdoch positions the party past as a crucial foundation for a viable sense of the active self today:

> Those ideas were so attractive and so inspiring . . . you had to be involved with them. . . . Those who were really involved in those formative years, particularly the most popular ones now, really punch above their weight. . . . People like Claire Fox, Frank Furedi, Mick Hume. . . . These people, because of their ideas and because of their formative years in the Revolutionary Communist Party, are really strong, very confident, and very able to hold their own.[24]

Veterans frequently attribute to their experiences in the RCP their leadership skills and analytical qualities. Former activists regularly recall how gruelling experiences of hostile political terrain instilled mettle and conviction. Para Mullan, for example, who arrived in the UK from Malaysia to study nursing, met the RCT through a student friend. Reflecting four decades later, having latterly worked as operations director for an international design consultancy, Mullan felt 'enriched' by her experiences as a senior member of the organization

> making me a questioning and thinking individual. It also made me a good organiser, made me resilient and tough. If I had just come to the UK to practice nursing, I would be a very different person to who I am now.[25]

Having jointly pursued momentous tasks in adverse circumstances, the majority of former RCPers maintain an enduring sense of camaraderie. Describing her time in the party as 'life-changing', Linda Murdoch evokes the togetherness of committed comrades:

> You're with all these other people who are like you. It's a great sense of trust, you know, huge trust that you will go into a room and if there's one other [RCP] person, and there's a hundred other people in that room, that other person will support you. That's a great feeling.[26]

Recalling especially her experiences as an embattled RCP organizer in Newcastle in the late 1980s, Claire Fox describes the party as 'a fantastic training ground

---

24 Linda Murdoch, 21 December 2021.
25 Para Mullan, 13 December 2021.
26 Linda Murdoch, 21 December 2021.

in resilience, and in teaching you not to give up . . . you can bear the slings and arrows'.²⁷

Especially among its former leadership, the degree to which the RCP constituted a defining social, intellectual and political milieu can barely be overstated. 'There's nobody who I would call a real friend that wasn't from that period in my life', Rob Killick reflects:

> It's still as intellectually stimulating as it ever was. Without it, I don't know . . . I would feel completely lost if I didn't have that, those connections to talk things through.²⁸

For Norman Lewis, shared experiences of adversity contributed to abiding friendships:

> We had twenty years together of struggling and we had some amazing, bad, and harrowing experiences too.²⁹

Another erstwhile leading member of the RCP, Ann Furedi, regards 'a significant number' of her former comrades as 'close enough to really think of as family'.³⁰

Continuity and change

Asserting thematic consistencies in their political thought throughout the decades, veterans locate their changing strategies and priorities in a profoundly altered external conjuncture since the late 1970s. A changing balance of forces over the succeeding decades, ex-cadres insist, diminished political subjectivities and compelled revolutionaries to pursue human emancipation differently. From the early 1990s, the party leadership declared that the receding subjective sense of class politics had frustrated the vanguard project. Transformed circumstances necessitated new tasks and methods. Meeting in 1997, the network's first major post-party conference identified restoring the human subject as a 'precondition for collectively changing society'.³¹ That so many former members of the RCP not only endorsed the dissolution but maintained constructive contact with ex-comrades confirmed the enduring primacy of ideas as a basis for action. Identifying *ideas* as the hallmarks of the RCP's distinction, most ex-cadres

---

27 Claire Fox, 1 September 2020.
28 Rob Killick, 20 August 2020.
29 Norman Lewis, 16 February 2021.
30 Ann Furedi, 7 October 2021.
31 'the next step: A conference to discuss where we go from here', *LM*, July–August 1997.

believed that post-party forms would be equally capable of developing the network's tradition.

Subsequently, from the mid-1990s, cadres identified a more foundational crisis of human self-belief. In the twenty-first century, at least until the Brexit vote in 2016, veterans lamented popular passivity and social disintegration: even the prerequisites for political contestation, they contended, were in a parlous state. John Gillott has aptly reviewed these successive setbacks for exponents of a revolutionary alternative:

> I know Frank [Furedi] has written in retrospect about two miserable decades – and he's really meaning the nineties and the thousands. And they were, for people who wanted to change the world, and who were interested in confrontation. It became a very frustrating period. . . . We were in a bit of a not going anywhere situation.[32]

Freeden's distinction between an ideology's 'core concepts' – its enduring, defining principles – and its secondary 'adjacent' and 'peripheral' concepts – which anchor core concepts in particular moments of contestation and change – is especially felicitous to analysing the RCP and its afterlives.[33] Disentangling consistencies and discontinuities in political thought, Freedenian analysis reveals the interaction between thinkers' core concepts and the more malleable dynamics of their application.[34] In this schema, the core concept of the RCP milieu's ideology was a revolutionary Marxism committed primarily to human emancipation, in line with Trotsky's aspirations: 'increasing the power of man over nature and the abolition of the power of man over man'.[35] This specific version of revolutionary humanism gave the organization its central meaning. Until the turn of the 1990s, the organization combined this core concept with adjacent and peripheral strategic methods and forms, namely those of class vanguardism. When cadres concluded that those adjacent and peripheral components were no longer suitable for the external conjuncture, the core radical humanism endured on a modified basis. Especially since the turn of the millennium, in vanguardism's stead, to combat the perceived diminution of subjectivity, the ex-RCP network substituted an array of political initiatives and themes, challenging, inter alia, technocracy, censorship and social atomization.

---

32 John Gillott, 6 October 2020.
33 Michael Freeden, 'The morphological analysis of ideology', in Michael Freeden and Marc Stears (eds), *The Oxford Handbook of Political Ideologies* (Oxford: Oxford University Press, 2013), 125.
34 Freeden, *Ideologies and Political Theory*, 37.
35 Leon Trotsky, 'Their morals and ours', *The New International*, 4, no. 6 (June 1938): 172.

Through the twenty-five years since the party dissolved, ex-RCPers broadly perceive the subjective dynamics to have deteriorated further. Critiquing a culture of fear, politics of limits and ideas which they deem misanthropic or divisive, ex-cadres suggest that the subject remains degraded in the present 'pre-political' age. Eventually, this entrenched assessment led veterans sometimes to promote political engagement itself as relief from passivity and inertia. Writing in 2007, for example, Dolan Cummings suggested that what was

> important for a healthy political culture is not so much the particular ideas people hold, as whether they are able to take part in critical discussion about them. . . . Our culture is sorely in need of more rather than less political mobilisation.[36]

Yet veterans of the RCP did not become relativists: on the contrary, they championed a battle of ideas specifically to advance specific emancipatory causes. By the 2010s, however, they engaged with external political forces far more catholically than they did during the RCP's lifespan. Expounding a discerning definition of the vanguard, the RCP brooked no concession to alternative radicalism: activists regarded left-wing reformists as significant obstacles to the revolutionary project. In 2016, by contrast, ex-cadres evinced much greater positivity towards exponents of different political traditions who supported a Leave vote in the EU referendum. Veterans celebrated Brexit rather wishfully as an enlightened and formative moment for a new stage of radical contestation.

The revolutionary Marxism which defined the RCP from its inception had as its premise a radical, emancipatory humanism. Expounding working-class independence from reformism, the party's class vanguardism articulated a specific form of humanism. From the outset, the revolutionary project was built upon the primacy of ideas, challenging the working class to adopt and act upon an independent position.[37] Moreover, cadres indicted capitalism less from a moralistic standpoint than from one of humanist idealism: capitalism's failure to maximize society's productive potential, they asserted, informed its inability to realize universal human freedom and fulfilment. With explicitly eudemonic aspirations, this was a political project founded upon relentlessly championing human potential.

'Freedom' from necessity and want remains a universal lodestar throughout the ex-RCP network. Critiquing a social system which circumscribes human potential, former activists sustain their ideological antipathy to capitalism.

---

36 Dolan Cummings, 'In defence of "radicalisation"', *spiked*, 12 October 2007.
37 Revolutionary Communist Tendency, *Our Tasks and Methods*, 14.

At the Battle of Ideas in 2017, for example, Josie Appleton recapitulated Marx's conception of the individual under capitalism being 'split asunder into conflicting elements'. The dictates of capitalist society, Appleton declared, continually represented 'imposition' and 'restriction', inhibiting the alienated individual's ability to thrive.[38] Writing nearly two decades after the RCP dissolved, Kenan Malik précised Marxism's radical humanist bedrock, which aspired to 'allow humans to flourish'.[39] Contributing to an online WORLDwrite event in December 2020, Norman Lewis underlined how 'freedom under capitalism is at best a formal appearance'. Quoting *Capital*, Lewis counterposed the universal, revolutionary ideal of 'real freedom' and the realities of life under capitalism, which fetters both the working class and the capitalist class.[40] As a former member of the Political Committee attests, veterans of the party remain fundamentally unreconciled to the status quo:

> Capitalism is still a problem. Its basic problems haven't gone away, right? Marx's critique of capital is still valid in terms of its strengths and its weaknesses. But obviously what hasn't happened in any way is any sense of a reconstitution of an anti-capitalist movement or an anti-capitalist force in society.[41]

Perhaps ironically, activists' perennial political dismay galvanizes their sense of survival and anchors their critiques.

Broadly perceiving political subjectivity in decline, since the 1990s ex-RCP activists have maintained their aspirations via modified strategic and organizational forms. In the twenty-first century, veterans expound a much more fundamental iteration of the ideas by which they define their 'tradition'. As a defining feature of the RCP and its post-party offshoots, the core concept of subjective agency remains integral to veterans' political philosophies. As Michael Fitzpatrick has argued, the organization's emphasis upon subjective *potential* reflected its diagnoses of 'persistently inauspicious' and 'highly unfavourable'

---

38 Josie Appleton, 'Self, society, alienation: From Marx to identity politics', in Angus Kennedy and James Panton (eds), *From Self to Selfie: A Critique of Contemporary Forms of Alienation* (Basingstoke: Palgrave Macmillan, 2019), 130–1.
39 Kenan Malik, *The Quest for a Moral Compass: A Global History of Ethics* (London: Atlantic Books, 2014), 233.
40 'What appears in the miser as the mania of an individual is in the capitalist the effect of a social mechanism in which he is merely a cog. Moreover, the development of capitalist production makes it necessary constantly to increase the amount of capital laid out in a given industrial undertaking, and competition subordinates every individual capitalist to the immanent laws of capitalist production, as external and coercive laws. It compels him to keep extending his capital, so as to preserve it, and he can only extend it by means of progressive accumulation'. Karl Marx, *Capital: A Critique of Political Economy – Volume One* (London: Penguin, 1976), 739.
41 Rob Killick, 11 January 2021.

objective circumstances.⁴² Paradoxically, the adversity of external forces has also informed the network's endurance: when the party declared a world-historical defeat for the working class in the 1990s, its network could expound a reduced but nevertheless perspicuous version of their radical humanist principles *after* class struggle. Veterans' contemporary maxim of 'taking people seriously' reflects their combative commitment to elevating subjective, ideological independence as a basis for political action. Delineating a confrontational strategy, the RCP's founders deliberately challenged prevailing tendencies in the working class, as a veteran of the organization reflects:

> We weren't there to pander to working-class prejudice; we were there to challenge the working class. We took the working class seriously and we took the idea seriously that the working class was totally capable of intellectually understanding these things and understanding where its interests lay. . . . Not in the sense of saying that they had a 'false consciousness': the whole point about Marx and our understanding of Marx was that the appearance of capitalist society was there for a reason. Capitalism is not a conspiracy designed to hoodwink ordinary people. The appearance of capitalist society is a real appearance which disguises an inner dynamic which everyone, including the capitalist class, are taken in by.⁴³

The RCP's critique of reformism generated considerable animosity on the left. Waging a crusade for independent revolutionary ideas, and deliberately polarizing discussions to clarify class interests, the organization antagonized and perplexed many leftists. When the RCT became the RCP in 1981, a leading British radical claimed that the new party abstractly expounded 'utopian' idealism, disconnected from the class struggle.⁴⁴ Intended as a barb, Alex Callinicos's comments presciently signalled two significant characteristics of the RCP and its afterlives. First, they indicated the party's self-consciously intertwined ideological and methodological distinction. Mike Freeman's keynote riposte articulated a revolutionary critique of left-wing economism. The SWP's 'self-activity' around particular industrial struggles, Freeman averred, might engender transient, spontaneous militancy in sections of the working class, but revolutionary politics would not truly be reinvigorated until workers identified their class interests clearly and consistently.⁴⁵ Inspired by

---

42 Fitzpatrick, 'The point is to change it', 218.
43 Norman Lewis, 16 February 2021.
44 Callinicos, 'Politics or abstract propagandism?'
45 Mike Freeman, '"Self-activity" makes you blind: A reply to Alex Callinicos and the SWP', in Revolutionary Communist Party, *World in Recession* (Revolutionary Communist Papers, No. 7, July 1981), 22–6.

Georg Lukács, the RCP envisioned a vanguard based upon programmatic clarity and maximal revolutionary consciousness.[46] Second, some four decades later, Callinicos's remarks provide a propitious analytical lens for examining the post-party offshoots. In the twenty-first century, the former RCP network's radical humanism often takes rather vague forms. But veterans lamenting degraded subjectivity find political sustenance in the key principles which have always shaped their various forms.

The RCP's ideological and strategic standpoints diverged profoundly from the orthodoxies of the late twentieth-century left. Yet if right-wing politics defends and galvanizes extant social systems and institutions, the RCP and its successors have not converged with the conservative right. On the contrary, although they readily acknowledge the absence of the requisite subjective force in society, to this day ex-RCPers maintain their overarching aspiration to social transformation. Since they argue that there is no short-term prospect of revolutionary change, their ideals – of a radical alternative maximizing human potential – are often vague in form. But herein lies the subtle but cardinal distinction between the former RCP network and the right-wingers their opponents depict. Whereas right-wing libertarians espouse individual freedoms as ends in themselves, ex-RCPers champion the same liberties as prerequisites for the subjective independence which could kindle overarching social transformation.

For the most part, neither the RCP nor its successors have been ideologically contrarian. Over the decades, veterans have generally devised positions to promote working-class independence or, increasingly since the 1990s, the history-making capacity of the human subject. Almost by definition, their standpoints have diverged from much contemporary orthodoxy – but those interventions have largely articulated genuine political perspectives. Former cadres' provocative methods originated in the RCP's foundational strategy: by polarizing debates, most notably around the Northern Ireland conflict and racism, activists sought to clarify workers' class interests and supplant labourism. For party strategists, training a vanguard meant instilling ideological independence in the working class – a project which repudiated reflexive contrarianism. In strategic terms, activists drew upon Lukács's insistence that the vanguard party would be

---

46 Lukács, *History and Class Consciousness*, 24, 70.

sometimes forced to adopt a stance opposed to that of the masses ... [the party] must show them the way by rejecting their immediate wishes.[47]

While veterans' politics have not been contrarian in *content*, they have, over the years, developed a tendency to be contrarian in *form*. The modus operandi represents an enduring inheritance from the vanguardist strategy: both during and after the party's lifespan, to a certain degree, activists revelled in piquing the wrath of, by turns, the radical left, liberals and authorities. James Woudhuysen succinctly attests how cadres employed provocative tactics to challenge workers to adopt a multifaceted revolutionary politics:

> We championed all the oppressed issues and we even made a point – although it was not written down – that if we talked to a black guy, we'd say we were with the homosexuals ... if we talked to an Irishman, we'd say *up with abortion*. We really wanted a sort of angular approach. And obviously if we'd talk to someone from England, we would talk about Ireland, as we did. So we really wanted a no-holds-barred defence of the oppressed.[48]

Superficially, external barbs reinforced activists' sense of their political alterity – and, for partisan adherents, their rectitude.

The charge of organizational elitism can more readily be levelled towards the RCP. In some respects, the party's tendency to become politically isolated reflected vanguardism's key strategic pitfall. Building a vanguard upon the primacy of independent ideas necessarily required cadres to articulate their own analyses without accommodating alternatives. Indeed, the organization was founded on the premise that radicals' historical compromises had deepened the reformist malaise and precipitated successive working-class defeats.

But the vanguardist emphasis upon ideological independence could engender a circular logic, especially in the 1980s. When cadres' interventions met with hostility or indifference in the working class, there was a tendency within the party to regard adverse reaction as confirmation of the RCP's foundational analysis: that the regressive forces of reformism and nationalism pervaded the working class after its successive defeats. Cadres could therefore interpret the party's continual unpopularity as a mere corollary of its perspicacious insight. Reviewing the party's career, a former member of the Political Committee elucidates vanguardism's 'unavoidable . . . perennial tension': castigating prevailing political tendencies in the working class, revolutionaries upholding

---

47 Ibid., 329.
48 James Woudhuysen, 7 December 2022.

the primacy of independent ideas risked inadvertently isolating themselves from a society they aspired to transform:

> In a way, of necessity, if you want to build the sort of organisation that we were trying to build . . . to rebuild the nucleus of a working-class movement that was anti-imperialist, anti-state, distinct, and breaking from this reformist tradition – that, of necessity, did mean isolating yourself. At the same time as trying to win over workers, you are isolating yourself from the labour movement. So it's a perennial tension . . . I sometimes think that in a way . . . it was probably unavoidable that what was being created was something that was actually, in many ways, quite insular . . . Maybe at the time you don't see that. But what you lose is exposure, probably, to a lot of normality, you know, the real world. Because you're kind of cutting yourself off from it in a way.[49]

Activists who were committed to reshaping working-class consciousness could thus drift into aloofness, as Frank Furedi accepts in hindsight. Reflecting in 2020, Furedi remembered militating against the tendency for cadres to turn away from the world which they aspired to transform:

> A lot of people in the RCP felt both different, and in some cases, superior to the rest of the left. And I think that was a problem because, you know, it's one thing to feel that you're more intellectually accomplished. . . . But there's a danger that you become complacent and there's a danger that instead of trying to communicate all the time you kind of, *oh, look at those idiots* – you know, that kind of approach. So that was something we always had to fight against because we didn't want to become caricatures of ourselves.[50]

Another leading veteran similarly counterposes the party's transformative ambitions and the recurring risk of becoming detached from working-class politics:

> We thought that the point was to go out there and be involved where things were happening and to force yourself into the situation. . . . You know, you learn a lot from doing that. . . . At the same time, you kind of create a kind of culture where you think that actually you know best. It's a kind of arrogance that has some basis to it, in the sense that you've done all this work: you've read all this stuff, you've studied, you have some understanding of history. . . . But in a way, there is something insular about it: you think that you know everything about a subject but actually there are a lot of people out there who really know a lot as well. You

---

49 Joan Hoey, 6 August 2022.
50 Frank Furedi interview with the author, 11 August 2020.

kind of cut yourself off from that. But I think that was probably the only way in which we could have created something.⁵¹

For a disillusioned former supporter who left in the mid-1990s, organizational elitism further manifested in some sections of the RCP as a

> contemptuous attitude towards the great mass of people who didn't agree with us, or who hadn't got the word, you know. This wasn't peculiar to the RCP: some other left groups showed this contempt too. I think it's a product of a vanguard-style organisation: *we know the truth, the real way forward*. It encourages a kind of feeling of superiority.⁵²

An experience of defeat?

Reviewing more than five decades of activism, Frank Furedi reflects upon 'a string of setbacks and defeats'.⁵³ Similarly, surveying her political career since the early 1980s, Claire Fox laments: 'There's no revolutionary party. My life's work was not able to be what I wanted it to be'.⁵⁴ At the strategic level, members of the RCP evidently experienced a defeat. Acknowledging the historic defeat of the revolutionary vanguard, veterans confront a degree of discomposure in their narratives. Surveying the party's history, veteran Michael Fitzpatrick has argued in retrospect that the RCP 'overestimate[d] its capacity' to rejuvenate revolutionary politics, which had been in worldwide retreat since the 1920s.⁵⁵

By their own measures, even veterans' substantially reduced objectives since the 1990s remain largely unfulfilled. Campaigning more fundamentally to reanimate the subject, former RCP activists continually inveigh against what they consider the regressive politics of misanthropy, pessimism and social fragmentation. A milieu forged in the 1970s – aspiring to transform working-class consciousness for revolution – today regrets the more profound absence of subjective belief in human agency.

Reviewed holistically, the failure of the RCP's vanguard project appears the unsurprising outcome of objective circumstances which were always, to a greater or less degree, severely adverse. Founding cadres formed the organization on the

---

51 Joan Hoey, 6 August 2022.
52 Paul Flewers, 3 November 2021.
53 Frank Furedi, 12 February 2021.
54 Claire Fox, 1 September 2020.
55 Mike Fitzpatrick quoted in 'Are political parties over?' Available at youtube.com/watch?v=dmzABn EbAZw (accessed 2 February 2022).

understanding that the Bolshevik revolutionary tradition had been receding for more than half a century. Even at its vanguardist peak, a founding member of the Political Committee told the party's weekly newspaper that while the project might yet fail, its qualitative distinction made it compelling:

> The history of revolution is one of victories and defeats. But at least we have a fighting chance – with reformists the working class always loses.[56]

As veterans reassert today, activists were acutely conscious of the unpropitious balance of forces:

> In a sense of course the whole premise was that there was a defeat of the working class . . . from the thirties onwards.[57]

Mitigating the demise of vanguardism, these emphases upon historical adversity infuse veterans' contemporary composure, functioning to assimilate past defeats in a resilient, if modified, political challenge today. A long-serving cadre who joined the RCP in 1982 similarly contextualizes the historical magnitude of its tasks:

> Obviously ultimately it was a failure: wanted to change the world; didn't achieve that objective. Never got to a size where it could make any decisive intervention in British politics. But the thing is it was always massively against the odds and faced enormous obstacles.[58]

For veterans who uphold the RCP's past positions, the party struggled courageously, through adverse circumstances, for clarion aspirations which remain ideological beacons today. These partisan retrospectives accentuate the humanist kernel of the RCP's politics. With the privilege of hindsight, veterans thematizing the party's past often emphasize the broad emphasis upon subjectivity which emerged more fully and explicitly after the RCP dissolved. A quarter of a century after the party disbanded, one former organizer depicted a committed organization developing a coherent tradition despite insurmountable external conjuncture:

> We bloody well gave it the best shot that we could possibly have given it. . . . I think we were just in the wrong time.[59]

---

56 Mike Freeman, 'Reform or revolution?', *tns*, 11 October 1985.
57 Alan Hudson, 22 October 2021.
58 Former RCP member interview with the author, August 2021.
59 Ann Furedi, 7 October 2021.

For former cadres who have remained within the orbit of the post-party network, the collective decision to disband the party in the mid-1990s crucially helped the network to pursue an imperative struggle for 'Enlightenment' humanism. In this schema, recognizing the subjective nadir of class politics was a difficult necessity which enabled veterans to defend embattled principles:

> At least we were honest about it and said, you know, *we're in the wrong place, we got it wrong, we have to do something else now*.[60]

Constituting the post-party self as a more sagacious version of the battle-hardened activist, veterans configure themselves as the principled products of formative challenges. For long-serving cadres who endorsed the turn to humanist fundamentals from the 1990s, relative to the old vanguardism, the subsequent project was reduced in scale but of perhaps greater importance. For Rob Killick, a former member of the Political Committee, once the RCP 'absorbed the defeat of the working class', it was vital to 'try to maintain some kind of progressive movement' or 'at least' to 'prevent' the political realm from 'sliding back into what you might call a pre-Enlightenment view'.[61]

Analysing how activists perceived historical reverses, and how they retrospectively narrate their longer-term trajectories, recalls the pioneering work of the radical historian Christopher Hill. Scrutinizing how the underground radicals of the 1650s interregnum negotiated their defeat, Hill examined how his subjects had defined their ideas and come to terms with the limits of their impact.[62] The evaluative dimension draws upon the salient insights of oral historians such as Luisa Passerini and Alessandro Portelli, who have conceptualized how retrospective testimonies render and represent complex experiences in stable, or at least cohesive, autobiographical arcs.[63]

For veterans of the former RCP's orthodox and periphery milieux, the RCP's experience of defeat evolved into a more enduring project to animate humanity's history-making potential. While acknowledging continually adverse external forces, ex-cadres find sustenance and stimulation in fusing emancipatory themes in their past and present politics. Norman Lewis charts an evolving struggle for

---

60 Linda Murdoch, 21 December 2021.
61 Rob Killick, 20 August 2020.
62 Christopher Hill, *The Experience of Defeat: Milton and Some Contemporaries* (London: Faber & Faber, 1984), 17.
63 See, for example, Luisa Passerini, *Autobiography of a Generation: Italy, 1968* (Hanover: Wesleyan University Press, 1996), 22–3, 126–7; Alessandro Portelli, *The Battle of Valle Giulia: Oral History and the Art of Dialogue* (Madison: University of Wisconsin Press, 1997), 79–80; Alessandro Portelli, 'Oral history as genre', in Mary Chamberlain and Paul Thompson (eds), *Narrative and Genre: Contexts and Types of Communication* (London: Routledge, 1998), 23–45.

liberatory politics, whereby setbacks have clarified and reinforced ideological tenets:

> It's like anything worth fighting for or doing in your life: there's no guarantee of success in anything that you do. The risk of failure is inherent in such commitments.... The more you have the courage of your convictions, the more it doesn't really matter if you fail – although we sincerely believed we would succeed. It doesn't become a marker or the end, it's just another way of learning, of going back to the drawing board and trying again. The intellectual rigour gained in such a process never weakens you; it is always a strength you can call upon in different circumstances.[64]

Reflecting on the ex-party network's trajectory, Mike Fitzpatrick similarly evokes a dialectical process by which adversity honed political priorities:

> It is true that the broad assumptions that were common to the whole of the left – that capitalism is a system that cannot develop the productive forces of society in a systematic way, and that the working class is the agency of its transformation – have not been vindicated by history.... We are left with a sense of failure in respect of those objectives.... But we survived to give expression to a spirit of ideological independence in the new era that followed the end of the Cold War.... A sense of agency and a commitment to human liberation endure.[65]

Recalling Graham Dawson's assessment of subject narratives positioning themselves in collective frameworks to strive for 'psychic comfort', these retrospectives configure a long process of political learning, through which overcoming past difficulties fortifies the individual and their milieu alike.[66]

But veterans who readily assert long-standing thematic continuities in their political 'tradition' are less cohesive when it comes to reviewing the feasibility of the RCP's foundational objectives. Former activists' retrospectives today differ as to whether they ever believed that they were capable of spearheading a revolution. For some ex-cadres, the question provokes a defensive response reasserting the organization's ideological conviction and seriousness:

> Obviously if I thought that it wasn't possible to change anything, why would you bother? Why would anybody get involved and put so much time and effort into doing something if you thought it had no chance of success? So yeah, I thought it would be possible.[67]

---

64 Norman Lewis, 16 February 2021.
65 Mike Fitzpatrick, 15 August 2020.
66 Dawson, *Soldier Heroes*, 23, 52.
67 Former RCP member interview with the author, August 2021.

In stark contrast, others claim that while they never truly believed that social transformation was feasible, the RCP's revolutionary aspirations were so strikingly visionary that the sheer pursuit of the vanguard commanded commitment:

> I'm very much of the school that although I loved the RCP and was dedicated to it, never for a second did I believe there was going to be a revolution in the years I was working for it. For me it was more like Martin Luther, you know: *here I stand, I can do no other.*[68]

Similarly, reassessing the party's programme, Para Mullan incorporates the RCP's past into the longer-term ideals unifying her network's political trajectory:

> Did I think there was going to be a revolution at some point? No, not really. But it was and still is important to raise the issues that are about standing up against oppression and the need for unity amongst people.[69]

Attesting these continuous imperatives enables activists narrating their life histories simultaneously to negotiate the defeat of the vanguard and to equip themselves for future political contestation.

The seeming variance of opinion underlines how the scale, ambition, and even idealism of the RCP's 'tasks and methods' energized its activists. Perceiving a political project of world-historical significance, cadres committed to mobilize minimal resources against major objective obstacles. Devoting themselves to salvaging revolutionary politics from the embers of defeat and retreat, members of the RCP drew inspiration from the distinct ideas which, they contended, equipped them to make an impact beyond their organizational limits. A founding cadre in the late 1970s, Phil Mullan, evokes how a sense of ideological independence stimulated activists who felt capable of making 'a difference':

> First with a propaganda group and then a party, we were trying to create an organisational form for political independent thought. . . . We were exhilarated by that, and that's why we worked so hard.[70]

Because the scale of the revolutionary task reflected its historic importance, activists could simultaneously acknowledge the enormity of their struggle while committing to it very seriously:

---

68 Former RCP member interview with the author, February 2021.
69 Para Mullan, 13 December 2021.
70 Phil Mullan, 11 March 2021.

> Our understanding was that it was the end of this left-wing tradition, this set of failures from Stalinism and social democracy, and we understood ourselves as a last chance for salvaging a transformative project, the last chance for a vanguard party to emerge. . . . So for us, it was a different project, a different world. . . . Now you might argue that that's a ridiculous project and you can't train a group of leaders so something can survive a world-historical defeat – otherwise it wouldn't be a world-historical defeat. But I think that was the understanding: that we were working to leave a legacy for the future, that the worldwide historical defeat of the proletarian project could be mitigated by our struggles, even though the chances seemed small. So even though it was a small group and even though it seemed that defeat was inevitable, whether it was an immediate thing or a long-term thing, I think we believed that we were still playing an important and unique role.[71]

Traditionally associated with the Italian Marxist Antonio Gramsci, 'pessimism of the intellect, optimism of the will' encapsulates the dominant outlook among most former RCP activists.[72] Veterans acknowledge the adversity of objective forces while upholding subjectivity's revolutionary potential. Championing Gramsci's dictum as a dialectic for the early twenty-first century, at the Battle of Ideas in 2010, former *Living Marxism* editor Mick Hume lamented that 'so few, including the left, appear still to have faith in the power of humanity' – while reasserting his own 'belief in the human capacity to meet new challenges'.[73]

On the one hand, former RCP activists denounce pervasive ideas, such as technocracy and identitarianism, which they regard as regressive. Paradigmatically, a party veteran complains:

> A lot of the misanthropic elements of various schools of thought are coming more to the fore and have become more and more pronounced and explicit.[74]

For Ann Furedi, the contemporary political sphere compares unfavourably with past periods of contestation and flux:

> Nobody wants to argue ideas anymore: you just get cancelled. Nobody wants to hear something that's outside of their comfort zone.[75]

---

71 Former RCP member interview with the author, November 2021.
72 Imprisoned by Mussolini's fascists from 1926, Gramsci, borrowing from the French pacifist Romain Rolland, espoused 'pessimism of the intellect, optimism of the will'. His rejoinder simultaneously rebuked both despairing leftists and bullish, sloganeering anarchists. Francesca Antonini, 'Pessimism of the intellect, optimism of the will: Gramsci's political thought in the last miscellaneous notebooks', *Rethinking Marxism*, 31 (2019): 42–57.
73 Mick Hume, 'Pessimism of the intellect, optimism of the will', *spiked*, 21 December 2010.
74 Former RCP member interview with the author, August 2021.
75 Ann Furedi, 7 October 2021.

Surveying his five decades of activism, James Woudhuysen similarly laments a societal loss of orientation towards the future:

> Everyone was obsessed with the future in the sixties. Now all we've got is presentism . . . the sixties sense of possibility is something we've entirely lost.[76]

Veterans aspiring to a radical alternative insist that cynical withdrawal cannot advance political critique:

> If you take Britain right now, there's such an unhelpful negativity of the people who were determined for Brexit to fail and were determined and take glee in every indication that Britain is not dealing with coronavirus well. And then you can that scale up to western civilization and there's a kind of pessimism there as well. I think it's really unhelpful. I think we need to be critical in a constructive way that suggests how we can do things better, rather than wallowing in pessimism, which I think is one of the cultural currents which is most problematic at the moment.[77]

Fulminating against the perceived misanthropy of political currents which eschew experimentation, former cadres critique a subjectively dormant political sphere. In a televised interview after the release of her documentary film *1917: Why the Russian Revolution Matters* (2017), Ceri Dingle averred:

> I don't think there's any idea of massive social change, changing the world, or what's required for real freedom: a belief in ordinary people's capacity to make their own destiny. Sadly we don't see that. I think that's of the past.[78]

Conversely, ex-RCP activists continually expound the *possibility* of an alternative, founded upon the history-making agency of the subject. Veterans' radical humanism underpins the enduring 'optimism of the will'. Although without a schematic programme, former cadres, most notably Frank Furedi, reassert their quintessential 'optimism about the human potential'.[79]

> I'm not optimistic in the sense that I expect things to change massively. But I am a firm believer in the human race and its ability to survive and to prosper. . . . You could say that that's the basis of my optimism.[80]

---

76 James Woudhuysen, 7 December 2022.
77 Dolan Cummings, 17 February 2021.
78 *Sky News*, 3 November 2017.
79 Frank Furedi, 12 February 2021.
80 Rob Killick, 11 January 2021.

Claire Fox similarly insists that she is 'not unrealistic about the circumstances' but 'always optimistic about the prospects for improving things'.[81]

An unwavering belief in humanity's ability to transform the world has always undergirded the ex-RCP milieu's politics. Since the late 1970s, activists have articulated this philosophy in significantly modified forms. But from the vantage point of hindsight, veterans can trace these core continuities in their world view. Today, the fundamental humanist precepts largely define the current iterations of the 'RCP tradition'. Espousing humanity's capacity to make history – albeit, in Marx's famous phrase, not in chosen circumstances – imbues veterans with a sense of their tradition's enduring vitality:

> A lot of the things I believed when I was young, I'd still go along with . . . I think we can have a much better world than we currently have, if things were organised differently. I think a better world is possible and the only way to achieve that is through the actions of ordinary people. I've always believed that and I still believe that today. I don't think there's any short cuts to achieving that. I don't think the problems that we've got are eternal or inevitable or natural. I think they're a product of the way society's organised, and we do have a possibility of changing that and people can remake the world. . . . The subject is always the important thing: subjective intervention in society can make history and change things, change the future. Nothing is predetermined. Nothing is written in advance.[82]

---

81 Claire Fox, 1 September 2020.
82 Former RCP member interview with the author, August 2021.

Bibliography

Interviews by the author

Jon Bryan, 15 March 2021
Dolan Cummings, 17 February 2021
Mike Fitzpatrick, 15 August 2020, 22 August 2020
Paul Flewers, 3 November 2021
Claire Fox, 1 September 2020
Ann Furedi, 7 October 2021
Frank Furedi, 11 August 2020, 18 August 2020, 12 February 2021
John Gillott, 6 October 2020
Joan Hoey, 6 August 2022
Alan Hudson, 22 October 2021
Rob Killick, 20 August 2020, 11 January 2021
Kirk Leech, 7 September 2020
Norman Lewis, 9 February 2021, 16 February 2021
Tim Martin, 1 December 2021
Para Mullan, 13 December 2021
Phil Mullan, 11 March 2021
Linda Murdoch, 21 December 2021
James Woudhuysen, 7 December 2022
Former RCP member and IFM activist, September 2020
Former RCP member, February 2021
Former RCP member, August 2021
Former RCP member, October 2021
Former RCP supporter and IFM activist, November 2021
Former RCP member, November 2021

Printed primary sources

Newspapers

Aberdeen Press & Journal
Andersonstown News
An Phoblacht/Republican News

Belfast Telegraph
Birmingham Daily Post
Cherwell
Christian Science Monitor
Courier: Newcastle University Student Newspaper
Daily Mirror
Daily Star
Daily Telegraph
Earlsdon Echo
Falmouth Packet
Fight Racism! Fight Imperialism!
Fulham Chronicle
Glasgow University Guardian
Green Left Weekly
Guardian
Hammersmith & Shepherds Bush Gazette
Herald
Illustrated London News
Independent
Independent on Sunday
Irish Independent
Irish News
Irish People
Lancashire Evening Post
Leeds Student
Leninist
Mancunion
Mercury: Newspaper of Warwick University Students Union
Militant: The Marxist Paper for Labour and Youth
Newcastle Evening Chronicle
Newcastle Journal
New European
News Line
the next step
Nottingham Evening Post
Palatinate: The Durham Student Newspaper
The Pink Paper
Reading Evening Post
Sandwell Evening Mail
Scotsman
Socialist Action
Socialist Newsletter: Journal of the Socialist Labour Group

Socialist Organiser
Socialist Press: Weekly paper of the Workers Socialist League
Socialist Worker
Spartacist Britain
Star
Stockport Express Advertiser
Student: Edinburgh University Student Newspaper
Sunday Life
Sunday Times
Telegraph & Argus
Times
Times Higher Education Supplement
Warwick Boar
weekly worker
Western Mail
Westminster & Pimlico News
Workers' Action
Workers Hammer
Workers' Liberty
Workers News: Paper of the Workers International League
workers power: monthly newspaper of the Workers Power group
Workers Press: Weekly Paper of the Workers Revolutionary Party

Periodicals

Academy of Ideas Newsletter
Against the Current
Anti-Apartheid News
Architects' Journal
Black Flag
British Medical Journal
Building Design
The Captive Voice/An Glór Gafa
Confrontation: Theoretical Journal of the Revolutionary Communist Party
Critic
Economist
Fortnight
Free Press: Journal of the Campaign for Press and Broadcasting Freedom
fuse: Magazine of the Students Union of the Polytechnic of North London
Gay Scotland

Hands Off Ireland!
IFM News: Bi-Monthly Bulletin of the Irish Freedom Movement
International Socialism
Ireland Socialist Review
Irish Freedom: Bulletin of the Irish Freedom Movement
The Irish Prisoner
Labour & Ireland
Last Magazine
Lingua Franca
Living Marxism
LM
London Review of Books
Marxism Today
miners' next step
Nation
New Statesman
Peace News
Prospect
Reason
Red Action
Revolutionary Communist: Theoretical Journal of the Revolutionary Communist Group
Socialist Outlook
Socialist Review
Socialist Worker Review
Spectator
Starry Plough/An Camchéachta
Times Literary Supplement
Troops Out: Magazine of the Troops Out Movement
UK Press Gazette
WAR News: Workers Against Racism Bulletin
Yorkshire miners' next step: strike bulletin

Pamphlets

Allen, Tony, Gareth Evans, Mike Freeman and Kate Marshall. *The Recession: Capitalist Offensive and the Working Class*. London: Revolutionary Communist Tendency, 1978.

Anti-Apartheid Movement. *Isolate Apartheid: Report of the Anti-Apartheid Movement Trade Union Conference Held on November 27, 1982*. London: Anti-Apartheid Movement, 1983.

Anti-Nazi League. *Document on the Politics of the National Front*. London: Anti-Nazi League, 1978.

Appleton, Josie. *Museums for "The People"?*. London: Academy of Ideas, 2001.

Appleton, Josie. *Toxic Sociality: Reflections on a Pandemic*. London: Academy of Ideas, 2022.

Auerbach, Paul. *The Left Intellectual Opposition in Britain, 1945–2000: The Case of the Alternative Economic Strategy*. London: Kingston University, 2003.

A Better Life For All Campaign. *The People's Declaration: 'A Better Life for All'*. Belfast: A Better Life For All Campaign, 1976.

Big Flame. *Ireland: Rising in the North*. Birmingham: Big Flame Publications, n.d. [1975].

Birchall, Ian H. *'The Smallest Mass Party in the World': Building the Socialist Workers Party, 1951–1979*. London: Socialists Unlimited, 1981.

Birth Control Campaign. *A Guide to Enoch Powell's Unborn Children (Protection) Bill: Why This Bill should Be Opposed*. London: Birth Control Campaign, 1985.

Blackie, Duncan and Ian Taylor. *AIDS: The Socialist View*. London: Socialist Workers Party, 1987.

Bristol Anti-Nazi League. *Defend St Pauls!*. Bristol: Bristol Anti-Nazi League, 1980.

Bristow, Jennie. *Growing Up in Lockdown*. London: Academy of Ideas, 2021.

Committee for a Communist Programme. *On the Split in the Revolutionary Communist Tendency and the Formation of the Committee for a Communist Programme*. London: Committee for a Communist Programme, 1977.

Cormacain, Ronan. *Parliamentary Scrutiny of Coronavirus Lockdown Regulations: A Rule of Law Analysis*. London: British Institute of International and Comparative Law, 2020.

Coventry Workers Against Racism. *Ghost Town*. London: Revolutionary Communist Party, 1981.

Cummings, Dolan. *Taking Conscience Seriously*. London: Academy of Ideas, 2021.

Democratic Unionist Party. *Our 5 Point Plan For Northern Ireland: Real Action on the Issues that Matter to You*. Belfast: Democratic Unionist Party, 2022.

Department of Health and Social Security. *AIDS: Don't Die of Ignorance*. London: Her Majesty's Stationery Office, 1986.

East London Workers Against Racism. *Our Flag Stays Red*. London: Revolutionary Communist Tendency, 1981.

Fitzpatrick, Mike and Don Milligan. *The Truth about the Aids Panic*. London: Junius, 1987.

Fox, Claire. *The Sovereign Subjects of History*. London: Academy of Ideas, 2021.

Freeman, Mike. *The Empire Strikes Back: Why We Need a New Anti-war Movement*. London: Junius, 1993.

Freeman, Mike. *Our Day Will Come: The Miners' Fight for Jobs*. London: Junius, 1985.

Furedi, Frank. *Freedom Is No Illusion*. London: Academy of Ideas, 2020.

Graham, Jenny. *The End of Apartheid? South Africa in the 1990s*. London: Junius, 1990.

Hayes, Dennis and Alan Hudson. *Basildon: The Mood of the Nation*. London: Demos, 2001.

Hume, Mick. *After the Brighton Bomb*. London: Junius, 1984.

Hume, Mick. *Whose War Is It Anyway? The Dangers of the Journalism of Attachment*. London: Informinc, 1997.

Hume, Mick. *Televictims: Emotional Correctness in the Media AF (After Diana)*. London: Informinc, 1998.

Hume, Mick and Derek Owen. *Is there a Scottish Solution? The Working Class and the Assembly Debate*. London: Junius, 1988.

Ireland: A Question for Us All: Report of a London District Communist Party Delegation to Belfast. London: Communist Party of Great Britain, 1983.

Irish Freedom Movement. *When the War Comes Home: The Irish War in British Politics*. London: Irish Freedom Movement, 1989.

Iron and Steel Trades Confederation. *What Is the Future? Steel – Rail – Coal*. London: Iron and Steel Trades Confederation, 1981.

Jenkins, Tiffany. *Human Remains: Objects to Study or Ancestors to Bury?* London: Academy of Ideas, 2004.

Labour and Trade Union Group. *Northern Ireland Labour and Trade Union Group*. Belfast: Labour and Trade Union Group, 1985.

Living Marxism. The Next Step conference programme. London: Living Marxism, 1997.

Malik, Kenan. *What Is It to be Human? What Science Can and Cannot Tell Us*. London: Academy of Ideas, 2001.

Manifesto Club. *27 Ways to Say: No Doesn't Really Mean No*. London: Manifesto Club, 2008.

Morris, Pat. Open *Letter to All Members of the Revolutionary Communist Group*. London: published by the author, 1977.

Myant, Chris. *Common Cause: Trade Unionists and Ireland*. London: Communist Party of Great Britain, 1984.

National Organisation of Revolutionary Communist Students. *Higher Education: Fight the Cuts – Defend Overseas Students*. London: Revolutionary Communist Tendency, 1979.

Norton, Sabina and Keith Tompson. *The Struggle for a Revolutionary Propaganda Group*. London: Revolutionary Communist Tendency, 1977.

Ó Brádaigh, Ruairí. *Our People, Our Future: What Éire Nua Means*. Dublin: Sinn Féin, 1973.

O'Malley, Craig and Stuart Waiton. *Who's Antisocial? New Labour and the Politics of Antisocial Behaviour*. London: Academy of Ideas, 2005.

Racial Oppression: How to Fight It. London: Revolutionary Communist Tendency, 1979.

Revolutionary Communist Group. *Ireland: British Labour and British Imperialism*. London: Revolutionary Communist Group, 1976.

Revolutionary Communist Party. *Prolonging the Death Agony: The Rise, Fall and Reconstitution of Social Democracy*. London: Revolutionary Communist Party, 1981.

Revolutionary Communist Party. *Slump Socialism: The Depression, the War and the Working Class*. London: Junius, 1981.

Revolutionary Communist Party. *World in Recession*. London: Revolutionary Communist Party, 1981.

Revolutionary Communist Party. *Malvinas Are Argentina's*. London: Revolutionary Communist Party, 1982.

Revolutionary Communist Party. *Poland's Black December*. London: Revolutionary Communist Party, 1982.

Revolutionary Communist Party. *Preparing for Power: The Programme of the Revolutionary Communist Party*. London: Junius, 1983.

Revolutionary Communist Party. *The Right to be Offensive*. London: Junius, 1993.

Revolutionary Communist Students. *On the Offensive for a Fighting Union*. London: Revolutionary Communist Students, 1990.

Revolutionary Communist Students. *Peace in the Gulf! Western Forces Out!* London: Revolutionary Communist Students, 1991.

Revolutionary Communist Students. *Students Towards 2000*. London: Revolutionary Communist Students, 1992.

Revolutionary Communist Tendency. *Documents on the Split within the Revolutionary Communist Group*. London: Revolutionary Communist Tendency, 1977.

Revolutionary Communist Tendency. *Isolation and the Radical Left – Statement on the Split within the RCT*. London: Revolutionary Communist Tendency, 1977.

Revolutionary Communist Tendency. *Ireland: It's a War, Not a Question of Human Rights*. London: Revolutionary Communist Tendency, 1978.

Revolutionary Communist Tendency. *The Recession, Capitalist Offensive and the Working Class*. London: Revolutionary Communist Tendency, 1978.

Revolutionary Communist Tendency. *Special Issue on Ireland*. London: Revolutionary Communist Tendency, 1978.

Revolutionary Communist Tendency. *The Battle for Africa*. London: Revolutionary Communist Tendency, 1979.

Revolutionary Communist Tendency. *Our Tasks and Methods*. London: Revolutionary Communist Tendency, 1979.

Revolutionary Communist Tendency. *Smash the Prevention of Terrorism Act!* London: Revolutionary Communist Tendency, 1979.

Revolutionary Communist Tendency. *Workers against Imperialism: The British Labour Movement and Ireland*. London: Revolutionary Communist Tendency, 1979.

Revolutionary Communist Tendency. *Ireland's Victory Means Britain's Defeat*. London: Revolutionary Communist Tendency, 1980.

Revolutionary Communist Tendency. *Khomeini's Capitalism: The Imperialists Close In*. London: Revolutionary Communist Tendency, 1980.

Richards, Frank. *Under a National Flag: Fascism, Racism and the Labour Movement*. London: Revolutionary Communist Tendency, 1978.

Richards, Frank. *The Miners' Next Step*. London: Junius, 1984.

Right to be Here: A Campaigning Guide to the Immigration Laws. London: GLC Anti-Deportation Working Group, 1985.

Sehgal Cuthbert, Alka. *The Dangers of the New Anti-racism*. London: Academy of Ideas, 2020.

Sinn Féin. *Éire Nua: Updated Text*. Dublin: Sinn Féin, n.d. [1980].

Sinn Féin. *Towards a Lasting Peace in Ireland*. Dublin: Sinn Féin, 1992.

Sinn Féin Publicity Department. *The Sinn Féin-SDLP Talks, January–September 1988*. Dublin: Sinn Féin, 1989.

Smash the Prevention of Terrorism Act Campaign. *TUC Hands Off Ireland!* London: Smash the Prevention of Terrorism Act Campaign, 1981.

Socialist Workers Party. *Why We Say Troops Out of Ireland!* London: Socialists Unlimited, 1980.

South London Workers Against Racism. *Police Out of Brixton!* London: Revolutionary Communist Tendency, 1981.

Steering Committee of the Revolutionary Communist Tendency. *Hands Off Ireland!* London: published by the authors, 1976.

Ulster Unionist Party. *Build a Better Northern Ireland*. Belfast: Ulster Unionist Party, 2022.

Williams, Austin. *Greens: The New Neo-Colonialists*. London: Academy of Ideas, 2021.

Workers Against Racism. *Cleansing Our Ranks: A Platform for Anti-racist Trade Unionists*. London: Junius, 1981.

Workers Power. *The British Left and the Irish War*. London: Workers Power, 1983.

Ahmed Iqbal Ullah RACE Centre, Manchester

Workers Against Racism. *Racist Attacks – Racist Deportations – Racist Police – Who Can Help?* Manchester: Manchester Workers Against Racism, n.d. [c.1991].

Archive of the Irish in Britain, London Metropolitan University

Anne Waring to Labour Committee on Ireland, 5 April 1985.

Ireland and the British Labour Movement. London: Smash the Prevention of Terrorism Act Campaign, n.d. [1980].

Niall Power to Anne Waring, n.d. [1985].

Working Class Movement Library, Salford

East London Workers Against Racism (n.d. [1982]).

Fighting for a Change! Vote Kate Marshall. London: Junius, n.d. [1987].

Police State Comes to Pontefract. RCP press release, 24 February 1986.

Revolutionary Communist Group. *Unemployment: The Dangers Ahead*. London: Revolutionary Communist Group, 1975.

Revolutionary Communist Group Discussion Bulletin, 2 (December 1974). London: RCG Publications, 1974.
Revolutionary Communist Group Discussion Bulletin, 3 (April 1975). London: RCG Publications, 1975.
Revolutionary Communist Group Special Discussion Bulletin, July 1975. London: RCG Publications, 1975.
Revolutionary Communist Party. *Our Day Will Come: The End of the Miners' Strike*. London: Revolutionary Communist Party, n.d. [1985].
South London Workers Against Racism, *Put the Police in the Dock!* (n.d. [1981]).

Warwick Digital Collections

UWA/PUB/S/HB/15/1: *University of Warwick Students' Union Handbook! 1981-1982*. Coventry: Warwick University Students' Union, 1981.
UWA/PUB/S/HB/18/1: *Warwick Life: The Students' Union Guide to the University of Warwick, 1984/1985*. Coventry: Warwick University Students' Union, 1984.
UWA/PUB/S/HB/26/1: *Warwick Life '93*. Coventry: Warwick University Students' Union, 1993.
UWA/PUB/S/HB/30/1: *Warwick Life '92*. Coventry: Warwick University Students' Union, 1992.

Websites

(All websites last accessed 27 September 2022)

blacklivesmatter.com/about/
conatusnews.com
crikey.com.au
medium.com
postrecession.wordpress.com
spiked-online.com
totalpolitics.com
youtube.com/user/battleofideas

'After Brexit: Reimagining Sovereignty – Gisela Stuart in conversation with Frank Furedi', 13 September 2017, youtube.com/watch?v=fRf9K4RFd00
'Arthur Scargill – 1985 NUM conference speech', ukpol.co.uk/arthur-scargill-1985-num-conference-speech/
Connor Ibbetson, 'Brits support new national lockdown', YouGov, 5 January 2021, yougov.co.uk/topics/politics/articles-reports/2021/01/05/brits-support-national-lockdown-jan-2021
'A death in the "Leninist" family: An internal RCP debate from 1995', 22 December 2020, communistpartyofgreatbritainhistory.wordpress.com/2020/12/22/internal-rcp-debate-1995/

Evan Smith, 'The British left and the end of the miners strike: A guide to online sources', *New Historical Express*, hatfulofhistory.wordpress.com/2015/03/07/the-british-left-and-the-end-of-the-miners-strike-a-guide-to-online-sources/

Evan Smith, '"Don't let them die!": The British Far Left and the Armagh Women's Prisoner Protest', hatfulofhistory.wordpress.com/2016/02/09/dont-let-them-die-the-british-far-left-and-the-armagh-womens-prisoner-protest/

Evan Smith, 'How the first Gulf War shaped the British left', *Red Pepper*, 11 March 2021, redpepper.org.uk/how-the-first-gulf-war-shaped-the-british-left/

'Facts about Srebenica', icty.org/x/file/Outreach/view_from_hague/jit_srebrenica_en.pdf

'Great Barrington Declaration', 4 October 2020, gbdeclaration.org/

'"Immigration was used by both sides to exploit the working class vote" – Kunle Olulode', 14 July 2016, youtube.com/watch?v=u6-pCetoASs

International Year of Ecotourism 2002 Launched at Headquarters Event: UN press release ENV/DEV/607, 28 January 2002, press.un.org/en/2002/envdev607.doc.htm

'ITN wins Bosnian war libel case', *BBC News*, 15 March 2000, news.bbc.co.uk/1/hi/uk/677481.stm

Margaret Thatcher Foundation: 'TV Interview for Granada *World in Action*', 27 January 1978, margaretthatcher.org/document/103485

The Marxist-Humanity Podcast: 'Episode 40 – COVID-19 Containment and the "Freedom-Loving" Backlash', 2 April 2021, marxisthumanistinitiative.org/episode-40-covid-19-containment-and-the-freedom-loving-backlash?fbclid=IwAR3FJE72bXkq_YoU0F6JB-_crODQWehW2t5rWhs-_3q2LQ4IHX-KhBl6GfQ

'Nasreen Saddique – "Anne Frank with a telephone"', *Journey To Justice*, jtojhumanrights.org.uk/local-stories/local-stories-posts/nasreen-saddique-anne-frank-with-a-telephone/

Oliver Kamm, 'The extraordinary journey of the Revolutionary Communist Party is a lesson in politics', *CapX*, 14 August 2020, capx.co/the-extraordinary-journey-of-the-revolutionary-communist-party-is-a-lesson-in-politics

'Open letter on Brexit that spiked rejected', *Marxist Humanist Initiative*, 25 March 2016, marxisthumanistinitiative.org/uk-news/open-letter-on-brexit-that-spiked-rejected html

Otto English, 'My trip down the Brexit Party rabbit hole', *Politico*, 2 September 2019, politico.eu/article/my-trip-down-the-brexit-party-rabbit-hole-nigel-farage/

Plan of Implementation of the World Summit on Sustainable Development, un.org/esa/sustdev/documents/WSSD_POI_PD/English/WSSD_PlanImpl.pdf

Rob Killick, 'UK after the recession', postrecession.wordpress.com

Slawek Blich, 'Fox: I am on the Left and I want to exit', *Krytyka Politczna*, 30 June 2016, politicalcritique.org/world/uk/2016/fox-i-am-on-the-left-and-i-want-to-exit/#

Triggernometry, 'Munira Mirza on Multiculturalism, "Institutional Racism", "White Privilege" and Diversity', 9 December 2018, youtube.com/watch?v=7ADPggwgJGQ

Wellcome Collection Dd 8934684 HSSH J0306 AR: Department of Health and Social Security, *AIDS: Don't Die of Ignorance*. London: Her Majesty's Stationery Office, 1986, wellcomecollection.org/works/kx943x59

Wellcome Collection SA/BCC/D/89: Birth Control Campaign, *A Guide to Enoch Powell's Unborn Children (Protection) Bill: Why this Bill should be Opposed* (1985), wellcomecollection.org/works/g57ngdfv

Books

Agar, Jon. *Science Policy under Thatcher*. London: UCL Press, 2019.

Alexander, Robert J. *International Trotskyism, 1929–1985: A Documented Analysis of the Movement*. Durham: Duke University Press, 1991.

Andrews, Geoff. *Endgames and New Times: The Final Years of British Communism*. London: Lawrence & Wishart, 2004.

Andrews, Geoff, Nina Fishman and Kevin Morgan, eds. *Opening the Books: Essays on the Social and Cultural History of the British Communist Party*. London: Pluto Press, 1995.

Appleton, Josie. *Officious: Rise of the Busybody State*. Winchester: Zero Books, 2015.

Bagguley, Paul and Yasmin Hussain. *Riotous Citizens: Ethnic Conflict in Multicultural Britain*. Aldershot: Ashgate, 2008.

Barry, Brian. *Culture and Equality: An Egalitarian Critique of Multiculturalism*. Cambridge: Polity Press, 2001.

Bean, Kevin. *The New Politics of Sinn Féin*. Liverpool: Liverpool University Press, 2007.

Beckett, Francis and David Hencke. *Marching to the Fault Line: The Miners' Strike and the Battle for Industrial Britain*. London: Constable, 2009.

Ben-Ami, Daniel. *Cowardly Capitalism*. Chichester: John Wiley & Sons, 2001.

Ben-Ami, Daniel. *Ferraris for All: In Defence of Economic Progress*. Bristol: Policy Press, 2010.

Berg, Sebastian. *Intellectual Radicalism after 1989: Crisis and Re-orientation in the British and American Left*. Bielefeld: Transcript Verlag, 2016.

Bloom, Allan. *The Closing of the American Mind: How Higher Education has Failed Democracy and Impoverished the Souls of Today's Students*. New York: Simon & Schuster, 1987.

Bristow, Jennie. *The Sociology of Generations: New Directions and Challenges*. Basingstoke: Palgrave Macmillan, 2016.

Bristow, Jennie. *Stop Mugging Grandma: The 'Generation Wars' and Why Boomer Blaming Won't Solve Anything*. New Haven: Yale University Press, 2019.

Bristow, Jennie and Emma Gilland. *The Corona Generation: Coming of Age in a Crisis*. Alresford: Zero Books, 2021.

Burgess, Adam. *Divided Europe: The New Domination of the East*. London: Pluto Press, 1997.
Burkett, Jodi, ed. *Students in Twentieth-Century Britain and Ireland*. Basingstoke: Palgrave Macmillan, 2018.
Calcutt, Andrew. *Arrested Development: Pop Culture and the Erosion of Adulthood*. London: Bloomsbury, 1998.
Calcutt, Andrew and Philip Hammond. *Journalism Studies: A Critical Introduction*. Abingdon: Routledge, 2011.
Callaghan, John. *The Far Left in British Politics*. Oxford: Basil Blackwell, 1987.
Callinicos, Alex. *South Africa: The Road to Revolution*. London: Socialist Workers Party, 1985.
Callinicos, Alex and Mike Simons. *The Great Strike: The Miners' Strike of 1984-5 and Its Lessons*. London: Bookmarks, 1985.
Campbell, Aidan. *Western Primitivism: African Ethnicity – A Study in Cultural Relations*. London: Cassell, 1997.
Carver, Terrell, ed. *Marx: Later Political Writings*. Cambridge: Cambridge University Press, 1996.
Chandler, David, ed. *Rethinking Human Rights: Critical Approaches to International Politics*, Basingstoke: Palgrave Macmillan, 2002.
Chandler, David. *From Kosovo to Kabul and Beyond: Human Rights and International Intervention*. London: Pluto Press, 2006.
Chun, Lin. *The British New Left*. Edinburgh: Edinburgh University Press, 1993.
Clements, Dave, Alastair Donald, Martin Earnshaw and Austin Williams, eds. *The Future of Community: Reports of a Death Greatly Exaggerated*. London: Pluto Press, 2008.
Cliff, Tony. *A World to Win: Life of a Revolutionary*. London: Bookmarks, 2000.
Cliff, Tony et al. *The Fourth International, Stalinism and the Origins of the International Socialists*. London: Pluto Press, 1971.
Cohen, Nick. *What's Left? How the Left Lost Its Way*. London: Harper Perennial, 2007.
Copsey, Nigel and David Renton, eds. *British Fascism, the Labour Movement and the State*. Basingstoke: Palgrave Macmillan, 2005.
Crick, Michael. *Militant*. London: Faber & Faber, 1984.
Crick, Michael. *The March of Militant*. London: Faber & Faber, 1986.
Cummings, Dolan, ed. *Debating Humanism*. Exeter: Societas, 2006.
Curtis, Ben. *The South Wales Miners, 1964-1985*. Cardiff: University of Wales Press, 2013.
Daniels, Robert V. *The Rise and Fall of Communism in Russia*. New Haven: Yale University Press, 2007.
Dawson, Graham. *Soldier Heroes: British Adventure, Empire and the Imagining of Masculinities*. Abingdon: Routledge, 1994.
Dawson, Graham, Jo Dover and Stephen Hopkins, eds. *The Northern Ireland Troubles in Britain: Impacts, Engagements, Legacies and Memories*. Manchester: Manchester University Press, 2017.

Delgado, Richard and Jean Stefancic, eds. *Critical Race Theory: The Cutting Edge*. Philadelphia: Temple University Press, 1995.
Dodsworth, Laura. *A State of Fear: How the UK Government Weaponised Fear during the Covid-19 Pandemic*. London: Pinter & Martin, 2021.
Engels, Frederick. *Socialism: Utopian and Scientific*. London: Junius, 1996.
Evans, Richard J. *Telling Lies about Hitler: The Holocaust, History and the David Irving Trial*. London: Verso, 2002.
Farrell, Michael. *Northern Ireland: The Orange State*. London: Pluto Press, 1976.
Ferrone, Vincenzo. *The Enlightenment: History of an Idea*. Princeton: Princeton University Press, 2015.
Field, Frank. *Neighbours from Hell*. London: Politico, 2003.
Fisher, Mark. *Capitalist Realism: Is there No Alternative?* Winchester: Zero Books, 2009.
Fitzpatrick, Michael. *The Tyranny of Health: Doctors and the Regulation of Lifestyle*. Abingdon: Routledge, 2000.
Flewers, Paul. *The New Civilisation: Understanding Stalin's Soviet Union, 1929–1941*. London: Francis Boutle, 2008.
Fox, Claire. *'I Find That Offensive!'* London: Biteback, 2016.
Freeden, Michael. *Ideologies and Political Theory: A Conceptual Approach*. Oxford: Clarendon Press, 1996.
Friend, Andrew and Andy Metcalf. *Slump City: The Politics of Mass Unemployment*. London: Pluto Press, 1981.
Fukuyama, Francis. *The End of History and the Last Man*. New York: The Free Press, 1992.
Furedi, Ann. *The Moral Case for Abortion*. Basingstoke: Palgrave Macmillan, 2016.
Furedi, Frank. *The Soviet Union Demystified: A Materialist Analysis*. London: Junius, 1986.
Furedi, Frank. *Mythical Past, Elusive Future: History and Society in an Anxious Age*. London: Pluto Press, 1992.
Furedi, Frank. *The New Ideology of Imperialism: Renewing the Moral Imperative*. London: Pluto Press, 1994.
Furedi, Frank. *Culture of Fear: Risk-Taking and the Morality of Low Expectation*. London: Cassell, 1997.
Furedi, Frank. *Population and Development: A Critical Introduction*. Cambridge: Polity Press, 1997.
Furedi, Frank. *Therapy Culture: Cultivating Vulnerability in an Uncertain Age*. London: Routledge, 2004.
Furedi, Frank. *Politics of Fear: Beyond Left and Right*. London: Continuum, 2005.
Furedi, Frank. *Where Have All the Intellectuals Gone?* London: Continuum, 2006.
Furedi, Frank. *Wasted: Why Education Isn't Educating*. London: Continuum, 2009.
Furedi, Frank. *On Tolerance: A Defence of Moral Independence*. London: Bloomsbury, 2011.
Furedi, Frank. *Authority: A Sociological History*. Cambridge: Cambridge University Press, 2013.

Furedi, Frank. *Moral Crusades in an Age of Mistrust: The Jimmy Savile Scandal*. Basingstoke: Palgrave Macmillan, 2013.
Furedi, Frank. *First World War: Still No End in Sight*. London: Bloomsbury, 2014.
Furedi, Frank. *Populism and the European Culture Wars: The Conflict of Values between Hungary and the EU*. London: Routledge, 2017.
Furedi, Frank. *What's Happened to the University? A Sociological Exploration of Its Infantilisation*. Abingdon: Routledge, 2017.
Furedi, Frank. *100 Years of Identity Crisis: Culture War over Socialisation*. Berlin: De Gruyter, 2021.
Furedi, Frank. *Why Borders Matter: Why Humanity Must Relearn the Art of Drawing Boundaries*. Abingdon: Routledge, 2021.
Gilligan, Chris and Jon Tonge, eds. *Peace or War? Understanding the Peace Process in Northern Ireland*. Farnham: Ashgate, 1997.
Gillott, John. *Bioscience, Governance and Politics*. Basingstoke: Palgrave Macmillan, 2014.
Gillott, John and Manjit Kumar. *Science and the Retreat from Reason*. London: Merlin Press, 1995.
Gilroy, Paul. *There Ain't No Black in the Union Jack: The Cultural Politics of Race and Nation*. London: Routledge, 2002.
Glenny, Misha. *The Fall of Yugoslavia: The Third Balkan War*. London: Penguin, 1992.
Glynn, Sarah. *Class, Ethnicity and Religion in the Bengali East End: A Political History*. Manchester: Manchester University Press, 2015.
Gramsci, Antonio. *Selections from the Prison Notebooks of Antonio Gramsci*, ed. and trans. Quentin Hoare and Geoffrey Nowell Smith. London: Lawrence & Wishart, 1971.
Grossman, Henryk. *The Law of Accumulation and Breakdown of the Capitalist System: Being also a Theory of Crises*. London: Pluto Press, 1992.
Guldberg, Helene. *Reclaiming Childhood: Freedom and Play in an Age of Fear*. London: Routledge, 2009.
Guldberg, Helene. *Just Another Ape?* Exeter: Societas, 2010.
Hannan, Daniel. *Why Vote Leave*. London: Head of Zeus, 2016.
Hardt, Michael and Antonio Negri, *Empire*. Cambridge, MA: Harvard University Press, 2000.
Heartfield, James. *The 'Death of the Subject' Explained*. Leicester: Perpetuity Press, 2002.
Heartfield, James. *The European Union and the End of Politics*. Winchester: Zero Books, 2013.
Heartfield, James and Kevin Rooney. *Who's Afraid of the Easter Rising? 1916–2016*. Winchester: Zero Books, 2015.
Hepworth, Jack. *'The Age-Old Struggle': Irish Republicanism from the Battle of the Bogside to the Belfast Agreement, 1969–1998*. Liverpool: Liverpool University Press, 2021.

Higgins, Jim. *More Years for the Locust: The Origins of the SWP*. London: IS Group, 1997.

Hill, Christopher. *The Experience of Defeat: Milton and Some Contemporaries*. London: Faber & Faber, 1984.

Hill, Christopher. *The World Turned Upside Down: Radical Ideas during the English Revolution*. Harmondsworth: Penguin, 1991.

Hudson, Cheryl and Joanna Williams, eds. *Why Academic Freedom Matters: A Response to Our Current Challenges*. London: Civitas, 2016.

Hume, Mick. *There Is No Such Thing as a Free Press . . . and We Need One More Than Ever*. London: Societas, 2012.

Hume, Mick. *Trigger Warning: Is the Fear of being Offensive Killing Free Speech?* London: William Collins, 2015.

Hume, Mick. *Revolting! How the Establishment Are Undermining Democracy and What They're Afraid Of*. London: William Collins, 2017.

Institute of Ideas. *Abortion: Whose Right?* London: Hodder & Stoughton, 2002.

Institute of Ideas. *Alternative Medicine: Should We Swallow It?* London: Hodder & Stoughton, 2002.

Institute of Ideas. *Animal Experimentation: Good or Bad?* London: Hodder & Stoughton, 2002.

Institute of Ideas. *Art: What Is It Good For?* London: Hodder & Stoughton, 2002.

Institute of Ideas. *Compensation Crazy: Do We Blame and Claim Too Much?* London: Hodder & Stoughton, 2002.

Institute of Ideas. *Ethical Tourism: Who Benefits?* London: Hodder & Stoughton, 2002.

Institute of Ideas. *The Internet: Brave New World?* London: Hodder & Stoughton, 2002.

Institute of Ideas. *Nature's Revenge? Hurricanes, Floods and Climate Change*. London: Hodder & Stoughton, 2002.

Irish Freedom Movement. *The Irish War: The Irish Freedom Movement Handbook*. London: Junius, 1985.

Israel, Jonathan. *A Revolution of the Mind: Radical Enlightenment and the Intellectual Origins of Modern Democracy*. Princeton: Princeton University Press, 2009.

Jackson, Ben and Robert Saunders, eds. *Making Thatcher's Britain*. Cambridge: Cambridge University Press, 2012.

Jacoby, Russell. *The End of Utopia: Politics and Culture in an Age of Apathy*. New York: Basic Books, 1999.

Jakubowski, Franz. *Ideology and Superstructure in Historical Materialism*. London: Pluto Press, 1990.

Jenkins, Tiffany. *Contesting Human Remains in Museum Collections: The Crisis of Cultural Authority*. Abingdon: Routledge, 2010.

Jenkins, Tiffany. *Keeping their Marbles: How the Treasures of the Past Ended Up in Museums – And Why They Should Stay There*. Oxford: Oxford University Press, 2016.

Judt, Tony. *Postwar: A History of Europe since 1945*. London: Vintage, 2005.

Kelly, John. *Contemporary Trotskyism: Parties, Sects and Social Movements in Britain*. Abingdon: Routledge, 2018.
Kennedy, Angus and James Panton, eds. *From Self to Selfie: A Critique of Contemporary Forms of Alienation*. Basingstoke: Palgrave Macmillan, 2019.
Kenny, Michael. *The First New Left: British Intellectuals after Stalin*. London: Lawrence & Wishart, 1995.
Klimke, Martin and Joachim Scharloth, eds. *1968 in Europe: A History of Protest and Activism, 1956-1977*. Basingstoke: Palgrave Macmillan, 2008.
Knight, Robert. *Stalinism in cr#isis*. London: Pluto Press, 1991.
Korsch, Karl. *Three Essays on Marxism*. London: Pluto Press, 1971.
Korsch, Karl. *Karl Marx*. Leiden: Brill, 2016.
Krastev, Ivan. *Democracy Disrupted: The Politics of Global Protest*. Philadelphia: University of Pennsylvania Press, 2014.
Laclau, Ernesto and Chantal Mouffe. *Hegemony and Socialist Strategy: Towards a Radical Democratic Politics*. London: Verso, 2014.
Lapavitsas, Costas. *The Left Case against the EU*. Cambridge: Polity Press, 2018.
Lasch, Christopher. *The Minimal Self: Psychic Survival in Troubled Times*. London: Picador, 1984.
Laybourn, Keith. *Marxism in Britain: Dissent, Decline and Re-emergence, 1945-c.2000*. London: Routledge, 2006.
Lenin, V. I. *Collected Works*, 45 vols. Moscow: Progress Publishers, 1960-1976.
Lenin, V. I. *The State and Revolution: The Marxist Theory of the State and the Tasks of the Proletariat in the Revolution*. London: Junius, 1994.
Lenin, V. I. *Imperialism: The Highest Stage of Capitalism*. London: Junius/*Living Marxism*, 1996.
Lewis, Penny, Vicky Richardson and James Woudhuysen. *In Defence of the Dome: The Case for Human Agency in the New Millennium*. London: Adam Smith Institute, 1999.
LM. *The Point is to Change It: A Manifesto for a World Fit for People*. London: Junius, 1996.
Longford, Charles. *South Africa: Black Blood on British Hands*. London: Junius, 1985.
Lucas, Ian. *OutRage! An Oral History*. London: Cassell, 1998.
Lukács, Georg. *History and Class Consciousness: Studies in Marxist Dialectics*. London: Merlin, 1971.
Macvarish, Jan. *Neuroparenting: The Expert Invasion of Family Life*. Basingstoke: Palgrave Macmillan, 2016.
Malik, Kenan. *The Meaning of Race: Race, History and Culture in Western Society*. Basingstoke: Palgrave Macmillan, 1996.
Malik, Kenan. *From Fatwa to Jihad: The Rushdie affair and Its Legacy*. London: Atlantic Books, 2009.
Malik, Kenan. *The Quest for a Moral Compass: A Global History of Ethics*. London: Atlantic Books, 2014.

Marley, Laurence, ed. *The British Labour Party and Twentieth-Century Ireland: The Cause of Ireland, the Cause of Labour*. Manchester: Manchester University Press, 2016.

Marshall, Kate. *Real Freedom: Women's Liberation and Socialism*. London: Junius, 1982.

Marshall, Kate. *Moral Panics and Victorian Values: Women and the Family in Thatcher's Britain*. London: Junius, 1985.

Marx, Karl. *Grundrisse*. Harmondsworth: Penguin, 1973.

Marx, Karl. *Early Writings*. Harmondsworth: Penguin, 1976.

Marx, Karl. *Capital: A Critique of Political Economy – Volume One*. London: Penguin, 1976.

Marx, Karl. *Capital: A Critique of Political Economy – Volume Three*. London: Penguin, 1991.

Marx, Karl. *Capital: A Critique of Political Economy – Volume Two*. London: Penguin, 1992.

Marx, Karl and Frederick Engels. *The Communist Manifesto*. London: Junius/*Living Marxism*, 1996.

Matthews, Roger, Helen Easton, Daniel Briggs and Ken Pease. *Assessing the Use and Impact of Anti-Social Behaviour Orders*. Bristol: Policy Press, 2009.

Matthews, Wade. *The New Left, National Identity, and the Break-Up of Britain*. Leiden: Brill, 2013.

Mattick, Paul. *Economic Crisis and Crisis Theory*. Abingdon: Routledge, 2015.

Mayes, Tessa. *Restraint or Revelation? Free Speech and Privacy in a Confessional Age*. London: *spiked*, 2002.

McCormack, Tara. *Critique, Security and Power: The Political Limits to Emancipatory Approaches*. Abingdon: Routledge, 2009.

McCormack, Tara. *Britain's War Powers: The Fall and Rise of Executive Authority?* Cham: Palgrave Macmillan, 2019.

McLaughlin, Greg. *The War Correspondent*. London: Pluto Press, 2002.

McLaughlin, Kenneth. *Social Work, Politics and Society: From Radicalism to Orthodoxy*. Bristol: Policy Press, 2008.

Mészáros, István. *Marx's Theory of Alienation*. London: Merlin, 1975.

Milligan, Don. *Sex-Life: A Critical Commentary on the History of Sexuality*. London: Pluto Press, 1992.

Mirza, Munira, ed. *Culture Vultures: Is UK Arts Policy Damaging the Arts?* London: Policy Exchange, 2006.

Mirza, Munira. *The Politics of Culture: The Case of Universalism*. Basingstoke: Palgrave Macmillan, 2012.

Moore, Charles. *Margaret Thatcher: The Authorized Biography – Volume One: Not for Turning*. London: Allen Lane, 2013.

Moore, Charles. *Margaret Thatcher: The Authorized Biography – Volume Two: Everything She Wants*. London: Allen Lane, 2015.

Moore, Charles. *Margaret Thatcher: The Authorized Biography – Volume Three: Herself Alone*. London: Allen Lane, 2019.

Mulholland, Marc. *Bourgeois Liberty and the Politics of Fear: From Absolutism to Neo-Conservatism*. Oxford: Oxford University Press, 2013.

Mullan, Phil. *The Imaginary Time-Bomb: Why an Ageing Population Is not a Social Problem*. London: I. B. Tauris, 2000.

Mullan, Phil. *Creative Destruction: How to Start an Economic Renaissance*. Bristol: Policy Press, 2017.

Mullan, Phil. *Beyond Confrontation: Globalists, Nationalists and their Discontents*. Bingley: Emerald Publishing, 2020.

O'Neill, Brendan. *A Duty to Offend: Selected Essays*. Ballarat: Connor Court, 2015.

Passerini, Luisa. *Autobiography of a Generation: Italy, 1968*. Hanover: Wesleyan University Press, 1996.

Pelling, Henry. *A Short History of the Labour Party*. Basingstoke: Macmillan, 1985.

Perry, Matt. *Marxism and History*. Basingstoke: Palgrave Macmillan, 2002.

Phillips, Joan. *Policing the Family: Social Control in Thatcher's Britain*. London: Junius, 1988.

Pimlott, H. F. *Wars of Position? Marxism Today, Cultural Politics and the Remaking of the Left Press, 1979–1990*. Leiden: Brill, 2022.

Portelli, Alessandro. *The Battle of Valle Giulia: Oral History and the Art of Dialogue*. Madison: University of Wisconsin Press, 1997.

Pugh, Jonathan, ed. *What Is Radical Politics Today?* Basingstoke: Palgrave Macmillan, 2009.

Purvis, Stewart and Jeff Hulbert. *When Reporters Cross the Line: The Heroes, the Villains, the Hackers and the Spies*. London: Biteback, 2013.

Rakovsky, Christian. *Selected Writings on Opposition in the USSR, 1923–1930*. London: Allison & Busby, 1980.

Revolutionary Communist Party. *Preparing for Power: The Programme of the Revolutionary Communist Party*. London: Junius, 1984.

Revolutionary Communist Party. *The Red Front: A Platform for Working Class Unity*. London: Junius, 1987.

Robinson, Lucy. *Gay men and the Left in Post-War Britain: How the Personal Got Political*. Manchester: Manchester University Press, 2007.

Rooney, Kevin and James Heartfield. *The Blood-Stained Poppy: A Critique of the Politics of Commemoration*. Winchester: Zero Books, 2019.

Ryan, Mark. *War and Peace in Ireland: Britain and the IRA in the New World Order*. London: Pluto Press, 1994.

Schaff, Adam. *Marxism and the Human Individual*. New York: McGraw Hill, 1970.

Scott, Helen, ed. *The Essential Rosa Luxemburg*. Chicago: Haymarket, 2008.

Screpanti, Ernesto. *Libertarian Communism: Marx, Engels and the Political Economy of Freedom*. Basingstoke: Palgrave Macmillan, 2007.

Service, Robert. *Comrades: Communism – A World History*. London: Pan, 2007.

Skinner, Quentin. *Visions of Politics, Volume I: Regarding Method*. Cambridge: Cambridge University Press, 2002.
Slater, Tom, ed. *The Year the World Went Mad:* spiked *Writers on 2020*. London: *spiked*, 2020.
Smith, Evan. *British Communism and the Politics of Race*. Leiden: Brill, 2018.
Smith, Evan. *No Platform: A History of Anti-fascism, Universities and the Limits of Free Speech*. Abingdon: Routledge, 2020.
Smith, Evan and Matthew Worley, eds. *Against the Grain: The British Far Left from 1956*. Manchester: Manchester University Press, 2014.
Smith, Evan and Matthew Worley, eds. *Waiting for the Revolution: The British Far Left from 1956*. Manchester: Manchester University Press, 2017.
Summerfield, Penny. *Reconstructing Women's Wartime Lives: Discourse and Subjectivity in Oral Histories of the Second World War*. Manchester: Manchester University Press, 1998.
Taaffe, Peter. *The Rise of Militant: Militant's Thirty Years, 1964–1994*. London: Militant Publications, 1995.
Thompson, Kenneth. *Moral Panics*. London: Routledge, 1998.
Tompson, Keith. *Under Siege: Racism and Violence in Britain Today*. London: Penguin, 1988.
Tonkin, Elizabeth. *Narrating Our Pasts: The Social Construction of Oral History*. Cambridge: Cambridge University Press, 1992.
Tripp, Charles. *A History of Iraq*. Cambridge: Cambridge University Press, 2014.
Turner, Alwyn W. *A Classless Society: Britain in the 1990s*. London: Aurum Press, 2013.
van der Linden, Marcel. *Western Marxism and the Soviet Union: A Survey of Critical Theories and Debates since 1917*. Leiden: Brill, 2007.
Victor, Peter. *Managing without Growth: Slower by Design, Not Disaster*. Cheltenham: Edward Elgar Publishing, 2008.
Vulliamy, Ed. *The War is Dead, Long Live the War: Bosnia – The Reckoning*. London: Vintage, 2013.
Waiton, Stuart. *The Politics of Antisocial Behaviour: Amoral Panics*. London: Routledge, 2008.
Walgrave, Stefaan and Dieter Rucht, eds. *The World Says No to War: Demonstrations against the War on Iraq*. Minneapolis: University of Minnesota Press, 2010.
Walker, Martin. *The National Front*. London: Fontana, 1977.
Watson, Geoffrey R. *The Oslo Accords*. Oxford: Oxford University Press, 2000.
Wermenbol, Grace. *A Tale of Two Narratives: The Holocaust, the Nakba, and the Israeli-Palestinian Battle of Memories*. Cambridge: Cambridge University Press, 2021.
Westad, Odd Arne. *The Global Cold War: Third World Interventions and the Making of Our Times*. Cambridge: Cambridge University Press, 2007.
Workers Against Racism. *The Roots of Racism*. London: Junius, 1985.
Woudhuysen, James, ed. *Big Potatoes: The London Manifesto for Innovation*. London: The Big Potatoes Group, 2010.

Woudhuysen, James and Ian Abley. *Why Is Construction So Backward?* Chichester: Wiley-Academy, 2004.

Zwolinski, Matt and Benjamin Ferguson, eds. *The Routledge Companion to Libertarianism*. Abingdon: Routledge, 2022.

Journal articles

'The politics of Furedi'. *Policy* 22 (2006): 43–9.

'Was *LM* bullied into oblivion . . .'. *British Journalism Review* 11 (2000): 40–4.

Ahmed, Sabeen. 'Communism as *eudaimonia*: An Aristotelian reading of human emancipation'. *International Journal of Philosophy & Social Values* 1 (2018): 31–48.

Antonini, Francesca. 'Pessimism of the intellect, optimism of the will: Gramsci's political thought in the last miscellaneous notebooks'. *Rethinking Marxism* 31 (2019): 42–57.

Bell, Derrick. 'Racial realism'. *Connecticut Law Review* 24 (1992): 363–79.

Brien, Kevin M. 'Marx's radical humanism'. *International Critical Thought* 1 (2011): 186–203.

Bristow, Jennie. 'The making of "boomergeddon": The construction of the baby boomer generation as a social problem in Britain'. *British Journal of Sociology* 67 (2016): 575–91.

Burgess, Adam. 'The development of risk politics in the UK: Thatcher's "remarkable" but forgotten "Don't Die of Ignorance" AIDS campaign'. *Health, Risk & Society* 19 (2017): 227–45.

Callinicos, Alex. 'Politics or abstract propagandism?'. *International Socialism* 2 (Winter 1981): 111–28.

Callinicos, Alex. 'Looking for alternatives to reformism'. *International Socialism* 34 (Winter 1987): 106–17.

Callinicos, Alex. 'Race and class'. *International Socialism* 2 (Summer 1992): 3–39.

Campbell, David. 'Atrocity, memory, photography: Imaging the concentration camps of Bosnia – The case of ITN versus *Living Marxism*, part 1'. *Journal of Human Rights* 1 (2002): 1–33.

Campbell, David. 'Atrocity, memory, photography: Imaging the concentration camps of Bosnia – The case of ITN versus *Living Marxism*, part 2'. *Journal of Human Rights* 1 (2002): 143–72.

Chandler, David. 'The Bosnian protectorate and the implications for Kosovo'. *New Left Review* 235 (May–June 1999): 124–34.

Chanin, Eileen. 'Interview with Frank Furedi'. *Australian Quarterly* 78 (2006): 34–7.

Collignon, Sofia, Iakovos Makropoulos and Wolfgang Rüdig. 'Consensus secured? Elite and public attitudes to "lockdown" measures to combat Covid-19 in England'. *Journal of Elections, Public Opinion and Parties* 31 (2021): 109–21.

Crenshaw, Kimberlé W. 'Race, reform, and retrenchment: Transformation and legitimation in antidiscrimination law'. *Harvard Law Review* 101 (1988): 1331–87.
Cummings, Dolan. 'Round-table rumbles at the national'. *New Theatre Quarterly* 22 (2006): 96–8.
Davis, Madeleine. 'The Marxism of the British new left'. *Journal of Political Ideologies* 11 (2006): 335–58.
Fermont, Clare. 'Bookwatch: *Palestine* and the Middle East "Peace Process"'. *International Socialism* 72 (Autumn 1996): 113–25.
Fukuyama, Francis. 'The end of history?' *The National Interest* 16 (1989): 3–18.
Furedi, Frank. 'Britain's colonial wars: Playing the ethnic card', *Journal of Commonwealth & Comparative Politics* 28 (1990): 70–89.
Furedi, Frank. 'Creating a breathing space: The political management of colonial emergencies'. *Journal of Imperial and Commonwealth History* 21 (1993): 89–106.
Furedi, Frank. 'Fear and security: A vulnerability-led policy response'. *Social Policy & Administration* 42 (2008): 645–61.
Gilligan, Chris. 'The Irish question and the concept "identity" in the 1980s'. *Nations and Nationalism* 13 (2007): 599–617.
Gillott, John. 'The changing governance of embryo research?' *New Genetics and Society* 32 (2013): 190–206.
Habermas, Jürgen. 'New social movements'. *Telos* 49 (1981): 33–7.
Hardt, Michael and Antonio Negri. '*Empire*, twenty years on', *New Left Review* 120 (November–December 2019).
Hayes, Dave. 'Thirty years on: The Socialist Workers Party and the great miners' strike'. *International Socialism* 142 (Spring 2014): 27–56.
Heartfield, James. 'The politics of food: Two cheers for agribusiness'. *Review of Radical Political Economics* 32 (2000): 317–30.
Heartfield, James. 'Capitalism and anti-capitalism'. *Interventions* 5 (2003): 271–89.
Heartfield, James. 'Demobilising the nation: The decline of sovereignty in western Europe'. *International Politics* 46 (2009): 712–31.
Heartfield, James. 'Nick Cohen: *What's left? How the left lost its way*'. *Critique* 37 (2009): 149–53.
Hepworth, Jack. '"The moral rearmament of imperialism": The Revolutionary Communist Party, the Northern Ireland conflict, and the new world order, 1981-1994'. *Contemporary British History* 36 (2022): 591–621.
Hepworth, Jack. '"Progress will not occur if we continually adopt positions of principle": Irish republican prisoners and strategic reorientation, c.1976-1998'. *Irish Political Studies* 37 (2022). doi.org/10.1080/07907184.2022.2074978.
Higgs, Michael. 'From the street to the state: Making anti-fascism anti-racist in 1970s Britain'. *Race & Class* 58 (2016): 66–84.
Hillyard, Paddy. 'Irish people and the British criminal justice system'. *Journal of Law and Society* 21 (1994): 39–56.

Hoare, Marko Attila. 'Genocide in the former Yugoslavia: A critique of left revisionism's denial'. *Journal of Genocide Research* 5 (2003): 543–63.

Holbrook, Jon. 'NATO's humanitarian war'. *Socialist Lawyer* 32 (2000): 12–14.

Hook, Sidney. 'The Enlightenment and Marxism'. *Journal of the History of Ideas* 29 (1968): 93–108.

Hudson, Alan. 'Intellectuals for our times'. *Critical Review of International Social and Political Philosophy* 6 (2003): 33–50.

Hume, Mick. 'Keep your nose out of the press'. *English Journalism Review* 24 (2013): 25–30.

Joseph-Salisbury, Remi, Laura Connelly and Peninah Wangari-Jones. '"The UK is not innocent": Black Lives Matter, policing and abolition in the UK'. *Equality, Diversity and Inclusion* 40 (2021): 21–8.

Killick, Rob and Sandy Starr. 'Freedom net'. *Economic Affairs* 20 (2000): 29–32.

Kim, Nam-Kook. 'Deliberative multiculturalism in New Labour's Britain'. *Citizenship Studies* 15 (2011): 125–44.

Klug, Francesca, Keir Starmer and Stuart Weir. 'Civil liberties and the parliamentary watchdog: The passage of the Criminal Justice and Public Order Act 1994'. *Parliamentary Affairs* 49 (1996): 536–49.

Lacy Rogers, Kim. 'Memory, struggle, and power: On interviewing political activists'. *Oral History Review* 15 (1987): 165–84.

Lai, Brian and Dan Reiter. 'Rally 'round the Union Jack? Public opinion and the use of force in the United Kingdom, 1948-2001'. *International Studies Quarterly* 49 (2005): 255–72.

Latour, Vincent. 'Between consensus, consolidation and crisis: Immigration and integration in 1970s Britain'. *Revue Française de Civilisation Britannique* 22 (2017). doi.org/10.4000/rfcb.1719.

Malik, Kenan. 'Universalism and difference in discourses of race'. *Review of International Studies* 26 (2000): 155–77.

Malik, Kenan. 'Making a difference: Culture, race and social policy'. *Patterns of Prejudice* 39 (2005): 361–78.

Malik, Kenan. 'Ethical odyssey'. *RSA Journal* 154 (February 2007): 50–5.

March, Luke and Cas Mudde. 'What's left of the radical left? The European radical left after 1989: Decline *and* mutation'. *Comparative European Politics* 3 (2005): 23–49.

Meredith, Stephen. 'A "brooding oppressive shadow"? The Labour Alliance, the "trade union question", and the trajectory of revisionist social democracy, c. 1969-1975'. *Labour History Review* 82 (2017): 251–76.

Message, Bill. 'The miners and the Labour government'. *International Socialism* 91 (September 1976): 9–14.

Mirza, Munira. 'The therapeutic state: Addressing the emotional needs of the citizen through the arts'. *International Journal of Cultural Policy* 11 (2005): 261–73.

Mirza, Munira. 'Review essay: James Heartfield, *The death of the subject explained*'. *International Journal of Cultural Policy* 16 (2010): 58–9.

Mulholland, Marc. 'Northern Ireland and the far left, c.1965-1975'. *Contemporary British History* 32 (2018): 542-63.
Nielsen, Kai. 'Marx and the Enlightenment project'. *Critical Review* 2 (1988): 59-75.
Nugent, Brodie and Evan Smith. 'Intersectional solidarity? The Armagh women, the British left and women's liberation'. *Contemporary British History* 31 (2017): 611-35.
O'Kelly, Cronain. 'British socialists and Irish republicans'. *Studies in Ethnicity and Nationalism* 1 (2001): 17-25.
Olulode, Kunle. 'Airbrushing racism: Why racist words shouldn't be edited from history'. *Index on Censorship* 44 (2015): 34-6.
Park, James. 'Who are we today?'. *Psychotherapy and Politics International* 6 (2008): 63-5.
Pencheva, Denny and Kostas Maronitis. 'Fetishizing sovereignty in the remain and leave campaigns'. *European Politics and Society* 19 (2018): 529-39.
Portelli, Alessandro. 'The peculiarities of oral history'. *History Workshop Journal* 12 (1981): 96-107.
Rosenberg, Chanie. 'The Labour Party and the fight against fascism'. *International Socialism* 2 (Summer 1988): 55-93.
Schneider, Wendy Ellen. 'Past imperfect: Irving v Penguin Books Ltd., No. 1996-I-1113, 2000 WL 362478 (Q. B. Apr. 11), appeal denied (Dec. 18, 2000)'. *Yale Law Journal* 110 (2001): 1531-45.
Screpanti, Ernesto. 'Freedom and social goods: Rethinking Marx's theory of communism'. *Rethinking Marxism* 16 (2004): 185-206.
Summerfield, Penny. 'Culture and composure: Creating narratives of the gendered self in oral history interviews'. *Cultural and Social History* 1 (2004): 65-93.
Ticktin, Hillel. 'The class structure of the USSR and the elite'. *Critique* 9 (1978): 37-61.
Tranmer, Jeremy. 'A force to be reckoned with? The radical left in the 1970s'. *Revue Française de Civilisation Britannique* 22 (2017): 1-15.
Trotsky, Leon. 'Learn to think: A friendly suggestion to certain ultra-leftists'. *The New International* 4, no. 7 (July 1938): 206-7.
Trotsky, Leon. 'Their morals and ours'. *The New International* 4, no. 6 (June 1938): 163-73.
Twiss, Thomas M. 'Trotsky's analysis of Stalinism'. *Critique* 38 (2010): 545-63.
Vladisavljević, Nebojša. 'Nationalism, social movement theory and the grassroots movement of Kosovo Serbs, 1985-1988'. *Europe-Asia Studies* 54 (2002): 771-90.
von Oppen, Karoline. 'Reporting from Bosnia: Reconceptualising the notion of a "journalism of attachment"'. *Journal of Contemporary European Studies* 17 (2009): 21-33.
Vulliamy, Ed. '"Neutrality" and the absence of reckoning: A journalist's account'. *Journal of International Affairs* 52 (1999): 603-20.
Waddington, Jeremy. 'Trade union membership in Britain, 1980-1987: Unemployment and restructuring'. *British Journal of Industrial Relations* 30 (1992): 287-324.

Walby, Sylvia. 'The COVID pandemic and social theory: Social democracy and public health in the crisis'. *European Journal of Social Theory* 24 (2021): 22–43.

Walker, Dave. 'Libertarian humanism or critical utopianism? The demise of the Revolutionary Communist Party'. *New Interventions* 8, Issue 3 (1998).

Warmington, Paul. 'Critical race theory in England: Impact and opposition'. *Identities* 27 (2020): 20–37.

Winterton, Jonathan. 'The 1984–85 miners' strike and technological change'. *British Journal of the History of Science* 26 (1993): 5–14.

Wolton, Suke. 'Immigration policy and the "crisis of British values"'. *Citizenship Studies* 10 (2006): 453–67.

Wolton, Suke. 'The contradiction in the *Prevent Duty*: Democracy vs "British values"'. *Education, Citizenship and Social Justice* 12 (2017): 123–42.

Book chapters

Bean, Kevin. 'More than the border? Looking at Brexit through Irish eyes'. In *Contested Britain: Brexit, Austerity and Agency*, edited by Marius Guderjan, Hugh Mackay and Gesa Stedman, 219–32. Bristol: Bristol University Press, 2021.

Conversi, Daniele. 'Moral relativism and equidistance in British attitudes to the war in the former Yugoslavia'. In *This Time We Knew: Western Responses to Genocide in Bosnia*, edited by Thomas Cushman and Stjepan G. Meštrović, 244–81. New York: New York University Press, 1996.

Dean, Hartley. 'Eudaimonia and "species being": A Marxist perspective'. In *Handbook of Eudaimonic Well-Being*, edited by Joar Vitterrsø, 507–20. Cham: Springer, 2016.

Freeden, Michael. 'The morphological analysis of ideology'. In *The Oxford Handbook of Political Ideologies*, edited by Michael Freeden and Marc Stears, 115–37. Oxford: Oxford University Press, 2013.

Furedi, Frank. 'Terrorism and the politics of fear'. In *Criminology*, edited by Chris Hale, Keith Hayward, Azrini Wahidin and Emma Wincup, 267–86. Oxford: Oxford University Press, 2013.

Lee, Simon. 'No Plan B: The coalition agenda for cutting the deficit and rebalancing the economy'. In *The Cameron-Clegg Government: Coalition Politics in an Age of Austerity*, edited by Simon Lee and Matt Beech, 75–88. Basingstoke: Palgrave Macmillan, 2011.

Molnar, Peter. 'Interview with Kenan Malik'. In *The Content and Context of Hate Speech: Rethinking Regulation and Responses*, edited by Michael Herz and Peter Molnar, 81–91. Cambridge: Cambridge University Press, 2012.

Portelli, Alessandro. 'Oral history as genre'. In *Narrative and Genre: Contexts and Types of Communication*, edited by Mary Chamberlain and Paul Thompson, 23–45. London: Routledge, 1998.

Schinkel, Willem. 'Governing through moral panic: The governmental uses of fear'. In *The Ashgate Research Companion to Moral Panics*, edited by Charles Krinsky, 293–304. Abingdon: Routledge, 2013.

Virdee, Satnam. 'Racism and resistance in British trade unions, 1948–1979'. In *Racializing Class, Classifying Race: Labour and Difference in Britain, the USA and Africa*, edited by Peter Alexander and Rick Halpern, 122–49. Basingstoke: Macmillan, 2000.

Wright, Nicholas. 'Brexit and Ireland: Collateral damage?' In *Brexit and Beyond: Rethinking the Futures of Europe*, edited by Benjamin Martill and Uta Staiger, 105–13. London: UCL Press, 2018.

Unpublished documents and manuscripts

Building the New Leadership. RCP conference bulletin (1982).

Fiona Foster, 'Contribution to OTAM' (n.d. [*c*.1995]).

FR, *Introduction to Preparing for Power to be Discussed in Branch Educationals: Marxism in Our Time* (1983).

London International Research Exchange, *Journalists at War* (n.d. [1994]).

London International Research Exchange flyer (n.d. [1995]).

London International Research Exchange news update (n.d. [1997]).

Mike Fitzpatrick, 'Waking from the nightmare' (2015).

Our Tasks and Methods: Discussion no. 1 (n.d. [*c*.1995]).

The RCP and the Problem of Democratic Centralism. RCP conference bulletin (1983).

Revolutionary Communist Party, Yorkshire *Capital* Reading Group schedule (n.d. [*c*.1986]).

Flyers and ephemera

Break Out of the Grey: Election Manifesto of the Revolutionary Communist Party (London: Junius, n.d. [1992]).

The Criminal Justice and Public Order Bill: The Control of Young People (Campaign Against Militarism briefing, 8, May 1994).

Kevin Green election flyer (Revolutionary Communist Tendency, 1981).

LM Demands that ITN News Team is Stripped of Awards. *LM* press release, 10 February 1997.

Revolutionary Communist Group Executive Committee, *Statement on the Expulsion of a Chauvinist Grouping in the RCG*, 17 November 1976.

Revolutionary Communist Group Paper to Troops Out Movement Conference, 5 June 1977.
Revolutionary Communist Party, *Free the Shirebrook 10!* (n.d. [1985]).
Revolutionary Communist Party, *Stand Up Fight Back: Vote Red Front* (1987).
Revolutionary Communist Party, *Towards 2000: Revolutionary Ideas for the Nineties* (1991).
Revolutionary Communist Tendency, *Internationalism and the Dictatorship of the Proletariat* (1978).
Revolutionary Communist Tendency, *The Trade Unions and the Struggle against Racism* (1978).
Revolutionary Communist Tendency, *Public Forums* (n.d. [1979]).
Workers March Against Racism Flyer (Workers Against Racism, 1982).

Undercover Policing Inquiry

MPS-0731471: 'Special Branch report on an RCP public meeting as part of their campaign in the Bermondsey by-election', 18 February 1983.
UPI0000015238: 'Special Branch report stating that the Revolutionary Communist Tendency are disappointed by the lack of impact made by the Smash the Prevention of Terrorism Act Campaign amongst the working class', 19 December 1980.
UPI0000015249: 'Special Branch report on a public meeting held by East London Workers Against Racism in support of their candidate in the Greater London Council elections', 29 April 1981.
UPI0000015545: 'Special Branch report on a national conference of the Revolutionary Communist Party titled "Workers Defence Takes Off"', 19 August 1981.
UPI0000015575: 'Special Branch report on an internal conference of the Revolutionary Communist Tendency to discuss forthcoming policies and actions', 1 September 1981.
UPI0000016193: 'Special Branch report on a public meeting of the East London Workers Against Racism including talks by Fran Eden and Joan Lamont on fascism and immigration', 28 January 1981.
UPI0000016491: 'Special Branch report on an educational meeting held by the Revolutionary Communist Tendency on the subject "Ireland – How can we build an effective solidarity movement in this country?"', 3 March 1981.
UPI0000016584: 'Special Branch report concerning national conference of Revolutionary Communist Tendency signed by HN68', 3 April 1981.
UPI0000017977: 'Special Branch report on a public meeting of the South London Workers Against Racism discussing the police', 31 March 1982.
UPI0000018684: 'Special Branch report on a public meeting of the East London Workers Against Racism discussing the forthcoming deportation of Afia Begum', 5 October 1982.

UPI0000019003: 'Special Branch report on a public meeting of Workers Against Racism and the Greater London Council's Committee for Women to discuss the forthcoming deportation of Afia Begum', 19 April 1983.

UPI0000029221: 'Security Service minute sheet for policy file enclosing brief for coverage at upcoming RCP conference', 7 July 1983.

UPI0000034280: 'Debriefing of a Revolutionary Communist Party (RCP) Source', 17 October 1983.

North of England Institute of Mining and Mechanical Engineers, Newcastle
Dave Douglass Archive: Miners' Strike Box 1.

West Yorkshire Archives Service, Bradford
WYB339/4/9/4: RCP election flyer, *Vote Revolutionary Communist Party*. Bradford: Revolutionary Communist Party, 1986.

Linen Hall Library, Belfast
Northern Ireland Political Collection: Irish in Britain Box 1.

Television and radio broadcasts

Against Nature, 30 November 1997, 7 December 1997, 14 December 1997
'Brendan O'Neill: What makes us human?', BBC Radio 2, 9 October 2013
The James Whale Show, 4 August 1995
Let 'em All In, Channel 4, 7 March 2005
Question Time, BBC, 26 November 2020
Sky News, 3 November 2017
Sunday Politics South East, BBC, 27 October 2019

Index

Aaronovitch, David 4
Abley, Ian 118, 177
abortion rights 1, 49 n.31, 89, 90, 227
Academy of Ideas 185, 187, 204 n.91, 210. *See also* Battle of Ideas; Institute of Ideas
Acheson, Donald 90
Adams, Gerry 33, 123, 125
African National Congress 120–2, 127
Afzal, Farekh 49 n.31, 60, 62, 66
Against Nature 145–6
Ahmed, Sabeen 27
AIDS 88–95, 101, 207 n.111, 215
Aire Valley Yarns, Farsley 66
Alaso, Rose 64–5
Alić, Fikret 155
Allen, Tony 19, 83
Allirajah, Duleep 152
Alternative Economic Strategy 20
Alton Bill, 1988 90
American Civil Liberties Union 160
Anderson, Eve 91, 110, 122, 124
Angle Gallery, Birmingham 141
Anti-Apartheid Movement 15, 68–70, 121
Anti-Nazi League 57–8, 68, 142–3
anti-racism 7, 11, 27, 42, 43, 54 n.56, 55–68, 71, 88, 101, 135, 136, 170, 172, 198–201
Anti-Social Behaviour Orders (ASBOs) 168–9
Appleton, Josie 167, 170, 187, 189, 205, 224
Arafat, Yasser 121–2
Ardern, Richard 54 n.56
Arnould, Yasmin 54 n.56

Balkans 112–18, 127, 156–8
Ball, Johnathan 42
Barrett, Cathy 49 n.31
Barry, Brian 170
Basildon 168, 176

Battersea 34
Battle of Ideas 8, 165, 179, 185, 193, 194, 211, 224
Begum, Afia 62, 88
Bell, Martin 156
Ben-Ami, Daniel 179, 181–2, 206
Benn, Tony 20, 62, 65, 111, 122–3
Berger, John 159 n.129
Berlin Wall 102
Bermondsey by-election (1983) 47–9
Big Flame 31
Birmingham 33 n.109, 41, 49 n.31, 54 n.56, 55 n.58, 64, 115, 131 n.4, 141
Birth Control Campaign 89
Blackie, Duncan 92 n.107, 116
Black Lives Matter 186, 198–200
Blackpool 35, 106
Blair, Tony 154, 166, 167
Bloody Sunday 126
Blunkett, David 37, 167, 171
Bolshevism 24, 31, 44, 49, 50, 102 n.2, 187, 213, 230
Bosnia 2 n.3, 112–18, 155–61
Bosnian Muslims 118, 155
Bosnian Serbs 112, 117, 118 n.90, 155–7, 161
Boyd, William 159 n.129
Brack, Ben 113 n.60, 148
Brand, Chris 142–3
Brent, Ben 131 n.4
Brexit 4, 5, 10, 186, 190–8, 202, 205, 206, 209, 211 n.127, 212, 213, 218, 222, 223, 235
Brexit Party 4, 186, 191, 195, 218
Brick, Carlton 152
Brighton 14, 53, 65, 148
Bring the Boys Back from Ulster 28 n.82
Bristol 53, 58, 64, 131 n.4, 199
Bristow, Jennie 142, 160 n.134, 167, 188, 189, 204–6
British Library 160

British National Party   39 n.141, 135–6
British Steel   21
Brixton   48, 56, 59–61
Brooke, Peter   120, 131 n.4, 133
Brussels   189, 190, 192–4, 197
Bryan, Jon   83–4, 86
Burgess, Adam   91, 143
Burnley   171
Burton, Ann   46, 54
Bush, George H. W.   109, 112

Cadre names   13 n.3
Calcutt, Andrew   144
Cale, Kirsten   110, 134
Callaghan, James   20
Callaghan, John   30
Callinicos, Alex   23, 69, 75, 77, 96–7, 225–6
Cambridge University   37, 116
Cameron, David   189
Campaign Against Militarism   118, 136–7, 178
Campaign for Nuclear Disarmament   111
Campaign for Press and Broadcasting Freedom   161
Campbell, Aidan   145
Campbell, David   2 n.3, 156 n.112, 162
Canterbury   25, 26, 68, 181
Cantle Report   171
Carr, Winston   61
censorship   17, 90, 141, 142, 157, 159–61, 222
Chadburn, Ray   75, 76 n.25
Chandler, David   107, 170
Change Politics For Good   195
Channel 4   145, 168
Chauvin, Derek   198
chauvinism   15, 21, 25, 27, 28, 32, 34, 39, 43, 55, 58, 119, 124, 141
Chetniks   117
Clarkson, Andy   29 n.86, 40, 86, 114–15
Cliff, Tony   6 n.30, 14, 19
Clifford, Theresa   131 n.4
climate change   146, 178
Clough, Robert   160 n.132
Cohen, Nick   3, 4 n.19, 5, 215 n.3

College of Europe   166 n.14
Colston, Edward   199
Commission on Race and Ethnic Disparities   200–1
Committee for a Communist Programme   18
Committee to Stop War in the Gulf (CWSG)   111
Communist Manifesto, The   130 n.3, 143, 144, 145 n.70, 176, 212 n.130
Communist Party of Great Britain (CPGB)   6, 15, 16, 17 n.17, 25, 30–2, 33 n.110, 39, 46, 66–7, 72, 84, 97, 216
Condorcet   139
Conservative Party   4 n.18, 21, 41, 57, 112, 136, 154, 182, 186, 189 n.19, 191, 195, 203, 207 n.111
Contracts Ltd   86–7
contrarianism   4–6, 19 n.28, 72, 76, 165, 211, 215, 216, 226–7
Conway Hall   21
Copley, Keith   46
Coronation Street   98
Coventry   26, 35, 43, 55 n.58, 61, 65, 68
Coventry Workers Against Racism   61, 65
Covid-19   10, 186, 202–10, 211 n.127, 212
Criminal Justice Act (2003)   167 n.18
Criminal Justice and Public Order Bill (1994)   136
critical race theory   7, 186, 199, 200
critique of liberalism   32, 36, 58, 62, 85, 88, 89, 107, 111, 112, 114, 117, 129, 149, 180
critique of statism   16, 21, 38, 44, 55, 77, 216
critique of the left   6, 13–26, 46, 47, 61, 67, 70, 72, 92, 95, 97, 99, 102, 112, 134, 153, 203, 216, 228, 232, 234
Croatia   113–16
culture of fear   130, 139, 143, 146, 155, 168, 205–9, 223
Culture Wars   160, 187, 203, 210–11
Cummings, Dolan   134–5, 150, 168–9, 206, 219, 223, 235

Cuthbert, Alka Sehgal 4 n.18, 200
Cybercafé Ltd 177
Czechoslovakia 102

Davenport, Neil 173
Davies, Chris 15–16, 28 n.80
Dawson, Graham 9, 232
Dean, Hartley 27
Deichmann, Thomas 155–7, 161
de Klerk, F. W. 121
democracy 14
  and the critique of the EU as anti-
    democratic 186–98
  democratic rights 42
  democratic socialism 40
  and Francis Fukuyama 129
  industrial democracy 20
  and the Northern Ireland peace
    process 126
  and revolutionary critique of
    'bourgeois democracy' 42–3,
    48, 58, 102, 107, 141
  transition to democracy in South
    Africa 121
democratic centralism 14, 26, 53 n.51,
  217
Democratic Unionist Party 197–8
Denehy, Alan 105
Department for Trade and
  Industry 115 n.77
Desai, Jayaben 65–6
Deverill, Khalid 132
d'Holbach 139
dictatorship of the proletariat 24, 99,
  138
Diderot 139
Dingle, Ceri 141, 178, 190, 235
Dodsworth, Laura 205
Douglass, David 37, 80–1
Downing Street Declaration (1993) 125
Drabble, Margaret 159 n.129
Dublin 125, 189
Duffy, Terry 79
Dunscroft 79
Durham 39, 84, 87 n.81

Eastbourne 102
eastern Europe 102, 115, 119
East Germany 102

East London Workers Against Racism
  (ELWAR) 43, 48, 55–63, 136
Eden, Fran 35, 48–9, 61 n.98, 83
educationals 18, 23, 43, 49–52
Ehsan, Rakib 200 n.73
Éire Nua 40
Elizabeth II 203
'the end of history' 108, 129, 131
Engels, Frederick 129, 143 n.59,
  145 n.70, 176 n.75, 211–12
  n.130
Enlightenment 103–5, 138–40, 143,
  147–8, 170 n.41, 175, 193, 194,
  213, 231
environmentalism 3, 7, 144–6, 158, 178,
  183, 185, 217
eudaimonia 27
European Central Bank 189
European Community 114, 123, 126
European Parliament 39, 63, 191
European Union 10, 186, 189–98
Euroscepticism 189 n.19, 190–2, 196
Evans, Gareth 19 n.27, 83

Falklands War 47, 109, 112
Farage, Nigel 4
Farrell, Alex 120, 123, 131 n.4, 132, 133
Farrell, Michael 29
fascism 13 n.3, 17 n.17, 32, 39, 47,
  57–61, 65, 117, 234 n.72
Ferrone, Vincenzo 139, 147
Field, Frank 169
financial crash, 2008 178–82
First World War 21 n.44, 31, 109
Fitches, John 65
Fitzpatrick, John 4 n.18, 36, 87, 96, 218
Fitzpatrick, Michael 6, 18–20, 22–4,
  44, 49, 86, 92–5, 134, 153, 166,
  207–9, 212, 215, 216, 224–5,
  229, 232
Fitzpatrick, Yasmin 4 n.18
Flewers, Paul 115, 137, 149, 154, 211–12,
  216, 219, 229
Floyd, George 186, 198–9
Flude, Justin 90 n.95
Foot, Michael 46 n.17, 47, 62
Ford, Eddie 216
Foster, Claire 87 n.80, 106
Foster, Fiona 123, 126, 127, 146

Fowler, Norman   91
Fox, Claire   2–4, 41, 42, 51, 155, 158, 160, 162, 163, 165, 166, 174, 187, 188, 190, 191, 195, 196, 204, 210, 215, 218, 220–1, 229, 236
Frayn, Liz   142
Fréchette, Louise   178
Freeden, Michael   7–9, 27, 108, 217, 222
Freeman, Mike   15, 19 n.27, 21, 22, 31–2, 39–41, 48, 54, 82, 96, 97, 104, 111, 117, 225, 230 n.56
free speech   1, 5, 141–2, 149, 159–61, 204 n.91, 215
Free Speech Wars   160
Fukuyama, Francis   107–8, 129, 131
Furedi, Ann   45–6, 51, 72, 74, 221, 230, 234
Furedi, Frank   43, 52, 53, 89, 105, 108, 143, 144, 150, 151, 154, 169, 170, 172, 173, 175, 186, 187, 193, 194, 206, 210, 215, 218, 220, 228, 229, 235

Gateshead   87
gay rights movement   88 n.86, 89, 91, 93–4
Gaza   122
Gear, Sarah   87 n.80, 89 n.88
general elections
    1979 general election   22, 58
    1983 general election   20, 49
    1987 general election   90, 95, 101
    1992 general election   108, 120, 131–3
    1997 general election   154
    2010 general election   182
    2015 general election   187
    2019 general election   195
Gilland, Emma   205
Gilligan, Chris   192
Gillott, John   50, 80, 89, 140, 145, 177–8, 207–9, 222
Gilroy, Paul   58 n.78
Givan, Paul   197
Glasgow   51, 53, 69–70, 85, 86, 91, 98, 102 n.2, 131 n.4, 137, 142–3
globalism   10, 179, 194–5
Gold, Helene   131 n.4
Good Friday Agreement   197 n.57
Graham, Jenny   91, 121

Gramsci, Antonio   10–11, 217, 234
Great Barrington Declaration   204
Greater London Council   55, 60 n.91, 61, 62 n.100
Greece   192
Greenslade, Roy   159 n.129
Greenwich by-election (1987)   95
Grossman, Henryk   50, 180–1
Grunwick   65, 66
Guldberg, Helene   142–3, 156, 158, 161, 188, 219
Guldberg, Karen   64, 95 n.127
Gulf War   105, 109–12, 119
Gupta, Sunetra   204
Gutman, Roy   156

Habermas, Jürgen   144
Hackney   48, 56
Hadaway, Pauline   198
Hadden, Peter   30 n.90
Hall, Stuart   97
Hallsworth, Dave   25, 34, 36, 37, 49 n.31, 87
Hammond, Keith   85
Hands Off The Middle East Committee   111–12
Hannan, Daniel   191
Harding, Alan   138
Hardt, Michael   194
Harman, Chris   79
Harrington, Patrick   67–8, 106
Harrison, Judy   14, 15, 16 n.11, 48, 56, 62, 83
Hartley-Brewer, Julia   159 n.130
Hayes, Dennis   168, 176
Heartfield, James   4 n.18, 103 n.11, 110, 136, 140, 173, 177, 181, 189–90
Heath, Edward   14, 15
Heathfield, Slough   66
Hegel   147
HFW Plastics strike, 1987   87
Higgins, Jim   19 n.29
High Court   67, 160–2, 164
Hill, Christopher   195–6, 231
Hill, Susannah   131 n.4
Hoare, Marko Attila   116, 161
Hodder & Stoughton   165
Hoey, Joan   50 n.39, 73, 80, 83, 193, 228–9

Holbrook, Jon   197
Holland, Stuart   20
Holocaust   117, 155, 158
Home Office   62, 63 n.109, 168 n.28
House of Lords   5, 204, 215
Howard, Michael   136
Hudson, Alan   72, 81, 143, 151, 165–6, 168, 176, 190–1, 230
humanism   11, 27, 99, 104, 108, 130, 138–40, 143, 150, 152 n.102, 164, 170, 174, 175, 178, 183, 185, 200, 210–13, 217–19, 222, 223, 226, 231, 235
Hume, Mick   2, 38, 86, 103, 107, 109–10, 116, 122, 129, 143, 144, 152, 156–7, 159, 161, 163–7, 174, 176, 177, 180–2, 184, 188, 195, 210, 220, 234
Hungary   103, 193–4
Hussein, Saddam   105, 109–11, 115
Hyde Park   28, 111

Ideas for Freedom   173
identity politics   144, 170, 172, 185, 186, 199–200, 212, 216, 234
Iman, Inaya Folarin   199–200
immigration controls   21, 49 n.31, 59, 62–5, 68, 88
Independent Television Commission   145
Independent Television News (ITN)   2–3, 130, 155–61
Indian Workers' Association   60
Industrial Relations Act (1971)   14
Institute of Ideas   4, 160–5, 169, 173–4, 178
International Marxist Group (IMG)   17 n.17, 20, 33 n.110
International Monetary Fund   189
International Socialists (IS)   13, 14, 19 n.29, 30, 33 n.110
Iraq   105, 109–12, 122, 167
Irish Freedom Movement   30–42, 71, 72, 101, 118, 120, 122–7, 131 n.4, 132, 135, 197
Irish National Liberation Army   35 n.121
Irish Republican Army (IRA)   4, 31–6, 39–42, 125–7

Irving, David   117
Isaković, Bojana   115 n.77
Israel   120–2
Israel, Jonathan   138–9

Jacoby, Russell   171–2
Jakubowski, Franz   89 n.90
Jarvie, Jenny   143
Jenkins, Roy   33 n.109
Jenkins, Tiffany   151–2
Jericho   122
Johnson, Boris   171 n.49, 200, 202–5
journalism of attachment   156–7

Kamm, Oliver   2
Kangesan, Sunder   61
Kant, Immanuel   148
Karadžić, Radovan   157
Karey, Suke   84
Kasparova, V.   50
Kelly, John   2 n.5, 53 n.49, 134
Kelly, Kevin   123
Kennedy, Mick   125–6
Kent, Bruce   111
Keynesianism   169, 192
Khan, Parveen   56
Killick, Rob   25, 39, 56, 65, 177, 179–82, 195, 218, 221, 224, 231, 235
Kilminster, John   67
Kinnock, Neil   78
Knight, Rob   66, 103, 110, 144
Korsch, Karl   148–9
Kosovo   113
Kossior, Vladislav   50 n.37
Krastev, Ivan   187
Krstić, Radislav   161
Kumar, Manjit   140, 145
Kundnani, Arun   172
Kurds   110–12
Kuwait   105, 109–10

Labour Committee on Ireland (LCI)   37
labourism   36, 47–9, 54, 70, 74, 77, 78, 81, 84, 96–7, 103, 138, 153, 185, 226
Labour Party   2, 14, 20, 22, 35, 36 n.129, 37, 39, 46 n.17, 47–9, 54, 57, 78, 95, 96, 154, 187
Laclau, Ernesto   217

Lambeth   34, 54 n.56
Lanchester Polytechnic   35
Landa, Inez   65, 66
Lapavitsas, Costas   192
Lasch, Christopher   188
Last Magazine   160 n.137, 170 n.41
Lawrence, Pam   131 n.4, 149
Laybourn, Keith   5
Leader, Robert   158, 216
LeBor, Adam   4, 67 n.129, 71 n.4, 98 n.146
Lee, Ellie   106
Lee, Gordon   97–8
Leech, Kirk   13 n.3, 25, 53, 68, 71, 106, 133–4, 151, 178
Leeds   43, 63, 64, 66, 67, 70, 89, 90, 160 n.132, 171
Left Opposition   49–50
Lenin, Vladimir Ilyich
   anti-imperialism   21, 28–31, 40, 50, 110
   critique of economism   17
   critique of labourism   19
   critique of the state   136
Leninist   32, 39, 72, 76, 104 n.17, 111
Lessing, Doris   159 n.129
Leveson Report   188
Lewis, Nigel   131 n.4
Lewis, Norman   26, 50, 57, 152–3, 182, 206, 221, 224–5, 231–2
Lexit   192
liberal democracy   102, 107–8, 129
Libya   26
Lipstadt, Deborah   117 n.88
Liverpool   31, 46, 64
Living Marxism   2, 3, 5, 84, 98–9, 101, 104, 105, 108–10, 115–18, 130, 132, 134, 139, 142, 143, 148, 150, 152, 156–62
lockdown   10, 186, 202–9, 212
London International Research Exchange   157
Longford, Charles   56, 63–4, 69 n.142, 70 n.149, 120–1
Long Kesh   35
Lott, Tim   4
Lukács, Georg   43, 50, 52, 140, 225–7
Luton   46
Luxemberg, Rosa   16, 50

Maastricht Treaty   189
McCormack, Tara   187
McElhinney, Frank   70
McGuinness, Martin   123
McLaughlin, Kenneth   168
McNally, Tony   72
McNamara, Paula   106 n.22
Mac Stíofáin, Seán   40
Mafethal, Billy   121
Major, John   112, 114 n.68, 189 n.19
Malik, Kenan   109, 119, 124, 131 n.4, 143, 168, 171–2, 175, 177, 200, 201, 203, 210, 211 n.128, 224
Malthusianism   145
Manchester   15, 26, 33–5, 43, 47, 55 n.58, 60, 63–4, 68, 69, 72, 78, 87, 131 n.4, 191, 219
Mandela, Nelson   121
Manifesto Club   172, 189
Mansfield   81
Marconi   69–70
Margam, Kate   118
Marshall, Kate   19 n.27, 21–3, 54, 77, 88–90, 95, 140 n.39
Marshall, Penny   155, 158, 161
Martin, Tim   138, 211
Marx
   and alienation   27, 152
   Capital   29 n.87, 49–50
   capitalism's inability to maximise society's productive potential   145
   critique of 'utopian' socialism   212
   and the critique of bourgeois liberty   148
   and the decisive role of the subject   180–1
   The Eighteenth Brumaire of Louis Bonaparte   32, 174 n.64
   and the Enlightenment   103–4, 147
   and modernity   129
   and radical humanism   163, 223–4
   and revolution   96, 143, 153, 225
   superseding capitalism   176–7, 180
   theory of crisis   50, 180
Marxism Today   46, 97
Massey, Wystan   115, 131 n.4
Masters, Mary   23, 40
Mattick, Paul   50, 98 n.146, 180

Mellish, Bob   47–8
Merrik, Alan   32
Miah, Mukith   136
'Midnight in the century'   102 n.1, 104, 105 n.18, 107, 129, 131, 137–8, 211
Militant tendency   30, 71 n.1, 81–2
Milligan, Don   91–4, 207 n.111
Milošević, Slobodan   113–16
Minneapolis   186, 198
Mirza, Munira   5, 169–72, 200–1
misanthropy   144, 145, 164, 168, 173–5, 183, 201, 210, 223, 229, 234, 235
Molloy, Mary Ann   64, 69
Monbiot, George   3, 5, 146, 158
Monks, John   36
Monster Raving Loony Party   48
Moorcock, Kate   152
moral authoritarianism   74, 88–94
Morland, Justice (Michael)   160–1
Morrison, Blake   159 n.129, 169
Morrison, Danny   125
Mos-Shogbamimu, Shola   200
Mouffe, Chantal   217
Mullan, Para   62–3, 87–8, 218, 220, 233
Mullan, Phil   45, 73, 150–1, 173, 177, 190, 194–5, 206, 212, 233
Muralov, Nikolai   50 n.37
Murdoch, Linda   51–2, 73, 85, 86, 98, 220, 231
Murphy, Phil   29, 40, 123
Museum of Applied Arts, Belgrade   115 n.77

Nassim, Daniel   120–1
National Association of Local Government Officers (NALGO)   36, 64–5, 85, 87
National Coal Board (NCB)   74–5, 78, 82, 85
National Front   39 n.141, 55, 57–9, 66, 67
National Health Service   203, 205
National Union of Mineworkers (NUM)   21 n.41, 74–5, 78–82, 84, 85
National Union of Public Employees (NUPE)   63, 64, 87
National Union of Students (NUS)   17 n.17, 34, 70, 106, 110

National Union of Teachers (NUT)   63
NATO   112, 114, 115, 117, 194
Negri, Antonio   194
Nevan, Julie   95
Newcastle   26, 46, 69, 83, 87, 89, 109, 118, 220
Newham Monitoring Project   61
Newham Rights Centre   59
New Left   6 n.32, 144
new social movements   144, 217
New Statesman and Society   114, 117
the next step   23, 25, 44, 46, 54, 68, 82–4, 86, 88, 96, 98, 102, 104, 106, 109, 111, 113, 119, 124, 171
No More Hiroshimas   141
No platform   17, 142
Northern Ireland   1, 7, 10, 28–37, 120, 122, 125, 131 n.4, 197–8, 215, 226
Northern Ireland Committee, Irish Congress of Trade Unions   34
Northern Ireland Labour and Trade Union Group   30 n.90
Northern Ireland Protocol   197–8
Norton, Sabina   18, 22, 25, 69
Nottingham   34, 39, 53, 158, 216
Novo Argumente   155
Nurrish, Julie   106 n.22

Off The Fence   158–9
O'Grady, John   48
O'Kelly, Cronain   38 n.136, 137, 149
Oldham   171
Olulode, Kunle   197, 201–2
O'Malley, Craig   169
Omarska   157 n.120
O'Neill, Brendan   167, 176–7, 180–1, 185–6, 188–9, 195, 197–9, 201–3, 208, 210, 218, 219
Operation Desert Storm   112
Operation Spanner   141
Orbán, Viktor   193–4
Osborne, Russell   113
Oslo Accords   121–2
Our tasks and methods   13, 16 n.12, 27, 87, 149–50, 223
OutRage!   94
Oxford   84, 131 n.4, 137, 148, 171 n.49, 204, 209

Paine, Tom   139, 188
Palestine Liberation Organisation
    (PLO)   120–2, 124
Paris   109, 115
Parris, Matthew   159
Parry, Colin   4
Parry, Tim   4, 42
Passerini, Luisa   231
Patel, Priti   198
Perks, Martyn   182
petit-bourgeois nationalism   31, 32, 40, 124
Phillips, Joan   62 n.99, 85, 86, 88–9, 97, 102, 113–16, 156, 189 n.17
Pilger, John   59 n.84
Pirani, Simon   32
Plan for Coal   74–5, 78
Poland   103
Political Committee   8, 13 n.3, 16, 18 n.24, 24, 26, 41, 50, 53, 83, 95, 97, 103, 104, 107, 135, 137, 140, 144, 146 n.80, 147, 188, 224, 227, 230, 231
Polytechnic of North London (PNL)   67–8, 106
Pontefract   81, 85
populism   193–4
Portelli, Alessandro   231
Portsmouth   53
Pottins, Charlie   117
Powell, Enoch   89
Preparing for Power (conference)   41, 43 n.2, 54, 77, 95, 96, 97 n.137, 103, 107
Preparing for Power
    (programme)   49 n.32
Preston   58
Prevention of Terrorism Act (PTA)   29, 33
primitivism   145, 178
Protestant working class (Northern Ireland)   29–31

Rabin, Yitzhak   121
Radcliffe, Bob   79
radical humanism   11, 99, 104, 108, 130, 138–40, 150, 164, 178, 179, 183, 210, 217, 222
Rakovsky, Christian   50

RCP (dissolution)   3, 76, 102, 130, 134, 149–54, 216, 217
Red Action   76, 95 n.126
Red Front   93, 95–7, 101, 201
reformism   10, 13–16, 20–2, 25, 37, 42–4, 47–9, 55, 59, 61, 66, 70, 80, 82, 85, 89, 95, 97–8, 106, 121, 124, 216, 217, 223, 225, 227
relativism   140, 166, 223
Republic of Ireland   189, 197
Revell, Lynn   69
Revolutionary Communist Group
    (RCG)   13–17, 28, 33, 111–12, 126
Revolutionary Communist Students
    (RCS)   26, 34, 58 n.75, 61, 71, 90 n.95, 106–10, 113 n.60, 119, 132, 142–3, 160 n.132
Revolutionary Democratic
    Group   95 n.126
revolutions of 1848   103
Richards, Dave   148 n.89
Richards, Frank   13, 15, 17, 19, 20, 40, 43, 44, 46, 55, 58, 61, 71, 76–8, 81, 82, 95, 96, 99, 102, 104, 107, 129, 131, 141, 145, 149
Richardson, Henry   75
Roberts, Pat   28, 76, 79
Robinson, Lucy   48 n.24, 93
Robson, Penny   112
Romania   102
Rotherhithe   48
Roucou, George   63–4
Royal College of Art   1, 165
Royal Institution   160
Royal Shakespeare Company   160
Rundle, Guy   5
Russell, Denis   196
Ryan, Linda   97 n.136, 118
Ryan, Mark   122, 127

Saddique, Nasreen   59
Said, Edward   122
Salt, Hilary   150
sari squad   62–3
Sarkar, Ash   200
Scargill, Arthur   75, 76, 78, 80, 82
Scientific Advisory Group for
    Emergencies   207

Serbia   113–17, 157
Sewell Report   200–2
Sheffield   37, 46, 49 n.31, 72, 81, 131 n.4
Shirebrook Ten   85
Simons, Helen   65
Simpson, John   159 n.129
Singh, Sharmini   135–6
Singh Gill, Satnam   61
Sinn Féin
    left-wing critiques of   32
    politics   40–1
    and strategic reorientation   123–7
Skegness   79
Skinner, Quentin   7, 131
Slovenia   113–15
Smash the Prevention of Terrorism Act Campaign (SPTAC)   29, 33 n.109, 34–5, 39
Smith, Evan   5, 6, 17, 67 n.127, 142, 215
Smith, George Davey   93
social atomisation   90, 143–4, 163, 164, 168, 169, 172, 183, 204–6, 210, 222
Socialist Organiser   67
Socialist Workers Party (SWP)   14, 19, 20, 22, 23, 31, 46, 53 n.49, 57, 69, 71 n.1, 75, 77–9, 92, 93, 96, 106, 111, 116, 167, 174, 196, 225
Society of Arts   160
South Africa   15, 69–70, 102, 119–21, 124
South Bank Polytechnic   1
South London Workers Against Racism (SOLWAR)   60
South Shields   86–7
Soviet Union   50 n.37, 72 n.8, 101, 102, 113
Spartacist League   22, 32, 37, 67, 75, 76, 78, 93
spiked (foundation of)   2, 151, 163, 165
Spinoza, Baruch   139
Srebenica   118 n.90
Stalinism   15, 40, 50, 102–6, 113, 115, 138, 216, 234
Starkey, David   159
Starr, Sandy   177
Stedman Jones, Gareth   104
Steel, Mark   174
Stockport   38, 195
Stop the War Coalition (StWC)   167

Strossen, Nadine   160
subjectivity (diminution of)   10, 101, 130, 143, 144, 147–9, 155, 163, 172, 173, 177, 178, 183, 188, 193, 209, 222
Summerfield, Penny   9
Syriza   192

Taggart, Carol   35
Tait, Richard   157
Tameside Trades Council   25, 34–7, 87
Tatchell, Peter   48
Tate Modern   160
technocracy   7, 10, 165, 183, 185, 186, 189, 190, 192–4, 196, 202, 205, 207, 210, 213, 222, 234
Thatcher, Margaret   6, 31, 56, 73, 75, 78, 82, 88, 97, 109, 112, 166, 169, 191
Theroux, Paul   159 n.129
Ticktin, Hillel   102 n.2
Tóibín, Colm   159 n.129
Tompson, Keith   18, 22, 23, 37, 59, 67, 97, 131 n.4
Tower Hamlets   56, 62, 136
Trades Union Congress (TUC)   14, 20–1, 34–6, 65, 69, 79, 201
Transport and General Workers' Union (TGWU)   47, 66
Tribune   46
Trnopolje   155–7
Troops Out Movement (TOM)   33, 126
Trotsky, Leon   19 n.28, 50, 213
Trotskyism   2, 3, 5, 6, 14, 30 n.90, 32, 53 n.49, 84, 134, 184, 216
Turner, Jenny   1

UK Press Gazette   116 n.79
Unborn Children (Protection) Bill, 1985   89
Union of Construction, Allied Trades and Technicians (UCATT)   63–4
Union of Democratic Mineworkers (UDM)   84, 85
United Nations   69, 120, 194
universalism   139, 170–2, 175, 199, 200
University of Kent   169, 171 n.49
UN Johannesburg World Summit on Sustainable Development   178

vanguardism   10, 17, 73, 82, 97, 102–5, 109, 130–2, 135, 139, 149, 154, 210–11, 216, 222, 223, 227, 230, 231
Vauxhall by-election, 1989   91
Victor, Peter   178–9
Vote Leave   191–2
Vulliamy, Ed   158, 159 n.129

Waiton, Stuart   4 n.18, 169
Walby, Sylvia   207 n.110
Walden, George   159
Walker, Dave   3
Walthamstow   56
Wandsworth   34
Warrington bomb (1993)   4, 42
Warwick University   51, 90, 108, 119
Washington   109, 114, 115
Waterfield, Bruno   171
Watney, Simon   94
Waugh, Auberon   159
Weldon, Fay   159 n.129
West Bank   122
Whelan, Bernadette   152
Whelan, Ella   187, 213
Whittle, Geoffrey   33
Widgery, Dave   93
Williams, Ian   155, 158, 161

Williams, Kirk   67, 87
Williams, Rowan   181
Wilson, Harold   14, 74
winter of discontent   23
Wollstonecraft, Mary   139
Wolton, Suke   152 n.102
women's rights   88–90
Wood, Dominic   132
Wood, James   44
Workers Against Racism (WAR)   55, 59–61, 63–8, 71, 97, 131 n.4, 135, 170
Workers' Aid to Bosnia   116 n.81
Workers' Liberty   93
Workers March Against Racism   65
Workers March for Irish Freedom   35
Workers Power   32, 46
Workers Revolutionary Party (WRP)   31, 32, 39, 53 n.49, 71 n.1, 75, 78, 98, 106, 117
WORLDwrite   178, 190, 224
Woudhuysen, James   4 n.18, 14–15, 17–18, 56, 177, 182, 227, 235
Wythenshawe Hospital   63

Yaffe, David   14–15, 16 n.11
Young, Toby   159
Yugoslavia   112–18, 157, 161

www.ingramcontent.com/pod-product-compliance
Lightning Source LLC
Chambersburg PA
CBHW071810300426
44116CB00009B/1270